HOW CAN I
KEEP FROM
SINGING:
PETE SEEGER

McGRAW-HILL BOOK COMPANY

New York   St. Louis   San Francisco
Toronto   Mexico   Hamburg

HOW CAN I KEEP FROM SINGING:

PETE SEEGER

David King Dunaway

To those who gave their lives to sing of freedom:

"You may burn my flesh and bones
and throw the ashes to the four winds,"
smiled one of them.
"Yet my voice shall linger on
and in the years yet to come
the young shall ask what was the idea
for which you gave me death
and what was I saying
that I must die for what I said."
                    —Carl Sandburg, The People, Yes

1 2 3 4 5 6 7 8 9 D O D O 8 7 6 5 4 3 2 1

LIBRARY OF CONGRESS CATALOGING IN PUBLICATION DATA

Dunaway, David King.
How can I keep from singing.
Bibliography: p.
Includes index.
1. Seeger, Peter, 1919 (May 3)–   2. Folk
singers—United States—Biography.   I. Title.
ML420.S445D8   784.4'92'4 [B]   80-29374
ISBN 0-07-018150-0

Book design by Roberta Rezk

The People, Yes by Carl Sandburg,
copyright 1936 by Harcourt Brace Jovanovich, Inc.;
copyright © 1964 by Carl Sandburg.
The selection used on the facing page
is reprinted by permission of the publisher.

Acknowledgments

BOOKS are cooperative undertakings, as writers often point out when they thank those who inspired and sustained their labor. My first debt is to the people I spoke and corresponded with over the last six years, including Pete Seeger's contemporaries, relatives, and friends, who willingly shared their past with me. Fifty allowed their interviews to be tape-recorded, and many more contributed guidance and materials. (Specific interview credits are included in the notes on each chapter.)

I particularly thank the musicians for their patience with an untrained strummer: Oscar Brand, Guy Carawan, Norman Cazden, Jimmy Collier, Mike Cooney, Judy Collins, Sis Cunningham, Barbara Dane, Rambling Jack Elliot, Ronnie Gilbert, Arlo Guthrie, Bess Lomax Hawes, Lee Hays, Fred Hellerman, Wally Hille, Reverend Frederick Douglass Kirkpatrick, Don McLean, Country Joe McDonald, Bernice Reagon, Malvina Reynolds, Earl Robinson, Charles, Peter, Mike, and Peggy Seeger, and Mary Travers.

I thank the associates of Pete Seeger—particularly Toshi Ohta Seeger and Harold Leventhal (and his staff) for their cooperation and frankness, even in their moments of doubt about my project; Marjorie Guthrie, for helping me explore and publish materials from the Woody Guthrie Archives in New York City; and Howie Richmond and his associates at TRO for their patient assistance in tracking down copyrights.

I thank the researchers whose insights I have borrowed and whose discussions have been an invaluable contribution: Richard Reuss, Archie Green, Norman Studer, Robert Rosenstone, Ron Loewinsohn, Alan Dundes, Willa K. Baum, and Lawrence Levine. Any errors or omissions are my responsibility, and not the fault of these thoughtful, generous advisers.

I thank those who volunteered their comments on the manuscript, and particularly Angus Cameron, Eve Merriam, Steve Mayer, John Berger, and Nancy Guinn, and my editor at McGraw-Hill, Lou Ashworth. I have a special debt to Ellie Shapiro and all those who helped in the research and typing of the book: Ellen Campbell, Jack Liederman, Bobbie Raymond, and Abbey Asher. My thanks to the photographers for their fine work; to the typists, typesetters, printers, graphic artists, sales staff, book sellers, and all who labor anonymously to bring the public its reading matter. The work of so many people goes into a book, yet only the author has a byline; I thank one and all for their dedication.

Finally I thank my community of old and new friends for their understanding, and particularly my parents and Nina Wallerstein—my doctor and companion in the book's dark hours.

El Cerrito, California   DAVID KING DUNAWAY
October 1980

Contents

Permissions

With the following exceptions, the song lyrics quoted in this book are in the public domain. Some of these songs were written collectively, many were never copyrighted or the copyright holders have disappeared.

The Almanac Singers produced "Ballad of October 16," "On Account of That *New* Situation," "Jim Crow," "Arctic Circle," and "Dear Mr. President." All are on file at the Library of Congress.

"Picket Line Priscilla" – words and music by Saul Aarons and Michael Stratton. Modern Recording Co.

"A Visit with Harry," "The Same Merry-Go-Round," "Swinging on a Scab" were first printed in the pages of *People's Songs,* as was "Wallace Man," written by Woody Guthrie.

"Never Turn Back" – Adaptation of traditional materials with new words and music by Bertha Gober. © Copyright 1963, Bertha Gober.

"Round and Round Hitler's Grave" – Words and Music by The Almanac Singers, © Copyright 1941 by The Almanac Singers. Copyright assigned to MCA MUSIC, a Division of MCA, Inc., New York, NY. Copyright renewed. All Rights Reserved. Used by Permission.

"Round and Round Hitler's Grave" – Woody Guthrie and Millard Lampell. © Copyright 1958 by STORMKING MUSIC, INC. All Rights Reserved. Used by Permission.

"Ballad of a Party Singer" and "Talking Management Blues" were written and composed by Roy Berkeley and appeared in *Bosses Songbook,* edited and published by Pat and Dick Ellington.

"Keep Your Eyes on the Prize," "I Love Everybody," and "Oh, Wallace" were communally composed by members of the Civil Rights movement and published in *We Shall Overcome* and *Freedom Is a Constant Struggle,* edited by Guy and Candie Carawan, Oak Publishers, 1963 and 1968.

"Wake Up, Jacob" (Cowboy's Gettin'-Up Holler). Collected, adapted and arranged by John A. Lomax and Alan Lomax. TRO – © Copyright 1938 and renewed 1966 LUDLOW MUSIC, INC., New York, NY. Used by Permission.

"Union Maid" – Words and Music by Woody Guthrie. TRO – © Copyright 1961 and 1963 LUDLOW MUSIC, INC., New York, NY. Used by Permission.

"The Hammer Song" – Words and Music by Lee Hays and Pete Seeger. TRO – © Copyright 1962 and 1968 LUDLOW MUSIC, INC., New York, NY. Used by Permission.

"De Grey Goose" – Words and Music by Huddie Ledbetter. Collected and adapted by John A. Lomax and Alan Lomax. TRO – © Copyright 1936 and renewed 1964 FOLKWAYS MUSIC PUBLISHERS, Inc., New York, NY. Used by Permission.

"The Big Muddy" (Waist Deep in the Big Muddy). Words and Music by Pete Seeger. TRO – © Copyright MELODY TRAILS, INC., New York, NY. Used by Permission.

"Sailing Down This Golden River" – Words and Music by Pete Seeger. TRO – © Copyright 1971 MELODY TRAILS, INC., New York, NY. Used by Permission.

"The Torn Flag" – Words and Music by Pete Seeger. TRO – © Copyright 1970 MELODY TRAILS, INC., New York, NY. Used by Permission.

"Tomorrow Is a Highway" – Words and Music by Lee Hays and Pete Seeger. TRO – © Copyright 1950 FOLKWAYS MUSIC PUBLISHERS, INC., New York, NY. Used by Permission.

"If You Love Your Uncle Sam (Bring Them Home)" – by Pete Seeger. © Copyright 1966 by STORMKING MUSIC, INC. All Rights Reserved. Used by Permission.

Introduction

"THOSE who know the words, sing out, so your neighbors will take courage," says Pete Seeger, unshouldering his banjo. Stepping out toward the audience from the lights, he frowns. "Well, we've got a bunch of good singers here. But *some* of you are holding back. Preserving their academic ob-jeck-tivity."

In their college auditorium the overeducated crowd roars appreciatively. Before them stands a rail-thin fifty-seven-year-old in a sailor's cap, frailing his banjo nonchalantly and acting more like a concerned friend than an entertainer. Three thousand New Englanders are gathered to raise bail for demonstrators arrested at a nuclear power plant. Eager promoters have oversold the house; the air feels hot and thick.

The crowd is watching a musician who has been concertizing for forty years. At a conservative estimate, the total audience of Pete Seeger—those in seeing, hearing, and microphone distance—might total between four and five million people in forty countries. His career has spanned nine Presidents of the United States, from Roosevelt to Reagan.

If Frank Sinatra seems at home in the casinos of Las Vegas, Seeger's abode is the impromptu political benefit. Over the years, he has worked with so many social movements that journalists have paid more attention to his politics than to his music. Wherever he sings, controversy follows. "Khrushchev's songbird" critics have called him, arguing about whether he is a revolutionary or a victim of red-hunting, a subversive or a patriot.

To his followers, Seeger is an institution—a preacher with a banjo in place of a psalm book. If at times his songs ring flat, and his music strikes a strident or inauthentic chord, well, the audience comes for the presence, not the show. "I go to a Pete Seeger concert for a hit of *him*," one fellow in a flannel shirt says. "He could stand up there and play the chair for all I care."

Seeger rolls up his sleeves and gets to work. Thick-soled hiking boots clump out the rhythm, jiggling the microphone. He swings his long-necked banjo toward the crowd, and they echo a chorus. They put their voice in his charge, confident he will not ask the impossible, or try to sell them his latest album. Pete drops his voice into a lower octave to harmonize; the room lights up, and the audience becomes a reverberating instrument in his hands.

When he sings the old ballads, his graying beard points off into the balcony and his eyes fix out of reach in the ether. He pours forth good spirits like a cornucopia, unrelentingly optimistic. Before the audience has a chance to applaud, he unobtrusively changes key and introduces the next song. The audience is content. Seeger is in high form tonight, doing just what made him famous.

The listeners understand Seeger has been blacklisted; this is common knowledge. It even adds a touch of danger to his performance, like books read under the covers. Yet for all his notoriety, despite being the most picketed, boycotted performer in American history, Seeger's life remains a closely guarded secret. No television network features him as an entertainer. No scandal sheets report his comings and goings.

Even to his friends Seeger is a mystery. After having known him for thirty years, his friend Gordon Friesen comments, "He's not a man I sit and chew the fat with." Family members tell of his immense reserve, insisting they've never been close. Despite his warmth on stage, there seems to be little left to meet humanity one-to-one.

For a performer whose voice and instrumental skill are dwarfed by those of his contemporaries, Pete Seeger has a popularity that is at first glance as mysterious as the rumors that circulate about him. Colleagues hint that Seeger has broken down, given up. The most surprising story comes from a woman who has known the musician since he was seventeen. In the last decade, she is convinced, he secretly "doesn't think he made the right choice somewhere," and feels "his career didn't matter or mean anything."

I wonder at this as I look out over the excited faces in the audience. Tuning his guitar with deliberate slowness, Pete is calming the crowd for a quiet song about living by the Hudson River. Then he closes with his tune "If I Had a Hammer," and even the hard-hearts sing. *I'd hammer out danger, I'd hammer out warning*—the song takes life; awakened from memory it rises and moves offstage, into the aisles. People stand and sway with arms around one another; the walls seem to shake like tentflaps at an old-fashioned camp meeting.

For the encore, Seeger does a Puritan hymn, "Amazing Grace." He teaches the audience to sing it New England-style, in surges of sound that roll across the hall:

> *Shall I be wafted to the skies*
> *On flowery beds of ease*
> *While others strive to win the prize*
> *And sail through bloody seas.*

As he leaves the hall he sees a very attractive woman with long auburn hair waiting by his dressing room. She says she wants to talk to him privately and follows him into the room.

Inside, she hesitates. "I just wanted to tell you how much you've made folk music come alive for me and my friends." Hoarse from singing and interviews, Seeger nods and bends down to give her shoulder a squeeze. His timing is perfect, the touch fatherly and gentle. He smiles and ducks out of the room. Watching this by now familiar cameo, I notice how Seeger's eyes flick into the distance, how he listens bemused, bobbing his head. This too is a performance.

I drive Pete home across Massachusetts and upstate New York; the russet-brown Berkshires whirl by the window. Dressed in a T-shirt, he snoozes in the back seat, his glasses hanging around his neck on an elastic band. Without the sailor's cap, his thinning hair adds ten years to his looks. His knees raised to the roof, Pete manages to fit most of himself into the small sedan seat; his head bounces along on an arm rest. He sleeps until the turnoff outside Beacon, where I struggle up his rocky driveway.

As we pull up, his grandson Tao is sitting in the sun with a plastic shovel. Toshi, his Japanese-American wife, gardens nearby, behind the log cabin where they live. A few years younger than Pete, she is also a good foot shorter, with shiny black hair and dark, restless eyes. They met at a square dance and married nearly forty years ago.

His wife talks over her shoulder as she unpacks the maple-syrup buckets we purchased on the way home. The frosted aluminum sparkles in the sunlight. She stacks the pails with the air of one habitually well organized, then stops to look me over. As Seeger's manager, press aide, and bookkeeper, Toshi has spent years shielding his privacy; she has become watchful of writers. She asks how his CBS interview went.

"Oh, I talked too much," Pete answers unenthusiastically. "Started to argue politics with the fellow."

She throws him a glare. It's dinnertime, and we sit on cushions at a low table. Their eldest daughter, Mika, has been to the health food store, and the fusty odor of soy milk fills the room.

As I awake the next morning, the smell of wet leaves and river fog hangs over the grounds. To my right is the cabin, forty feet by twenty, divided into three rooms. Over to the left stands the barn, with offices and darkroom upstairs. A Japanese garden hangs over the edge of the sloping yard. At the bottom of the hill the Hudson flows like a wide highway through the mountains. In the distance, the river disappears into a gray cloud with pins sticking through: New York City.

A performer withdrawn from friends and his public often confides in his journal, and with fresh hopes I pass the morning alone in the barn, poring over the files in Seeger's study. In a little office over his wife's pottery studio Seeger spends much of his time: answering mail, writing lyrics, and doodling on his banjo. On top of a stack of tapes is a prominent songwriter's new album. Hundreds demand Seeger's opinion about their songs, stories, and causes; and he initiates his own projects so rapidly they cram the wooden chests of his small, square study.

In these chests and boxes reside Seeger's dreams. Like many frustrated journalists, Pete Seeger has written thousands of pages of unpublished journals, song notebooks, and sketches—even two book-length manuscripts, including the provocatively titled *Fantasies of a Revisionist.* "Look here," he says, pulling open a drawer to reveal a handmade flute. Reels of tape spill from their boxes "A record on Chinese flute music I wanted to edit—three years ago." He points at a brown box in the corner.

"My banjo book. It's so out of date I hate to mail out copies. I wrote it in hotel rooms during Henry Wallace's campaign in 1948. 'What the heck,' I decided. 'Might as well publish it myself.' First year, I sold a hundred mimeographed copies. The ninth year, nine thousand. By now, we've sent out a quarter million. The last five years I've been trying to find a month free of mail to revise a few points. No luck," he says bitterly.

The performer's public cheerfulness sours. Mail seems to be the root of his personal evil: requests for benefits, missing lyrics, tunes for a worthy quatrain—he feels a duty to answer them all himself. Writers in twenty countries have pushed Seeger's correspondence out of control, leaving him with a three-month backlog of letters.

His problems with correspondence may be a foil for deeper concerns. It turns out Pete questions his role in a folk-song revival which, according to writer Jon Pankake, had young enthusiasts rifling America's folk traditions "like so many grubby urchins grabbing at pennies thrown in the street."

His uncertainties lie buried in the mounds of paper before me. Amid thirty years of files lie Seeger's hopes and bitterness about politics and fellow performers, clues to a man both complex and unfamiliar to his public.

I start with the journals.

In the first of these, the sixteen-year-old noted a telling dream about music. After a performance of the New York Philharmonic, ten thousand people appeared at the box office of the Roxy Music Hall to demand their money back. Although Toscanini conducted with a phosphorescent baton, "he did not wave it about enough," according to the crowd. (Pete's violinist mother had hopes of raising a virtuoso; he didn't much care for the idea.)

Another entry reveals Seeger's astonishingly precocious interest in radical politics. At thirteen, he already had a subscription to the Communist literary magazine *New Masses;* he was a "red-diaper" baby a generation before Dr. Spock. "Fascism is the last stage of capitalism," Pete wrote with the orthodox fire of adolescence. "The greatest danger [to revolutionaries] is the Greenwich Village type, the bohemian." These are stern words from someone who eventually spent seven years living in the Village.

In letters from his army days in World War II, he complains of the lines at boot camp and how his Yankee accent stands out in a southern regiment. Yet on his first day in the army, "New York" (as bunkmates called him) won friends and a banjo contest by picking southern tunes.

I am momentarily distracted by a sound outside the window. Seeger is standing at the edge of his garden, head tilted up to the sky. He's yodeling into the wind. "Yodl-ay-dee-ohh." I watch fascinated, half expecting to hear the sound returned from the river. "Ohh dl-ay-dee-ohh." I am reminded of a tune he once composed for Shakespeare's *Tempest*: the song of Ariel, the breezy spirit who plays on invisible instruments.

Turning back to the stack of papers, I come across an unfunded grant proposal. At the height of Seeger's commercial success, when "Goodnight Irene" was America's most popular song, he applied for a Guggenheim fellowship to research "Instrumental Styles in American Folk Music." Soon after the grant went in, however, Seeger's name came up before the House Committee on Un-American Activities (HUAC). He received a polite note from the foundation that the climate wasn't right for such a project, perhaps in a few years . . .

Seeger's thickest files are those labeled BLACKLIST. The volume of his collection is astounding—at least four hundred documents. One letter, typed on the thickly embossed stationery of the New York Historical Society, catches my eye. According to their letter, the Society cancelled a 1957 concert due to last-minute indications of "political unpleasantness." The entertainer's reply shows his self-protective irony. It was a shame, he wrote, the Society caved in to a few threats. Not only had he and his parents lived in New York for years; a great-uncle, after all, had been the mayor, the man who christened the Brooklyn Bridge.

There is an even larger collection of documents, which Seeger has yet to see: his FBI files. To America's intelligence agencies, Seeger and his friends were a public menace; the FBI infiltrated, eavesdropped, and maintained mail and trash covers on the organizations Seeger set up. Three years of litigation under the Freedom of Information Act has yielded ten feet of reports on informers in the folk-music community, imagined cabals of folk musicians, even details of the Bureau's behind-the-scenes role in Seeger's blacklisting. But the FBI does not have all of Seeger's correspondence. For decades, politicians have been writing him: Senator Frank Harris of Oklahoma promises to find a marker for Woody Guthrie's home in Okemah; in 1948, Mayor Paul O'Dwyer thanks him for helping out New York's municipal radio station; Reverend Martin Luther King, Jr., warmly acknowledges his help, back in 1956.

Some of Seeger's letters show an unsuspected bleakness, as in 1974, when he wrote songwriter Malvina Reynolds:

> I guess my problem is really not too different from an awful lot of other people. It's simply that I'm weary of never catching up on a huge pile of mail. The months and years go by and I somehow never get the songs written that I intend to.
>
> It's a relief to go on a trip where all I have to do is stare at a hotel room instead of a study that has about ten unfinished jobs.

As I look around the study, the unfinished tasks are still there. The tapes sit silently, waiting for a sympathetic hand to insert them into the tape player. The past lies in scraps around the room; dreams of political change, fantasies of a quiet stint as a folklorist, frustrations at the boycotts that shadow his singing.

"You must be about drowned in all this paper." The voice startles me. "One of these days I'm going to throw all this out," Seeger laughs.

He's been chopping firewood, a favorite exercise, and his cheeks are red from effort. "Fellow my age should get out of breath once a day," he insists. A nondrinker, a nonsmoker, Pete unwinds by ice-skating, wood-chopping, and playing music. "Let's get some lunch, and we'll talk afterwards. But not too much. If I talk for a whole afternoon, I can't perform for the next two nights." He stops short, wistfully. "Nowadays I even have to eat by myself on nights I perform."

He lopes down the stairs and across to the cabin, where he grates a hunk of white cheddar into some eggs and the flat beer he keeps especially for rarebits. As the tasty goop steams, he spots Tao, his four-year-old grandson, in the corner. Picking up his recorder, Pete begins a jig, softly at first. Tao looks up, and his grandfather smiles. The boy dances, and his grandfather plays faster until Tao gets so excited he wobbles. Seeger slows the music and his grandson falls on the floor, giggling. Grandpa picks up Tao, swinging him around the room, and walks to the stove for a taste. He licks his finger, stirs in more mustard, and ladles it out for the half-dozen friends and relatives the smell has assembled.

I compliment Pete on his rarebit, cheesy and sharp. He grins proudly. Someone has been teaching him to cook; just this morning I read the twenty-year-old's "great new way of cooking cakes—one egg and five teaspoons of baking powder."

There's no small talk at the table; we discuss an article on free speech in *The New Yorker*. I ask Toshi about the fantastic stories concerning her father Takashi, who was exiled from Japan and who once fought with Sun Yatsen.

"Oh, Peter shouldn't have told that story," she laughed, with an edge to her voice. "That's family business. And besides, he tells it *all wrong*." Seeger is oblivious to her comment; he sits straight as a deacon on the comfortable cushions. Absentmindedly passing the butter, he practically leaves it in midair.

After lunch we climb the curving barn stairs to his study. Strapping the microphones in place, I wonder how to tackle the hard questions. How do you bring up the Communist Party with a man once sentenced to ten years in jail for refusing to discuss his political associations? What has he actually done to be so heavily targeted by right-wing groups?

"Instead of me, you really ought to write about Aunt Molly Jackson" (a Kentucky mine organizer and balladeer). "I've gotten too much attention already," he begins, launching into the disclaimer: "Too many people listen to me and not enough to the people I learned from." His words carry an improbable modesty, and the anti-psychology, anti-individual canons of an older generation of leftists. "If Seeger ever wrote his autobiography," fellow songwriter Country Joe McDonald mused, "he'd content himself with a half-dozen entries in the index."

He was also deeply influenced by the Anonymous Movement, a group of artists in Paris in the 1920s who refused to sign paintings: they insisted that works of art must stand on their own merits, not on the artist's personality. Thus, talking with Seeger about his past is like starting a detective novel halfway through; you're never sure whom to follow in the plot.

Not that Pete is evasive. In conversation he is chatty, but reserved; he doesn't wait for questions. He throws off a string of anecdotes: the upper-crust boarding schools he attended, how he got started in music and in politics, bumming cross-country with Woody Guthrie, fighting the blacklist. For the first time, Seeger volunteers information about his involvement with the Communist Party. In matters of fact and situation, his candor is complete.

Without his banjo, the man's arms become an instrument. With the thin wire of a microphone trailing him, Seeger wanders about his study, gesturing haplessly at the quart-sized basket with today's mail, discussing his fears that his voice will give out. His words are mesmerizing, but I can't help feeling his attention has flown away. His stories are set pieces, each capped with a moral. The concern about office work is genuine but trivial; he could afford three secretaries if he wanted them. Seeger speaks in parables, he pulsates energy and ideals—but he's not all there.

At the end of the session, I pack up my equipment while he rests, head cradled in his palms. After a moment, Seeger perks up and stretches. He walks over to a bookshelf and pushes files aside until he comes up with a black notebook the size of a well-worn wallet. Holding it gingerly, he flips the pages for a minute, his back to me. When Pete turns around, he has a sheepish grin.

"Look at this, David." He opens the notebook so I can read the neatly printed song lists.

"I sat down thirty years ago to copy names of songs I know all the way through. Here they are, maybe six hundred of them." Then he looks up hopefully, pressing his lips together and scanning the song titles: "Let's see how many I still remember."

Pete Seeger wonders how he forgot lyrics, and I despair of finding an avenue into his past. His communicator is set on long-range broadcast, a farsighted man who holds the world at arm's length.

After our interview, Seeger suggests I help out with the chores. "Sure," I nod, and he smiles broadly. He throws me a pair of cotton gloves, damp to my fingers. Backing up the pickup, we head for the dump with a contribution to the world's waste problem.

There's something democratic about garbage dumping. Everyone—

the lowly and the great—creates and disposes of waste. Some stuff it down the sink and push a button, reducing leftovers to a mush. Most Americans pile it in a bag, take that out to a can, and forget about it. A few, including the Seegers, recycle glass, metal, and newspapers—and take the rest to the dump. In garbage, like wine, there is truth. As the biographer Plutarch tells us, attention to small tasks often characterizes people more truly than their heroic moments.

It is a bright sunny afternoon as we wind down the hillside, with the wind blowing sweetly off the Hudson—the sort of fair and pleasant day when knights and pilgrims meet in English ballads. The cans rattle in the back of the pickup as Seeger stops to add a load at the Beacon Sloop Club, his home-away-from-home, where he picks up odds and ends left by teenagers from the last sailing class. The clubhouse, with a nonpolluting toilet that produces mulch (and uses no water), sits on a forlorn strip of land opposite the railway station.

Here the Hudson is over a mile wide, gliding silently past the little pier where the boats dock. A hundred years ago, riverboats stopped in this shallow; today the sloop Seeger helped build, the *Clearwater,* casts anchor here for sailing lessons and meetings, or to publicize the club's annual strawberry shortcake fest: heaping mounds of hot sourcake biscuits and icy, sweet strawberries. On these days, the club overflows with locals and citybillies out for a fair. Folks promenade the riverbank, sing, picnic under the trees, use the nonpolluting toilet, and, of course, stuff the garbage cans full.

This afternoon the river laps quietly at the Beacon waterfront. The ovens for cooking shortcake lean like giant breadboxes against the clubhouse, and commuters' cars crowd the shoreline. We heft the cans up on the tailgate and drive off.

I'm curious why Seeger bothers with all this community service. A half-dozen good causes across the country are probably trying to get through to him right now, and we're out hauling trash.

At the dump, he pulls into the loading spot with a ritualized slowness. This is a contained dump, where the garbage is kept in a warehouse and later compacted and shipped out to be buried. We knock at the keeper's window, and somebody who looks like a second-generation farmhand nods. Pete hops back in the cab and backs the pickup into place.

I start to tip the nearest can into the pit when I feel a restraining hand on my shoulder. "Whoa," he says gently, "better not tilt it like that, or the whole can'll go in. And you with it." His mood is improving.

He rolls the can at an angle three feet from the edge and tilts it cautiously toward the opening. Grasping the rim, he rocks back and forth, his long arms pushing the can away, then snapping it back so a third of the contents falls out. Like salt from an oversized shaker, the heavy can empties in a few rhythmic motions. Pete bends over like a fisherman reeling in line, then straightens up, pivoting until the empty can spins back next to a full one. He performs this efficient dance with the same attention he works audiences.

The job done, he snaps up the tailgate and quickly pulls the truck to one side so a neighbor can get in. He turns the pickup into a long driveway with a guard's hut on one side. Seeger tells a white-haired man that some-one has busted the lock behind the river park.

"It's those kids from the next town," the attendant sighs, with a boys-will-be-boys smile. "Guess it's time to put in a heavy chain." Pete agrees, suggesting that a sign telling vandals the cost of lock and fence might help. The other man nods, he'll get to it tomorrow or at the latest, the day after. That's quick enough for fences in Beacon, and Pete swings back toward home, with the empties clanging as we go up the bumpy dirt road.

"Funny thing about the man we were just talking to," Seeger says. "Not long ago, he used to gripe about the young longhairs moving into town. Now he comes to the Sloop Club. Sends his kids. He maintains the chain himself; some weekends he brings the family down to the waterfront. And you know," Pete grins, "twelve years ago he may have signed a petition to stop me from singing at the local high school."

I sit silently as he threads the truck expertly up his driveway. So *this* is where he has been all afternoon. While we talked of labor organizing in the forties and Czechoslovakia in '68, he's had this broken bit of chain on his mind. He has moved from international to local concerns. Seeger keeps on preaching, but now he reaches local teenagers, huddled around a wood stove in the clubhouse by the river.

But why would a forty-year veteran of political campaigns turn to cleaning up a river? A loss of zeal? Seeger knows river fairs don't redistrib-ute power or wealth. A journalist who worked with Pete in the forties suggested the *Clearwater* may be the closest thing today to Don Quixote's horse. Others insist the *Clearwater* (and environmental activism) is a start on the occupational health and anti-cancer movements of the 1980s.

As we unload at the cabin, I realize what a long day it has been. Pete's earlier diffidence has burned off with the morning fog, and he's back rib-bing academic ob-jeck-tiv-ity like any successful college dropout. For a mo-ment I see him on stage again, "a sixty year old smiling public man" as Yeats described himself, with thousands awaiting every syllable. Then the image of Seeger rocking the garbage cans imposes itself. As I start to leave I notice a stone the size of a soft ball cemented into the chimney. It destroys the symmetry. The more I look at the stone, the more out of place it seems. I ask Pete where it came from.

"That rock nearly hit my son Danny," he begins softly. "Came through the car window on a strange, violent afternoon, nearly thirty years ago. I glued the rock up there so I'd never forget."

Outside, dusk is settling and mosquitos buzz faintly in the evening air. We sit silently, both staring at the stone. I imagine the force that hurled it through his window, until Seeger breaks in on my thoughts.

"Let me tell you the story of Peekskill," he says grimly. "People threw stones at women and children, with intent to kill. At my own family. I had two little babies in the car . . ."

Hold the Line

1

AT DAWN on Sunday morning, September 4, 1949, the first convoys of cars headed north from New York City for Peekskill, a summer resort town where Paul Robeson and others were to sing. By nine A.M. the roads were blocked with veterans' groups and local anti-Communists who had vowed to stop the concert. New York labor unions sent a security force of three thousand to keep the concert grounds open. Outside the gates, one thousand armed police lined up in formation. Across town in the woods, a half-dozen men piled rocks the size of softballs into a car trunk. From a nearby church a woman watched them, noticing the hand-lettered signs that read: WAKE UP AMERICA, PEEKSKILL DID.

America *was* awakening, from dreams of wartime prosperity into a national shortage of jobs, houses, and schools; from hopes of united nations into cold war, a global morality play of markets and propaganda. Everything Soviet was sinister, and tolerance of radical thinking gave way to curses and right-wing violence.

As Pete Seeger drove to the concert with his wife and their two infants, rumors of an ambush spread. Asked if there'd be trouble at Peekskill, a state trooper answered: "I don't know. But someone told me the whole road was lined with rocks. I hope it's the vets who picked them up." Seeger was heading straight into the first full-scale riot of America's cold war.

The concert had originated two weeks earlier with a notice in the Communist *Daily Worker:* Readers were invited for a pleasant evening in the country at the Lakeland Picnic Grounds. The name hinted at a quiet affair—beer and sandwiches, with a blanket to keep out the cool night air.

The FBI clipped the notice for their files. The *Peekskill Evening Star* called Robeson "violently and loudly pro-Russian"; their editorial was unusually bitter: "The time for tolerant silence that signifies approval is running out." A few residents wrote the editor, calling this an invitation to violence. That, for a time, was that. If the local citizens agreed with the *Star,* they weren't vocal about it.

On his newly purchased country land, Seeger didn't always see the morning papers. When he did, the news was scary. Communist Party leaders faced jail for teaching and writing about Marxism. Radio commentators called for another war to stop Communism. Anti-Communists beat up left-wing actors outside a theater in New York. Half the cast of *They Shall Not Pass*—a play about the trial of the Scottsboro boys—ended up in the hospital. There were no arrests.

Nineteen forty-nine had not been a good year for Pete. That spring, right after he turned thirty, People's Songs—an organization he had built from scratch and run for three years—went bankrupt. He felt responsible for its debts. His new singing group, an unknown quartet called the Weavers, was falling apart from lack of work. Neighbors in upstate New York distrusted the Seegers as "city folks." And then in August, Pete's prim mother arrived for a visit, but the only accommodation he could offer was a tiny trailer lacking water or electricity.

Pete and his wife Toshi had spent the summer clearing their land by the Hudson. The work was toilsome and unfamiliar, and days passed without a chance to relax and watch the boats pass. During his mother's visit, Pete and his family had to sleep in a tent. Still, they were better off than they had been in New York. Pete had fewer political meetings and more time with his banjo. Toshi looked forward to a Japanese garden and making pottery. The kids could grow up in the woods.

His bookings were not numerous, but he survived. The night before he was scheduled to sing at Peekskill, he led a performance of teenagers, the Good Neighbor Chorus. He had to drive into the city and set up, take the kids home after the show, and cart off the instruments; it was probably two A.M. before he got to bed. Fortunately, the concert was not until eight the next night, and only ten miles away. After dinner that evening, Pete packed his banjo in the car, helped his sixty-year-old mother into the front seat, and cheerfully headed south.

He ignored predictions of violence, though Peekskill had a reputation as a center of Ku Klux Klan activities. A pre-concert parade was being organized by the Joint Veterans Council of Westchester County. Suspecting the parade might get rough, the leader of a teenage marching band had withdrawn, telling the *Peekskill Star* he would not bring his boys anywhere they could get hurt.

It was one of those seductively warm, Indian summer evenings, but the road to the concert was empty. Pete expected the concert to go on: "It *was* legal and there might be a few who'd object, but after all, there were policemen there." He planned to sing a few songs and show that people can say what they want in America.

Mother and son had a pleasant ride along the parkway. Constance Seeger knew the area well; she'd given birth to Peter a few dozen miles away. They arrived early, but at the exit from the highway, a patrol car blocked their way. A state trooper motioned them to turn around. Seeger pulled his car to one side and walked over.

"Officer," he said politely, "I'm one of the performers here tonight. Do you think you could help me get to the head of the line?"

"He looked at me rather peculiarly. 'There's not going to be any concert,' he said. I asked him what's up and he answered, 'It's completely jammed, the concert's been called off.' " Seeger was puzzled. He could see press cars hurriedly pulling up, while police idled at the entrance to the picnic grounds.

He later found out what had happened. Novelist Howard Fast was master of ceremonies, and he had arrived an hour or so before Pete. For once, everything had gone smoothly—The sound system worked, the lights were set. Fast had been rather proud of how well things were going. That was at seven o'clock. A few minutes later, matters looked quite different, as Fast wrote in *Peekskill USA*.

A boy ran up to say there was trouble up at the top of the road, where the veterans' parade was gathered. When Fast and his crew ran up to the entrance, veterans charged them, three hundred vigilantes with billies and brass knuckles and rocks in clenched fists and American Legion caps. It became clear why no more people or entertainers were coming into the concert. One of the forks of the road was piled high with rocks, a great barricade of stone, and the other had a Legion truck parked across it.

It was straight out of an old-time western: Fast and his friends were cornered in a box canyon with nowhere to turn. Picnic dinners were forgotten. Outside, Pete and his mother talked with the trooper; from the road, they could see nothing of the trap.

The veterans in the parade weren't gangsters. These were respectable folk: well-dressed real-estate men, grocery clerks, and filling-station hands: men and women who feared losing what little they had, vets frustrated at not having a good job after the war. They blamed the city intellectuals in their summer houses, the Negroes, and the Jews.

Fast sent off a scout to find help. Up at the entrance, the trooper again told Seeger to leave. Not knowing what else to do, he drove his car up on the grass and turned back, departing just as the scout reached the main gate. Exactly what happened next has never been determined. In the last light of the day, the veterans were bearing in, shouting, "We'll finish Hitler's job!" and "Give us Robeson. We'll lynch the nigger up!" Soon Fast and the others were backed against a truck while the crowd swung into them with bats and fence posts.

Someone aimed a blow at Fast. A friend deflected it, but the attacker leaped on the writer, tearing off his glasses. Others went down in the free-for-all. Someone yelled, "They're killing Fast, God damn it."

Fast limped up from beneath a pile of bodies, his clothes torn. Then he did something Seeger might have done in his place; he began to sing. The concertgoers locked arms to form a line and started:

> We shall not–we shall not be moved!
> We shall not–we shall not be moved!
> Just like a tree that's standing by the water,
> We shall not be moved!

The road in front of them was bathed in the glare of headlights, but all else was in darkness. Across the beams came the "new Americans," brandishing fence rails. In the shadows, a man was stabbed.

Off in one corner, three men in suits scribbled furiously in their notebooks. They were from the Justice Department, and to them, this was a bold new experiment in red-hunting.

As the vets closed in, they were met with a new resistance. Emboldened by the music, the concert organizers halted their retreat. Joining arms and singing gave them an extra measure of courage. They fended off the attackers for two more hours, until the mob battered their way to the stage. Frustrated that Robeson wasn't there (he'd been warned of the attack), the vigilantes broke up wooden chairs and set fire to pamphlets and songbooks. They left behind a flaming cross.

At ten o'clock, the police began to help. The wounded were taken to a hospital, the buses rumbled back to the city in the dark, and the long chill night was ended.

Next morning Seeger read the half-dozen stories in *The New York Times*: RIOTS STOP CONCERT. The local D.A., an ambitious fellow named Fanelli, said the audience provoked the violence by showing up where they weren't wanted. Veterans' groups claimed no responsibility for the attack; their parade had officially disbanded before dark. There were no arrests. Pete signed a group telegram urging Governor Dewey (the recently defeated presidential candidate) to investigate. The governor named District Attorney Fanelli as his neutral observer.

This was Monday. The veterans' riot had taken place on Saturday, and the furor still hadn't let up. Not content with congressional hearings or labeling subversive books in libraries, anti-Communists had opened a new front: street violence.

On Wednesday, August 31, the FBI started checking into People's Artists, one of the sponsors of the concert. They found that Seeger served on the board of directors. The New York office questioned eight informers on People's Artists, without effect. Then a patriotic citizen called the FBI to complain of a mailing from People's Artists. The special agent in charge "recruited" the caller and sent off an immediate report to Washington.

On Friday, Seeger found out Robeson wanted another chance. The Civil Rights Congress held a mass rally in Harlem. "If the police won't protect the audience," Robeson promised in his velvety bass, "we will protect ourselves." A decision was made at the highest levels of the Communist Party: the concert *would* take place—on Labor Day, two days hence, half a mile from the scene of the previous violence. "From now on, we take the offensive, and that offensive begins tonight," Robeson told the cheering crowd.

It was a gutsy move. Seeger and a half-dozen others agreed to perform; they weren't giving up their right to be heard, even if it meant a fight. Fifteen veterans' groups in Westchester and surrounding counties announced a counter-demonstration. The FBI teletyped J. Edgar Hoover with the news. Pete met with the other directors of People's Artists to talk over their next move. They decided to seek an injunction against the veterans' demonstration. The case came up on a hot Friday afternoon, just before the court's recess. Judge John W. Clancy turned down the injunction, blandly asking, "I don't know why you think the veterans are going to disobey the law."

And so the weekend began. All over Peekskill the bumper stickers appeared: WAKE UP AMERICA, PEEKSKILL DID! On street corners and in the bars, local residents boasted of what they would do to Commies. Carloads of teenagers were seen loading up rocks.

The mood in Peekskill was sullen and grim; local citizens felt their town was being invaded. "No Parking" signs were posted, and American flags appeared outside homes. Some residents felt remorse, and others regretted the bad name the previous week's violence had brought. The majority seemed to agree with a spokesman for the veterans: "Our objective was to prevent the Paul Robeson concert, and I think our objective was reached." According to the *Star,* the worst part of the disturbance "was that it played into the hands of the Commies." Meanwhile, the largest number of police in the history of Westchester County arrived in Peekskill. By busload after busload they came, jamming the roads, cleaning their guns in the parks.

The citizens of Peekskill had a fear and a small-town distrust of outsiders; their situation resembled that of modern inhabitants of once-rural areas facing emigrants from California or New York. Fear also infected many in Seeger's circle, who increasingly expected "the beginning of a fascist onslaught," he recalled. "This was no more than Hitler did in 1933, when he burned down the Reichstag and said, 'I must have emergency power, the traitors are destroying our country.'" Many Party members seriously believed a right-wing coup was in the offing. The day before the second concert, the Klan was bold enough to write and thank Seeger (and People's Artists) for stimulating 722 new membership applications in the week since the riot.

The morning of the concert, Pete and Toshi were back sleeping in their trailer; Pete's mother had returned home. Outside the drafty sliding window, a gray mist covered the river. The air was still, broken only by the splash of a creek.

In ten years of singing professionally, Seeger had found himself in tough spots before, but he had never brought his family into danger. Now he and Toshi argued over who should go to the concert. Pete felt his children should see whatever happened. Toshi reminded him their boy was barely three, and the baby only one year old. Pete assured her everything would go smoothly; dozens of reporters would be there and twenty thousand people. The whole world would be watching. Toshi, who had a quick temper, told Pete not to be naïve; there would be trouble. Did he want to be responsible?

"Ok," they finally agreed, "Let's do it. If one of us goes, we all go." Toshi's father joined them, and so did an old army buddy, Mario Cassetta, and his girl friend: seven of them, with Seeger at the wheel. If there was trouble, the kids would lie on the floor. He drove the stretch of freeway to Peekskill less cheerfully than before.

Not all his friends thought he had made the right decision. "There's a kind of ruthlessness in the Seegers' feelings of principle," long-time friend Bess Lomax reflected. "Once he decided he was right, his course was set. He wouldn't brutalize his family, but he thought about their safety and serenity *after* he made his decision.

"There were some very scary rumors about the Robeson concert. It was going to be a real tough scene, that much was widely known. We had a year-old baby and there was no way we could justify bringing her. Toshi and Peter took the kids and were very proud of it. Not proud—they talked about how important it was for children to see this happen. I thought it was something an infant *shouldn't* see."

The Seegers approached the parking lot at eleven A.M., a few hours before the program was to begin. From the main gate, Pete peered down into a bowl-shaped amphitheater where the stage was set in an empty meadow, open to attack. On the surrounding hill, he saw what looked from a distance like the Great Wall: a line of 2,500 union men, elbow to elbow in a human chain around the grounds. The veterans outside were more vocal than violent, shouting curses, and "You'll get in—but you won't get out." Twenty-five thousand heard Paul Robeson sing "Old Man River"; he earned an ovation with the lines "I must keep fightin'/Until I'm dyin'." At 2:50, as Seeger began to sing, the demonstration outside was scheduled to end; if police had dispersed the vets at the appointed time, the day might have ended as originally planned.

The program was cut short to be sure to get everyone out before dark. Seeger had time for only a few songs, including one he and Lee Hays had written six months earlier, "If I Had a Hammer." This song had premiered at a benefit for Communists on trial under the notorious Smith Act; the lyrics were so controversial, no commercial publisher would touch it. Neither Hays nor Seeger imagined the Hit Parade would find the song, or that it would eventually be attacked by both right- and left-wingers. To its composer, the song offered an affirmation of the Left's sustaining power; to the audience, it was an anti-cold-war mantra.

They sang the song loudly, out past the anti-sniper patrols and union defenders, out across the neighboring valleys and dusty roads where local residents were gathering.

After the singing and announcements, people congratulated each other and finished off the contents of their picnic baskets; cars massed at the exit. At 4:10, Westchester police began diverting traffic up a steep, winding road, to the confusion of those leaving. Pete wanted to turn left toward home, but the police told him, "No. Everybody this way." It was a setup. There was a heaviness in the air and a sinking sensation, like the opening plunge of a roller coaster. Pete described what happened next.

"Fifty or a hundred people were hollering: 'Go home you white niggers,' 'Kikes,' 'Go on back to Russia.' The cars moved very slowly down the road.

"We hadn't gone a hundred yards from the gate when I saw glass on the road. And in my innocence I said to the family, 'Hey, watch out, they may be throwing stones at us.' Hell, I had no idea how well organized it was. Around the next corner was a guy with a pile of stones, waist high, each about the size of a baseball. As the cars came by, four or five feet away, WHAM! Around the next corner was another group with another pile of stones."

Seeger drove a jeep wagon, an unprotected car with glass all around. "Now," he told his children, "get *down*." Their windows caved in, spitting splinters of glass everywhere.

It was a battle of two Americas: the city and the country, the liberal and the conservative. Goaded by redbaiting in the daily press and radio, the attackers blamed the gadflies for the frustration of wartime dreams. The attackers were true Americans, as patriotic as the Know-Nothings who tortured the Irish and Catholics during the Civil War, as American as the 1920 Palmer raiders who arrested thousands of "anarchists" in immigrant communities coast to coast.

Up ahead a state trooper said, "Let's get the bastards," pointing to a car where a man from New Jersey sat helplessly. The trooper took careful aim and shoved his nightstick, point first, at the driver's left eye. The man ducked, too late. The club missed the eyeball, but caught the corner of the lid. It began to bleed, and when the man brought his head up, the trooper aimed at the eye again.

The police ordered passengers out of the car and beat them with nightsticks. One trooper noticed a bandage on the driver's left hand, which had been burned a week before. He jumped on the hand and ground his heel into the bandage, fracturing one of the burned fingers.

Hysterical cries and the sound of breaking glass spread panic along the line of trapped cars. Pete couldn't stand it. Despite stones raining in his jeep's windows, he stopped the car and got out, pale and shaking with rage.

Such moments didn't happen often. Even in the middle of violence, Pete Seeger maintained his New England reserve. Songs were his chosen weapons, not baseball bats. He fought in symbols—a union, a tall thin banjo—for the causes of others. Now he was getting his own taste of the lash.

Until he left the car, he had managed well, if one "manages" driving a terrified family through acres of blood and broken glass. "I don't remember shouting," he said later. "When there's a real crisis I get very cold." About a hundred feet beyond the next pile of stones stood a police officer, arms folded across his chest. Pete ran over.

"Officer," he cried at him, "Aren't you going to do something? What are you *waiting* for?" The trooper just shook his head and took a step back. For a split second it looked like Seeger, who towered over the man, would pick him up and shake him.

"I look around and the guy in back of me is getting it. Because I'm stopped, he's got to stop. And he's getting stone after stone right through his window. So I moved on."

Pete's friend Mario was caught in the back of the Seeger car: "The veterans stood on an embankment and heaved a boulder from up there. It hit the windshield like a cannonball. The highway was strewn with these rocks; steering through them was like crossing a minefield. We could feel the buffeting and the rocking and the terrible noise of these huge stones ringing against the car.

"I was scared to death. I expected any moment that damned car would roll over. Then I heard this terrible noise, a crack. Somebody said, 'My God, Greta's been hit.' A big rock had come through the window and hit her just above the eye. Danny, Pete's boy, was huddled under the seat covered with glass.

"We got to the end of the run and there was a clearing. We stopped. Some people were sitting, and we asked, 'Do you know the nearest hospital?' And they all started laughing and cackling. *Cackling.* I remember one woman rocking back and forth slapping her knees, like she'd heard a good joke. It was unbelievable, like I imagine Nazis would have been in those early street gang days in Berlin. All the way into the Bronx—more than twenty miles—you could see the injured, a long bloody alley."

When they returned to Beacon, glass covered their clothes. They could barely move without cutting themselves. Pete knelt by his three-year-old son, calming him as he pulled slivers of glass from his hair and skin: "We turned off at a nearby camp because where we were staying, we didn't have water. Hundreds of people went to the showers and carefully washed broken glass out of their hair." Obviously the rock throwers, whoever they were, existed everywhere, even in Beacon. Whom could he trust? Seeger knew almost nobody in town, not even the grocery clerk. With the kids safely in bed, Pete spread out a newspaper and methodically hammered every bit of glass from his car windows: "Unless somebody looked closely, they didn't notice we didn't have windows." Only one neighbor stopped by to see if they were injured. Seeger resolved to win his neighbors' acceptance—though it took him thirty years.

A well-known guitarist later told Seeger, "You know, I was raised in Peekskill, and I know the whole story behind that riot. The Klan organized it."

"How?" Pete asked. "I never knew for sure the Klan was up there."

"Oh, yes," he replied, "and they were in cahoots with the police. They had that place surrounded with walkie-talkies, just like a battlefield. You didn't have a chance."

"How do you know?"

"My father was on the Peekskill police force."

The Peekskill riots were an unsubtle threat that drew leftists together. "The people in Peekskill were calling out to the rest of America," said Seeger, remembering his alarm. "Whenever you find a Commie around, do something about it—don't wait for the long process of the law, do it right away, because our country is in danger."

Two weeks after the event, Pete and some friends had worked up a new song, "Hold the Line."

> Let me tell you the story of a line that was held, ©
> And many men and women whose courage we know
>   well;
> As they held the line at Peekskill on that long
>   September day,
> We will hold the line forever till the people have their
>   way.
>
> Hold the line! Hold the line!
> As we held the line at Peekskill we will hold it
>   everywhere.

Which line was really held? The one separating radicals from the rest of America? The Party's? Or perhaps the barrier separating civil liberties from mob rule—this too had broken down.

At first glance, "Hold the Line" seems a bluff. The cold war was heating up, and only five months later the junior senator from Wisconsin, Joe McCarthy, would begin waving his list of secret Communists. But Seeger was terribly serious about the song; optimism and perseverance were the bedrock of his art, a music born of political adversity. His songs were blunt weapons, but he lanced them with all his might.

Both sides claimed Peekskill as a victory, but neither won. Yellowed newspaper photos still show the hate-filled faces and terrified concertgoers, the air frozen about them in great, still blocks. On that day, the observer in Seeger departed and the activist burst forth, only to retreat as he urged a policeman to enforce the law. He inhabited De Tocqueville's America, alternately violent and pacifist, naïve and worldly wise. Yet, in the name of patriotism, conservatives would attack Seeger in every way short of assassination.

His character manifested itself in a peculiar farsightedness and the ruthlessness of principle that made him bring his children to a riot. He was a stubborn man, a tall skinny fellow who didn't like to be pushed around. The stones thrown at Peekskill (and the pickets and blacklisters who followed later) couldn't penetrate his shell of idealism. Peekskill only forced him *toward* those who throw the first stone, a passion that led him over and over to a cycle of confrontation, controversy, and, eventually, to grave discontent.

Wasn't That a Time 2

THE ROCK throwers at Peekskill might have been surprised to learn that Seeger was actually a local boy, born just ten miles away, or that his family considered itself "enormously Christian, in the Puritan, Calvinist New England tradition." By background, Seeger had more in common with local conservatives than with the immigrants, blacks, and Jews he sang with.

"When I was a teenager, I was not much interested in any of my ancestors," Pete once told an audience in introducing the song "Wasn't That a Time." "My grandmother, a member of the Mayflower Society, told me a funny story about a man who came to address them once: 'Ladies,' he said, 'those of us who come from common ancestors, let us remember that most of them were very, very common.'

"My ancestors came to this country because they didn't want to answer questions put to them by the then Un-English committees. One of them, Elder Brewster, was on the *Mayflower* with Governor Bradford, one of the leaders of the Plymouth Colony. His descendants that came my way were staunch upholders of independence among the colonists. Not one was a royalist. One of them is said to have walked down Bunker Hill backward because he wouldn't turn his back on the redcoats. One was a quartermaster and another a major on General Putnam's staff. He might have been at Valley Forge:

> *Our fathers bled at Valley Forge* ©
> *The snow was red with blood*
> *Their faith was warm, at Valley Forge*
> *Their faith was brotherhood.*
>
> *Wasn't that a time*
> *Wasn't that a time, a time to try the soul of man*
> *Wasn't that a terrible time?*

These lyrics later gave Seeger trouble before an investigating committee; the implicit patriotism of "Wasn't That a Time" infuriated conservatives. "The nerve of singers like Seeger," they would say, "to try and claim they are a part of the American story."

"These ancestors of mine," Pete continued, "were all subversives in the eyes of the established government of the British colonies. If they had lost the War of Independence, they might have each and severally been hung. . . . Later, my ancestors were to a man and woman abolitionists. My great-grandfather Seeger was a doctor like his father; he lost many patients in the town of Springfield, Massachusetts, because of his abolitionist stance. One of my great-grandmothers died as a result of having to escape from Charleston after the firing on Fort Sumter."

> And brave men died at Gettysburg
> And lie in soldiers' graves
> But there they stemmed the slavery tide
> And there the faith was saved. . . .
> Wasn't that a terrible time.

"I spent much of my life trying to forget my antecedents, I confess it. I tried to ignore them, to disparage them. I felt they were all upper-class." Seeger's family tradition dwarfed him. One relative Pete did admire was his father, Charles Seeger, "the one person that all my life I was able to talk and argue with." Yet the man closest to him also cast a shadow that Pete dodged as he grew up. "The biggest danger for Peter," his brother John said (with the insight only a sibling possesses), "was whether he'd be swallowed up in father's dreams."

In 1919, when his third son Peter was born, Charles Seeger had become as much of an outcast as the radicals in Peekskill. Yet Charles was brought up not as a radical, but as a gentleman scholar: erect and precise. Growing up on the Seeger estate on Staten Island, Charles traced his ancestors back to Gebhard Von Seeg of the Crusades and divided the world into three categories of worth: "The Seegers, friends of the Seegers, and everyone else." The Seegers had four servants and a plot of land large enough for twenty houses. Pete's grandfather had made a small fortune in sugar-refining in Mexico, and he lived in semi-retirement, writing his memoirs and playing Wagner by ear. The family took pride in being Yankee and Puritan: probity, self-control, and strict table manners were taken for granted. Like the rest of his family, Charles had the hard slim nose and high cheekbones of New Englanders who speak when spoken to.

Charles studied music at Harvard and became an aesthete scornful of politics until 1914, when at age twenty-five, he had an experience that shaped his (and Pete's) life. One evening at a wine-and-cheese party of young faculty and graduate students, an economist quietly joined their circle. As Charles and a friend finished a diatribe against socialism, the newcomer laid into them.

"You don't live in a real world, sitting in your libraries. You could talk your heads off and it wouldn't make *any* difference to *anything*," he admonished.

The young economist, Carlton Parker, stayed afterwards to introduce himself. He hadn't meant to offend, he explained, and if they were willing, he'd show them what he was talking about.

His remarks came as a shock to Charles, who thought himself worldly. He had, after all, conducted the Cologne Opera before becoming the youngest full professor in the history of the University of California, Berkeley. Charles wore a trim mustache and spectacles with gold frames; in Europe, his speech had acquired a Germanic clip. Proud, fastidious, he nonetheless had a mischievous sparkle in his eye, as if warning people not to take him *too* seriously.

In New York Charles had been introduced to an equally slim violinist of excellent family, Constance de Clyver Edson. Their courtship was quick and musical; the couple played parlor concerts in high society. As it was considered improper for a young lady to be seen by those she hadn't met, Charles and Constance performed behind a screen. In 1911 they married, and soon afterward set up their household in what seemed another continent, California.

Constance was a shy but headstrong girl, raised in Tunisia and Paris: blond, with linen-white skin and a delicate smile. Grime wouldn't stick to her. Her grandfather ran one of the most fashionable schools in New York, the Charliere Institute. Though related to the wealthy Curtises of Philadelphia, she grew up with more noblesse oblige than money; her mother was an incurable spendthrift. Constance practiced extremely hard and watched the family finances. She was a student (and eventually a teacher) at what would be the Juilliard School, and classical music dominated her life. She communicated through her violin; in person, she often struck people as dour and self-conscious, with a poor sense of humor. She hesitated to exchange her New York social life and her fine antiques for California's primitive comforts; but the financial security of Charles's job made the sacrifice worthwhile.

Berkeley was not then a city of coffee palaces and boutiques along Telegraph Avenue. The Seegers lived in a quiet town of farmland and tall eucalyptus forests; wildcats and packs of dogs roamed the hills behind the house. Their windows looked out on San Francisco Bay, a flat glassy table of blue. The couple gave dinner parties and recitals; after the birth of their two sons, Charles III and John, they hired a governess. Constance hated housework, and Charles refused to be disturbed in the morning before he was ready. "Father liked things just so: the table napkins, the settings, everything had to be perfect," Charles III remembered.

Two weeks after the faculty party where Charles had been challenged, he and the economist Carlton Parker drove up the long, dusty driveway of a hops ranch in the San Joaquin Valley. The wagons of migrant workers lined the road; off to one side were tents, farm animals, a lot of children— and a latrine, nothing but a board over a ditch. Charles had never seen anything like it.

This was an unlikely spot for a political conversion. Everyone over the age of six picked busily. In the middle of this activity, Charles spotted a double of his son John, the same color eyes and hair. After days in the field, however, this boy looked wretched and pockmarked: "We talked to some of the workers, and they told us of the miserable wages and the hard working conditions," explaining how they walked for days through the hot, dusty valleys—only to find the promised jobs gone when they arrived. Charles returned to Berkeley a different man.

"Deeply shocked, Seeger was giving a speech about what he had seen," his son reported, "when a burly voice from the audience said, 'Sit down, you lily-livered bastard. You've just found out about these things. We've known them all our lives.'"

The fellow who said this probably belonged to the Industrial Workers of the World (IWW) who were then organizing in the fields. This union of bindle stiffs, miners, loggers, and rebel workers had an enthusiastic (and musical) membership out West; when songs wouldn't get better working conditions, they weren't shy about sabotage. Charles stopped by their office, and before he knew it, he was a regular on the trolley linking Berkeley and the San Francisco waterfront, near IWW headquarters. Charles tried to juggle his new-found radicalism and his academic career, a precarious task.

In his first years of teaching, Charles had managed well. He had coauthored a respectable book on harmony and built up enrollment in his courses. His dean had been pleased. Seeger's one eccentricity was his insistence on approaching music from a historical and social perspective, introducing the discipline now known as musicology into America. His attempts at linking music and society had produced good-natured chuckles among his colleagues, who underestimated the self-confident, nattily dressed intellectual. Charles was a scrapper. In faculty meetings, he could be fanatically stubborn when convinced he was right. When a professor sponsored a concert that included whistling, Charles insulted his choice "in no uncertain terms," and later panned one of his rival's concerts without hearing a note. Eventually his elderly opponent fell ill and left school; Seeger triumphed, but he left enemies behind. He had an infuriating way of tuning out: If he didn't want to see someone, when that person walked into the room, Charles simply walked out.

Charles's haughtiness softened after his conversion in the San Joaquin Valley, but the Seegers kept up their social obligations. Friends had provided letters of introduction to San Francisco's prominent families, and when Charles was not visiting the IWW office on Market Street or stalking the docks with longshoremen, he hobnobbed on Nob Hill. Between his lectures on music in the Renaissance he found time to compose an operetta and pass out leaflets. His contradictions amused him, but his balancing act could not continue for long. The war in Europe upset this equilibrium.

Since 1914 news of the European war had steadily increased, but California, so far from the front, had remained neutral. By 1917, though, the university community was becoming solidly pro-Ally—except for the music department, which revered Germans from Bach to Wagner. Seldom one to shy away from controversy, Charles told his dean (a native Englishman) that Germany and England were both imperialist powers, and as far as *he* was concerned, they could fight each other to a stalemate.

Charles opposed war as fervently as Pete would fight American involvement in Vietnam. His IWW friends complained about the government's Committee on Public Information, which had launched the most extensive pro-war advertising campaign in history. Even Constance moved to the Left. She called herself a socialist, but she was not really a political person: she liked Norman Thomas because he drove an old, cheap car.

The growing pro-war sentiment only drove Charles closer to the IWW. Once he arrived for a talk and found a police cordon and a huge crowd surrounding the entrance. Plainclothesmen filled up the standing room, "down to the last square inch." Seeger lectured on Bertrand Russell's pacifism and at the end, the moderator asked him to join the IWW. Charles declined with irony, claiming he was unworthy "of mixing my bourgeois background with your proletarian ancestries."

Word traveled back across the Bay: That young professor was "going a bit beyond the bounds of decency." A formerly friendly biologist cut him dead as they passed on campus. Charles turned sharply and caught his arm, asking, "What's the matter?"

"I do not recognize people who approve of bayoneting Belgian children to barn doors," the biologist replied. Charles, trying to be equally uncivil, turned on his heel.

He ignored the stares as best he could. To escape the campus, he bought a gleaming, black Model T Ford. Adding a primitive camper with a hammock, Charles, with Constance and their boys, Charles and John, traveled through the open wilderness that was prewar California, up the dirt roads and canyons to the waterfalls of Yosemite. The trailer bumped along back roads to cross the Sierras at Tioga Pass, two miles above sea level. Below stood a forest of sequoias, the oldest in the nation: dark, leafy giants, tall as skyscrapers. The hostilities of Charles's life in Berkeley fell away among the rivers and snowy mountains.

At other times Charles sought music in the wilds. The anthropologist Alfred Kroeber had played him Indian music recorded on phonocylinders, and the Seegers hunted songs among the Hoopa Indians on the foggy northern coast of California, where the Klamath River churns to the sea.

Each time the family returned to Berkeley, however, they found their situation worsened. The university administration began hinting it was time for a sabbatical, to be followed by a permanent leave of absence. Then, in April 1917, war was declared. President Wilson signed the Espionage Act, and a wave of sedition trials began against war resisters. Vigilantes calling themselves Sedition Stompers cursed and attacked pacifists, particularly those with German-sounding names like Seeger. Brass bands played "I'd Like to See the Kaiser with a Lily in His Hand." Everything German became taboo, and sauerkraut had to have a new name: "liberty cabbage."

In September 1917, Charles's IWW friends in San Francisco were arrested as part of a national raid against "un-Americans." Local anarchist Tom Mooney was sentenced to death on highly suspect evidence. In Boston, a mob of sailors broke into the headquarters of the Boston Socialist Party and wrecked the offices.

As the unpopularity of his position grew, Seeger hardened in his opinions, showing the discipline and love of a good fight that Pete later emulated. Charles's friends warned him he would get into trouble. Uniformed student-soldiers (ROTC) loudly paraded outside the offices of "unpatriotic" professors like Seeger. His savings were few, and he and Constance had two kids to support; but instead of backing off for a more prudent course, Charles grew intransigent. Asked to buy a war bond on campus, he answered hotly, "I don't approve of war and will *never* contribute voluntarily." Remarks like this spread quickly.

When his draft board asked him to register, Charles declared himself a conscientious objector. In 1918 alternative military service was not widely accepted, and the first reaction of many draft boards was to slap COs into prison or call them traitors. A confrontation could have been avoided. Charles was thirty and underweight. In the last trying year he'd lost twenty pounds; his suit jacket drooped about him like clothes on a hanger. All in all, Charles didn't look like much of a soldier. The judge taking his deposition begged him to change his application—there was no need of the CO business—the army would refuse him anyway. But Charles Seeger was in no mood to make life easy; he insisted on registering as a CO.

Pete's grandparents were disappointed about Charles's attitude. He was an embarrassment, unlike his older brother Alan, who couldn't wait for the U.S. to join the war.

Thin, energetic, an effusive idealist, Alan Seeger always said life was not worth living past thirty. Everything was the moment for him, and war attracted him like a beacon. Alan had Byron's genius of merging poetry and life; change itself seemed ennobling and glorious to him, "the old order irrevocably vanished." After graduating from Harvard, he lived among bohemians in Greenwich Village, writing poetry and sleeping on the couch of his pro-Bolshevik classmate John Reed, author of *Ten Days That Shook the World*. Charles was the family's intellectual and Alan its adventurer.

Uncle Alan, as Pete Seeger would lovingly call him, volunteered for the French Foreign Legion when the war was only a few weeks old. On July 4, 1916, as he was preparing to read an ode at a public ceremony in Paris, Alan was shot down by machine guns while leading a charge. "I have a rendez-vous with Death" he wrote in his *Last Poems*. Alan became a legend in the family; his flamboyant courage made a high standard to match. "Pete [who bore a striking physical resemblance to his uncle] always said that if he could play one person in a film, he wanted to play Alan," his wife remarked later.

In Berkeley, a young economist Charles knew was ordered to report to military camp in the Sierras. Like Charles, he was a CO, and his prospects weren't good. Rumors traveled about what happened to war resisters in these camps. Not everybody who went came back, and those who returned told of suffering and even torture. In one camp Charles heard of, COs were lined up twenty-five at a time and blasted with fire hoses. The force of the water broke bones and dislocated backs. After the pacifists picked themselves up, they were hit a second time. At Fort Riley in Kansas, COs had ropes "put about their necks, hoisting them off their feet until they were at the point of collapse. Meanwhile officers punched them in their ankles and shins. . . . A garden hose was played on their faces with the nozzle six inches from them, until they collapsed completely and were carried and dumped screaming and moaning into their cells." Only one of seven hundred withstood this treatment and ended up classified as a CO.

As a full professor, Charles might have avoided this fate, but why wait to see if he was called up? Charles and Constance decided to leave California. The departure was overdue; the president of the university, "a properly chauvinistic Britisher," had all but fired Seeger. On a hot September afternoon in 1918, the Seegers left their house keys with a tenant and headed east. Charles's "sabbatical" lasted forty years.

Losing his professorship for his activism affected Charles profoundly; he wouldn't bow to expediency, but he "retreated," as his eldest son put it, feeling "a bitter defeat." On the other hand, the experience would lead Charles to encourage Peter to do the things he had been afraid to do. He hoped his children would see the point of his principles.

Riding a slow train across the country, Charles and Constance had plenty of time to take stock of their lives. Charles's health had begun to fail; Constance had only one skill, her violin. The couple had no income, and Constance fretted over how they would live. All her life she had been pressured: as a prodigy, a debutante, a professor's wife. Now she had two kids to take care of, and a husband who threw over his job for his conscience. The strain told on her, and she developed a "deep, dark, dyeddown pessimistic" streak where money was concerned. She and Charles began to drift apart.

Charles's medical problems turned out to be serious. A physician who examined him said he was headed for a nervous breakdown. From the strain he had suffered in Berkeley, the musicologist had developed chronic indigestion. He was a sick man, shot to pieces: "I didn't think I would last long."

On top of all this, Constance discovered she was pregnant.

Abiyoyo  3

IN THE WINTER of 1918 the family arrived at Charles's parents' estate in Patterson, fifty miles north of New York City. They had come to a land thick with birch woods and creeks, where the towns had the names of Indians and Dutch settlers. Thirty miles away, the Hudson River glistened and slapped at its rocky banks. Charles's parents lived on a dozen quiet acres near the Taconic Mountains with a barn, a garage, an expanse of lawn, and a main house with balconies of wood carved to resemble wrought iron. Charles and Constance settled into separate bedrooms, and on May 3, 1919, soon after the treaty ending World War I went to the printers, Pete Seeger was born.

His father still felt defeated by the events in Berkeley: "I couldn't write. I couldn't compose music. I couldn't earn a living. I couldn't do anything." He lost his taste for performing; repeating the same tired pieces at parlor concerts bored him. Charles hit on the idea of a trip "to bring music to the poor people of America, who didn't have any music." He and Constance would build a trailer and explore the musical back roads of America. The trip would be a needed tonic, for Charles remained weak: "The doctor said I wouldn't live very long, so my wife and I staked everything that we had— and our marriage too—on that trip."

Charles borrowed money from his folks and built a trailer in the most meticulous way, cutting tongue-in-groove joints into maple, adding wagon wheels and tires of solid rubber. Stuffed into special compartments were gallons of local maple syrup, pumpkins, and sacks of potatoes—all of New York they could carry into the unknown. In November 1920, with Peter a year and a half old, the Seegers set out for the South.

Driving through New York City, Charles couldn't resist showing the sophisticated set a mobile home, 1920-style. The Ford's custom transmission roared down Broadway pulling the one-ton trailer through the wide, uncrowded streets of midtown Manhattan. Peter and his brothers peeped out from inside. Their elegant mother rode in front, and beside her was their father in a new beard and wire-rims, tooting at the horsecarts.

Across New Jersey, Pennsylvania, and Maryland they rolled, the spinet piano bouncing heavily in the back. In Richmond, Virginia, the weather was so hot, the trailer left grooves in the asphalt streets. Back into the Virginia hills they climbed and out across the coastal lowlands, green from winter rains. Finally they came to rest in Pinehurst, North Carolina, twenty miles from the present site of Fort Bragg.

On the road, the children got restless, and Charles made up stories and songs to keep them in bed. Peter, his blond hair falling about like a thatched roof, adored his father's "nutty stories"; the earliest one he remembered was about a little trailer in a long, wet puddle.

"One *very* rainy day, the road was covered with water. But the trailer wouldn't back up, so the driver figured, well, the puddle is probably not too deep. They kept on going. It was raining so hard they couldn't see the end of the puddle. It just got deeper and deeper. It was up to the hubcaps. The rain kept coming down, and a mist settled around them.

"They stayed on the road by seeing the telephone poles or the fences on either side. No one knew how deep it was going to get. Finally, to their relief, the road emerged from the puddle. They reached solid ground, and off they went."

Peter bounced along in his cradle-bed, listening to the story over and over, as the rhythms of the wheels blended into the tale. Charles made "quite a suspense out of it"; but always the road reemerged, and the child drifted off to sleep.

After settling in, the Seegers hiked through the fragrant hills, inviting local residents to free concerts. Amazingly enough, the mountain people came, and went away in awe: imagine a fiddle making sounds like that! After the show, Constance would do the wash by their campfire; it wasn't the most comfortable situation, but she didn't complain. Hands accustomed to the polished wood of violins stirred clothes in a metal tub. Pictures show Peter dancing by the fire to his father's music.

These were golden days for the Seegers, but their musical social work had little effect. The family opened the ears of their new community, but they were more of a novelty than an inspiration, and novelty fades. Pete's parents brought their culture as an ennobling gift; but they touched off no Handel revivals in North Carolina. Music transplants poorly, they discovered, especially in the name of civilization. The failure at Pinehurst began for Charles a long, lonely period, trying to join music and the social concerns born that hot afternoon in the San Joaquin Valley. Charles knew music could shape society. He could almost touch the connection, but its form eluded him.

On the Seegers' last night, the wagon was packed and ready to go, except for their fold-down stage. At nightfall, the hollow was crowded as the North Carolinans wished their odd friends Godspeed. That evening's concert had an unexpected finale: The locals actually *did* have music. They produced fiddles and guitars and played the surprised Seegers hillbilly music. By complete accident, Peter heard his first authentic folk music when he was two.

Six years later, on a clear morning in the summer of 1927, Peter woke before anyone else and wandered through the grounds of his grandparents' home in Patterson. He was eight, with long, silky hair and sky-blue eyes. He left the barn where his brothers and father slept and lounged under the arching elms which separated the outbuildings from the main house. Across the lawn drifted the smells of fresh rolls and country bacon from the sun-warmed parlor. Peter crept back into the barn and smiled up at his sleeping brothers. At the top of his lungs, he called out a cowboy holler:

> *Wake up, Jacob, day's a breakin'*   ©
> *Peas in the pot and the hoecakes bakin'*
> *Early in the morning, almost day*
> *Better come soon, gonna throw 'em away.*

His brothers bounded down the ladders from the haylofts, yelling at Peter, and a pleasant morning commotion began. "We'd bounce tennis balls up against the wall and call it barn squash—like father, who occasionally played squash at the Harvard Club," Pete said. "Afterwards we'd close off the door to the courtyard, take off all our clothes, and pail water over ourselves."

In 1927, while the Seeger boys chased tennis balls in the country, the headlines followed Babe Ruth, headed for his sixty-home-run season. Charles Lindbergh had just returned from the first transatlantic flight. In rural communities like Patterson, families gathered around the new wonder box, radio. Wind-up gramophones were still a novelty; the Seeger boys, in their grandparents' absence, listened to pop tunes like "Red, Red Robin" and "S'Wonderful."

Once a week the boys came in from the barn for a sit-down dinner. Dressed up in sailor suits, the boys were careful not to sprawl on the sofa, and they used their finger bowls, as the cook had taught them. There was no Gershwin on when grandmother was around; she thought the tunes "dreadfully vulgar." Grandmother Elsie looked like a *New Yorker* cartoon. She entered the room like a galleon in full sail; her feet didn't seem to move, she just swept in. Sometimes she would look at Peter and exclaim: "You come from very good stock. Don't *ever* forget it—very good stock."

Grandfather Charles was equally proud of his ancestry. He had made his money first in sugarcane and now in rubber, and dreamed of retiring to France to cultivate a Parisian mustache. He looked like dukes are supposed to look, but never do.

The family assumed Peter and the other boys would distinguish themselves, like Alan or Charles—and more than wealth or fame, they expected high moral standards. "Your word should be as good as any piece of paper," Peter learned in elementary school. As to profession, Pete's grandfather wanted a businessman, his mother a musical virtuoso. Pete, however, was not keen on either idea; he meant to sidestep family tradition, which remained as strong as when Charles had grown up, in the days when the Seegers printed a family newspaper modestly titled *The Prophet*.

Peter had been sent off to boarding school at four, an unusually early age. Soon after the Pinehurst trip, Charles and Constance found themselves fighting over money. Constance had set up a secret bank account; when Charles found out, he exploded. The summer the boys were at Patterson—1927—they divorced. In Peter's case, neither really had custody; he was always off at school. The closest he ever came to a home was the barn in Patterson.

Like many children of divorce, he was caught between parents and developed a lifelong aversion to family quarrels. Constance felt wronged by Charles, who still hadn't found a full-time job. She had her smooth, milky complexion, but ever since Charles had been fired in Berkeley, the pressure of supporting a family had soured her inside. The couple also had radically different ideas about music; Peter's musical education was "the last big fight" the couple had. Was Peter to be trained properly, Constance demanded, or was he going to grow up a musical illiterate?

Charles's laissez-faire answer reflected the changing currents of music in the twenties. While Constance remained faithful to the three Bs (Beethoven, Brahms, and Bach), Charles was intrigued by musical experimentation: the twelve-tone compositions of Schönberg and Webern, and Bartok's experiments with folk music in orchestral settings. One of Charles's favorite composers, Shostakovich, eulogized the Soviet Union in stirring music. These currents propelled Charles on his search for a social dimension to music; and Peter absorbed his scorn for "fine" music.

Of the three sons, Peter was the only one who refused piano or voice lessons. Yet he wasn't unmusical, just undisciplined: "Whistles, anything that made music I banged on. I didn't want to study, I was just having fun. . . . The idea of reading notes was as boring to me as painting by numbers." Another problem was Peter's foot. According to the way Constance taught, the whole body was kept motionless, so that the energy would pour out in the music. But no matter what he did, Peter couldn't keep his foot from tapping. In his eighth year, his parents gave him two instruments: a ukulele and a quartersize violin. One was for "good" music, the other for fooling around. Peter never practiced the violin, even when it had the friendlier name of fiddle. The uke, on the other hand, seemed daring, with its light, unelaborated sound. Peter played it constantly, till his brothers lost their patience; then he would sneak up on them from behind the sofa and start in again.

Years later, Peter made up a story-song about a boy who played the ukulele. The boy lived happily with his magician father, whom the townspeople shunned. Then one day a giant appeared, Abiyoyo, a monster as tall as the sun. With the help of a song and the father, the boy saved the town from destruction. In the end of the fantasy, based on a Bantu legend from South Africa, the boy became a hero, and the townsfolk cried: "Come back! Bring your damn ukulele, we don't care." A close friend later called this tale of ukuleles, magical fathers, and victorious songs "the key to Pete Seeger's imagination."

Afternoons when there was nothing to do at Patterson, when the wooden boats had all been carved and the vegetable plot tended, Peter often disappeared into the woods. He loved to play Indian, creeping through the bushes in a loincloth, his face painted with a paste of berries and red-iron soil. Once he made himself a miniature tepee, meticulously sewing canvas with a wooden needle and leather strips. Other times Peter stalked rabbits with his homemade bow and arrow. He carefully stepped on rotted wood, but the rabbits proved too quick. The best he could do was to scare them, howling like a coyote or hissing like a rattler. Then, surrounded by the rich, hot summer smells, Peter would dip his feet in the stream and read his favorite book, the Canadian naturalist Ernest Thompson Seton's *Two Little Savages.*

This largely forgotten romance of woodcraft and Indian lore fascinated Peter absolutely. The boys in Seton's book make music by stretching a calfskin drum, Indian-style. They cook over a wood fire and make their own tepee. When the boys finally huddle inside, lighting a fire without matches, they have a reward Peter craved: "the pleasure of achievement in the line of great ambition." "Seton was one of the big influences on my life. I read every one of his books. I came across a picture of Seton saying, 'Could you survive in the woods with just yourself and an axe?' Seton—a founder of the Boy Scouts—thought boys should pattern their ideal on the American tradition: self-reliant, strong, moral, and clean. Whatever you had you shared."

Seton's teachings gave Seeger dual ideals: the independent axeman, who survived outside society by his strength; and a tribal communism of uncompromising moral purity. In time Peter became both: the self-sufficient craftsman and a communalist, looking for his tribe.

"Talk about ivory towers, I grew up in a woodland tower. . . . I knew all about plants and could identify birds and snakes, but I didn't know that anti-Semitism existed or what a Jew was until I was fourteen years old. My contact with black people was literally nil. . . . If someone asked me what I was going to be when I grew up, I'd say Indian or farmer or forest ranger. Maybe an artist. I'd always loved to draw." A slim, dreamy child, he would rather hike in the snow to sketch animal prints than sip tea in grandmother's parlor. He would spend rainy afternoons poring over magazine ads of Scottish moors, mountain resorts in Carolina, or safaris across Africa. He read romances by a British author, George Henty: tales of jousts of honor and the quest for the holy grail. Between this medieval chivalry and Seton's Indians, Peter steeped himself in woodsy absolutes.

Only through music did he come out of his shell, like the time he and his roommate, Bob Claiborne, led a group sing at their upper-crust boarding school, Spring Hill, in Litchfield, Connecticut. Pete's mother gave him a book of sea chanties, and the pair rigged up a blue backdrop and a ship's railing. Another friend held a bottle while they sang "What Shall We Do with the Drunken Sailor"; by the last song, they had the whole auditorium singing. With his uke Pete easily became the center of attention, no matter how awful he sounded. For a half-hour his shyness would melt, and he would bask in the attention, only to feel a letdown as the singing ended. Then it was back to feeling alone and hiking off by himself. Part of his isolation came from his family situation, for Peter never had much home life. From his fourth till his seventeenth year, he saw his family only at Christmas, Easter, and summers. One of his former schoolmates, George Draper of the *San Francisco Chronicle,* described what separations like these mean to a child: "No tears allowed at family separations—that you get used to early. You have this emotional blindness. . . . You don't grow up to see all the compromises of a family."

John Seeger watched his kid brother grow up far from the family, without need for emotional support, terribly independent. Family life, when he had it, was never terribly warm. "In the second and third decades of this century, when I was brought up," Peter recalled, "the modern way to think was 'Don't baby your child. Give him a good schedule and obey it strictly.' . . . There wasn't any cuddling in our family; they held our hand, yes, but a lot of people would think it a very cold childhood."

One gray and snowy day on Christmas break in 1932, Peter tromped through the frozen grass in Central Park. Only policemen on their horses ambled through the icy meadows. Peter, thirteen, felt out of place. He spent half the vacation with his mother and the rest with his father, wandering like Holden Caulfield in a city he recognized but no longer knew.

He had arranged to meet his father and new stepmother on East Eighty-ninth Street, a good walk from his mother's studio on West Sixty-fifth Street. Peter enjoyed the fresh air. After listening to Constance's pupils play scales, he had felt suffocated. Before he could leave, Constance had sat him down for a talk: "You must take lessons. You've got the hands that can do it. I'm sorry, but we're going to insist. . . ." Then, in the hallway, his mother had quizzed him on ways to save money. He practically leapt out the door.

"My father was the one person I really related to," Peter said. "For good or bad, I had very few relationships with anybody else. I was cordial with everybody—I didn't like to fight and I didn't like to argue. My brothers? We got along; but they were much older than me—six and seven years older—and in a different world." He might have gone on to admit, as Henry Adams did, that "his education was chiefly inheritance, and during the next five or six years, his father alone counted for much."

Arriving at the apartment of Charles and his new wife, Ruth Crawford Seeger, Peter found them leaving to hear Aaron Copland speak at the left-wing Pierre DeGeyter Club.

The couple took the boy to an unheated loft in Greenwich Village. As Peter watched from the back of the room, two dozen prominent New York composers arrived, dressed in corduroys and leather jackets, carrying scores and instruments. Trained in the best music schools in the country, they were the renegades of the Philharmonic, passionately political. "The social system is going to hell," they told each other. "Music might be able to do something about it. Let's see if we can try. We *must* try."

Charles had finally found a way to mix music and activism. He belonged to a group within the DeGeyter Club, the Composers Collective, which tried to compose songs for picket and unemployment lines. As devotees of the new dissonance, however, the musicians sought to uplift workers' musical tastes while stirring up revolution. The Composers Collective was probably the first group in the world to attempt a twelve-tone protest song.

Peter did his best to follow Copland's address, but neither the politics nor the music made sense to him, what with the talk of German composer Hanns Eisler and the slogan "Music is a weapon in the class struggle." He did sense how important the Collective's mission was to his father; Charles now wrote music columns for the *Daily Worker* under a pseudonym. Peter later heard about his father's entry in a contest for the best May Day song. When the submissions were played through, the Collective chose Copland's "Into the Streets May 1st," with its loud, rhythmic chords on the piano. Charles agreed that musically, Copland's song was best; but his was more singable, he insisted. These were marching songs, after all, and how were workers going to carry a piano on a march?

Charles's colleagues—like most of the Left before 1935—disliked folk music, which they called "defeatist melancholy, morbidity, hysteria, and triviality" because the music predated Marx. Doctrinaire radicals like Eisler thought folk songs "a badge of servitude"; Charles himself called them "dead relics." Ironically, Pete heard these sentiments at a time of tremendous American musical growth. Gene Autry, "America's number one singing cowboy," was captivating the nation with his movies and "western" music (later called "country and western"). In Kentucky, the Monroe brothers had developed a sound later named after their band, the Bluegrass Boys; Bob Wills broadcast "western swing" over KVOO in Tulsa.

Like his father, Peter knew nothing about country and hillbilly music. He was caught between musical eras; his choices were among classical, experimental, pop music, jazz—and none of these interested him. He left Copland's talk confused, but thrilled by the composers' high passions: "I got the feeling that here were people out to change the world. The world might be corrupt, but they were confident they could change it." Charles's experiments in protest songs were too highbrow to succeed, but at least he was out challenging tradition, not hiding from it in the woods.

Pete went away with one of his father's radical rounds, which he and John sang on hiking trips:

> *Oh, Joy upon the earth* ©
> *To live and see the day*
> *When Rockefeller Senior*
> *Shall up to me and say:*
> *Comrade, can you spare a dime?*

His father's radicalism actually fit Peter as well as Seton had, different as the two philosophies were. Resistance was part of the New England nature; Peter could look back on the side of his family he preferred to think about, the generations of predecessors who viewed the world as a thing to be reformed, filled with evil forces to be abolished. The duty to keep at that battle continued, endlessly. The Depression swept in on Peter's woodland tower like a hurricane, shattering its isolation. In the next months he began reading radical newspapers, watching Eisenstein's films, and generally soaking up the radical education New York offered in the 1930s.

For a firsthand look into the Depression, Charles walked his sons through New York's Lower East Side, telling them: "The streets aren't so well lit as where we live." Skeletons of buildings stood empty, the floors covered with broken glass. Shutters fell off their hinges. Father and son walked for miles until their feet ached. The Lower East Side stretched endlessly, compared to the sliver of well-to-do life on Fifth and Madison Avenues. The garbage-filled alleys were so different from Peter's schools in New England that he visited them as a conscience-stricken tourist.

If the Lower East Side was poor, by 1932, the rest of the country was hard on its heels. Banks called in loans and foreclosed farms by the thousands. With mortgages gone and the dust bowl blowing, families wandered the land. One in four was out of work—and the country had no unemployment insurance, no Social Security.

Through the Composers Collective, Peter met some people who called themselves Communists: "It was quite different from the cartoons of a person with a beard and a bomb. I found these were very organized, highly intelligent, and argumentative people. But my actual experience in relating to the American people was zero, I mean *zero.*"

His new comrades told him of textile strikes in Gastonia and Marion, North Carolina; of the Scottsboro boys, blacks imprisoned for rape on weak evidence; of songs and coal strikes in Harlan County; and of Norman Thomas, the Socialist who received 900,000 votes for President in 1932. The Communist Party had captivated Charles and his friends; joining the Socialists, as John Dos Passos said, had about the same effect "as drinking a bottle of near-beer." In the streets, Pete could watch volunteer squads from the CP-led unemployment councils restore the furniture of evicted tenants; these people were *heroes.*

Soon Charles was taking Peter to his first May Day demonstration. They crowded in line on Fifth Avenue singing IWW tunes like "Pie in the Sky" and Maurice Sugar's "Soup Song." New York's finest rode by, their nightsticks slapping against the horses' flanks. A delicious defiance floated in the air. The singing and laughing made Peter feel part of a high-minded family, far different from his own. He didn't notice that a few blocks away, another contingent paraded separately from the Communist—the Socialists. The "family" Peter had joined was not on speaking terms with its relatives.

Back at school, Peter came across a Bolshevik children's book in the library, *New Russia's Primer*. Written with a Whitmanesque grandeur, this children's book promised a new world in the next Five Year Plan—new chemical brigades to hasten production and cut pollution. Futuristic tales of Russian scouts in uncharted forests were not lost on Peter, who saw the pioneer spirit of *Two Little Savages* harnessed to a socialist ideal.

It was a heady moment when Ernest Thompson Seton met Lenin's Young Pioneers on Peter's bookshelf. But for this Depression-born radicalism, he might have become a teacher, like John, or a scientist, like Charles III. Yet any connection between strumming his uke and the *Daily Worker's* politics escaped Peter's notice, though father and son now heard their first concert of folk songs.

This happened at an opening of the murals of Thomas Hart Benton, Charles's fellow instructor at the New School. Home on vacation, Peter drank in the bohemian crowd of composers and painters sipping wine and chatting noisily. In one corner of the gallery, Benton amazed the boy and his father with "John Henry." Pete's foot started tapping immediately. This was the stuff— much better than mother's dreary violin exercises. Even in a room echoing with conversation and overshadowed by fifteen-foot murals, the music cut right through him. Peter didn't understand what attracted him; later he decided it was the rhythm. Afterward, Benton lent Charles some records, but the music didn't take. When Pete first heard the folk banjo—Dock Boggs's version of "Pretty Polly"—he thought the melody sounded Chinese.

In the fall of 1932 Peter entered high school at Avon Old Farms. Avon trained boys to take their place in the company of men, to preserve "the elite of the well-ordered mind." Peter was going as a scholarship student, but Avon's dress code disturbed him: Brooks Brothers suits, with starched wing collars and bow ties required for supper every night.

When he arrived at the school Peter could scarcely believe his surroundings, which resembled an English manor in the 1500s. The school's patron, an eccentric steel heiress, had spent five million dollars creating a Tudor village in the Connecticut woods. Peter couldn't help admiring this fortress. After unpacking, he explored the three-thousand-acre park; the woods delighted him. He wondered at the blue-gray slate roof and ran his hands over rough red-brick walls, two feet thick. The splendor simultaneously repulsed and appealed to him.

Peter had a hard time adjusting to this new life. One moment he read about Lenin and the next he sang in a chapel of hand-hewn oak beams and panes of leaded glass. The boys teased him about his "sweet girlish complexion," as schoolmate Bill Leonard, later president of CBS News, remembered it. Even at sixteen, Peter stood only five feet one, with long curls; he ended up with the female roles in Avon's theatricals, including "Consuela, the Bare-backed Tango Queen." In addition, he found himself chronically short of cash among the free-spending children of executives. Instead of feeling inferior, though, he earned pocket money by shining classmates' shoes—and took pride in his self-reliance. He never entered into the camaraderie of boarding-school life, and scholarship, the refuge of the anti-social, never held his attention; he earned mostly Bs and Cs.

One of his more memorable events at Avon occurred soon after his arrival. Peter met a teacher, Charles Langmuir, who owned a four-string banjo he wasn't using. (The four-string, or tenor, banjo was popular for Dixieland jazz.) Peter toyed with the banjo and decided he *must* have one. His strategy was to ask his mother; she'd prefer a classical instrument but would be happy to have him playing anything.

Constance had written, "Did you receive the package with the shirts, the wing collars, the patent leather shoes? . . ." She got no answer. Her next letter ended: "Please check what clothes you received." Still no answer. With the third letter came another checklist. Peter answered, "Mother, please, nobody wears those patent leather shoes, they're awful—and a complete waste of money." In between he wrote, "There's a master here who would like to sell his banjo to me for ten dollars. Please, may I have it?" His mother's letters never mentioned the banjo. Finally, near the end of term, she sent a checklist of all the things he was supposed to have written home about—"Did you receive my package, the sweater, the underwear? . . ." and Peter doggedly replied, "Yes, yes, yes"; then he made his own checkbox: "Please, mother, can I have that banjo?"

Peter got his instrument, and music gradually caught his fancy. He started playing in Avon's five-piece Hot Jazz Club, learning tunes like "Night and Day," "Blue Skies," and "I Got Rhythm." In this, his first musical group, he was exposed to one of the melodically richest periods of American pop music. Even in later years, when his musical tastes had changed, he found himself doodling on Gershwin tunes.

As a child Peter had banged away at the autoharp or ukulele for emotional release. As an adolescent he slowly came to appreciate how music frames a mood and affects people. His Glee Club instructor, Dr. David Boyden, worked with Peter's clear but ordinary soprano voice, remembering his talent as "unfocused." Boyden taught him fundamentals of harmony and drilled the chorus with Palestrina and spirituals. But music was still little more than a game to Pete, something to tease with or provoke authority. Singing harmony was frowned on in chapel, but when Peter had an anti-authority impulse, he stepped to the back of the group and harmonized during vespers.

Long before receiving his first banjo, Peter had chosen a nonmusical career: journalism. In elementary school, he had published a penny paper, the *Spring Hill Telegraph*. At Avon Peter started the chatty *Avon Weekly*. He had read muckraker Lincoln Steffens's autobiography with great excitement and threw himself into journalism, quickly earning a reputation for overworking his contributors. "Watch out for Pete," his sports columnist Dan North was warned. "He'll have you doing his own work if you're not careful." As an editor, Seeger occasionally ran afoul of the school administration; he wrote one devastating story about a snake loose in the dorms, the property of poet Archibald MacLeish's son, Kenneth.

"It was one of my funniest stories," Peter chuckled later, "and they censored it out. MacLeish had a big snake, which had broken a rib. He'd taken the animal to his room to nurse it, but the snake escaped. Kids in the dorm said, 'I'm not going to live in that building with an eight-foot Texas bull snake loose.' Well, they looked everywhere and couldn't find it. Commander Hunter, the assistant provost, got upset. 'MacLeish,' he said, 'you'll stay in your room until that snake is found.' Of course how could the boy find the snake when he's in the room?"

The incident gave the aspiring journalist his first lesson in politics. He typed up his story, but Commander Hunter told him not to publish it. When the young editor protested, Hunter insisted, complaining that the publicity would ruin the school. Peter naïvely agreed, all the while developing a vehement distaste for censorship. Next time, he promised himself, he'd stand on his rights.

He didn't wait long for a second round. A Jewish student wrote his paper a letter on anti-Semitism: "There's a lot of talk about democracy and freedom in this country and in the school, but when it comes down to the way people actually act, face it, they don't always live by their pretty words." The student told Peter he could print the letter—if he dared—but he had to keep it anonymous. He agreed, running off the paper himself on the battered old mimeograph.

In the early thirties anti-Semitism was growing in America. The pro-Hilter Liberty League raved about Jewish bankers; Pete's classmates—and ten million others—heard Father Coughlin attack President Roosevelt's "Jew Deal" on the radio. In gentile society the issue was hushed up. "The guys who'd been making anti-Semitic cracks were furious," Peter remembered. These were husky fellows, and they cornered Seeger one afternoon: "Who wrote that letter?" Pete refused to say.

Commander Hunter asked him the same question. Peter again refused to name his source. Hunter, an ex-Navy man who took pride in discipline, called the boy into his book-lined study and gave him hell. Peter sat there and fumed. He walked away in a slow burn, hating the "bluff old phony" but uncertain what to do. He had given his word, but the provost was threatening to take away the paper, or expel him.

His situation paralleled that of unfriendly witnesses before the House Committee on Un-American Activities. Resistance was symbolic, for the provost undoubtedly guessed the letter writer's identity—there were only a few full-blooded Jews at Avon. The point was apparently to humiliate Peter publicly. Had he been ambitious, he might have arranged to exempt himself from academic requirements in exchange for giving the name. Had he more political cunning, he might have exacted limits on future censorship.

Seeger gave in, without conditions.

"I guess I showed a talent for compromise," he said wistfully forty-five years later. "I didn't want to be a *cause célèbre* and figured OK, I wouldn't butt in on the provost head first, I'd try and find some way to get around him or ignore him." Seeger had tried his character and found it wanting; the decision haunted him. These disputes over censorship returned throughout his adult life, and each time the stakes got higher.

In the next few years, Peter had an ever harder time keeping his woodsy isolation. Looking back forty years later, he remembered one conversation as the turning point, when he began to leave Seton behind. He and his mother were visiting two of her students, the Kantrowitzes, a few months after his fight with the provost. The censorship still rankled, and he vented his frustration one summer night at their house in rural Connecticut, when the three boys sat out on the porch.

"With all the dishonesty in the world, how can anyone lead an honest life?" Peter asked.

"Come on, Pete, not everyone's dishonest," replied one of the Kantrowitz boys.

"No, but society sure is. The only ones who can be honest are those who don't have to compromise: the hermits. I wouldn't mind being one." He stared into the warm darkness, shielded by mosquito netting.

"But, Peter," his friend replied gently, "what kind of morality is that? Be pure and let the rest of the world go to hell?"

In the 1300s Pete Seeger might actually have become a hermit; nature had given him a character that in earlier times would have marked him for the clergy. He yearned for a morally consistent life, and the complications and compromises of daily life made him want to retreat. Yet he always had another side, which felt a duty to stay and fight. His friends' arguments and his father's commitment slowly swayed the thirteen-year-old: "I thought about that conversation for some time, and finally decided the Kantrowitz boys were right." He began to look to newspapers for more than excitement. That fall Peter returned to Avon with a subscription to the Communist magazine *New Masses.* He quickly became a devotee of a firebrand journalist, Michael Gold.

Gold was everything Peter wasn't: ethnic, working-class, and politically committed. The author of *Jews Without Money* grew up on the Lower East Side, quit school at twelve to work, and hung out with New York bohemians like John Reed and Peter's uncle, Alan.

Though he wasn't the only boy at school reading Mike Gold, from the beginning Peter kept his radical sympathies secret. A favorite English teacher lampooned *New Masses,* but Peter sat in the back of the class, never saying a word. He had become a closet radical, lounging in a herringbone suit—which never managed to fit his scrawny frame—and smiling superiorly while his dormmates analyzed the Harvard-Yale game or their fathers' cars. Their wealth had a flaccid, decadent quality. Peter kept to his room, working on the *Avon Weekly.* To others he seemed a goody-goody, and aloof; he thought himself a rebel. At nights in the dorm, the precocious journalist had to put aside his typing. He had hours of work left for tomorrow's paper, but he wasn't worried: "It was against the rules to have lights on past a certain hour, but no one said anything about getting up early."

When Peter needed rest and isolation, he visited a clearing overlooking Beaver Pond, where his woodscraft teacher lived. Peter used Verne Priest's log cabin for a trailhead, disappearing in the woods for a day at a time with two apples and a book.

A woodsy recluse straight out of Seton's pages, Priest knew the land surrounding Avon as if born there. He needed fuel for his pancake suppers, and Peter chopped the wood gladly on fall afternoons when the leaves turned yellow and red, and the air smelled like bitter chocolate. Few activities exhilarated him more than cutting and stacking a five-foot pile of logs. On one of his many afternoons there Peter finished chopping and swept up the broken bark. He slid into a favorite chair, where his back found a notch it fit perfectly. Rain fell lightly on the wooden roof, and the firs stood tall, outlined by the drops. Contented to be on his own, Peter sketched and dozed, as the wind rustled the wet branches.

But just as Charles had tried to balance his academic career and his social concerns in Berkeley, his son Peter could not long remain a radical in the woods. He might have been isolated at Avon, but as the economy hit its deepest trough, hundreds of thousands were joining Socialist and Communist campaigns. Rebels "are no less products of the society than those who uphold it," British historian E. H. Carr once wrote. "They owe their role in history to the mass of their followers and are significant as social phenomena or not at all."

Long after the thirties passed, the events of his formative decade marked Peter's consciousness and repertoire. In the mid-thirties, intellectuals "discovered" American folk music; a handful of folklorists formed a coterie to give the music a wider audience—Robert Gordon, Ben Botkin, John and Alan Lomax, and, surprisingly enough, Charles Seeger. Their movement combined nationalism and patriotism, a sense that here at last was America's *true* music. This occurred during the Popular Front era, when the Communist Left (and its intellectuals) united behind President Roosevelt and tried to sink roots in American tradition. Radicals turned a new ear to traditional folk tunes; the hostility of groups like the Composers Collective softened. It was a chorus-filled era, in politics as well as music, the beginning of what conservatives would call the left-wing folk song conspiracy.

In these developments, Peter's mentor played an important part. After leaving New York and the Composers' Collective in 1935, Charles administered music programs for the Resettlement (later Farm Security) Administration. Peter spent the summer of his graduation, 1936, with his father, one of those languorous stretches near the end of adolescence where seventeen-year-olds stand between childhood and adulthood, with the privileges of both. With Senate investigations of labor spies and railroad monopolies, New Deal Washington was an exciting place for leftists and a welcome change from Avon. Peter met Charles's new friends, including Alan Lomax, a tall, swarthy fellow a few years Pete's senior; already famous for his song-collecting expeditions with his father, John, Alan's voice boomed as he talked, as if shouting into an imaginary microphone. Peter met Party members debating the new slogan "Communism is twentieth-century Americanism"; Paine and Jefferson were resurrected as American radicals. The Seeger boy fit right into this new patriotism, with his all-American stock and wholesome habits. He came of age in one of the rare moments when American radicals succeeded by working in coalition rather than in small sects. He never forgot this: folk songs, radicalism, and patriotism blended in his mind.

At Charles's new home in Silver Spring, Maryland, Peter visited with his stepmother Ruth and relaxed by the oversize fireplace in the living room. It was like living in the office of a great cause: He had only to sit still, and raw, field-recorded music came his way. No raja's son could have had better access to America's musical treasury, a privilege he later shared with Ruth's first children, Mike and Peggy Seeger.

With nothing better to do on the long muggy evenings, flies buzzing in the Maryland heat, he listened as Dio (Ruth) transcribed Library of Congress recordings for the Lomaxes. Dio fascinated Peter; she warmed the house with her presence; she was round-faced and laughing, but extremely serious about music. As a young composer she had already produced her eerie "String Quartet No. 1" and received a Guggenheim grant to study composition in Berlin. By the mid-thirties, she had been infected with Charles's new passion for folk music; she transcribed with a maniacal precision, sometimes listening to a song a hundred times to see if a note was closer to C or C-sharp.

But when Peter sat down to learn these tunes on his four-string banjo, to his embarrassment he found he couldn't do it. He had learned about music, finally, but these "simple" tunes escaped him. He didn't realize that everyone on the recordings played a five- rather than a four-string banjo. At the end of one particularly browbeating session, his father walked in: "Peter had the four-string in his lap, and I asked 'What are you playing that for?' (I was quite new in the field, and convinced the five-string was *the* proper one.) Peter looked up at me and asked, 'Well, father, what *should* I play?'" Charles suggested they talk it over with banjo picker Bascom Lunsford in North Carolina. A few weeks later, father and son packed up their big blue Chevy and drove south.

Soon the mountainous Piedmont stretched before them. The North Carolina hills "were lordly, with a plan," as Thomas Wolfe wrote. "Westward, they widened into the sun." Nestled among the Blue Ridge and Smoky Mountains, Asheville's clean air attracted five hundred guests to the Ninth Annual Folk Song and Dance Festival in 1936. To Peter, the scene was as exotic as a market Sunday in the Middle Ages; crowds of mountain people jostled past them to fill seats in a canvas-topped baseball field. Sellers hawked steaming corn on the cob and sarsaparilla. In sessions running late into the night, old-time string bands played for dance teams from towns named Rattlesnake Knob and Greenbriar Creek. Two banjoists impressed Peter: Samantha Baumgartner from Dillsboro, and Lunsford, the master of ceremonies.

From the first banjo tunes, he was transfixed. The crisp rhythms and rippling notes clamped him to his seat. Lunsford carried his instrument like a favorite coat; sitting down to pick, his banjo became an extra arm.

Seeing the five-string banjo on its native ground made an instant convert of Peter. His ukulele wouldn't do. The tenor banjo's Dixieland plunk-plunk-plunk paled. "I discovered there was some good music in my country which I never heard on the radio. . . . I liked the strident vocal tone of the singers, the vigorous dancing. The words of the [folk] songs had all the meat of life in them. Their humor had a bite, it was not trivial. Their tragedy was real, not sentimental. In comparison, most of the pop music of the thirties seemed to me weak and soft, with its endless variations on 'Baby, baby I need you.' "

In England, pioneer folklorist Cecil Sharp had a similar moment, when he looked out a window near Oxford and saw a procession of men in costumes on a snowy country lane. Sharp watched with astonishment as they broke into song and did a morris dance; he dated the English folk music revival from that moment.

Pete's third passion, after his woodland tower and the radicalism inherited from his father, was rural, working-class music—which was, in some ways, a combination of the first two. By the end of the summer he burned to find out more about this odd five-string banjo. He couldn't figure out how they got that rhythmic, percussive effect. (Because of the extra string half-way up the neck, the instrument is played differently: plucked or frailed instead of strummed with a pick.) Charles considered it the most dramatic folk instrument, but by the time Pete heard the five-string, the instrument had all but disappeared, fading with the minstrel shows at the turn of the century.

As Charles Seeger's son, Peter had immediate access to recordings at the Library of Congress. Besides, who could turn him away—a ruddy-cheeked, gangly kid so eager to learn? The banjo surprised him with its long history: Egyptian dancers played similar instruments for pharaohs. Slaves brought banjos to America from West Africa, and Thomas Jefferson described the "banjar" as a chief instrument among Negroes in the 1700s.

The fifth string, he discovered, developed in the 1800s and gave the banjo a Scottish drone, integrating British and African heritages into a truly American instrument.

Next Peter traced contemporary banjoists with a reporter's zeal. Through their records and songs Peter entered a world vastly different from boarding-school life.

Bascom Lamar Lunsford—who lent Charles the five-string Pete first practiced on—lived like Johnny Appleseed, selling fruit trees before becoming a teacher and lawyer. He learned two-finger picking by playing banjo at apple-butter stirrings and house-raisings. Kentuckian Pete Steele, whose clean, crisp up-picking style Peter admired, learned on a squirrel-skin banjo. Pete listened again to Dock Boggs, but now the modal scales he had heard on Tom Benton's records made sense. Uncle Dave Macon expanded Pete's feel for tunings and taught him country-political songs. Buell Kazee, Wade Ward, Lilly Mae Ledford, the list goes on for pages; one day he hoped to meet them all. The seventeen-year-old practically obliterated what records he could find, putting his thumb on the edge to slow them to a growl. He played the discs over and over until, like Yeats's prescription for developing a style—"sedentary toil and imitation of the great masters"—he got the hang of it. This took years, during which he continued on the four-string. Peter had no instruction books or cassette tapes; he had to figure it out on his own.

Despite all this work, Pete wasn't interested in music as a profession. There was no living to be had: "It was better just to play for fun." While these were beautiful tunes, as a journalist he could support himself *and* change the world.

Despite Depression-stretched resources, the family was determined that Peter should receive a proper education—which meant attending Harvard, as his older brother, father, and uncle Alan had. He started in the fall of 1936 with a partial scholarship and a job washing dishes in a boarding-house. Lunch money was in short supply. His mother's lessons in frugality helped, but once he complained, "It's a bit hard, Father. The other boys are going out to dances—but I don't have a tuxedo."

Bookish but not brilliant, Peter basically didn't like Harvard; the life that pleased his ancestors didn't work for him. They didn't teach journalism, so he studied sociology, which bored him. He was easily distracted: One minute he studied, and the next he put down his books to work on a play or redesign the furniture in his dorm room. He began to write tunes, contributing one to the Hasty Pudding Club Show.

In the journal he kept, his ambition surfaced continually—a hunger not for wealth, power, or girls, but for distinction. "What makes a man great?" Peter repeatedly asked himself, answering: "When he is at the top of the value scale of the majority; when people think him great." Fame or fortune could not fulfill these aspirations. He prided himself on having a "temperament that looks forward," even admitting: "You know damn well, Pete Seeger, that the only reason you are writing in these notebooks is that you want future people to read them and say, 'There's an OK guy.' " Seeger's hopes for posterity seem extreme for an acne-faced eighteen-year-old, too shy to ask a girl out.

College life was more than textbooks and the Tenor Banjo Club. It was bicycling along the Charles River with autumn leaves blowing into the channel; carrying his sketchbook in hopes of catching the eye of a Radcliffe girl; lonely nights in his dorm room, playing banjo or trying to read Marx but ending up tangled in economic theory. When he read Spengler, his thoughts swirled in vast historical currents, and he missed classes and supper. When he read Goethe, he was awash in romance and sexual frustration. He rushed through his assigned readings to read works he cared about, like Carl Sandburg's *The People, Yes;* few books in the late thirties moved him more.

The summer of his freshman year, Peter worked at a summer camp run by socialist friends of the family. His fellow counselors were far more politically involved than he: midsummer, one quit to join the Abraham Lincoln Brigade in Spain; a friend from Avon also volunteered. Like the abolitionists who streamed into Kansas to keep the state free of slavery, Peter's generation of radicals were challenged to commit themselves by the Spanish Civil War. The fighting in Spain became a testing ground of World War II. Three hundred American volunteers had already fallen outside Madrid, fighting Italian and Nazi troops. Before Peter returned to college that fall, an older counselor took him to task for his political reticence: "What? You're not a member of the student union?"

Peter promised to consider signing up: "But as far as politics, I was keeping my distance. I liked the idea of not actually being involved myself, but observing the action. . . . If someone had offered me a job as a reporter, though, I'd have jumped at it." Pete didn't feel he belonged in battle; observing was one thing and participating another. Just as his father had refused to join the IWW, Peter hedged about Spain. He used his age as an excuse, but by now he had matured physically. He was nearly six feet tall, thin as a fence post, and shy, the sort who sits alone at parties. People mistook his aloofness for conceit. Aquaintances argued politics with him at the commons, but they didn't invite him to their rooms to drink and talk about girls.

Peter wasn't the only unsocial journalist Harvard had seen; thirty years before, John Reed had been every bit as lonely. Seeger and the chronicler of the Russian Revolution had much in common: Both turned to art and revolution from upper-crust backgrounds; neither managed studies or dating well. And both were romantic radicals, with a bit of Don Quixote in them. Peter, on the other hand, never had Reed's self-assertiveness. John Reed tolerated contradictions that Pete's puritanism would never allow. Reed could comfortably leave a benefit for striking IWW workers to weekend on a yacht; a tall beer after the show would have been Peter's extravagance.

Gradually, by his sophomore year, politics overtook Pete's other interests. On winter afternoons, Pete passed out leaflets for Spanish war relief in front of Widener Library, stamping his feet in the cold. Wrapped in greatcoats of Scottish wool, the Harvard men passed him by. He founded a radical paper, *The Harvard Progressive,* with Arthur Kinoy (later a radical lawyer who defended the Chicago Eight). Trading the Banjo Club for the Young Communist League (YCL), Pete started reading Lenin's *Imperialism.* The YCL represented a good-natured extremism, advertising themselves with appeals to sports and clean fun. Yet joining still had a spark for Peter; it meant a commitment, in the lavish words of Pete's future friend, Walter Lowenfels, "to open all your pores to wind and men."

"As an individual," Pete wrote in his journal, "what do I count for? In the YCL, I have the Comintern behind me." The YCL leadership was fighting for control of the liberal American Student Union (ASU); Young Communists joined the ASU and formed secret caucuses. Peter ran for and was elected secretary of Harvard's ASU chapter—without discussing his more radical affiliation. The politicking gave him moral indigestion. "I am not a politician, a fighter, an organizer," he noted in one of those acute self-realizations which are later ignored.

At eighteen, Pete's politics were a strange mix of revolution and *Robert's Rules of Order.* His political activity was confined to Harvard Yard, though he once led an expedition to leaflet Grant's department store in the wilds of Boston. Neither black, Jewish, nor Catholic, Peter didn't face discrimination of his own. He empathized with other people's causes.

"Where *is* Peter going?" his grandparents asked, confused at the radical turn he had taken. His aunt told him he was "a damn loafer" for getting Cs in college, but Pete shrugged if off. His interest in his studies withered like the renowned organs of the state. Soon a letter from the dean's office notified him of academic probation. If he flunked out, too bad, he decided; he had more important things to consider.

Coming home from a crowded recital one night, Peter wondered why formal concerts bored him. He noted the reasons in his journal: The instruments were strained to their loudest pitch; hot, stuffy concert halls put him to sleep; and "the audience should be a great chorus." This last phrase is a curious one—what did he expect of audiences? Did he imagine he could change them?

Peter was ambitious, and school only stood in the way. Sociology was *not* the same as journalism, and he chafed at Harvard's refusal to let him study his profession. He found the professors pompous and his readings irrelevant. He had particular problems with P. K. Sorokin, one of the giants of sociology. Pete found his credentials unimpressive; he was just someone who had been thrown out of Russia by the Bolsheviks, and who used a lot of big words. After Sociology 3 one afternoon, Peter stopped by his office. "Professor Sorokin," he asked, "why do you use these particular words in your lectures? Why can't you use ordinary English words?" The professor looked up with a smile, saying, "You have to impress people, you know." "He really meant it," Pete reflected: " 'Well,' I thought to myself, 'If this is the sort that's teaching here, I'm not going to bother studying any more.' "

Peter lost his scholarship because of poor grades and left Harvard in the spring of 1938; he was in such a hurry, he didn't even take his exams. He took leave of the Charles River and his few friends. What would replace Harvard in his life he didn't know. One afternoon before he left, he passed John F. Kennedy bustling across the Yard with his personal secretary. If JFK became the most famous graduate of the Class of '40, Pete Seeger was surely its best-known dropout.

66 Highway Blues

4

PETE LEFT HARVARD hoping, like generations of nineteen-year-olds before him, to make his career in the city. He imagined himself a hard-writing reporter for the *Times* or, perhaps, Gilbert Seldes's *New York Journal*. Before he tried his luck, however, he wanted a vacation. He visited his mother in Sarasota, Florida, and helped her move back to New York City. Rather than stay in her new apartment, he hit upon an original idea: to paint his way across New York State by bicycling from one farm to another and trading his watercolors for a night's lodging. His bike was an old, broken-down affair, but it would have to do; he would survive on his talent. Prudently waiting until the nights were warm enough to sleep outside, Pete left for his first summer by himself, pedaling across the Catskills in the summer of 1938.

He still had that rosy-cheeked, long-legged look. He had now grown so much that the seat on his bicycle rode sixteen inches high, with an easel and canvas frames strapped underneath. He would choose a pretty house and approach it from behind, painting a landscape of cows and barns. He supplied plenty of pretty clouds, even on a gray day. Then he would knock on the front door.

"Hey Mary, come look at this," the astonished homeowner would say. "Some guy's painted a picture of our house!" Once a farmer caught him in the cow field before Pete had finished. "My barn, you make it look too short," he scolded the nineteen-year-old. Pete had to start all over, until the barn appeared as large as a palace. The farmers almost always gave him a place to sleep and food. Once he received a clucking chicken, and by the time he figured out how to kill, pluck, and cook his prize, he got so hungry he ate it "darn near raw."

After the overintellectualized atmosphere of Harvard, Pete was relieved to wind through the mountains on his bike: "College was fine for those who want it, but I was just not interested; I wanted to be a journalist."

After a couple of months, Pete returned to the city thin enough to slide through the subway turnstiles without paying. Without funds of his own, he moved into his brothers' apartment, where he slept on a couch and washed dishes for his share of the rent. He walked the streets looking for work, having left his watercolors in farmhouses across the Catskills. Years afterward, when his name appeared in headlines, he received letters asking if he was the same Seeger who painted the barn the wrong color.

Autumn made its brief New York appearance, and the leaves in Central Park turned orange and brown before blowing away in the wind. New Yorkers paused on street corners to marvel at the new season. The city whirled around him; he would call a paper in the morning, take a subway to the editor's office that afternoon, and find there was no job for him—all in the same day. He sat on subways with clerks in suits and housewives with sagging shopping bags from Macy's, all rocking together anonymously through the musty tunnels. After Connecticut and Cambridge, New York loomed exotic. The Seeger boys lived on the Lower East Side, at 118 East Eleventh Street, and Pete shopped the ethnic stores and bakeries, sampling piroshki, bagels, and sour cream for the first time. He peered in at Ukrainian churches and Irish bars. With so much to explore, he thought he would never tire of the city. His imagination hopped from one project to the next: On the same page of his journal he discussed the ideal tenure for elected officers; why furniture makers favor square edges over round ones; and remarked how saving thirty cents a day made a hundred dollars a year.

To make ends meet, he picked newspapers from the trash bins and read books at the library. His brother Charles's wife, Inez, dared Pete to perform in the streets. Painfully nervous, acne blooming on his face, Pete Seeger stood on Park Avenue with his four-string banjo. (He still hadn't mastered the rhythm of the five-string.) A small crowd gathered when the reedy-looking boy opened his case and started plunking "Old Man River" and "Cindy." Pete's voice cracked, his Adam's apple bobbed up and down, but he kept on singing. Passersby on New York's fanciest boulevard left little in the way of donations—seventy-five cents for three hours. If Pete had ideas of being a professional musician, that experience put a match to them. Music ran a poor third in Seeger's life, behind painting and journalism. When he wasn't visiting newspaper offices, he took classes at the American Artists' School. He had always loved to sketch, from his earliest expeditions tracing animal tracks; now he studied oil and watercolors. His greatest talent was for the latter, he decided; besides, oils were costly.

To his dismay, Pete discovered that papers weren't hiring college dropouts, even Harvard-educated ones. Part of his problem was his presentation. His wrists poked out from his jackets; his trousers were too short and his movements awkward. Interview after interview passed without an offer. While his paintings showed promise—particularly to anyone fond of barns—no exhibitions came his way. Dead broke and frustrated at not finding a position, he visited his aunt Elsie Seeger, for many years principal of the Dalton School. She helped him out with a job playing at a dance, which brought in five dollars and invitations to sing at other schools and at Margot Mayo's folk-dance group on Thirteenth Street. One Sunday in 1939 the troupe was supposed to have a work party and wash the skylights of their loft. Pete and a pretty girl named Toshi Ohta were the only ones who showed up.

Toshi—the name means "beginning of a new era"—had luxuriant jet-black hair and an adventuresome streak inherited from her mother, the radical in an old Virginian family that included Jim Bowie of the Bowie knife. Pete shyly asked her about herself. She told him how, over her grandparents' wishes, her mother had married a Japanese exile of noble birth and eloped to Europe, where she was born. Because of the Oriental Exclusion Act (which prevented children of fifty percent or more Oriental blood from entering the U.S.) she hadn't been allowed in the country until her mother smuggled her in, lying to the customs officer that the vivacious baby was one hundred percent Caucasian.

Toshi grew up in the art colonies of Provincetown and Woodstock and attended "progressive" schools, including Greenwich Village's Little Red School House. Both had canvassed for Loyalist Spain, they discovered. Pete was attracted to her, but shy; they went out for a hamburger a few times. The friendship drifted as Alan Lomax—now in New York on business—introduced Pete to a fascinating world of musicians. Lomax brought him into the Lower East Side apartment of Aunt Molly Jackson, an Appalachian coal miner's wife. Peter knew Molly's songs from his Washington summer: "I Am a Union Woman (Join the CIO)," and "Pity the Coal Miner." Aunt Molly knew Pete's father from the Composers Collective; the musicians there had gracelessly called her a "living anachronism," a coal miner organizer who wrote songs without even reading music.

Despite these memories, Molly received Pete warmly. Her rough clear voice bowled Pete over, the first live "protesty" songs (based on folk tunes) he heard. Her songs had fire and direct, everyday lyrics, and Pete immediately sat down and transcribed them. Lomax had an even greater success in introducing Seeger to the "King of the Twelve-String Guitar," Huddie Ledbetter.

Born on a Louisiana farm the same year as Pete's father, Ledbetter learned play-songs and spirituals at home and received his musical training on the seamier side of Shreveport, where he had periodic conflicts with the law. Alan told Pete how he and his father had discovered the singer known as Leadbelly on a song-collecting trip to a southern jail in 1933, and how they helped him out of prison. Leadbelly and his wife had joined the Lomax household—as servants, by one account—then moved to New York. Despite his gentle side and a tenderness for children, the reputation for violence followed Leadbelly onstage like a sessionman no one paid. Peter didn't know what to expect.

One afternoon—the date is unclear—the young banjo picker had his chance; when Alan called, Pete grabbed his banjo and took off out the door. When he got to Ledbetter's apartment, Pete marveled at Leadbelly's square frame and his arms as thick as stove pipes. He was barrel-chested, with close-cropped salt-and-pepper hair. His eyes were as bright as porcelain. Beside him Pete seemed pitifully frail. Leadbelly had no use for the overalls Pete affected, and he loved liquor and high times. Until Leadbelly pulled out his guitar, the pair didn't have much in common.

Huddie's music bound him to the city boy without a callous on his hand. The composer and adapter of "Goodnight Irene," "Midnight Special," and hundreds of other songs, Leadbelly had a rhyming, improvisational genius. Pete couldn't always understand his Louisiana twang, but he caught the infectious joy of his music, and its powerful rhythms. Leadbelly talked to his guitar as he played—and he meant it. To Pete, who had met only a handful of blacks in his life, Leadbelly was a sensation; Pete compared his music to Beethoven. Leadbelly also provided living proof of the power of song. A dark-skinned Orpheus, he had composed a song to soften the heart of Texas governor O. K. Allen and literally won his freedom with a song.

This was one of the truly momentous meetings of Seeger's life. He stuck to Leadbelly even after his novelty wore off. Pete had traded Harvard's faculty for guitar lessons, and he was convinced he had the best of the deal: "There I was, trying my best to shed my Harvard upbringing, scorning to waste money on clothes other than blue jeans. But Leadbelly had on a clean shirt and starched collar, well-pressed suit, and shined shoes. . . . I was proud that he accepted me. Perhaps he wondered at my earnestness, trying to learn folk music."

After meeting Leadbelly, Pete returned to worrying about his modest expenses. He was meeting interesting people, but finding a job in Depression New York was proving more difficult than he had anticipated. Painting was his ambition until one day when an art teacher, Arthur Stern, casually asked what else he did.

"Well, I play the banjo," Peter answered brightly.

"I've never heard you play the banjo," the instructor said, "but I'd suggest you stick to that."

And so, after years of ambivalence, after chance encounters with an art teacher, a Louisiana farmhand, and a coal miner's wife, Pete began to look at music as a more promising career. Nevertheless, he postponed a decision. On one page of his journal in early 1939 he listed people to call for work as a journalist. On another, taking a cue from his mother, Peter wrote out twenty ways to save money with a stern "Do this!"

A friend asked him to play with a summer music-and-puppet troupe, the Vagabond Puppeteers. Weary of looking for a job, Pete agreed; there was no money in it, but the project looked like fun. The group bought a 1929 Oldsmobile, built a collapsible stage on the car's back flap, and made puppets out of papier-mâché. The idea was a cross between the Pinehurst experiment and the rural education campaigns of postrevolutionary Mexico, where two of the group had been trained. After writing up tentative scripts, the foursome booked themselves by poster across upstate New York, passing the hat as they went.

The puppeteers played church socials and union halls for three months in mid-1939, sleeping in barns or beneath the stars on folding cots. By chance, the troupe ran head-on into the most serious milk strike in New York history. Independent dairy farmers were fighting the low milk prices paid by Borden and Sheffield, the large chain dairies. In bloody clashes with scab drivers, farmers poured thousands of gallons of milk onto highways. The puppeteers met with Dairy Farmers' Union officials, who grudgingly accepted their services. The trip went fine until Peter announced he wouldn't step out in front of the stage to perform while the others remained in back. Pete offered all sorts of arguments to support his refusal, but the basic problem was stage fright. Nevertheless farmers kept coming up to ask who the banjo player was, and Peter had to come out. He fumed, though; it wasn't right to make him the "star"; he didn't enjoy solos. Eventually he agreed to step out at the end and coax people to sing with him, as he had when he was eight.

Pete wasn't as staunchly political as some of the others, but he was as ascetic as a monk, insisting: "A person shouldn't have more property than he can squeeze between his banjo and the outside wall of his banjo case."

One afternoon in August 1939 the Vagabond Puppeteers put on their milk skit for pickets outside a dairy in Ithaca. The men watched with one eye on the puppets and the other on the highway. The strikers had heard about a load of scab milk heading their way.

The skit opened with a farmer arguing with his fussy cow. "Repaint my barn," the cow (Peter) mooed, threatening to tell the state milk inspector. The farmer sulked. Then the cow berated him for selling her milk so cheaply. The farmer brought on mustached Mr. Shorden Beffield, milk dealer, to explain his prices. At "Shorden Beffield," mutterings of "What the hell is this—a puppet show"—turned to guffaws. Their attention distracted, no one noticed the distant line of dust slowly crossing the dry valley.

On stage, the cow exposed Beffield as a gouger and goaded the farmer into joining a strike. Beffield threatened to boycott the cow's milk, hit the now-subdued farmer on the head, and exited. (Boos from the crowd.) The farmer angrily chased the cow until his wife interrupted: "Patch the roof," she scolded him, whacking him over the head with a butter churn.

Just then, a neighbor happened by to explain the Dairy Farmers' Union. The farmer signed up. The cow was happy, the farmer's wife was happy, and everyone sang the finale, "The Farmer Is the Man Who Feeds Us All." The puppeteers left amid general congratulations. Pickets mooed at each other, and women made sandwiches and coffee for the night shift.

Under the cover of darkness, the scab trucks waited. The first one rumbled up the road to the dairy a few hours later. The pickets jumped to their feet.

The truck rattled along slowly, lights extinguished. The milk cans clanged as the truck swayed over the bumps. The pickets stood in a human chain across the road. At the entrance, the driver threw on his lights, down-shifted, and started to honk. The men blocked the road, motionless. Then the truck hit the line, hurling a union steward eight feet. That night, he died from internal injuries at a local hospital.

"We heard the news when we came in for breakfast next morning," recalled one of the original troupe. "We couldn't believe it. Night before last, that same steward had put us up. We were pretty shaken." Pete began to take music and politics more seriously.

Yet even as he turned to music for a living, he remained divided between the two impulses of his youth: the woodland path that stretched from the tepee at Patterson to Vern Priest's woodshed; and the worldly road of Mike Gold and his father's radical friends in Washington and the Composers Collective. For the rest of his life, Seeger searched for the meeting of the two ways: Involved in political campaigns, he yearned to sit by the river with his banjo; and even into the woods, he carried hopes of political change.

Returning to New York City, Pete finally admitted to himself that he hadn't become the reporter he had pictured at Harvard. He spent more time practicing banjo than calling up editors, but he couldn't shake the feeling that music meant recreation, not a profession; and after earning seventy-five cents his first day out, no one could blame him. He was just another twenty-year-old singer in a city of would-be crooners. He took a job as a porter in the 1939 World's Fair, sweeping up cigarette butts and watching the jitterbug contests. He picked up a few extra dollars grading aptitude tests. Mostly Pete needed to succeed at *something,* and with painting and journalism behind him, music was all he had left. His brother Charles III soon noticed a change in Pete. One afternoon Charles came into his room and found Pete sitting at his spinet harpsichord. After a few passes, Pete did a fair job of picking out jazz tunes. Then he stood up in frustration and scowled at his brother: "God damn it, I've got to stop playing so *many* instruments and learn to play some of them well."

Alan Lomax came to his aid. He had been listening to Pete improve on the banjo and heard a talent there. Finally he pointed out the inevitable: "Pete, what do you want to be an artist for! You ought to learn more about folk music." Pete was invited to join Alan at the Archive of American Folk song at the Library of Congress—a natural consequence of Charles Seeger's influence. The pay wasn't great, but it beat sweeping up after tourists.

"I went down to Washington to work at the Archive for fifteen dollars a week," Seeger remembered. "I lived in an old rooming house around the corner and kept to myself. Saved my money and bicycled out to see my parents occasionally," visiting with their eldest children, Mike and Peggy Seeger. As usual, Pete watched his pennies. His idea of luxury was to go out and buy a new set of banjo strings—which he often needed, as he experimented with different tunings. Pete's duties were untaxing and he handled them conscientiously: cataloging the dusty archives and transcribing songs. In the process, he absorbed an entire repertoire. The songs lived for him; rather than notes on paper, like those his mother had offered him, these were new friends. He got to know Old Joe Clark, Casey Jones, the Arkansas Traveler, Joe Bowers, and Jesse James; he even met girls: Pretty Polly, the Buffalo Gals, and Jennie Jenkins.

"I remember visiting Pete at Alan's house that winter," said Bess, Alan's sister. "He had begun to play the five-string almost continuously. One night Alan had to throw him out; Pete just never shut up, and it was driving everybody mad. Oh, he was *terrible.* It was very definitely practicing, and it got to be intolerable. He played all night, and he played all day, and after a while you wanted to ship him off somewhere. One morning, I had to catch the train to Philadelphia at a very early hour. Pete was sitting outside on the radiator of Alan's car, playing the recorder very quietly at four-thirty A.M. He said he didn't want to disturb anybody." At length, Lomax encouraged him to perform at a fund-raising concert in New York.

Only four years older than his new assistant, Alan Lomax was as self-confident as Pete was timid. Both had left Harvard, but the *wunderkind* of folk music, Alan, had his B.A. and mentioned it more. As a teenager, Alan had gone on his father's recording trips and studied briefly under ballad scholar George Lyman Kittredge. At twenty-two, he was hired at the Archive of American Folk song. And while still in his twenties, Lomax produced two major radio series on folk music. His many abilities did not include tact, however, and Lomax rarely let Pete (or anyone else) forget his position. Alan had connections and a reputation as an activist and a folklorist; when he decided Pete was ready for the stage, Seeger could be sure of being noticed.

Like the arms of a nebula compacting as it turns, a folk-political song movement began to take shape. If an observer from another world had trained his eye on a two-mile-square area bounded by Greenwich Village to the south and Times Square to the north, with the participants drawing together from Louisiana, the Connecticut woods, and the dust bowl, he would have witnessed an art form—the protest song—in the making.

Topical rhymes and songs were not new, of course. During the early Middle Ages, defrocked monks sallied about with anticlerical songs. "Little Jack Horner" was originally a protest over Henry VIII's scheme to take over church lands. Labor songs by the hundreds were sung in nineteenth-century America, and IWW songwriter Joe Hill wrote his parody of "Casey Jones" twenty-five years before Leadbelly set foot in New York. Yet the widespread association of folk music and social causes dates from the mid-1930s and the Popular Front era. Wobblies had rewritten hymns, and labor musicals like *Pin and Needles* had used show tunes for social commentary, but traditional folk tunes went unexplored. No political commissar decreed folk songs in vogue; the change came about through trial and error (and through the negative example of the Composers Collective). It was as spontaneous as musicians sitting down together to sing, among them a trouble-tough Louisiana black; a New England boy, bouncy as a kid in sneakers; and soon, a wandering Okie.

By themselves, these three could not have moved American musical history. But their tastes coincided with the New Deal's radical patriotism and folklore activities; and as works like Earl Robinson's "Ballad for Americans" came along, political music—combined with labor drives—reached a new height. ("Ballad for Americans" was so chauvinistic that the Republicans actually asked Paul Robeson to sing it at their 1940 presidential convention.) As Arlo Guthrie, Woody's son, later wrote of draft resistance, "If one person does it, they may think he's really sick . . . if two people do it, in harmony, they won't take either one of them. And if three people do it, they may think it's an organization—a movement." This *was* a movement, the All-American Left-Wing Folk-Song Revival Movement.

On the third of March, 1940, Pete Seeger waited backstage for his first concert performance. The occasion was a "Grapes of Wrath" benefit for California migrant workers at the old Forrest Theatre, the same cause which had propelled Pete's father into the IWW. Seeger fidgeted in the wings for hours, for the show was crowded with America's most distinguished folk-song performers: Burl Ives, Josh White, Richard Dyer-Bennett, Aunt Molly Jackson, and Leadbelly. People milled around him, tuning guitars and peering out at the audience. The lights hummed faintly, and the heat mixed with the backstage aromas of sawdust and spilled whiskey. Performers entered and exited past Pete till the audience yawned from the lateness of the hour.

Finally he heard his name, and he walked out in front of the crowd, blinking at the lights. He couldn't see anyone beyond the first row. He retuned his banjo (though it was already in tune), bolstered his courage, and tried to play. He couldn't. His fingers twisted out of his control and hit the wrong strings. Then he forgot a verse.

"I was a bust," Seeger grimaced thirty-five years later. ". . . . You see, I didn't know how to play the five-string banjo. I tried to do it too fast, and my fingers froze up on me. And I forgot words. It was the 'Ballad of John Hardy'; I got a polite applause for trying and retired in confusion."

He had made a poor beginning of what turned out to be one of the important nights of his life. Fortunately, Pete was not too disappointed to appreciate the evening's surprise star: "Woody Guthrie just ambled out, offhand and casual . . . a short fellow complete with a western hat, boots, blue jeans, and needing a shave, spinning out stories and singing songs he'd made up." He sang in a dust-dry voice made of tires on hot asphalt, the midnight howl of a coyote, the rhythm of a train clacking across the plains. The effect was stunning, "Well, I just naturally wanted to know more about him. He was a big piece of my education."

Woodrow Wilson Guthrie was born on Bastille Day, July 14, 1912, in Okemah, Oklahoma, later moving to Pampa, Texas, before making the dust-bowl migration to California. Despite a hard childhood, with his mother in an asylum, his sister burned in an explosion, and his father nearly bankrupt, Woody had an optimistic, come-what-may spirit. Yet a hard loner quality filled his voice; he could never really belly laugh.

Like Pete, he had little home life, and he earned attention through music. He started singing as a boy, quitting school early to pick grapes and haul wood. What licks he didn't learn from his father Charles or his fiddling uncle Jeff, he picked up off Carter Family and Jimmie Rodgers records. As with the Russian writer Maxim Gorky, barbershops and saloons were his university.

Four years before meeting Pete, Woody had landed in Los Angeles, where he made a reputation with his dust bowl ballads and radio programs. There he also met Communist intellectuals, who saw in Guthrie a native proletarian; he toured the migrant workers' camps where the treatment of the Okies and Arkies—his own people—infuriated him. As Woody's fame grew, radical actor Will Geer mailed Pete a book of Woody's songs. Though Pete was curious to meet Woody, the night they sang in New York he didn't push his way through the crowd around Guthrie. Only later, at one of those cocktail parties where wealthy patrons meet performers, did Alan Lomax finally pull Pete forward and say, "Here. Woody Guthrie, I want you to meet Pete Seeger."

That night Pete left the theater feeling he'd failed again. The disappointment smarted. The next morning as he scanned the papers, perhaps expecting to see himself denounced by the *New York Times* music critic, he found news of everything except what he was looking for. Seabiscuit looked like a sure bet for the $100,000 Santa Ana purse. In Atlanta the Ku Klux Klan was campaigning to outlaw the Communist Party "and other un-American activities." A snowstorm swept across Finland, slowing the Russian infantry's advance toward the Nazi border. At last Pete found the review: JOHN STEINBECK COMMITTEE TO AID DUST-BOWL REFUGEES. The *Times* ran a list of entertainers—his name was not there—and one comment: "The house was almost full." So much for his concert debut. New Yorkers preferred Frank Sinatra in Tommy Dorsey's new band.

If Pete was disappointed, at least Alan Lomax thought it a momentous occasion: "Go back to that night when Pete first met Woody Guthrie. You can date the renaissance of American folk song from that night. Pete knew it was his kind of music, and he began working to make it everbody's kind of music. . . . It was a pure, genuine fervor, the kind that saves souls.

Alan convinced Woody and the young soul-saver to join him in a cherished project; for years, Alan told them, folklorists had omitted songs they considered political or obscene from published collections. With Alan, Pete and Woody compiled a book of political songs, beginning in New York in April. *Hard Hitting Songs for Hard Hit People,* as the manuscript was called, had them working feverishly. For two months, Woody sat at the typewriter, day and night, writing notes to the songs, while Pete transcribed melodies. Then Alan contacted publishers, who found the book politically "hot." (Twenty-six years passed before the manuscript was published.)

Their part done, Woody suggested that Pete head out west with him and discover America. Seeger agreed, overcome by wanderlust. "When I first met Woody, I'd hardly been west of the Hudson River. Like most Yankees, I really didn't see why it was so very important to go west. But Woody said, 'It's a big country out there, Pete, you ought to see it, and if you haven't got money for a ticket, use the rule of the thumb.' Woody came driving through in a car and said he was going to visit his family in Oklahoma and Texas. The car was not paid for by a long shot. Woody called the trip 'hitch-hiking on credit.' "

At the time, Pete shared a place in Arlington, Virginia, with Alan and Nicholas Ray (later known as the director of *Rebel Without a Cause*). He didn't have anything to hold him; he was ready for an adventure. Pete said goodbye to Ruth and his father—who jealously called Woody's accent and cowboy manners "affected"—and the pair took off for Oklahoma by way of Tennessee.

They made an unlikely pair. Pete had just turned twenty-one and stood a head taller than Woody; he had innocent eyes and an unquenchable enthusiasm. "That guy Seeger," Woody once told a friend. "I can't make him out. He doesn't look at girls, he doesn't drink, he doesn't smoke, the fellow's weird." Woody, on the other hand, acted hard-bitten. He ate with his cowboy hat on. Sometimes he didn't bother taking off his pointed boots in bed, massacring the sheets. His reputation as the "dust bowl balladeer" preceded him, and record companies and radio stations chased him almost as hard as his creditors.

Woody's element was fire, and Pete's air. Guthrie burned across the roads of America; his singing could ignite a barroom in minutes. Volatile in his moods, Woody walked around perpetually in heat. His humor was the dry, crackly kind, and few people were warmer with children. Pete was Woody's opposite, down to his tall, airy frame. His head pointed skyward as he frailed his banjo; his passions rarely settled down to earth. For the next few years, the pair would need each other as a flame needs oxygen.

They started down through Virginia and then across Tennessee, picking up every hitch-hiker they saw until the car couldn't hold any more, six, seven people at a time. One hitch-hiker, a one-legged man on crutches called "Brooklyn Speedy," persuaded Pete to buy him paregoric; Pete didn't realize people drank the drug for the opium in it.

Pete nervously walked into a drugstore: 'Like he told me, I said, 'I need it for the baby.' The druggist looked at me sharply, said, 'This will put any baby to sleep for two years. Why do you need this much?' Nevertheless, he sold it to me and I signed a fake name and took the paregoric back to Brooklyn Speedy. He drank it in one long gulp, the whole two ounces, and then as we drove on he closed his eyes and leaned back contentedly."

"What does that stuff *do* for you?" Pete asked, half curious, half censoring. The young puritan couldn't understand why anyone would take drugs to feel good.

"It just relaxes me and helps me forget all my troubles," Speedy answered. "I'm sitting here in this car and the road is moving past me and that's all I know."

After dropping off their riders and stopping to discuss music at the Highlander Folk School outside Chattanooga, they drove on. Pete breathed in the America he had dreamed of: hitch-hiking, bumming meals, doing everything Americans are supposed to do while searching for the national soul. A decade before the Beats and twenty years ahead of the hippies, Pete and Woody breezed across the hot asphalt, spring turning to summer as they traveled south. Like the characters of *On the Road,* there was no state that bored them, no town that did not call out a rhyme or song. They savored motion itself, hungry for new faces and streets and songs.

No sooner would they stop the car and pull themselves out, stretching and wiggling their toes after the long drive, than someone would ask if they could play those instruments. "Sure," they'd say, and despite promises to make good time, they were soon sitting on a porch swapping licks. They needed no American Express or Visa cards; their songs were always good for a round of drinks and a bowl of chili.

They made a game of how far they could stretch their musical credit, with Pete getting his haircuts for a song. Once when they were hungry in a river town in Mississippi they sauntered into a cafe, two strangers asking for coffee (Woody) and two glasses of buttermilk (Pete). As their eyes got used to the darkened lunchroom, they noticed they were the only whites there. They were hungry, though, and the smells of gravy dripping from a pot of chitlins, red beans, cornbread, and beef-rib stew were irresistible. The countergirl avoided them for a while, then told them to go; if they stayed, racists would have torn down her cafe.

They left, and Pete learned about America the hard way, as the characters of *Easy Rider* did thirty years later. He was finding what he had left New York for, a taste of "real people," an unfiltered water glass of Folk.

From Mississippi they cut west toward Woody's home in Texas. They drove Highway 66, "the long concrete path across the country," as John Steinbeck called it, the migrant's road, the Okie trail, the road of Tom Joad and his family in *The Grapes of Wrath*. The car radio blared Gene Autry and Bob Wills, and the gospel stations woke them up Sunday mornings, after a long all-night drive. Gas money was scarce, but that made things more exciting. Pete was eager to sing in his first saloon, and he pestered Woody for a chance. "Let's drive on," said Woody, always a man to postpone necessity; "I think we still have a little cash."

And drive they did, across hilly Arkansas and dust-dry Oklahoma and Texas. Hamburger stands lined the road, glorified wooden shacks with two gas pumps in front and a giant Coke sign. Inside were pies on wire racks, steaming coffee urns, and pyramids of corn flakes in tiny boxes. They would walk in yodeling and come out with cheeseburgers with all the trimmings.

All this singing began to make a musician of Seeger. From 1939 to 1941 he learned basic musicianship from Woody and Leadbelly. Leadbelly introduced him to the twelve-string guitar, teaching him bass runs for its doubled bass notes tuned an octave apart; Lead had patterned them after the piano breaks in Louisiana boogie-woogie. From him Pete learned the importance of rhythm. Woody taught him to play simple and straight; Guthrie sometimes played a ten-verse song without changing chords. Pete and Woody differed in vocal color and tone, the qualities that distinguish two voices singing the same notes together. Woody's voice had a flat, clear resonance; try as he might, Seeger never duplicated it, or Woody's other mannerisms. Once during a long drive, Pete unsuccessfully tried to tell a story to introduce a song.

"Pete," Woody said, "I can't stand it when you just keep on talking like that! Can't you cut it short sometimes?"

"Well, why don't *you* ever cut it short?" Pete asked.

"Ah, well, that's different," Woody said.

Woody knew what he was talking about; it *was* different. Pete didn't have the same timing. Woody grew up with the country music of Oklahoma and Texas; when he opened his mouth everthing just poured out: all the dust and beer halls and flop houses, everything.

"Now Pete thinks he sings Woody's way," a former singing partner said. "He professes not to believe in dynamics or effect—yet he's one of the most contrived, dramatic performers I've seen." Seeger's musical genius would prove interpretive rather than imitative: knowing when to flat a seventh or how to slow a tempo at the right moment to move an audience to sing. Pete eventually paid Woody back for his teaching by exposing millions to Guthrie's music. Woody was awfully rich ore, but without the miner and the mill, many would never have seen the gold.

Music was not all Guthrie taught Seeger. Pete absorbed his healthy disinterest in commercial success, from episodes like Woody's experience with the Model Tobacco Company, which paid him a princely two hundred dollars a week to sing on a radio show on the condition he keep his radicalism off the air and stop improvising. Woody decided he liked his freedom better than Model Tobacco, and the two parted ways. Guthrie wasn't above commercial work, so long as it did not disturb his life style. Seeger, more of a moralist than his friend, made a creed of noncommercialism. He used this year of wandering, when politics were postponed for experience, to practice his musicianship.

Seeger and Guthrie finally approached their destination; two hundred miles east of Pampa, they put up at a flop house in Oklahoma City. Though exhausted from driving, they made up a song, the first complete tune Pete remembered composing: "66 Highway Blues." The song appeared in *Hard Hitting Songs,* with Woody's fanciful introduction: "I had part of this tune in my head, but couldn't get no front end for it. Pete fixed that up. He furnished the engine, and me the cars, and then we loaded in the words and we whistled out of the yards from New York City to Oklahoma City, and when we got there we took down our banjo and git-fiddle and chugged her off just like you see it here. She's a high roller, an easy rider, a flat wheel bouncer and a tight brake lady with a whiskey driver."

> *There is a Highway from coast to coast,* ©
> *New York to Los Angeles,*
> *I'm goin' down that road with troubles on my*
>   *mind,*
> *I got them 66 Highway Blues. . . .*

Been on this road for a mighty long time,
Ten million men like me.
You drive us from yo' town, we ramble around,
And got them 66 Highway Blues.

Sometimes I think I'll blow down a cop,
Lord, you treat me so mean,
I done lost my gal, I ain't got a dime.
I got them 66 Highway Blues. . . .

I'm gonna start me a hungry man's union,
Ainta gonna charge no dues,
Gonna march down that road to the Wall Street
    Walls
A singin' those 66 Highway Blues.

The following day they met Bob and Ina Wood (who may have been the inspiration for the song "Union Maid"). The Woods were local Communist Party organizers, and they immediately recruited Pete and Woody to sing at a meeting of striking oil workers.

"There were hardly 50 or 60 people present," Pete later wrote, "but it included some women and children who evidently couldn't get babysitters. It also included some strange men who walked in and lined up along the back of the hall without sitting down. Bob Wood leaned over and said, 'I'm not sure if these guys are going to try to break up this meeting or not. It's an open meeting and we can't kick them out. See if you can get the whole crowd singing."

This was quite a challenge for a twenty-one-year-old on his first trip west. For centuries writers have claimed that music tames the savage instincts, but few writing this were musicians, and fewer still had to practice before a gang of union busters.

"Woody and I got the crowd singing, and you know, those guys never did break up the meeting. We found out later they had rather intended to. Perhaps it was the presence of so many women and children that deterred them—perhaps it was the singing." This was Pete's first time using music to avoid violence, and he received another lesson in the power of song: Music sometimes has a graver responsibility than entertaining or selling soap flakes.

Finally they arrived at Woody's home in Pampa to see his three kids and his wife, Mary, a blonde with the lean flat face of a plains woman.

She'd been taking care of their family since Woody had disappeared for New York, and she was furious. "When is Woody going to get a job and settle down?" she yelled at Pete. "He can't travel forever!" Pete and Woody looked so ragged, Mary's parents almost turned them away from their door. After this disastrous reception, Pete—uncomfortable in the gritty poverty of Woody's family—headed back to Oklahoma City. Woody was under pressure to stay with Mary and the kids, which he did—for a few days.

Just before departing, Pete asked, "Woody, what kind of songs will get me some coins if I sing them?"

"Well, try 'Makes No Difference Now,' or 'Be Nobody's Darling But Mine.' And a few Jimmie Rodgers blues can't go wrong." This was exactly the sort of tip Pete needed.

"Now don't start singing right away," Woody continued. "Just keep that banjo slung on your back. You nurse a nickel beer as long as you can, sooner or later somebody's gonna say, 'Hey, kid, can you play that thing?' Don't be in too big a hurry. Say, 'Well, not much.' And keep sipping your beer. Pretty soon they'll say, 'Come on, I'll give you a quarter if you'll play me a tune.' *Now* you unlimber it."

Though Pete and Woody rarely talked about style and presentation ("We just sang; if it came out right, it came out right"), Pete had quietly absorbed Woody's repertoire: the dust-bowl ballads and Carter Family songs, such as "Worried Man Blues." Guthrie himself borrowed freely, without regard for tradition or copyright. "Aw, he just stole from me," he once admitted, "but I steal from everybody. Why, I'm the biggest song stealer there ever was."

Pete looked to Woody for authenticity, and Woody in every way fit the definition of the hillbilly or regional singer: his modes, the way he made no concession to dynamics—everything functioned on one level—railroads, love, war, death, politics, hoboes, freight trains. Woody grew up on country music and Pete on the pop tunes of the 1920s, two completely separate musical styles. When the same company owned both pop and country releases, it issued them on different labels with different artists, and sold them in different areas. From the union of Pete and Woody came a *new* music, a citybilly blend of politics, country music, and ballads.

Soon after returning from his first trip, in the spring of 1940, Pete was eager to set out again, this time hitching cross-country alone. His father escorted him to the edge of Washington, D.C., where Pete thumbed a ride carrying a small knapsack and his banjo.

"Now Peter, have you got some reserve funds tucked away?"

"Ah . . . no," Pete said petulantly. "Father, I'd just spend it."

"Come on, take five dollars."

"NO."

"Well, how much *do* you have?"

Pete tried to be civil, but his patience gave way. He said he had some change in his pocket and *please,* that would be enough, he'd manage on his own. Then he admitted he'd been thinking of riding the rails, and Charles exploded: "For God's sake. There's a sheriff just this side of Scottsboro, Alabama, that's retired and lives next to a cemetery. He sits on his front porch and takes potshots at the hoboes riding the rails." Pete got in a passing car and waved goodbye.

First he looked up a girl he'd met on another brief trip a few months before. After hitching a thousand miles, though, he discovered her passion didn't match his. "She was flirting with me up in Wisconsin," Pete complained with the vehemence of a twenty-one-year-old disappointed in love. "Down in Missouri she was cordial—no more than cordial." What must the girl and her parents have thought, having a scruffy kid with a banjo arrive at the door, uninvited, overripe with desire after bouncing across the Ozarks on a truck.

Pete kept right on moving, searching for the America of the songs he loved. As one folklorist described his journey, "He saw the little old sod shanty in the west, hopped the midnight special train from Sourwood Mountain to the dreary Black Hills, walked out in the streets of Laredo and beyond the Red River Valley." Out of these adventures, Seeger fashioned his art.

"I still run into people who remember meeting Pete in those days," said Mike Seeger. " 'Hey, I met your brother,' they tell me. 'We called him Slim, and he hopped off a freight train. He introduced himself to my husband and me, and told us that he was out trying to meet the people of the United States, the real people. So he came and stayed with us. We had lots of music, stayed up talking till late hours of the night.' "

Without Woody, however, traveling didn't turn out as smoothly as before. Preparing to jump off his first freight, banjo in one hand and knapsack in the other, he lost his balance. He didn't position his feet right, and when he landed, he knocked his breath out. Behind him there was a loud *crack*! For a few moments he sat in a heap beside the rails, afraid to look. He had smashed the neck off his banjo. He had no money in his pocket, and no way of earning more with music.

Fall was blowing his way, and the nights got colder as he traveled north across the plains. Pete chopped wood and did odd jobs to stay alive. Just as in the Vagabond Puppeteers, he bent over backward to travel light; instead of a sleeping bag, he slept in a floppy Salvation Army overcoat.

"Finally in Rapid City, South Dakota, I did it. I'd had to pawn my camera—worth sixteen dollars and hocked for five—to get a cheap guitar, because I'd broken my banjo. There I was, a thousand miles from home. I had to earn some money right away, so I hit the saloons. The first night I made five dollars and got the camera back with the song 'Makes No Difference Now.'

"Gene Autry had a big hit from it. A woman bartender gave me a whole silver dollar and said, 'Sing it again.' I had to sing it five times, but I got five silver dollars. I never had quite such good luck anywhere." Pete floated out the smoky saloon doors, deliciously satisfied with himself. The evening breezes gave Pete relief from the August heat, and the heavy dollars jangled in his pockets. Outside, he breathed in the fragrant air and open sky. He wandered out to the edge of town, where the hay fields began: "There were piles of straw, and I just buried myself and slept like a kitten."

Seeger finally arrived in Butte, Montana. He marveled at the open copper and zinc mines and the fantastic clamor of the mining equipment; at midday, the sound was deafening, and smoke from the mills and processing plants blackened the sky. At night the slopes of the Rockies grew bitter cold under the wide, dark heavens.

"I knocked on the doors of the Mine, Mill, and Smelter Workers' Union and said, 'I know some union songs, would you like me to sing them at a meeting?' They said, 'Yeah, I guess that'd be kinda nice, come around next meeting, we're having one Tuesday.'

"Tuesday, the agenda was going late and I could hear the train whistling and I said to the chairman, 'You know, I really need to catch that train. If you want me to sing those songs, I have to do it now.' 'Okay.'

"I don't think I was very good, but I sang Aunt Molly's songs, and a couple of others. And they gave me a check. I said, 'Gee, what good'll this check do me, I'm catching the freight?' 'Oh, you can cash it in the bar downstairs.' I cashed it downstairs, got five silver dollars, and ran down the road with the train whistling. And the dollars kept falling out of my pocket and rolling down a hill. Finally one got lost in the weeds and I never did get it. I clutched four of them in my hand and jumped into this boxcar already moving. It shuttled back and forth all night long. I woke up in the same town."

Pete finally found a train east, landing in New York at the beginning of September 1940, the week Leon Trotsky was assassinated outside Mexico City. Travel had toughened him, and he knew he would never go hungry if he held on to his banjo. Walking and working had made him muscular. Most of all, Pete came back bubbling with Americana. He had found its folk and they had sung him their songs, sometimes in excess: A drunk in Montana had insisted he hear twenty-three beery verses of "Strawberry Roan." Seeger's pride and patriotism blended into his new songs until folk music itself seemed patriotic. But New York radicals, many of them immigrants, couldn't understand his enthusiasm; when a friend applied for a job as a music director in New York, radicals criticized him for being "too American" in his music, "just like Pete Seeger."

Pete was now ready to begin a career as a musician, but he didn't know where to start. He played at a few "cause parties," evenings where someone gave over their house to fund-raising, but this didn't cover the rent. He shared his problems with Leadbelly who, despite his enormous talents, eked out a bare living in New York. While Woody and Pete had traveled Route 66, Leadbelly had been in prison on Rikers Island on an assault charge, an embittering experience. The big city tantalized Huddie with a recognition that was never his. He played the few dates that came his way and stuck close to home. It upset Seeger to realize that, with less experience, he could go much further than Leadbelly—because he was white and talked the "right" English.

Pete received an invitation to sing with Woody at the American Peace Mobilization in Washington, D.C. At this point the Communist Party—and most of Pete's friends—had broken with Roosevelt over his refusal to support the Spanish Republic and over his preparations for war. All summer Pete had read about the fat defense contracts given Ford and other companies; tanks rolled off assembly lines in Detroit. Pete had never been enthusiastic about fighting, even in Spain. Now, like many Communist radicals in 1940, he opposed Hitler but denounced the war as "imperialist," a provocation to get the Nazis to fight the Soviet Union. Though it was easy to imagine Winston Churchill gloating over a Hitler-Stalin confrontation, overlooking Hitler's crimes wasn't easy. Pete focused his emotion on the evils of war, though this no more allowed him to escape the nation's war fever than his father had at Berkeley, before World War I. An unpleasant, irrational violence moved throught the country.

Seeger arrived in Washington insecure enough to borrow a tie and jacket from a friend, the first he'd worn in years. Afterward, he and Woody stayed up late improvising talking blues. The folk-song movement had by now spread outside of New York City. In a country of a hundred and twenty million, however, all the practitioners of folk-protest could fit into a single hall—and often did; the music had an extremely small following.

Yet as a profession, songwriting was on the rise; technological advances in record production had lessened the music industry's dependence on sheet sales; and while formulaic, Tin Pan Alley-style songwriting still dominated the industry (Twentieth Century Fox alone employed twenty-five songwriters for its films. Records had become less expensive to produce, thus opening opportunities for independent songwriters. "Anyone could write a popular song," said Irving Caeser (who with George Gershwin wrote "Swanee"). "That's no great shakes. But to be able to write a song any time of day or night, that's what a pro had to be able to do. I wrote my songs *any* time, on a bet."

In reworking folk songs, Seeger involved himself in a different process. Most songwriters aimed for a hit—or back to the piano. Pete and Woody put their lives and politics into songs. Sometimes it cost them jobs, sometimes their reputations.

Pete's appetite for travel approached gluttony; he could turn no proposal down. In October 1940 Pete visited a progressive family in Alabama. He was all legs in those days, full of Yankee stiffness and working-class affectations such as refusing to wash. "I was worried about my beds, he was so dirty," recalled his host, Mrs. Joe Gelders. To get him to clean up, the family had to promise washing would help the purplish-red acne that persisted in patches on his face.

He tried hard to lose his Yankee ways. On arriving in Birmingham, he had walked into a department store and bought a set of overalls. Unfortunately, his New England accent gave him away to the clerk as soon as he opened his mouth.

Pete had a bad case of proletarian chic. He envied Woody's ability to fade into a working-class bar; the only way he could be accepted by a southern railway worker was to play the banjo. He worked this contact for all he could, walking up to a farmhouse on a hot day, his banjo on one shoulder, and asking for some water. "Say, can you really play that thing?" the farmer invariably asked. "Well, I try," Pete would answer, and in the noonday sun, he would play a few tunes until everyone put down their tools and swapped verses. Pete didn't have an easy time walking up to strangers and asking if they'd show him a lick or two, but he had no other way to learn.

He kept a journalistic distance from his experiences; the *Southern News Almanac* published his first article (in a paper not his own), about visiting a family of musicians in rural Alabama.

"An old man came to the door [Pete wrote]. 'Yes, I'm Mr. Smith. . . . Hey Bill. There's a young feller here to see you!' This was all the introduction I had. We became acquainted right off when he saw I was carrying a banjo. 'Well, what do you say, we'll rattle off a tune together.' So the instruments came down off the walls, and out of the dresser drawers.

"Well, you can have your Radio City Music Hall, your Hotel Savoy, your Hollywood Klieg lights, and your tuxedos, but as far as I'm concerned some of the best music I ever heard came out of that old shack in Townley, Alabama. We played all that evening, and next day went the rounds of the neighbors, swapping songs, and me getting acquainted.

"But before I go on, I want to give you a picture of this place. The coal mine which used to support everybody at Townley closed down several years ago, and since then half the town has moved away. . . . Stores closed down, grass coming through the sidewalks, houses falling into disrepair, and a general gray color to everything. . . .

"[The next morning] I was watching the design made by a hundred glowing cracks in the top of the ancient stove. Joe mixed some biscuits. . . . We heard a train whistle down the tracks that run straight through town. 'There's your train callin' you!' I gobbled down my breakfast, grabbed up my banjo and my hat.

" 'See you next Wednesday!' I shouted at the door, and lit out in the early morning darkness, just in time to catch the blinds of the fast passenger express as she started to roar down the tracks to Birmingham."

Pete was still reading Lincoln Steffens—his collected letters—and he had a columnist's eye for events he participated in. But more and more he adopted the attitude of Woody, himself a columnist for the *Worker:* "There is something too slow and too plowy and ploddy for me to spend my time at fooling around with long novels. . . . I've never heard nobody yet get a whole room full of friends and enemies both to sing and to ring the plaster down singing out a novel."

Coming back to the city in November, Pete was a city boy who looked and sang country. Rural values (and music) inspired him as Seton's tribal communism had: here were honest ideals, far from city slickness, unspoiled by commerce. Pete's association of folk music and antimaterialism may have come from mistaken notions of country living, but he nonetheless made his life meet his image of the rustic singer. He became a character, traipsing down Broadway in his overalls and bending his friends' ears with reports of life down South.

Soon after his return to New York, someone who knew *Hard Hitting*

Songs—probably Peter Hawes—told him a fellow named Lee Hays was also putting out a collection of labor songs. "No sense having the books repeat," said Pete, arranging a meeting. They spent an evening together, and Lee suggested, "How about teaming up? I know some songs, and you know that banjo." Pete liked the tall, heavy-set fellow. Lee told him he'd been a cook and a song leader at a radical labor college in Commonwealth, Arkansas. Pete enjoyed his wry, down-home way of telling a story; Lee could engross his listeners so thoroughly that they didn't realize he had drunk half a bottle of their whiskey in the telling. As a result of post-surgery complications, he had gained an enormous amount of weight; Lee and Seeger were a sort of Laurel and Hardy of the Left.

The proposed partnership percolated while Pete considered other possibilities, among them a job Alan Lomax might get him on radio. Lomax now worked for CBS, producing a program on American folk music, "Back Where I Come From." Alan thought the producers might hire Pete to play banjo occasionally. It would be a small break, but an important one. In the days before TV, appearing on coast-to-coast radio gave a musician unsurpassed exposure. Plenty of professionals had waited years for just such an opportunity.

Unfortunately for Pete, he wasn't ready for the major leagues: "I couldn't sing with the banjo; I had to either play the banjo or sing, but couldn't do both." Alan knew this as well as anyone; when Pete had come back, Alan had asked, "What have you learned?" Pete showed him a few things on the banjo. "Well, you haven't learned much on the banjo," Lomax replied with characteristic bluntness. But then he heard Pete sing and complimented his voice.

CBS balked. They weren't convinced Seeger could make it as a pro. "In those days, radio was all live," Alan's sister Bess pointed out. "They'd point at you and say 'Now' and you had to perform instantly." On the other hand, Pete was one of the few people in New York who could play old-time banjo. Alan and Nick Ray, the show's director, prevailed. Pete just didn't have the skills, however, and he was let go after a few sessions.

Pete didn't let this become a setback. He had gone too far into this, his third profession, to turn back. He saw clearer than ever the connection between music and society that had eluded his father in Pinehurst. His notebooks were stuffed with song ideas and snatches of tunes that he wrote out in his thin, elegant hand. He started rehearsing with Lee Hays. This time there wouldn't be any problem about Pete stepping in front of the stage; travel had made him audience-wise; he had even helped stop a near-riot in Oklahoma with his singing.

In December 1940 Lee and Pete sang at the Jade Mountain Restaurant in New York City, their first booking together. Soon Lee's roommate, Millard Lampell, started coming along. The trio kidded around a lot, but Pete was serious; having traded his woodsy ideals for the life of a city radical, he was tired of drifting. Pete tied his ambition to causes larger than himself; he meant to Change the World, as Mike Gold called his column. In two months the group already had a repertoire and a name, the Almanac Singers.

Talking Union

5

ONE hot, muggy evening in late May 1941 New Yorkers crowded the stoops of brownstones. Inside Madison Square Garden, Pete Seeger and his five-month-old group, the Almanac Singers, tuned up backstage. At this, their first big rally, twenty thousand striking Transport Workers' Union members waited impatiently for the performers. Over the echoing conversations, the Almanacs could barely hear themselves tune.

They made a strange-looking ensemble. Instead of wearing tuxedos, the Almanacs had come from Greenwich Village in their street clothes. Pete Seeger was twenty-two, and the others weren't much older. After eight years of playing banjo, Pete had begun to resemble his instrument: long and straight-necked, with a topknot of hair. Lee Hays was singing bass, and Pete Hawes, a radical with a taste for breeding horses, added a tenor. Mill Lampell stood out in a clean shirt and suit jacket, an athletic, all-American sort. None of them knew what to expect. The striking drivers had brought their families, and the kids squirmed in the heat, fanning themselves with the programs. The crowd looked awfully big, and union chief Mike Quill, Pete realized, underestimated the controversy of the Almanacs' songs.

Two weeks before, Pete had been attacked while singing at a party in Greenwich Village. He had been finishing up an anti-war song poking fun of Winston Churchill when "a drunk guy came up, and WHAM, the next thing I know, he'd socked me right in the eye. Banged my head right against the mantelpiece. His friends pulled him away, and he said, 'I like Churchill!' " The assault only made Pete more outspokenly anti-war; he hated to be told what to sing.

A drunk was one matter, and an audience the size of tonight's was quite another; a run-in here could lead to more than a black eye. Instead of peace songs, the Almanacs had decided to sing their union tunes. They walked on stage to mild applause and snickers at their casual dress. Pete took a long breath and started "Talking Union":

> *If you want higher wages let me tell you what to do;*   ©
> *You got to talk to the workers in the shop with you;*
> *You got to build you a union, got to make it strong;*
> *But if you all stick together, boys, it won't be long*
> *You get shorter hours, better working conditions.*
> *Vacations with pay, take the kids to the seashore.*
>   . . .

The crowd perked up. No one had ever sung them a song about *unions*.

> *'Course the boss may persuade some poor damn fool*
> *To go to your meeting and act like a stool;*
> *But you can always tell a stool, though, that's a fact,*
> *He's got a rotten streak a-running down his back;*
> *He doesn't have to stool—he'll make a good living—*
> *On what he takes out of blind men's cups. . . .*

The audience laughed and hooted; Seeger speeded it up.

> *Suppose they're working you so hard it's just*
>   *outrageous,*
> *And they're paying you all starvation wages,*
> *You go to the boss, and the boss will yell,*
> *"Before I raise your pay I'd see you all in hell."*
> *Well, he's puffing a big cigar and feeling mighty*
>   *slick,*
> *'Cause he thinks he's got your union licked.*
> *He looks out the window, and what does he see*
> *But a thousand pickets, and they all agree*
> *He's a bastard—unfair—slavedriver—*
> *Bet he beats his wife. . . .*

The audience roared in appreciation. A year before, Pete had left the stage in defeat; now, after his travels, he received an ovation. The Almanacs had done a good job for "the only group that rehearses on stage," as Woody called them. The Almanac Singers didn't want all-expenses-paid trips to Hollywood; union rallies were what they craved. They opposed war and promoted unions the way early Christians believed in the Church.

     Next they had a song from their new anti-war album, "Songs for John Doe," a number that often shocked audiences by ridiculing the President (to the tune of "Jesse James"):

Oh, Franklin Roosevelt told the people how he felt.   ©
We damned near believed what he said.
He said, "I hate war and so does Eleanor, but
We won't be safe 'till everybody's dead. . . ."
                    —"*Ballad of October 16*"

The Almanacs weren't entirely alone in these opinions. The audience was of an age to remember relatives killed or wounded in World War I. Yet in 1941, only a few extremists opposed sending American troops to fight in Europe, many of these Communists who had been denouncing war since the 1939 Hitler-Stalin pact. The Almanacs led the stop-the-war effort with songs so militant their record company—Keynote—refused to stamp its name on the discs, issuing them as "Almanac Records."

Their union songs brought the loudest applause. The Almanacs swayed enough of the audience that when Mill Lampell approached Quill and Saul Mills of the Congress of Industrial Organizations, they agreed to help set up a national tour of CIO unions, a royal invitation.

The group had not been together long when all this occurred. Mill, Lee, and Pete had recently moved from a dark ground-floor apartment in Chelsea to a sixty-five-foot loft on Thirteenth Street, within spitting distance of the Bowery. They were an odd but vital combination: Lee brought southern hymns, a slow, country wit, and his organizing-religious background. Following the example of the radical minister Claude Williams, he had already begun adapting traditional lyrics (and would go on to collaborate on Seeger's best-known songs). As a roommate, Lee could be grumbly, and tended to pit people against each other; Pete, eager to learn song-leading from him, made allowances.

Mill Lampell came from a liberal Jewish family in New Jersey; short, quick-witted, and dapper, he was a radical Joe College. Mill was also a born operator, hustling publicity and engagements for the group. The Almanacs teased him about his smooth talking and fondness for dress-up clothes, but they appreciated his remarkable ability to improvise verses, sometimes producing a whole song in minutes. Women were often on his mind, and it may have been he who introduced Pete to Ellen Sillen, daughter of the Marxist professor and critic Sam Sillen. Pete and Mill would double-date, and at the end of the evening, Pete would hem and haw out on the stoop with Ellen, while Mill and his date casually marched up the stairs and into bed.

Peter Hawes grew up in Massachusetts, a baritone who loved sea chanteys and political theory. He had inherited money from one of the Boston

Houghtons and enjoyed discussing the proletarian dictatorship out on a sundeck with a tall drink in hand. His contradictions were no less pronounced than those of Bess Lomax, Alan's sister and daughter of the renowned folk song collector and banker, John Lomax. Bess was a proper, dark-haired Texan girl who took weekends off from Bryn Mawr to partake of New York's fringe Left. She had an infectious, throaty laugh and a sparkly quality, like a woman in love.

Pete Seeger was the real musician of the group, the central element that the others needed to function. "When Woody and I were together," Lee said, "nothing much happened; we drank wine and talked a lot, had a great time, but no sparks flew."

Everybody pitched in to fix up the loft. They even added an extra-high sink, so their long-armed banjoist could do the dishes. A friendly carpenter built them a fourteen-foot picnic table with benches, and soon, hungry musicians were dropping in for dinners from a stew pot long on potatoes and carrots but short on beef. They held Sunday afternoon rent parties, which packed in a hundred people at thirty-five cents a head, and their peace songs got them so many write-ups in the *Worker* that other left-wing musicians grumbled. The group's specialty was improvising verses to old tunes, which was how they wrote "Talking Union." One afternoon Mill and Lee were tossing around verses to a traditional talking blues.

> *If you want to get to heaven, let me tell you*
> *   what to do*
> *You got to grease your feet with mutton stew*
> *Slide out of the Devil's hands*
> *Ease on into the Promised Land.*

In an hour they had two-thirds of "Talking Union" worked out. Finding a positive ending stumped them; that task fell to Seeger, who worked it out on the roof in his undershirt, with his banjo and a bottle of pop. He came up with a moral, something he was always good at: "Take it easy, but take it." In time, "Talking Union" was itself parodied:

> *If you want higher profits let me tell you what to do,*　©
> *You got to talk to the people who work for you,*
> *Got to bust up the unions. They're much too strong,*
> *Fire anybody who dares belong!*
> *Get rid of the agitators,*
> *Hire friendly people*
> *Willing to work for an honest wage.*
>
> — "*Talking Management Blues*"

As chief organizer and musician, Pete had his hands full weeks before the CIO tour. The group had agreed to provide their own transportation, but they had no car, nor money to buy one. With the help of Alan Lomax, Pete arranged to record two albums of cowboy songs and sea chanteys for a small, jazz-oriented label, General Records. With the four hundred dollars from the session they bought a roomy 1929 Buick and enough gas to get to their first booking. Pete then turned his attention to coordinating the tour: He and Mill charged around writing letters and polishing songs. Pete would schedule early-morning house meetings, which the others disappointed him by sleeping through.

His zeal for unions was nearly religious, and many of the Almanac tunes had a gospel flavor appropriate to an era when labor organizing had the tough glamor of investigative journalism in the 1970s. The Thirties and Forties, when unions became Pete's obsession, were some of American labor's finest hours. Talented and bright radicals went broke organizing the CIO, but they got results: Henry Ford negotiated with a labor union for the first time; every week another major auto factory got CIOrganized. Riding this wave, the Almanacs hoped to be the songleaders of American labor.

Seeger had come a long ways since 1938, when the Harvard Jazz Band had turned him down for not reading notes fast enough; "Pete was absolutely absorbed in his banjo," Mill Lampell remembered. "He would get up in the morning, and before he'd eat or anything, he'd reach for the banjo and begin to play, sitting on his bed in his underwear." He also practiced the guitar, and when there was no one else to play with, the recorder. "Even at that early age, there was a charisma about Peter Seeger," a journalist commented. "The feeling was: Here's a young guy who's not just singing for everybody, he's singing especially for *us*." Audiences trusted him. At twenty-one, he already had a record out, and its title song, "The Ballad of John Doe," was his solo. "Back then, Pete had enormous energy," Mill continued. "He wasn't the greatest banjo player, he didn't have the greatest voice, but there was something catchy about him. . . . It was a time when the left wing was very romantic about America; in literature, these were the days of Carl Sandburg, Archibald MacLeish, and Stephen Benét. Then suddenly it was as if the *music* of America had arrived," carried on the shimmering strings of a young Yankee banjoist.

"Pete was superb with that banjo," added Earl Robinson. "I saw then what came out later: Pete would stand up in front of an audience and really get them going, and in the enthusiasm of the moment, he'd tear off about twelve seconds of totally brilliant cadenza-type banjo; music that would stand up on any concert stage. Then he'd pull back and say, 'Well, let's all sing a song, shall we?' He didn't want to act 'long-hair,' didn't want to be taken for a classical musician."

Seeger stood out from his colleagues, a situation the Almanacs hadn't expected and resisted as best they could. Inspired by the Anonymous movement in Paris, in which artists didn't sign their works, the group copyrighted their songs collectively and took turns singing leads; they even refused to list their names on their album covers. Despite these efforts, newspaper writers spotlighted Pete's "technically brilliant, haunting solos." *Time* noticed his "bitter sincerity": "Lanky Pete Bowers (a name Seeger took to protect his father's government job) talks union with plenty of persuasion."

A couple of weeks before their scheduled departure, on a warm Sunday afternoon, June 22, 1941, the Almanacs were holding a rent party. As usual, the crowd clapped and sang, dropping nickels in the can for cups of coffee. All of a sudden Alan Sloane, a friend of Mill's, burst into the room. "The Nazis have invaded Russia," he said, and the singing stopped dead. For a moment there was silence, as people tried to imagine what would happen next. Then everybody started arguing. For two years the Communist Left had followed Russia's lead in opposing the war. Now, partisans of the Soviet Union were cut adrift, hesitant either to go to war or to desert Russia. How could the Almanacs go on singing peace songs while the Soviet Union fought for its life? Maybe they would have to give up their tour.

Skilled as the Almanacs were at rewrites, history had changed faster than their songs. Political singers have always been the pinch-hitters of the musical world, able to field a political position on short notice. But the Almanacs lacked the true politician's facility for changing overnight, and the group soon found themselves in trouble with their radical colleagues—particularly with the Trotskyites, who gloated over the Party's ill fortune. Even friends such as Dorothy Millstone, progressive journalist for the *New York Post*, grew uneasy. "After hearing that Russia had been invaded, I hung up the phone, and the first thing I did was break my Almanac records."

Two years before, when the Hitler-Stalin pact had originally been signed, Pete had been touring New York State with the Vagabond Puppeteers. He'd had a hard time believing his ears. There was no *Daily Worker* for guidance, and he'd been shocked that the Nazis and the only socialist nation on earth should suddenly become allies; the Jewish members of the troupe were horrified. In the city, other Party members had a similar reaction. "There were those who said, 'Well, what're you going to say about this one,' " reported Alvah Bessie. "There were those who claimed to know immediately what it meant and were sounding off. But they didn't sound too convincing. Then there was the cautious voice which said, 'We haven't got all the facts. Let's wait and see. I'm willing to give the Soviet Union the benefit of the doubt.'

"At that point one guy got up and said, 'Well, I'm *not*! You can explain it all you want, but no matter how you slice it, it's still baloney!' "

Pete was in the wait-and-see camp. On his return, he had heard the Party's side: that the West hoped Hitler would attack Russia, but Stalin had outfoxed them and bought time for defense. He didn't know whether to believe his own gut reaction or the *Daily Worker*. Opposing the pact would have cut him off from friends and jobs in New York. The Soviet Union's *Realpolitik* was hard to overlook, but Seeger had forced himself.

Now the bargain was off. The invasion of Russia put him back where he started, with the Soviet Union and Nazi Germany in warring camps. Only today Pete had a national reputation for singing, "Franklin D. You Ain't Gonna Send Me Across the Sea."

Underlying his political back-and-forthing was the basic truth of Pete's anti-war songs: A good cause didn't make war any less horrible. Many would later criticize these flip-flops as cold-hearted, overlooking the deep roots of both anti-Nazi and anti-war instincts in the thirties. Radical youth then seesawed between pacifism and anti-fascism, first taking the anti-war Oxford Oath, then pledging to fight for Collective Security. In these contradictions Seeger was by no means alone, even if other New Yorkers his age were more interested in Joe Louis's approaching title fight or Joe DiMaggio's hitting streak with the Yankees. Pete saw both sides of the problem. All he'd gotten for giving up his dreams of hermithood was a conscience that hurt like a broken tooth. Glenn Miller could play the same sweet tunes no matter what happened to the world, but Pete Seeger faced the occupational hazard of political singers: song obsolescence.

Meanwhile, war spread from country to country, and nothing, not the threats of statesmen nor pleas of the church, could stop it. Though America wasn't at war, "We aren't going to let neutrality chloroform us into inactivity," Secretary of State Cordell Hull insisted. Scientists at the National Defense Research Committee began investigating a new field: atomic energy. Said one, "I hope they never succeed in tapping atomic power; it will be a hell of a thing for civilization."

"Woody was also continually frustrated by the curves of history which were wiping out our repertoire," said Bess. "He really wanted to write songs that would last; to express this, he parodied a song he knew . . . and called it 'On Account of that *New* Situation' ":

> *I started to sing a song*
> *To the entire population,*
> *But I ain't a' doing a thing tonight,*
> *On account of this new situation.*

To make matters worse, a Harvard professor, Carl Frederick, called the Almanacs "Poison in Our System" in an article in the June *Atlantic*. "These recordings are distributed under the innocuous appeal: 'Sing out for peace.' Yet they are strictly subversive and illegal. . . . You can never handle situations of this kind by mere suppression." The words "mere suppression" had an ugly ring, but Seeger wasn't about to change what he sang to please the professor.

Whenever Pete tried to bring politics and music together, it was like practicing woodlore in the city. He wanted to sing on the right side, but this kept changing; the problem with topical songs is *keeping* them topical, while remaining true to the original inspiration. Seeger grew more adept at this in later years, but now he felt pain and embarrassment.

In the best of times, communal living can be tense; among impoverished musicians trying to agree on politics, blowouts were inevitable. Lee claimed he had tuberculosis, which went undiagnosed because no one had money for a doctor; the Almanacs accused him of "malingering" and "divisionist tendencies." Once, as the group left for a booking, Lee decided he was too sick to sing and draped himself over a couch, one hand falling dramatically over the edge. Pete reached into his back pocket and pulled out his trusty recorder. He played "Taps," and everyone howled with laughter except Lee, supposedly too sick to get mad. Hays's "sicknesses" came so often, the others eventually expelled him from the Almanacs, replacing him with Arthur Stern.

Now, with Russia attacked and half their repertoire "inappropriate," everyday strains burst out in new ways. Hardly a day used to go by without a new song, but the group grew unproductive, dissipating energy in political debate rather than music. A day before their tour began, Pete shepherded everyone over to record for General, whose advance they had already spent. Fortunately, Woody Guthrie arrived from Oklahoma City just in time for the recordings, half-shaved and road-weary. Asked if he wanted to record and tour with them, he scratched his chin and said, "Well, I just *came* from there . . . but I don't guess I mind if I join up with you."

These were one of the few sessions Pete recorded with Woody. In *The Soil and the Sea* (originally two sets of 78s titled "Sod Buster Ballads" and "Deep Sea Shanties"), Guthrie's tastes for simple accompaniment went to extremes, but his voice made up for it, rolling out in eerily sustained waves, a Middle Eastern sound: half drone, half wail. Pete studied his friend's vocal control and phrasing, how he reached up and laid his voice on a note, covering it completely. Pete had none of this self-possession. His voice cracked nervously on the first phrases, but at least he could now sing and play banjo together. And where his voice hadn't quite knit, he knew how to cover himself with the banjo.

On July 3, having agreed to perform only folk and union songs on the trip, the Almanacs left New York on tour. Illness plagued them from the beginning. Peter Hawes contracted pneumonia as they were leaving, and they'd gotten only as far as Philadelphia when he quit—an inauspicious start. Some CIO officials greeted them with open arms, but others were unfriendly or downright hostile, treating the Almanacs more like cheerleaders than consciousness-raisers. The young radicals looked to unions as a golden stairway to decent pay and safe housing conditions, and they could not understand why they had to battle suspicious leaders for the privilege of singing for pennies. When the Almanacs reached San Francisco, having sung for radical groups and striking CIO locals in Chicago, Cleveland, and Minnesota, they had their grand finale, which Seeger later described: "When we walked down the aisle of a room where one thousand local members of the [San Francisco] longshoremen's union were meeting, we could see some of them turning around in surprise and even disapproval. 'What the hell is a bunch of hillbilly singers coming in here for? We got work to do.'

"But when we finished singing 'The Ballad of Harry Bridges' for them, their applause was deafening. We walked down the same aisle on our way out and they slapped Woody on the back so hard they nearly knocked him over."

Seeger didn't know it, but among those pounding Woody was an FBI operative. He didn't enjoy the show. In his report, he characterized the Almanacs as "extremely untidy, ragged, and dirty in appearance." Their songleading technique couldn't fool the FBI. "After going through the song once, the majority of the audience joined in the singing," noted the informant. "They joined in not from their own desire, but were led into it through mass psychology and apathy toward the utter control of the meeting by Communist officers and members." FBI headquarters took particular exception to one line in "The Ballad of Harry Bridges": "The FBI is worried, The bosses they are scared." Undaunted by such criticism, Washington sent out three communiqués warning field offices to watch out for any Almanac singers in their midst. From this point on, Pete's career held great interest for intelligence agencies. Each time the *Daily Worker* mentioned his name in an ad, the clipping found its way into a growing file—which would eventually be turned over to Seeger's enemies.

The strains of traveling fragmented the group. Lee rode a bus home, too sick to keep up. Mill met an old girl friend in Los Angeles and returned separately. The Almanacs were reduced to Woody and Pete, who were to make their way east via Washington and Montana. On a lark, before leaving they visited northern Mexico. Their host described the pair in that summer of 1941: "Pete was a slat of a lad, all Adam's apple and large trusting eyes, with sudden attacks of embarrassment that reddened his cheeks. . . . Woody was as light and wiry as one of the early planes made of sticks and canvas, and he was as light on his feet as a cat avoiding trouble." Pete apparently acted as Woody's private secretary, shopping for groceries, stowing their gear in the car, and reminding Woody of their schedule for the day. Woody usually ignored him and pounded on his typewriter, when he wasn't teasing him about Ellen.

They started their return in Portland (disappointing) and Seattle (where they attended a singing party called a "hootenanny"). Traveling together was like old times, except when Pete and Woody swung through Butte, Montana, where Pete knew his way around and Woody didn't. Guthrie wrote out his memories in a long, unpublished account of their trip.

"Pete Bowers and myself had just started back across the country from California to New York, singing in all kinds of places in all kinds of towns. . . .

"We pulled out through the hills north of Butte, and the sun was just about the middle of the afternoon, and when we got about forty or fifty miles out of town, the sun went down, and we hit the high winding mountain roads, full of all kinds of short turns and quick curves. We didn't have extra good brakes, so we didn't drive very fast. But as we drove on higher and higher up into the mountains, the weather got colder and colder, and we finally hit a big snowstorm, and the wind was blowing ninety miles an hour, pushing our old car all over the road, and the snow piled up in the highway and covered it over so we couldn't see it, because our lights weren't any too bright, anyway, and the snow kept freezing on the lights and we just barely had to creep along, creep along, and then the ice got to sticking on our windshield, and it got so thick it broke our wiper, and we had to stop about every mile or two and scrape and hack and dig the ice off. We couldn't see the road because it looked just like a big white herd of sheep out in front of us. Se we just barely oozed along. And driving this slow, our motor first got too hot and started boiling our water out, and the steam flew like a train engine, and we wondered what in the devil was going to happen next.

"The steam froze all over the front of the car and all over the radiator, and the wind couldn't get through to cool the motor off, so it kept boiling worse and worse. The whole thing seemed crazy, because it looked like everything in the world that could go wrong was doing it.

"We got to the tops of the mountains and coasted down faster, and the motor was running slower, and the whole works froze tight and solid. Like one big icebox under our hood. We had icicles a foot long all over our car, and the wiper and the lights not working, no brakes, and about 27 hundred and 50 miles to go to get back to New York.

"The snow stayed with us all of the way across Montana, North Dakota, the big wheat and farming country, and on till we come to Duluth, Minnesota. . . . We saw deer and antelope out in the forests, and all kinds of wild animals, because this was just about thirty miles from the Canadian border, and it was cold winter time, snow and ice all over the trees and the lakes and the roads. . . . Minnesota gets awful, awful cold. I remember that it was so cold that it just seemed to pop and crackle in the air. The trees would crack and pop and it would ring out like guns, and it always sounded like the men were out there somewhere swinging their axes."

At this point, Pete picked up the tale, providing a clear contrast between his journalistic style and Guthrie's more naturalistic one, which had a wealth of landscape but no people.

"An organizer for the lumberjacks union asked us if we would be willing to go around and sing in some of the camps, and we said, 'Sure.' He was on a routine inspection tour to make sure that the union contract was being obeyed by the bosses. . . . He introduced Woody and me. We walked up to the center, sang a song. There was dead silence. We sang another song, there was still dead silence. We looked at each other and said, 'Suppose we ought to sing another?' Well, we sang one more. There was still dead silence when we finished. We thanked the men for listening to us, and walked over to the side. One of the men said, 'Aren't you going to sing any more, boys?' A little reluctantly we went back and sang a couple more songs, again to complete dead silence, and then we figured we better not push our luck anymore and said good night.

"The next morning one of the men said to us, 'Boy, that music sure was wonderful. Wish you had sung a lot more, we could have listened to it all night.' "

Pete and Woody left the ice behind them and coasted toward New York. Cramped together in a car for weeks on end, the odd couple thrashed out their differences. "I can't stand him when he's around," Pete later told Lee Hays, "but I miss him when he's gone."

"Woody kind of jarred Pete's regular way of life, made Pete feel unnerved when he was around," Lee recalled. "Woody was hard to take; he was *not* housebroken. If he drank too much, he was obnoxious and rude, at best an unruly child." According to the woman they stayed with in Duluth, Irene Paull, "Pete was having a lot of trouble with Woody on that trip. Pete was the most patient guy in the world, but Woody! . . . If he wasn't in the mood to talk, nothing could make him do it. He'd sit, play the fiddle, and say, 'Dance.' "

As a young man, Pete Seeger was drawn to his opposites, working-class heroes like Mike Gold, Leadbelly, and Guthrie. In Woody, Pete had found a companion and teacher; but he no longer needed him as a model.

When the pair reached New York in the fall of 1941 they found the Almanacs on the verge of breaking up. No one mentioned anti-war songs; they had literally changed their tune. The group had learned a bitter lesson in politics: to survive in closed organizations like the Party, one has to read the wind. Those preoccupied with art instead of doctrine fall behind—often with humiliating results. For Pete, giving up his peace songs reminded him of the difficulty of keeping ideals pure; looking back, the best he could say of this period was that he hadn't "stood on any false consistency." Henceforth he avoided direct association with left-wing tactics; he lent his name but he rarely strategized.

Morale was generally low. Mill Lampell took Pete off to one side, soon after he arrived, and explained that in his absence, Ellen Sillen had fallen for Peter Hawes, and the couple were planning to be married. "Pete jumped up, wearing those big farmer's shoes, and took off into the night. He didn't say a word—but he was gone for several days. He never told anyone where he went, either," Mill said.

There didn't seem much reason for the group to go on. At the end of September, the Almanacs gathered at the New Hampshire vacation home of Peter Hawes and actually agreed to separate. They enjoyed each other's company too much, however, and by October, they had rented a townhouse on Tenth Street and Sixth Avenue and turned it into a frat house of musical revolutionaries. Pete and Bess shared an attic room, a curtain demurely dividing their beds. Needless to say, they lived chastely, though Bess had a heavy crush on Pete: he was so all-fired innocent and cute, if scrawny. The Lomax and Seeger families wouldn't have minded if the friendship became something more; Bess was one of Ruth's favorite people.

Woody stayed on the second floor, and the others bunked where they could. Mill took a place nearby for more privacy with his dates. A mix of show business people, journalists, and guitar-pickers gathered for suppers, feasting on bread and salad. Music was always coming out of one room or another, and the living room was cluttered with song sheets, instruments, and debris. Bess would come downstairs for breakfast and find Woody asleep over a typewriter on the dining table, a bottle of wine at one side and sheets of manuscripts scattered over the floor. She sometimes overlooked the romance of the situation as she hunted for a clean cup or a place to eat.

At the end of the day, Leadbelly or other musicians would drift in for a late-night jam session. A pint of whiskey would make the rounds, and everybody would sit on the floor and whoop it up, sometimes singing "John Henry" for three hours as people tossed out new verses. Once in a while someone would replenish the bottle or wander into the kitchen for a snack; all they'd find was salad or bread crumbs from Lee's homemade loaves.

On nights they had bookings the group raced through what they called "the subway circuit." Around nine, they went off to their first booking (worth perhaps ten dollars for a twenty-minute set); then they rode the subway to the next one, returning home at three or four A.M., after as many as five appearances. The Almanacs learned to tune fast; if they overstayed, they lost the next booking. They were quite picturesque; in those days walking around with guitars and banjos was like leading a giraffe. Pete loved the echoey subway stations; when they had some nice harmonies ringing—to the surprise of their fellow riders—Pete would get so giddy, he would dash up the down escalator, clomping around like a kid.

To pay the ninety-five-dollar rent for their three-story house, the group held "hootenannies," named after the ones Pete and Woody had seen in Seattle. On Sunday afternoons, audiences assembled in their basement; those in the know brought old coats or cardboard to sit on. The singing got so loud, the landlord complained about "the continuous stamping that seems to be going on at certain times during the day or night." Generally, the Almanac House ran on turmoil and music, the only items the group had in excess. Theirs was the poverty of rebellious intellectuals. Nights, the group sang protest songs like "Jim Crow":

> *Lincoln set the Negroes free*
> *Why are they still in slavery?*
> *Jim Crow!*

By day, their house was cleaned by Ethel, their black maid who earned four dollars for her twice-weekly labor.

As the months rolled by, an underlying frustration crept in on their work; the Almanacs weren't taken seriously—or heard—by working people. They played in an occasional union hall, but all too often Pete and the others were cheap, mid-meeting entertainment on the Party circuit, a situation as frustrating as a Bible-thumping revivalist unable to hold a crowd long enough to preach. The Almanacs mainly blamed this on a management plot: "Bosses have hired fake songwriters . . . but the people know inwardly that these 'hits' are no part of their working, slaving, worrying." Actually the problem went far deeper: the Almanacs assumed working-class immigrants would identify with folk songs, the way they did. Unfortunately, most city dwellers didn't know "John Henry," and even if they did, the song often sounded "country" to those emigrating from the South. Instead of union songs, New Yorkers listened to their own ethnic music, or to the show tunes and pop hits the Almanacs scorned. "I think we were in the wrong city," Bess said. "In New York, we sang Appalachian songs to Central European or Irish immigrants in the International Ladies' Garment Workers' and the Transport Workers' Unions." The traditions mixed as smoothly as an outing of Rotarians at a roller disco.

Except for Woody, the Almanacs sang in the name of a class they didn't belong to: the People, who stubbornly preferred Harold Arlen's "Blues in the Night" or the "Chattanooga Choo-Choo" to "Talking Union." If the Almanacs had wanted to reach the people, maybe they should have played saxophones or zithers instead of guitars. But they couldn't have. They worked with folk songs because they loved them—particularly Pete, who had become so absorbed in the banjo that even simple conversations grew difficult. Pete played for hours at a stretch, his back against the living room wall and his long legs jackknifed across the floor. Coming home from a night of bookings, he would play a few more tunes before bed.

Pete began to develop a style: using the banjo to punctuate lyrics by adding a strum off the beat, or by varying soft and loud strokes to build musical tension. He began strumming underneath his song introductions—evolving a folk *Sprechgesang* (speech-song) where introduction and song flow seamlessly into one another. Pete learned from the musicians who later brought folk music to mass audiences: Burl Ives, Oscar Brand, Josh White, and others. The greatest influence was still Woody, who at the time was working on his vocal delivery, off blues records of Blind Lemon Jefferson and T-Bone Slim. "Woody had his own little record player upstairs with about eight records he listened to absolutely continuously," Bess said. "Sitting in the kitchen you could hear him play the record, and at the end of the cut, he'd pick up the needle and move it back to the beginning. He'd play these songs maybe a hundred and fifty times, until he drove us crazy."

There was a big difference, however, between listening to the masters and capturing their style. Compared to Jim Garland (the Kentucky labor organizer who wrote "I Don't Want Your Millions Mister"), Pete Seeger was out of his depth. He could sing, play, and make up songs that pleased urban audiences, but because Garland's political songs came from his experience as a coal miner, they had a solid feel; Pete's attempts resembled furniture made of plywood with a folk veneer. Seeger was destined to be a middle-man between traditional country singers and city audiences accustomed to crooners like Bing Crosby.

The Almanacs sang mostly for members or close kin to the Communist Party and suffered the fate of most artists in political organizations: They were either ignored or suspect. The singers themselves vacillated between trying to make workers into unionists or unionists into revolutionaries. And Party functionaries couldn't help clarify this, for cultural politics are non-quantifiable; music and drama touch emotions, rather than dogma. Thus the Almanacs drifted and found themselves judged on their support of current slogans. One time Party representatives stuffily complained because a chorus ended with the words "Jim Crow," rather than the more militant "Jim Crow must go."

Why did the Almanacs put up with this treatment, and why did Pete now join the Party itself, graduating from the YCL? To be radical meant many things, but to be committed meant joining the Party to many in the thirties: Talk was cheap. "Can a sunrise or a revolution create a poem you don't live?" asked Pete's friend Walter Lowenfels in a poem, "On Joining the Party."

"Fellow travelers" supported the Party but didn't join up; that was like standing outside a Students for a Democratic Society meeting in the 1960s, while the insiders targeted the next demonstration. Being approached about membership carried a feeling of being chosen, of becoming a tough, sacrificing comrade; not everyone was invited.

The pleasures of belonging brought unpleasant side effects, however, such as the interminable and abstruse political discussions. When they weren't shuttling from one fund-raiser to the next, those Almanacs who considered themselves "organized" attended meetings. Occasionally they got to discuss topics like "How to Write a Good Worker's Song," but mostly the agenda concerned the Party's new campaigns. After a night of this, even forward-looking musicians needed a break. The Almanacs' meetings often "degenerated" into impromptu hoots as people hauled out instruments to illustrate a point.

Pete's problem was that ideology alone didn't hold his interest; he had to fight a tendency to get up and stretch every half hour. "If Pete went to a lecture on Leninism, he's the type that would stop and think about it, and eventually come up with a creative observation on how the idea works for the subway system," Bess said. His fingers would find an instrument, and he'd drift off into another world, leaving the comrades discussing Earl Browder's *The Way Out*. Pete had his own way out, and somehow it always came back to music.

"I remember driving with him one time," Bess continued, "and we went over a long section of metal grating. We hit this road and the pitch of the tires went way up. Pete started speculating on how [an engineer] could grade the surface of the road so that you could play a tune on coming into a city—the right song to put you in the right mood, with a sign that said 'Hit this at 42 miles per hour and you'll hear . . . ' "

No one in the Party knew what to do with a mind like this. Partly because of his value as a fund-raiser, administrators tended to let him have his head, reminding him to look at the *Worker* when they disagreed with one of his comments. On his part, Pete viewed the Party the way suburban mothers sometimes regard the local PTA: an organization worthy of support, but not great fun—in a word, duty.

On December 7, 1941, Pearl Harbor was attacked, and America finally entered the war. Though a relief, the declaration of war actually worsened the Almanacs' situation; the Party soon asked unions for a no-strike pledge and class-consciousness songs like "Talking Union" were put to pasture "for the duration." Six months before the Almanacs had lost their peace songs, and they fell back on union songs. Now these, too, were obsolete. Prisoners of their own talent, the Almanacs discovered that their songs would not disappear. Rank-and-file unionists (and Ku Klux Klan members, bent on embarrassing the Almanacs) kept asking for "Get Behind Me Satan," which equated bosses with the devil. Pete had a strange profession. No sooner did he write a good song and make it popular, than he stopped singing it. He might have fared better as a plumber; at least no one tore up the old pipes when it came time to begin a new line.

As unofficial office manager, Seeger felt the pressures of their situation. Few jobs came in, the rent was due, but to Pete's frustration, no one seemed to care. Woody laughed and answered the phone "Almanac House and Barn Shelter," but Pete didn't see the humor. Bess—the only Almanac who punched a time clock—lost her job as a secretary, and finances careened toward disaster. Seeger withdrew. "The only time Pete seemed to come out of his shell was during our work meetings," said Bess. "In the middle of an argument, Pete would simply get up and walk out. He was such a rock, everyone would try to fix it up by the time he got back."

One day toward the end of December 1941, two new members of the Almanacs, Gordon Friesen and Sis Cunningham, came in from a booking. As they passed the office, they found Pete sitting at his desk with his head in his arms. "Damn it, it's terrible," he sobbed. "Nobody cares about the Almanacs anymore."

The landlord cared very much about the Almanacs. He had gone to court to evict them for nonpayment of rent. Neither the landlord nor the utility company—now threatening to shut off service   showed much compassion for the down-and-out singers.

"Pete Seeger, diligent fire builder and stoker, finally had no fuel left to feed the furnace," wrote Gordon Friesen. "All efforts to keep the house heated on weekdays were abandoned; frigid temperatures took over; windows frosted; pipes froze; icicles grew like stalactites in the bathroom. The only source of heat (really quite feeble) was the gas oven in the kitchen, lit and turned up full force. Those huddled around the open stove door could hear the chattering teeth of guests fool enough to stay overnight. . . . Woody, always ready to record in song what went on around him, wrote a blues, one verse of which went:

> *I went into the bathroom and I pulled upon the*
> *   chain,*
> *Polar bears on icebergs came floating down the drain,*
> *Hey, pretty mama, I got those Arctic Circle Blues.*

Mistrusted by the unions they wanted to help, the Almanacs had hit bottom with an icy thud.

In January, Alan Lomax, Nick Ray, and other Almanac supporters warned the group to change its name; in wartime, they reasoned, the anti-Roosevelt, anti-war songs were not merely inappropriate, they were treasonous. Pete fought the change as a sellout, convincing the group not to hide their past. Like so many of Seeger's decisions of principle, this one eventually landed him in hot water. Lomax was proven right; the Almanacs' name would be a liability when they least expected it.

Pete usually kept himself aloof from arguments, but the Almanacs' reputation and house finances preoccupied him. The group kept their communal fortune in a box on the kitchen shelf; everyone was allowed a dollar a day, on the honor system, which didn't always work. Personal conveniences were the stumbling block, for one person's necessity was another's luxury. And Seeger's spartan habits made anyone's indulgences look wanton. "Pete was at that time quite puritanical. He didn't approve of liquor, cigarettes, coffee, even sex. Woody (and Lee) loved them all," Bess laughed. "Now Pete didn't come on about this all the time, but if you drink, it costs money. He just couldn't approve." Sometimes Pete would come home and find the cupboard bare. Woody and Lee would be sitting in a corner with a pint, looking like two cats who'd pulled a chicken out of the refrigerator. Seeger would blow up. "God damn it Woody," he'd yell, "you can't buy whiskey when we need new strings." Then he would stomp from the room, calling after him, "We just don't have enough money for this stuff! And don't do it again!" Pete didn't mind sacrificing as long as everybody else did.

"Oh, go on, Pete," Woody and Lee would taunt him. "You don't have a hair on your chest. Why, you're just a little boy. When you grow up, you'll learn to like a drop or two."

After an exchange like that, Seeger would storm off around the corner to the Jefferson Diner, where Woody had somehow convinced the owner that in his home state hamburgers came with all the free lettuce and tomatoes he could eat. Pete Seeger would sit there by himself, wolfing "Oklahomas" on credit until a delegation came to soften him up.

Whether urging them to clean up or cut down on their drinking, Seeger was the kind of roommate whose vacations are occasionally welcome. But for his politics, he might have been at home in a church choir or a 4-H Club. Though Pete still shared a bedroom with Bess, apparently nothing more racy occurred than playing banjo in his underwear. Besides, Pete already had a sweetheart: the girl he had met on first arriving in New York. There was one problem: Toshi was half Japanese in an era when Japanese-Americans had become the enemy within, a "yellow horde" herded off to detention camps in California. "We'll stomp their front teeth in," *Time* reported Americans saying after Pearl Harbor. When the Tennessee Conservation Department requested a hunting license for six million "Japs," an official returned the application with the note: "Open season on Japs, no license required."

Even the Party agreed on preventive detention for Japanese-Americans. Toshi's situation grew even more tense because her father, Takashi Ohta, was not one to hide his background. An adventuresome exile from a highly respected family in Japan, Takashi had traveled the world as a soldier of fortune, fighting under Sun Yat-sen, hiking the Gobi Desert, and serving in the British Merchant Marine. He fascinated Peter; his life was the stuff of romance. If Toshi's father had been on the West Coast, he would have been rounded up and put in a camp; in New York, the FBI came and took his binoculars, camera, and breadknife. To Pete, the controversy only made Toshi more desirable. The first time he brought her to meet his parents, Pete's half-sister Peggy rushed into the bathroom, not knowing Toshi was there: "She stood there with nothing on and her hair all the way down her back. I'd never seen anything like it. She was really exotic, beautiful."

Ruth and Charles accepted her, though Constance had her doubts. Once Pete told one of his brothers he was thinking about getting married. "You're getting married?" his sibling reportedly said. "She's got to be either Jewish or Negro—which is she?"

"She's Japanese," Pete answered.

Toshi visited the Almanac house regularly, and her teasing often brought Pete down to earth. The previous year he had appeared in a play opposite a vivacious young actress, Carol Channing. Toshi kidded him, "You're too shy to look her in the face—so you look her in the bosom." Another time, when he was performing in blue jeans and hiking boots, Toshi told him not to put on airs: "Look, you're not a working man, you're just pretending. Everybody sees through it." She also chided him about his gloves; in the coldest weather, he'd wear the cheapest cotton ones to give himself a proletarian air.

As winter thawed, the Almanacs dug themselves out of the ideological hole where they had been since the previous June, when Russia was invaded. Popular outrage at Japan and their own hatred for Hitler led the Almanacs to write war songs in earnest. The most successful of these was "Reuben James," the story of the ninety-five people drowned in the first American ship torpedoed in World War II. On first try, Woody had turned the passenger list into an impossibly long ballad, listing everyone who went down. Seeger doubted anyone would listen to the end. The Almanacs sat in a circle in the living room, discussing the song. Woody was adamant and ready to spend a week memorizing the verses. Finally Pete or Mill asked, "What *were* their names?" and that became the chorus. This was Almanac songwriting at its best—direct, nonrhetorical, focused on people instead of statistics.

Pro-war songs filled the hit parade: the pitch was irresistible; radio, television, and the papers portrayed a country in wartime unity. Unions and manufacturers met in Washington to plan the economy. Pete wanted to do his bit and wrote "dear Mr. President," a singing letter to Roosevelt in "expiation for those 'John Doe' songs," according to Earl Robinson. "Dear Mr. President" was the title song of the next Almanac album, released in February 1942. The song is an artful mix of patriotism and social protest; two of the verses demonstrated how Pete liked to think of himself:

> I'm an ordinary guy, worked most of my life,   ©
> Sometime I'll settle down with my kids and wife.
> I like to see a movie, or take a little drink,
> And I like being free to say what I think.
>   Sorta runs in the family . . . my Grandpa crossed
>   the ocean
>   For that same reason. . . .
>
> I never was one to try and shirk
> And let the other fellow do all of the work
> So when the time comes, I'll be on hand.
> And I can make good use of my two hands.
> Quit playing this banjo around with the boys,
> And exchange it for something that makes more noise.

He sang all this in the most heartfelt voice; he was now as devoted to war songs as he had been to peace and union songs.

After seven months of heatless nights and watery soup, the Almanacs' fortunes began to rise. Gifted songwriters from the start, the Almanacs now played on the government's side, and that made all the difference. Even the most unmusical administrator at the Office of War Information understood the value of songs in building morale. When the Almanacs had sung peace songs, critics had called it propaganda; now that they sang war songs, the government styled it patriotic art. After "Reuben James," word got around that they were hot again. Their hootenannies became stylish; at the beginning of February 1942 a photographer from *Life* visited one. On February 9 the prestigious William Morris Agency offered to manage the group. The Almanacs' moment of success had come. The rift between the Communist Left and Roosevelt closed up after the Pearl Harbor attack, and Popular Front patriotism reflowered. War bonds sold like popcorn at a Sunday matinee, and the nation wanted solid fighting songs.

The Almanacs did their best. One evening a delegation of firemen invited the group to learn how to put out fires in case of an air raid. Seeger insisted everyone go. The singers soon discovered how out-of-shape they were from their erratic diet and unusual hours. "About all they learned," wrote Gordon Friesen, "was to distinguish between the male and female couplings of a fire hose (one goes into the other, but it doesn't work vice versa)." Fortunately, they were better at singing than fire-fighting. When the government needed publicity about air-raid shelters, the Almanacs worked up a song about a romance between a young couple who met in a shelter, "Taking It Easy." A few weeks later the phone rang, and the Almanacs lost another good song. "The Civil Defense people said they didn't like the song . . . people were getting too casual about air raids—people shouldn't be taking it easy, they should get the heck into the bomb shelter," one Almanac laughed. They had better results with radio. Woody, Bess, Sis Cunningham, and Pete sang for a CBS program, "We the People," and were promised another spot. One success led to another, until the Almanacs were invited for an audition in the Rainbow Room, one of New York's swankest nightclubs high atop Rockefeller Center. A successful showing there could have started them on a nationwide concert tour and their own radio series. The agent at William Morris imagined the Almanacs singing headlines for fifteen minutes every day on CBS. They could be the first left-wing entertainers to reach a mass audience through electronic media.

The audition date was set, and one afternoon an elevator whisked the group high above Radio City, then the world's largest office complex. Only a year had passed since their Madison Square Garden appearance, but the Almanacs were far better musicians—though no better dressed. They still expressed their politics in work shirts and secondhand pants.

Walking into the nightclub was a dizzying experience. Manhattan stretched out before them, dropping away on all sides; the room resembled an enormous airplane cabin, empty except for the management. Rows of tables on pedestals spread out in a horseshoe, and matchbooks covered in glossy rainbows were displayed in a cut-crystal bowl. The opulence drove Woody wild.

"There was big drops of sweat standing on my forehead," he wrote, "and my fingers didn't feel like they was mine. I was floating in high finances, sixty-five stories above the ground, leaning my elbow on a stiff looking table cloth as white as a runaway ghost."

The Almanacs had never even *seen* a place like this. "We were absolutely unprepared for success of any kind," said Bess Lomax. "We were awfully young and green. The Almanacs made it on sincerity. That was part of the difference between us and the workers we tried to reach. They were poor and didn't want to be. We were poor and didn't notice it. . . . The people running the club were sharp businessmen; they thought of us as an act, and treated us as one. . . . But if we were anything, it was *not* an act."

"The man that had been our guide and got us up there in the first place," Woody continued, "walked across the rug with his nose in the air like a trained seal, grinned up at us waiting to take our tryouts, and said, 'Sssshhh. Quiet, everybody.' "

The Almanacs began singing their most popular anti-Nazi song (to the tune of "Old Joe Clark"):

> *Round and round Hitler's grave*   ©
> *Round and round we go,*
> *We're going to lay that poor boy down*
> *He won't get up no more.*
>
> *I wish I had a bushel*
> *I wish I had a peck*
> *I wish I had old Hitler*
> *With a rope around his neck.*
>
> —"*Round and*
> *Round Hitler's Grave*"

The club owners loved it, but complained that the group lacked showmanship. One suggested the Almanac men wear one-suspender overalls, and the women sunbonnets and gunny sacks.

That did it for Woody. Pete tried to steady him, using his banjo to even out the rhythm. Mill and Woody would not be calmed; they took the next song, Leadbelly's "New York City" and improvised:

> *At the Rainbow Room, the soup's on to boil*
> *They're stirring the salad with Standard Oil*
>
> *It's sixty stories high, they say,*
> *A long way back to the U.S.A.*

The managers thought this was hilarious—a clever part of the act. The Almanacs continued, even madder than before.

> *The Rainbow Room, it's mighty high*
> *You can see John D. a-flyin' by.*
>
> *The Rainbow Room is mighty fine*
> *You can spit from there to the Texas line.*

The more insulting they became, the more the owners laughed. It was a devastating experience: "I don't think Woody ever got over it. He'd finally gotten to a territory where he couldn't be outrageous enough," said Bess.

To play in nightclubs or on the radio, the Almanacs had to accept a new identity: entertainers. The owners of the Rainbow Room allowed themselves to be insulted—as long as it sold drinks—but Seeger (and the others) refused to be turned into vaudeville. Pete left the room humiliated, suspecting: "They'd never let us sing our songs anyway." If the management had their doubts, they also saw commercial potential; they made a tentative booking, to begin in two weeks. Once started, the Almanac bandwagon was difficult to stop. The labor singers finally joined a union, Local 802 of the American Federation of Musicians, after the William Morris Agency paid their dues. Bookings poured in, and the Almanacs began rehearsals for their tour and for the next big radio broadcast.

The way they got on radio is itself fascinating, involving internal changes in the music industry. Ever since the "talkies" began in the late Twenties, the Hollywood film industry had dominated music publishing, through the American Society of Composers, Authors and Publishers (ASCAP). When radio began making inroads on movie receipts, film companies simply doubled ASCAP's royalty rates, the fees stations paid for broadcasting music. The move backfired. On January 1, 1941, a coalition of radio stations set up their own publishing organization, Broadcast Music Incorporated (BMI). Stations began searching for previously unrecorded singers, anyone with talent and no ASCAP contract; these changes (and a bitter strike by the musicians' union) further opened up song publishing to nonprofessionals. Previously only 125 writer-composers accounted for most of the songs published and played on American radio. By 1941, when Seeger's career as a songwriter luckily began, everyone was looking for new musical talent.

On February 14, 1942, the Almanacs played for nearly thirty million listeners at the opening of a new series, "This Is War." The show was broadcast in prime time, Saturday night, on all networks from Maine to

California. The Almanacs' beat-Hitler songs made a sensation. Decca Records called to propose an exclusive contract on extremely favorable terms.

If the FBI had a say in the matter, the Almanacs wouldn't have gotten that contract—or any other. A bit behind the times, the Bureau had just discovered "Songs for John Doe," and decided the peace songs threatened wartime mobilization. Since the albums bore only the imprint "Almanac Records," though, the Bureau didn't know where to turn. J. Edgar Hoover sent out a memo, eventually forwarded to a Bridgeport police chief, asking if anybody knew anything about this Almanac gang.

On September 1, 1942, the special agent in charge of the FBI's New Haven office drove a hundred miles to a record-pressing firm in Newark, and discovered the masters of "John Doe" belonged to a company long extinct. Six months later, hot on the trail of the out-of-print records, the agent drove across Connecticut and the length of New Jersey to interrogate officials of the Radio Corporation of America. RCA, one of the most commercial record companies in the world, had never heard of the Almanacs. When the FBI agent asked them for a list of all the small record companies in the U.S., frustrated RCA executives suggested the FBI try reading *Variety* or *Billboard*.

While the FBI hunted the Almanacs' past, reporters in New York had done their own research, which soon hit the front pages. Seeger's insistence on keeping the Almanac name turned out to be a disaster. On February 17, three days after the "This Is War" show, Pete picked up the *New York Post* and read: PEACE CHOIR CHANGES TUNE. The *World-Telegram* proclaimed: SINGERS ON NEW MORALE SHOW ALSO WARBLED FOR COMMUNISTS. The stories rehashed the *Atlantic* article "Poison in Our System," published before the Nazi attack on Russia.

The Almanacs' commercial career crumbled as suddenly as it began. The William Morris people dropped their negotiations for a tour. Decca canceled its record offer. Pete made a flurry of calls and sent angry letters, but soon even he resigned himself: "We weren't willing to change, and the Rainbow Room and the others weren't willing to take us on our own terms. Besides, we were very busy singing at rallies." According to their booking calendar, however, jobs were few. Days and even weeks went by without a paid performance. Pete still didn't care much about wages, fans, or free drinks—all he could drink wouldn't fill a medium-size tumbler. And he didn't *like* nightclubs; he was just as happy helping the war effort by turning in early and getting up at six A.M. to scavenge tires for the rubber drive.

Underneath his bravado at losing a radio career, however, lay a mild concern that in time ripened into a mania: finding an audience for his music. At age twenty-two, Pete had no family to support and a fierce anti-materialist streak that wouldn't have allowed him to enjoy fame, even if it arrived without any effort on his part. He was a passionate amateur who welcomed the chance to be heard nationally. If things didn't fall into place this time, he would have other chances, he assumed.

What anger he did feel, he kept under wraps. In the rare instances when he let it out, Seeger had a violent temper, as one incident showed.

On a trip to Detroit to sing for the United Auto Workers in March or April, the Almanacs began to argue among themselves, following a particularly grueling stretch of driving: "We had taken down the back of the station wagon and Pete was lying there, stretched out. It had been a very strenuous week, and there'd been an awful lot of bickering about something stupid—were we going to stop for supper now, or drive on through. This had gone on for about an hour and everybody was very tired and antsy.

"All of a sudden there was this crash from the back," Bess Hawes continued. "Pete had put his foot through my mandolin. Smashed it completely. Nobody said a word—complete silence for the rest of the trip. When Pete breaks out, it's very scary."

The Almanacs' fall continued to be painful. After the incriminating headlines, even the friendliest club owners hesitated to hire them. Their calendar listed bookings in Seeger's fine hand, later crossed out with equally neat strokes. Finances looked like a corporate sales chart in a bad year: At first twelve-dollar bookings predominated, then ten-dollar ones; finally they were down to seven-fifty. The admission charge at one of their benefits came to twenty-eight cents. The inequality of talent within the group reemerged: only Pete and Woody had solo bookings. In February, their bookings were about equal. By June and July, dates marked "Pete" took up half the Almanacs' bookings. As the summer of 1942 began, notations in the margin read "if possible Pete." Seeger didn't pull rank or expect everybody to do his laundry now that he brought in much of the commune's income. In fact, his responsibility increased. "Other people could miss a meeting and we would go on," Bess said. "For Pete, we had to wait." Woody still teased him about his hairless chest, but Pete had matured and even outgrown his mentor. On commission, Woody wrote the rousing "Boomtown Bill" for the Oil Workers' Union. "But in the studio," Pete said, "either I pronounced the words clearer, or had more stamina for rehearsal after rehearsal. After a number of takes, Woody said, 'Pete, you better try this. I can't seem to do it.' " From this point on, Pete rarely took second billing behind Guthrie.

Pete had slowly reconstructed his personality to suit a performer's life, learning to tolerate his friends' minor vices. He seemed looser, more willing to try new places to eat or visit. Yet at the heart of his performances, he still had that sense of mission Alan Lomax had noticed. Whatever Seeger sang, he turned it into a cause. "In May 1942," wrote Gordon Freisen, "a friend got Woody, Pete and Sis Cunningham a booking at the Waldorf-Astoria for a national conference of big business executives and managers. Pete was leaving for the army in a few weeks.

"It was late in the evening when the three Almanacs began. The five hundred conventioneers were drunk, relishing the fat war contracts on the way. They were eating hurriedly, impatient for the next round of pleasure—the girls. The Almanacs sang a few anti-fascist songs but no one listened over the hub-bub. Pete's temper exploded. He grabbed the mike and said, 'What are you, human beings or a bunch of pigs? Here you sit slobbering whiskey, and hollerin' for whores. Don't you care that American boys are dying tonight to save your country for you? Great God Almighty, haven't you got any shame?'

"Frankly it was like shouting against the wind; a drunk millionaire at one of the front tables bawled: 'Aw shut up, and play some music. How about "She'll Be Coming 'Round the Mountain"?' Woody's guitar and Sis's accordion took up the song, and Pete cooled off by concentrating on the strings of his banjo. After a few minutes, Woody said: 'Let me take the next verse.'

"Stepping real close to the mike so his voice filled the room, he sang to the bosses:

> She'll be coming 'round the mountain when she
>   comes,
> She'll be coming 'round the mountain when she
>   comes,
> And she'll be wearing a union button,
> She'll be wearing a union button,
> She'll be wearing a union button when she comes."

The Almanacs picked up their instruments and walked out.

They were no longer a novelty among left-wing New York audiences. Without peace or union songs, their repertoire—in its third generation in a year—had stretched thin. The Almanacs also suffered the fate of many successful (or persistent) musical groups—hangers-on who wanted to sit in. In an excess of democracy, the group decided anyone could be an Almanac. One admirer from the Bronx sang quite loudly, in the Polish fashion; her Bronx-Polish accent made their Appalachian songs sound quite bizarre. Then there was one of Woody's girlfriends, who knew one chord on the guitar, D. "He used to take her out on bookings," Lee remembered, "and all of a sudden everything we were playing was in the key of D—and she wasn't even playing the other chords. But every time we'd come around to the D-chord, she'd wham the hell out of it."

Another time an organization fond of Pete Seeger booked the Almanacs months in advance. On the night of the concert, the only ones free to perform were Sis Cunningham, Sonny Terry (blind and led on stage carrying a cane), and Brownie McGhee. Afterward, one of the sponsors asked Brownie in an irritated voice, "Who are the Almanacs, and how many are there?" "Well, I don't know," Brownie answered. "We ain't counted them lately."

Pete received his draft notice in June; he wrote in his journal that he was "almost glad" to get out of the Almanacs before they fell apart. He griped about leaving Toshi, but figured he'd find a way to be with her again. Before he went off, though, he wanted one thing in good shape: his banjo. Seeger's musical intuition kept reminding him of the instrument's limitations—he couldn't play in F sharp, and other keys required constant retuning or placing a capo so high on the neck that he lost his bass notes. He persuaded master instrument maker John D'Angelico to saw off his banjo neck and extend it three frets. The resulting extra-long banjo eventually became Pete's trademark, and four decades later, his design was still used by manufacturers and musicians.

Parting was still difficult. It wasn't only friends he left, but the team that Pete had hoped would reach America's working class through music. Woody was joining the Merchant Marine along with two singing buddies, Jim Longhi and Cisco Houston. Half the Almanacs had already left New York for Detroit to work in war production.

Meanwhile, as the Almanacs said their goodbyes, the FBI stepped up its efforts to find the traitors behind "Songs for John Doe." After the RCA interview, various field offices tried to avoid jurisdiction; the New York office lost, and the file labeled "Gramophone Records of a Seditious Nature" reopened there. At this point, a year and a half had passed since the anti-war records had been issued. When the FBI finally walked into the office of Keynote Records, the manager baldly told them the discs were collector's items: "Things have changed since those were recorded."

Satisfied that subversion had been checked, on April 28, 1943, J. Edgar Hoover wrote the New York office to call off the chase. Hoover was irate because the three records that had started the investigation were now broken. "See to it," Hoover sternly noted, "that records are more carefully packed, in order that incidents of this type will not reoccur."

Right before entering the army, Pete was playing a booking with Sis Cunningham at a summer resort near Monticello, New York. Gordon Friesen had recently boosted his self-confidence by telling him of a conversation with Bob Miller, the Almanacs' publisher. "Gordon," Miller had said, "do you realize Pete's the second best banjo player in the country?" Gordon smiled. "Seriously," Miller continued, "there's only one better—Uncle Dave Macon of the Grand Ole Opry. And Macon's *seventy-one*." In Monticello, a string broke on Pete's banjo, curling up around his shoulder. "Ooooh," the audience murmured. Pete smiled sweetly. "Now don't worry," he told the crowd, "I can play this thing without strings."

Four months earlier, on "dear Mr. President," Pete had promised to trade his banjo for something that made more noise; after basic training began, he was less sure. Pete planned to keep talking union, but he worried that he might not live to return or might come back "wounded, crippled or blind."

RIGHT Pamphlet written by Peter's maternal grandfather

THE STORY OF THE

U. S. GUNBOAT GLOUCESTER

TOLD BY

DR. J. TRACY EDSON

Of the Class of '71, U. S. Naval Academy, late ENSIGN U. S. NAVY, Watch and Division
Officer of the Gloucester, at the Battle off Santiago, July 3d, 1898

BELOW The Seeger estate at Patterson

RIGHT Charles Seeger and infant son Peter

ABOVE Constance, Peter, and the baby's grandfather, Charles Seeger, Sr.

RIGHT Constance as a young violin student

Peter, under the influence of Ernest Thompson Seton's Indian lore (about 1928)

The young Pete Seeger (about 1930)   Portrait of Peter by his aunt, Elsie Seeger

Peter and his eldest brother Charles in Manhattan

Private Seeger performs for sailors and Eleanor Roosevelt, 1942

First publicity photo: 1946

The Almanac Singers perform for Harry Bridges;
from left: Woody Guthrie, Lee Hays, Mill Lampell,
Pete Seeger, 1941 (*People's World*)

Pete and Toshi Ohta Seeger, wedding, July 20, 1943 (*Berenice Abbott*)

Pete and his first daughter, Mika Seeger

With Woody Guthrie (about 1942)

A typical elementary school presentation in the 1950s

Michael   Charles

Penny   Ruth

Barbara   Peggy

New Years greetings
from six Seegers
1948-49

Charles Seeger's second family with Ruth Crawford Seeger (as indicated)

Union Maid

6

ON A HOT sticky day along the Mississippi gulf coast, Private Pete Seeger was about as bored as a person could be. His regiment had shipped out without him, and he sat in the orderly room, picking up cigarette butts and watching the soldiers drill at Keesler Field. The new recruits marched better than he did. Not long before, Seeger had been on close-order drill when down the road walked boxer Joe Louis, newly drafted into the army. Pete got so distracted watching him, he didn't listen to the platoon leader. He made a misstep and walked off in the wrong place. Louis laughed and said, "Look at that guy fucking up."

In his army fatigues and crew cut, Pete made quite a sight. Army chow didn't agree with him, and he had grown as lean as the broom he pushed around. This wasn't how he had imagined army life when he was with the Almanacs. Pete had thought he would fight fascists, instead of singing about them, do a little organizing, and get the boys singing progressive tunes. Down in steamy Biloxi, Pete soon found out different. Classified as a mechanic, he wasn't allowed to lead songs. Oh, he could bring out his banjo now and again, but it wasn't the same.

In his first months at Keesler Field, Seeger learned to take apart airplane engines, graduating second in his class; he had disappointed himself by not volunteering for combat duty, but hell, that was dangerous. Anyway, he'd be shipped out at any moment, he told himself. But week after week went by without a word. Everyone else had gone, but his orders never came. "What happens to a dream deferred?" Langston Hughes once asked; Seeger was finding out.

Lonely for singing partners, he began leading strangers in impromptu singing, despite the regulations. At dusk, in the half-hour between supper and his evening classes, he sat outside the barracks and sang. People wandered over, a new audience—one that didn't know a manifesto from a manifold. He soon had a chorus going, and he wrote the

Almanacs about his method for rousing both New Yorkers and Southerners with "common denominator" songs: "We have concentrated on ones that at least the majority will know, ranging from 'Farther Along' and other hymns which the Southern boys all like, to 'East Side, West Side' for New Yorkers." In a postscript typed sideways on the page, he added: "Even though the song may not be the greatest, when the audience feels sure of themselves, then they really sing out with confidence, and it sounds swell."

"Finally, after six months I decided for all I knew, I was going to spend the entire war there. I wrote Toshi: 'Let's get married on my furlough.' " They wed in a little church in Greenwich Village, and Toshi proved herself indispensable: When Pete didn't have the money for a wedding ring, she borrowed her grandmother's. The groom was short three dollars for the license—Toshi lent it to him. After the ceremony, they walked back to Toshi's parents' house on MacDougal Street. Leadbelly and the Lomaxes came over, and their singing echoed up the steep brick walls of the back-yard in the July heat.

Toshi's parents tried to dissuade her from moving to Mississippi with Pete. Anti-Japanese sentiment was still high; and in Mississippi, she'd be "colored," perhaps even subject to laws forbidding interracial marriages. Toshi forced the issue and told her parents she could take care of herself. "We moved our suitcase into a room off-base, put towels on the racks in the bathroom, and had supper sent up." After a few delicious days, the new groom reported for duty. "Seeger!" they cried. "Where've you been? We've been looking all over for you. You're shipping out tomorrow."

"We heard later that an order had come through that no left-winger was to be near the sea coast. So they sent us to Amarillo, Texas. Toshi was all set to head for Texas when three days later they said, 'Seeger! You're being transferred to Fort Meade, Maryland.' I quickly called Toshi and told her not to get on the train." Actually Pete had used his father's Washington contacts to transfer into the Special Services Division (for performers). A few months later, Pete was stationed close to his family, and Toshi got a job tying packages at Garfinckel's department store in Washington.

Pete felt "far away from our old work," as he wrote Ben Botkin at the Archive of Folksong, hungering for news of the Almanacs. In his new Special Services unit, he found himself surrounded by show business pros unimpressed by his talent: "I wasn't looked on as a serious performer. 'It's fun sitting around the barracks singing old-time songs with Seeger,' the pros thought, 'but this isn't what makes a fast-paced show.' I was a kind of freak. I didn't perform in any of the shows: I remember being rather hurt by it. One time, at a party, they said 'Oh, Pete's here. Let's ask him to do a song.' " Before they could ask twice, he had his banjo out for Uncle Dave Macon's "Cumberland Mountain Bear Chase." Pete pulled out all the stops, trilling the strings to imitate a hoot owl and a hound's bark and frailing furiously; but when he finished and looked up expectantly, "a little polite applause" was all he received. The vaudeville and orchestral musicians found his music quaint. "I felt so terrible—and Toshi was there!" It was more than he could bear. Pete walked out of the building as the next performer began, back to where no one but Toshi could see him, and burst into tears. Toshi reached up her arms and comforted him as best she could.

Seeger lived at full tilt. It wasn't enough to be talented; he needed an audience, a community, a cause. "Though I don't drink or smoke, I have got one helluva dissipation," he later wrote Toshi, "and that is music. I can get quite drunk on it—I hope you are a patient wife." Toshi proved more than patient. Her new husband sent her a tax receipt from a recording session to hold for him. She kept that receipt and the thousands that followed.

"You want to know the difference between Seeger and some of the guys back then?" a friend asked. "Between him and Josh White? Maybe the biggest is having Toshi Ohta behind him—for forty years!" If the women's liberation movement had developed earlier, Toshi might have acted differently. Eventually she'd question her supportive role, but for now, she had only one receipt to guard for her husband.

The move to Fort Meade proved handy to Seeger's career: New York was just a train ride away, and during 1943 and 1944 he appeared at three recording sessions: Earl Robinson's "Lonesome Train," a cantata based on the death of Abraham Lincoln; an album of songs of the Spanish Civil War (Pete later wrote the producer worrying if he had slandered Generalissimo Franco); and "Solidarity Forever" in a version aimed at the 1944 election:

> *It's a mighty long time since the early days*
> *When it took a bunch of pickets to get a raise*
> *We've built a union—stands millions strong*
> *We taught the bosses how to get along*
> *With the working class . . . more respectful like*
> *Friendly conferences and mutual understanding . . .*

Pete had unabashedly joined the national stampede to wartime unity; the man that once sang "Talking Union" now saw "friendly conferences" between bosses and the working class.

While Pete moonlighted from the army, the Federal Bureau of Investigation continued to be one of his most active followers. The FBI added Seeger's first mention before the House Committee on Un-American Activities (HUAC) to their file on "Gramophone Records of Seditious Nature." For the moment the FBI had nothing on Seeger except his songs, but they kept after him; as Shakespeare wrote, "Perseverance keeps honor bright."

According to the arrangement Charles had negotiated, Pete was not to go overseas; nevertheless the army shipped him out, and to his surprise, on the troop ship overseas, he found he had more to offer the enlisted men than his colleagues who snubbed him: "I realized that I had an advantage over the pros, with their limited amount of material. A juggler had his one act. Once you'd seen it, you'd seen it. Even the clown had a limited number of jokes. But I had three hundred songs in my head. . . . The first night it was 'Down in the Valley,' and 'My Little Margie' and 'Tea for Two,' my common denominator songs. . . . For two weeks, I sang every night for half an hour without repeating myself: Latin and calypso songs, blues, old pop tunes and hillbilly songs."

Seeger had his audience, and the pros marveled at his memory. Even his reputation improved: Previously, Seeger was known as the prude of the barracks. A musician who kept a mistress had once called his relationship "liberating"; Pete stood up and called her a whore. This might have done for a boy's school, but not the army. He must have been the only guy in the barracks who didn't talk about sweethearts and sex; it took him several months to admit to his bunkmates that he was married. Crossing the Pacific, though, Pete loosened up. In a skit, he shuffled on stage with a straw hat on, carrying a jug. He upended it to whistles from the crowd and played "hillbilly" banjo.

On Saipan, Seeger felt needed. He was put in charge of hospital entertainment, with an office and a borrowed jeep. A lieutenant offered him a chance for Officer Candidate School, but Seeger refused; he preferred private first class.

By mid-1944, he had learned the basic skills of an organizer: coordinating schedules, jollying administrators and secretaries, spending hours on the phone. He wasn't terribly proud of himself, though; the only enemy he fought was army red tape. Watching the wounded pour in made him feel guilty; in his dreams oversize telephones rang, and huge, uniformed hands grabbed him, as he wrote Toshi: "A dozen times in the past year and a half, I have seriously thought of transferring to the infantry and losing myself in the war. . . . I have decided against it for many reasons; the first is fear of getting my head shot off. . . . I'm not proud of it, but it's true. I'm not volunteering for death—yet." He consoled himself by hard work and by experimenting with music-rehabilitation therapy: healing patients by getting them singing.

Evenings he traveled the unpaved jungle roads with the entertainers he booked: a barbershop quartet, some Frank Sinatra imitators, and a string band he played with, the Rainbow Boys. They would rumble along in a truck with broken springs, singing in officers' clubs or as a warm-up act for an open-air movie. Soldiers accustomed to the Andrews Sisters or Bing Crosby had a surprise in store when Seeger pulled out his banjo.

On WXLD, the local radio station, he attracted the attention of old Almanac fans like station manager Mario Cassetta, who was listening in the compound. "I thought to myself, my God, this guy is right here, a few yards from me. I literally ran pell-mell to the station and peeked through the glass. I saw this skinny guy with his head up, frailing away."

Pete and "Boots" Cassetta became fast friends. Together they commiserated about the commercial "patriotic" discs that flooded the airwaves, jingles like "Good-bye Mama, I'm Off to Yokohama," "Little Bo Peep Has Lost Her Jeep," or the offensive "Don't Be a Sap, Mister Jap." The two of them pulled together an informal singing group of progressives. Off in the abandoned hospital barracks, officers swapped songs with enlisted men, taking off their bars to avoid breaching army discipline:

> *Fuck 'em all! Fuck 'em all!*
> *The long and the short and the tall*
> *Bless all the admirals in the back*
> *They don't give a shit if we never get back;*
> *So we're saying good-bye to them all*
> *As over the gangplank we crawl*
> *There'll be no promotions*
> *This side of the ocean*
> *So cheer up my lads, fuck 'em all!*

Or they sang about the time the enlisted men broke into the officers' beer stash: (to the tune of "Old Chisholm Trail")

> *Who broke the lock on the foreward hold?*
> *We'll find out before we go.*
>
> *Took it by the can and they took it by the case*
> *Everybody had a smile on his face.*

> *A first lieutenant came snooping around*
> *And boy was he surprised at what he'd found.*
>
> *Who broke the lock, the question was asked*
> *As far as I'm concerned, they can kiss my ass.*

These songs had an important lesson for Seeger, though he was slow to learn it. Propaganda becomes unnecessary when inequality is obvious; no one had to write a song, for instance, to convince GIs to break into the officers' beer. This distinction—between songs created *by* people instead of *for* them—would prove crucial to his hopes of getting union members singing.

On a warm night in 1944 Pete and his friends were having a party under the coconut palms. Boots was there, a friend named Felix Landau, and a USO singer new to Saipan, Betty Sanders. A cook bootlegged some food, the officers brought the beer, and everybody sang their lungs out in the balmy tropical air. After a while, the conversation turned to the Almanacs, and to what would happen after the war. According to Mario Cassetta, Pete sketched out "a loosely knit organization, some structure where people could get together to exchange and print songs. He told me, 'Boots, you could work with Earl [Robinson]! I'll do it in New York and you can do it in L.A.' "

Out of this casual beginning came a new organization, People's Songs, Inc. (PSI), which would publish a new letter of union songs and form a national network, singing on picket lines and demonstrations. The Almanacs had been fine as far as they went, but labor needed a larger effort to make America a singing, progressive country.

A miscalculation lurked in these ideas—not the simple character tragedy of high-mindedness, of wanting people to unite around music, but something deeper: the assumption that a movement of political songs could change society. While Seeger sang anti-brass songs on Saipan, Greek and French partisans also sang—but few Greeks imagined defeating the enemy with songs alone. Seeger's chosen medium was mere entertainment to most of America. To Pete, singing helped people fight, and the fighting gave them power: thus, the gift of song appeared a gift of power, the social glue of community. As he would painfully discover, the chain linking song to action is not so direct.

He arrived at his ideas late. In the nineteenth century, many labor songs came from laborers themselves, or from nonprofessional songwriters. By the 1940s, however, the United States had more listeners and record buyers than singers, and laboring audiences knew few of Seeger's cherished Appalachian tunes. Though he associated the "folk" with the working class, he had an uphill struggle convincing American workers of this heritage.

There was another problem—his hopes for a singing labor movement rested on two organizations (the CIO and the Communist Party) which had gone through wartime developments that Pete, in his isolation on Saipan, did not fully understand.

The Communist Party U.S.A. had its greatest influence and success during the Thirties and Forties. In these years, the CP fought for unemployment benefits, campaigned against lynching in the South, sponsored the heroic (if unsuccessful) American participation in the Spanish Civil War, and established anti-fascist coalitions. The Party had Americanized itself out of its isolation of the 1920s. To be a socially conscious writer, actor, or musician in the Depression meant contact with the Party, which through its cultural fronts and publications offered art a social context as part of a worldwide movement.

Back in 1937 Seeger had felt this wholeness in the Young Communist League, with "the Comintern behind me." The Party had a special appeal to artists and thinkers: those who live at the edge of society, who work alone. As one of Seeger's contemporaries expressed it:

> Marxism was the transforming stuff, the new color, the new space, the new texture, the one that brought to the surface the life until then obscured. Do you know what that means? That's what the artist waits a lifetime for. . . . But the *tool* with which to shape the stuff of Marxism . . . that was the Communist Party.

The Communist Party of 1943 was quite different from that of 1937. With nearly a hundred thousand members—fifty-six percent of them trade unionists—the Party represented America's wartime ally, the Soviet Union. The Sunday *Worker* boasted a national circulation of a hundred thousand. Communists held rallies in Madison Square Garden, commanded four political/labor schools, a publishing house, and a host of weekly, daily, and monthly publications. The price of the Party's success was collaboration with its previous enemies, such as the National Association of Manufacturers.

The same was true for the CIO, now bigger than ever before. When Party leader Earl Browder announced support for a no-strike pledge for unions—which Russia needed to keep the U.S. fighting at its hardest—the CIO soon followed suit. Labor leaders sat down with manufacturers at the feast of war profits. In exchange for speed-ups and overtime, unions built up their benefits: health care, sick leave, vacations. This seemed a fair trade-off for national unity—at least in the beginning. But as war profits doubled and tripled, CP and CIO leadership in the plants was discredited; rank-and-file unionists grew disaffected with "radicals" who avoided strikes.

In the summer of 1944 Pete ill understood these changes; he expected to return and find the Left-labor alliance unchanged: "I just assumed we were all coming back with long-deferred projects, and I would dive in to pick up where we left off." Seeger had other things on his mind. He was about to be a father.

When news of the birth of Peter Ohta Seeger reached Saipan in August 1944, Pete let out a whoop that rang through his barracks. He was so proud of Toshi and "Pitou" that he gave in to tradition and passed out cigars. For Toshi, he drew an "Album of Daydreams" in cartoon form, all about his postwar hopes: a large vegetable garden, a fully equipped tool shop, instruments hanging on the wall, and "a kitchen full of good crockery." To pass the time till his return, Seeger collected songs, starting with the bawdy songs his group sang. Sundays, a folklorist in fatigues, he crossed the island to the security camps where Saipan's native Chamorros and Kanakas lived. He and the major sat around trading songs: The islanders loved "You Are My Sunshine." In the barracks, people would come up and sing him their favorite tunes for the pleasure of having Pete sing them back. He would learn from anyone: Roy Acuff tunes from the hillbillies, blues from the hipsters. He made his friends through music and discovered the side effects of community singing: the trust (and gratitude) between song leader and singers, the chesty warmth that comes from strangers resonating in harmony.

All this only made him ambitious for larger audiences. "After the war," he wrote Toshi, "I want to organize a very large chorus of untrained voices." When he saw a film biography of George Gershwin, *Rhapsody in Blue*, this ambition cut into him like a whip. Any film about a songwriter would have fascinated Seeger, but he had admired Gershwin since he learned his tunes on the ukulele at Patterson. At one point in the film, a character tells the young songwriter: "George, you can give America a voice!" The filmmaker had touched a hidden nerve; Pete immediately wrote one of his most introspective letters of the war years. Feelings of inadequacy, of not getting anywhere, flooded in on him. He had never quite overcome his mother's bias in favor of classical music, and now he worried that his lack of formal musical training would keep him from ever writing "serious" music:

"I used to think there was nothing in the world I couldn't do if I wanted to. I've since learned some limitations: an overlight and nervous physique and other things. . . . Now I know [my profession] won't spring from intuition and unschooled genius, but take hard study and perseverance and concentration."

"There have been so many failures," he wrote Toshi. "You don't know. Every song I started to write and gave up was a failure. I started to paint because I failed to get a job as a journalist. I started singing and playing more because I was a failure as a painter. I went into the army as willingly as I did because I was having more and more failure musically."

At twenty-six, despite his four albums, a national tour, and appearances on coast-to-coast radio, Pete felt like a failure: No worldly success could satisfy him. He suffered from the emotion his Puritan ancestors called humility: the modest pride that let a John Brown rouse a congregation against slavery, then weep quietly at his own unworthiness. This emerged in other ways, in what a fellow soldier called Seeger's "personal intransigence," citing one legendary incident.

Late one afternoon Seeger and his string band were driving across Saipan in a jeep. They'd just given a concert of country music for the native settlers of Saipan; the islanders had loved the show—particularly Pete's yodeling. As they rode back to the barracks, the band talked of their lives back home, as Pete relaxed in the warm breezes: "I was feeling proud that I'd gotten these otherwise prejudiced Southerners to change their opinions. Because originally they'd said, 'What do you want to sing for those gooks for?' I'd answered them, 'Oh, you'll like it. They're nice people.'"

It started getting dark, and nightfall made Saipan bleak and menacing; several hundred Japanese survivors still hid in caves, coming out only at night. Pete had been warned more than once not to stop the jeep for anything. Enemy soldiers were known to set up roadside ambushes, with one man pretending to be wounded.

They got to talking about the "jigs": "The niggers this, and the niggers that." Then the lieutenant from Texas told Pete, "You know, back home we have to string one up every now and then, just to keep the rest of them in line."

"You just let me out of here," Pete said. "I can't stand this any more." The men began to worry that Seeger would turn them in. He insisted they stop the jeep and he walked back to camp, out across the fearsome island. Pete never reported the conversation (though news of it spread through camp); his concern was keeping his conscience clear.

A few months later he learned that his four-month-old son had died. From nine thousand miles away, there was nothing he could do. He rarely mentioned the death in his letters, didn't complain, blame, or soothe his wife. All he wrote in his journal was one matter-of-fact line: "Over a month ago my and Toshi's baby died." The words that comforted him most were his father's: "Something good that has happened cannot be made to un-happen." The pain drove him toward home and his new projects: "The whole last year," he wrote the following April, "has been a bit of a night-mare. Weeks rush by with disconcerting speed and yet time drags horribly. . . . I only want to go home home home."

"When Pete came back from the war," Bess Lomax recalled, "he was a very different man. He had matured physically and become a stronger singer. Now he was physically vibrant. He'd always been tense, lean, and bony, but the years of physical activity had put some weight on him. He was as hard as nails. . . . He'd worked for all kinds of audiences and come back with People's Songs in his head and the same burning intensity. He had a national idea in mind now."

In short order Pete Seeger scheduled two meetings of folk musicians, CIO representatives, and others, collecting one hundred fifty-five dollars to start the new organization. The same performers who had overshadowed Pete at his concert debut six years ago now elected him president. Lee Hays became vice-president, and work began on the *People's Song Bulletin*. In an article about their "back from the war party," Woody gently poked fun at Pete's new seriousness: "We will print up a bulletin, a little bulletin," Toshi said, explaining Pete's dreams.

" 'Not too little,' Pete put in.

" 'Anyhow, a bulletin, either by mimeograph or photo offset.'

" 'Or off the presses of the *Daily News*,' Pete said again.

" 'Well, not just overnight, anyhow,' Toshi smiled, lit up a cigarette, and knocked the ashes off into an incense burner. . . . 'Of course later on, we will buy out the *Daily Mirror*. . . . Me, I want to raise a houseful of children for Peter to sing to sleep. But maybe I can find some sort of organizing career here working with People's Songs.'

" 'Your job is to keep me organized,' I heard Pete laugh."

This she did, providing him the guidance he accepted from only one other person, his father: "Toshi played a very strong role in Pete's political education," one friend pointed out. "She was responsible for much of Pete's staunchness of approach and political direction."

In one respect, though, he needed no direction. Asked about his purpose in life in January 1946, he answered: "Make a singing labor movement. Period. . . . I was hoping to have hundreds, thousands, tens of thousands of union choruses. Just as every church has a choir, why not every union?" He assumed unions would need the same thing they had before the war: singers for picket-line duty, publicity, and building attendance at meetings.

Pete's isolation in the South Pacific had built up a tremendous emotional charge, which now burst forth. In 1946 alone, he ran People's Songs, Inc., edited the *Bulletin*, taught courses in radical songwriting, spoke at conferences on folklore and civil rights, made a film, composed music, and set up and performed at People's Songs hootenannies. After two months, PSI boasted one thousand paid members in twenty states. The more the organization grew, the higher his hopes rose.

If the people of People's Songs wanted to hear "No Business Like Show Business," however, they would have to find another people's songster, for Pete still associated the folk with a mythic proletariat or a rustic peasantry. He also continued to be torn between his desire to sing or compose, and his duty to political discipline. Playing the banjo or hiking in the woods, he'd remember the destructiveness of racism; but sitting in a discussion on colonialism in the South's Black Belt, he sometimes wished he was home with the banjo.

To resolve his confusion, Seeger again turned to the Communist Party. Reports of Stalin's crimes fell on ears echoing Lincoln Steffens's report from Moscow thirty years before: "I have seen the future, and it works." "Back then, the Party held no conflicts for musicians," Seeger's friend Earl Robinson commented, "I was following the Party line for guidance in my composition—particularly 'Communism is twentieth-century Americanism.' "

After the war, Seeger eagerly enlisted the Party in his efforts, unconscious of the tensions following the recent denunciation of CP leader Earl Browder, for collaborating with big business. In January 1946, a few days after PSI began, Seeger met with a representative of the Party's cultural section and showered him with ideas: progressive songbooks for every union, workers making their own culture and spreading it through People's Songs. Apparently embarrassed at such an outpouring, the functionary asked Seeger to step around the corner for a cup of coffee. "It was a young guy I met, not V. J. [Jerome, unofficial cultural consultant to the Party]. He said 'Sure, fine, great idea, put us on your mailing list'—but he didn't seem to care much one way or the other."

The meeting disappointed him; he had tried hard to go through the right channels, but the Party representative was more preoccupied with surviving internal power struggles than a singing labor force. Pete might well have heeded the CP's indifference; People's Songs saw itself as more than "red" entertainment, but cultural officials only nodded and tapped their toes to the music. This forced Seeger (and others of the lyrical Left) to compartmentalize their art, alternately producing songs for specific campaigns, and more lasting (and more fulfilling) ones. The Communist Party did not use People's Songs, because PSI believed in the Party more than the Party believed in it. On the other hand, Party organizers felt free to criticize: Once when Seeger played Kentucky banjo tunes alongside topical songs at fund-raisers, a Party dignitary took him aside and said, "Pete, here in New York hardly anybody knows that kind of music. . . . If you are going to work with the workers of New York City, you should be in the jazz field."

This cheeky comment—as if Seeger would change his repertoire because some ideologue preferred the clarinet to the banjo—had its grain of truth; New York's ethnic audiences knew jazz, Yiddish, or Slovak tunes better than Appalachian ones. Still, Seeger was a musician first, and a politician second. He continued to keep up his ties, however—and when the Party organized a "club" composed largely of PSI staff, Pete joined. His cross-country travels excused him from most responsibilities; as a musician, he got off easy. He never had to sell the *Daily Worker*, never handed out leaflets on the street. Everyone was asked, repeatedly, to recruit new members into the Party; though Seeger started to draw up a list, he never got very far. Because of his independence—and musical taste was only a part of this—Seeger had a reputation as an "unreliable"; at least one committee on "backsliders" chided him for not having the right attitude. To make PSI succeed, Pete Seeger listened to their counsel, even when he didn't follow it. He needed all the allies he could find.

In the beginning, there was no stopping People's Songs. Circulation on the *Bulletin* rose weekly and was soon up to two thousand members. Favorable publicity on the group appeared in *Time, The New York Times,* even *Fortune.* The organization seemed to float on Pete's enthusiasm: "When a bunch of people are seen walking down the street singing, it should go almost without saying that they are a bunch of union people on their way home from a meeting. . . . Music, too, is a weapon," he wrote in *New Masses,* paying a debt from his boarding-school nights.

No sooner had People's Songs set up offices on Times Square than the

FBI opened a file on the group. All this talk of peace, unions, and racial brotherhood sounded suspicious. At first, the collection amounted to only a few flyers in a rough scrapbook.

The FBI notwithstanding, events in 1946 seemed to favor People's Songs: America had its greatest labor unrest since the mid-Thirties. Two million went out on strike in January 1946; before the year ended, five million had laid down their tools. Just like old times—in the papers Seeger watched the National Association of Manufacturers denounce labor unions. Despite fiery rhetoric on both sides, however, the worldwide expansion of U.S. commerce satisfied manufacturers, unions, and government alike. Labor settlements of this period produced a now-familiar pattern: Union leaders got regular pay increases for their members, and employers recouped these through inflated prices, automation, and government subsidies. The last thing either unions or manufacturers wanted was labor disorder.

The decline in labor militancy had begun with the war. While Pete stumbled through close-order drill in Mississippi, the ingredients of a multinational postwar economy had been readied. The twenty million war workers would need employment after the war ended, and this many jobs, as even Earl Browder predicted, would require foreign markets for American goods. While Seeger wandered through Saipan collecting songs, Walter Reuther prepared an attack on leftists in the United Auto Workers, both to fend off outside pressures and to assume the power and seniority of the "reds." As Pete shipped out for home, radical unionist Joe Curran was purging "reds" from the National Maritime Union.

After the war, as PSI opened shop, redbaiting in the unions increased with a vengeance. At a United Steelworkers meeting in May 1946, Philip Murray used the term "outside interference" to describe the Communist organizers who had set up his union. Six months later, after a fierce battle, the CIO passed an anti-Communist resolution. It seemed like decades since Roosevelt, Churchill, and Stalin had pledged postwar cooperation in Teheran; since Walter Winchell had remarked that "the fear of Russia" was a "bogey"; since *Life* had devoted an entire issue to Soviet-American cooperation—but all this was only four years past. The cold-war sun was rising steadily; and though early in the day, the heat had begun to build.

People's Songs thus began at a dramatically inappropriate time. Its successes would be those of its founder: good musical taste, originality, and dedication. Unfortunately, its grandiose aims and an ambivalence between organizing and musicianship also characterized Seeger: a man with his fingers on an instrument and his head a long way from the ground.

In September 1946, after a summer when Pete was so busy with organizational tasks he scarcely saw anything of his wife, the couple made the gossip column in *New Masses*: "The Pete Seegers are expecting a young folksinger." Danny Seeger was born a few days before Labor Day.

Pete and Toshi Seeger managed well together; Toshi held her own in the People's Songs executive meetings, which convened in her basement. Her style was to listen carefully before saying a word, then passionately leap into the discussion. The couple lived rather traditionally; Toshi took care of the children and filled a salad bowl the size of a horse trough for hungry guests, while Pete came and went "like a boarder." In the army, Seeger couldn't wait to be a father; now he put work before family life: "I felt shot through with adrenalin as I dashed around from appointment to appointment. Just think of getting so much done in a short time! . . . Poor Toshi. She stayed home changing diapers and I'd get home at one A.M. from one committee meeting, then be off at seven the next morning to another. It was a real case of the male supremacist organizer who expects the wife to run the house while he's changing the world."

The initial success of People's Songs did keep Seeger on the run. In its second year, PSI opened western and midwestern branches. Boots Cassetta and Earl Robinson played at strikes in the Hollywood studios. Members sang at a Westinghouse strike in Pittsburgh; on street corners in New York to protest the end of price controls; and in a California housing caravan. The *Bulletin* had more songs than they could print; Malvina Reynolds (who later wrote "Little Boxes") couldn't get a song in against competition like "Picket Line Priscilla":

> *Picket Line Priscilla*   ©
> *Had a line, a killer*
> *Workers in marine adore her*
> *Steel and textile fall before her*
> *She could make those vigilantes*
> *Run like anties was in their panties . . .*
> *When Priscilla starts to function*
> *Bosses need a new injunction!*

As 1947 wore on, People's Songs ran a race against time. Seeger barreled ahead, waging his internal battle between the hours spent on organizing and those on music. At People's Songs, at least, the two weren't mutually exclusive, but three-hour discussions on white chauvinism just weren't as much fun as learning a new lick on the guitar. The Party's "must" demands multiplied as its membership shrank, and Seeger noticed a hardening in the Party since his Almanac days, when meetings had flowed into hoots. Union leaders were equally unenthusiastic. In the beginning, People's Songs worked with the CIO and a few locals in the more conservative AFL. But soon even previously friendly union leaders stopped returning Seeger's calls. Toward the end of 1947, CIO education director Palmer Webber quietly severed his ties with the group. Once Pete traveled to Washington to ask a union official to sponsor a songbook. "Well, no," the union man hedged, "we're working on our own."

Alan Lomax tried to round up support for the troubled organization among his contacts. (He now had a Guggenheim fellowship and a relatively well-paying job with Decca Records.) Radio personality Studs Terkel sent his greetings, and a "Board of Sponsors" blossomed on the *Bulletin's* masthead: Aaron Copland, Leonard Bernstein, John Hammond, Oscar Hammerstein II, Dorothy Parker, Sam Wanamaker, and Harold Rome. Though the PSI staff disagreed about the value of including such luminaries, no one denied the list looked impressive.

It's doubtful any of these notables ever wandered into the ramshackle office off Times Square. If they did, they would have found four people cramped into one room, the People's Songs library on one side, a front desk, and a file cabinet spilling over with graphics. In one corner Wally Hille, music editor of the *Bulletin,* would transcribe songs, sitting on his desk with guitar and a pencil stuck behind his ear. Pete Seeger spent his time on the phone, trying to convince groups to pay the musicians, for goodness' sake. Volunteers in jeans straggled in, the phone rang constantly, and the hubbub of Times Square filtered up. The office had more in common with a draft resistance center in the 1960s than a music publisher in the 1940s.

One noticeably missing from this scene was Woody; though he signed on for the People's Songs board, he didn't take an active role. He was writing songs and was hard at work on a long mystical novel eventually published as *Seeds of Man.* The pair were still close; Woody planned to name his next boy Pete. The disease that later paralyzed Guthrie began to appear, though his symptoms were mistaken for drunkenness.

In May 1947 Irwin Silber, a short, energetic fellow with thick glasses and a commanding, nasal voice, joined People's Songs as executive secretary. He soon made the office shape up. Unlike Seeger or Hille, Irwin was not a musician. Fresh out of Brooklyn College and the American Folksay Group, he enjoyed folk songs and square dancing, but organizing was his calling. Through his activities in the Party hierarchy, Irwin made himself quite a reputation; today, ex-comrades flinch at his name, recalling him as "staunch," and "a dedicated-but-not-brilliant worker, a Jimmy Higgins type." Irwin had a keen, incisive mind, always ready to leap into political arguments; unfortunately, his pronouncements were steel-edged with theory rather than compassion.

Some took an immediate dislike to his heavy-handedness; one West Coast member called him "a sectarian personality. . . . I had a lot of confidence in Pete, but after a while I got the feeling Irwin was running things." Irwin minded the store while Pete toured, and according to Hille, a neutral party, the two argued over which songs to print. Silber favored politically correct songs and Seeger more musical ones. Irwin had files for everything and he put in long hours; Pete had the spark that drew members. For the next twenty years, their friend/adversary relation continued as Irwin Silber went on to edit the folk-song magazine *Sing Out!*

Silber wasn't the only one Seeger had trouble with at PSI. Lee Hays joined People's Songs expecting equal billing, but times had changed; Pete's prominence was incontestable. In fact, friends wondered if his head would swell, if he'd be the same old Pete. Lee Hays was one of the few who teased Pete, joking about his "arrogant modesty." Lee would sit in the office and chat with whoever dropped in, joking about his 250-pound frame and telling funny stories about Arkansas. After a while, his old habits returned. He had a way of creating disruptions, talking about people behind their back. One staff member gave Lee five dollars, making him promise faithfully not to spend it on liquor. A half-hour later, he was back with a bottle.

When tipsy, Hays could be genial and fascinating; but Seeger had too much at stake to let this situation last. He complained to Alan Lomax of Lee's "sectarian maliciousness" and apologized for an incident when Lee insulted Alan (the two had never gotten along). Pete avoided the moment as long as he could, but finally he asked Lee to step down as vice-president. Reflecting on how he showed Lee the door, Pete admitted: "Occasionally Toshi reminds me of something we've gone through that's been very unpleasant; but I haven't the faintest memory of the occasion. It's as if I have some protective device inside my brain; instead of causing grief by remembering it, I simply erase it. Maybe I've got a little mental eraser that just blots things out."

An interesting and handy device. Puritans in colonial America believed in something similar, a "reprover," which kept a lookout for wayward impulses and pride. Seeger's "little eraser" let him float over office politics, trusting that the good cause would keep people working together. "Pete never liked to say no," Earl Robinson once said. "He'd much rather you didn't ask him twice."

"I feel very optimistic and confident," Seeger wrote at the close of 1946, with the exuberance that was simultaneously his strength and flaw, "that we will keep growing for a long time to come." Not all of New York's Left was as excited. Radicals outside the Party poked fun of PSI and Pete (to the tune of "The Wreck of the Old 97"):

> *Well, they gave him his orders* ©
> *Up at Party Headquarters,*
> *Saying, "Pete, you're way behind the times.*
> *This is not '38, this is 1947,*
> *And there's been a change in that old party line."*
>
> *Well, it's a long, long haul*
> *From "Greensleeves" to "Freiheit,"*
> *And the distance is more than long,*
> *But that wonderful outfit they call the People's*
>   *Artists*
> *Is on hand with those good old People's Songs.*

Pete brushed such jibes aside as his career took off in two directions at once: as a People's Artist and as a nightclub entertainer. He had just completed his first solo engagement at the Village Vanguard, and *Billboard* had praised him as the "trim, slim Sinatra of the folksong clan." *The New Yorker* called his singing "fresh" and "contagious." In the first years of People's Songs, Seeger could afford the exquisite luxury of holding a commercial career at bay; he turned down nightclub jobs to teach nights at the Marxist Jefferson School. It didn't disturb him to play for the same small union that could pay him no more now than they had in 1941; he wasn't worried about being "overexposed"; he did not push himself to play ever larger halls. In his own quiet way, he had balanced a professional reputation with keeping his friends and his convictions, much as Charles had balanced university life and the IWW. While many of his friends were growing tired of living from hand to mouth and ached for a family and a house, Pete seemed content. He had no pressing need for money, his parents could support themselves, and anyway, he had no other profession to fall back for an income. He also never seemed to age: While his peers fretted about receding hairlines, Pete had barely gotten over his acne. In a film that year, *To Hear Your Banjo Play*, Seeger appeared in a workshirt, his hair swirled back into a pompadour. He resembled a nineteen-year-old farm boy fresh from a hay ride; his front teeth stuck out, and he banged his foot so hard the stage shook.

In these postwar years, Seeger lived with Toshi's politically progressive parents: "For twenty-three years Peter had one family. Then, after the war, he adopted mine," said Toshi. The Ohtas had more in common with Pete than his own parents (Toshi's grandfather had translated Marx into Japanese). Constance Seeger had now retired to Florida, where she gave violin lessons and hoped for Peter to establish himself as a respectable musician. Pete and Toshi visited regularly, but Constance got on their nerves with occasional anti-Semitic or prejudiced remarks. After one particularly bad spat, they all decided to drive to the beach. In a fit of pique, Toshi turned off at the entrance marked "Colored." Constance recoiled. "Where *are* you going!" she asked. "Well, down here," Toshi answered, "they call *me* colored, you know."

Relations with Charles had grown similarly distant. As close as the pair had been in Peter's childhood (and considering both worked with folk music—Charles at the Pan American Union), their separation was mysterious, perhaps caused by Charles's disaffection with political radicals.

In October 1947 People's Songs held its first national gathering: in Chicago, at Hull House. Publicity began a full three months before the event.

Before the delegates could gather, however, FBI Director J. Edgar Hoover received an urgent telegram on the convention from his New York office, which had been watching PSI since March 1947, when the Bureau reported: "They play folksongs . . . where the hoity-toity red intellectuals gather." In April, the Los Angeles office had sent an agent to investigate PSI's West Coast operation, discovering the organization was run by one "Peter Suger." The agent chatted with Boots Cassetta, a slim energetic man persuasive enough to sell Good Humor ice cream to Alaskans. This time Boots outdid himself. Before the agent could get out the door, Boots had extracted a small contribution and thrust PSI's first-anniversary issue in his hand. In May, the Bureau had filed the United States Army's *Weekly Domestic Intelligence Summary,* which cited People's Songs as a Communist front. On July 21, the FBI had discovered Walter Steele, who had the exotic title of Chairman, National Security Committee of the American Coalition of Patriotic, Civic and Fraternal Societies. Steele's HUAC testimony—that People's Songs performed for Communist-led groups—landed verbatim in FBI files.

Unaware of this investigation, Seeger publicly spoke of opening a new international division. On the eve of the PSI convention, he flew into Chicago from Los Angeles, trailing success. A writer for the *Los Angeles Examiner* somehow sensed the Seton in Pete, describing his singing as "a refreshing excursion out of the mental and physical smog of urban life . . .

an enlightening and exciting essay in Americana." Pete wore a suit and tie and accepted the pretentious title of chairman of the board. Big Bill Broonzy, Earl Robinson, Woody Guthrie, Seeger, and Alan Lomax put on a bang-up hootenanny. And, to Seeger's delight, CIO locals in Chicago sent representatives. The new chairman went away thinking: "New branches will open in cities in the United States and Canada. . . . Performers will leave the big cities and head out over the countryside." Seeger didn't seem to mind that only sixty people had attended—at least one of them an FBI agent.

Despite their urgent telegram to Hoover, the FBI had decided to keep a low profile at the convention. Attending the gala hootenanny, the Bureau's informant noted the program "had a definite 'pinkish tinge,' " and reported the convention was arranged "by some group of Jewish women." What the FBI lacked in accuracy they made up in bulk. In the next two years the Bureau compiled five hundred pages on People's Songs, including stolen and photocopied documents; phone calls recorded without warrants; and infiltration of PSI board meetings. The FBI took People's Songs more seriously than the Communist Party did.

In its humdrum way, the Bureau was an accurate critic: Its analysts realized (more fully than Seeger did) the limits of song in producing change without a mass social movement. They understood that Seeger sang for "red intellectuals," rather than a sector of the working class. Yet the FBI concluded that PSI threatened national security: Its songs nourished the radical community.

The FBI was not the only agency worried about People's Songs. In Canada, the provincial government of Quebec seized copies of the new *People's Songbook* (edited by Wally Hille), declaring the song "Joe Hill" subversive; also confiscated in the raid were Tolstoy's *War and Peace* and Whitman's *Leaves of Grass*. Seeger issued an unusually rhetorical statement: "Do you think, Mr. Duplessis [Quebec's governor], you can escape the judgment of history? Long after the warmakers are relegated to the history books . . . people's music will be sung by the free peoples of the earth."

"For People's Songs, 1948 was the year of the Progressive Party and Henry Wallace," Irwin Silber said. "Today it seems like a footnote to history, but there's no way to describe the importance attached to it by the Party and people on the Left. . . . The wartime alliance was over. There was an excitement that gripped our organization and Pete stood in the thick of it. In the beginning, we thought Wallace would get ten million votes."

Henry Wallace, Roosevelt's former secretary of agriculture and vice-president, was a Midwesterner known for his folksy editorials and his Pioneer Hi-Bred Corn, a farmer-statesman. Passed over for renomination as vice-president in 1944 because of his liberal views, he made anti-cold-war speeches a major part of his 1948 presidential bid. His Progressive Party ticket depended on Communist support, however, and organized labor doomed the campaign by refusing to back Wallace.

Seeger could have predicted the costs of supporting the candidate. Given the Party's support, working for the campaign was both inevitable and a bad bet; nothing was surer to sever People's Songs' ties to unions. Nevertheless the cause was right, and Pete stood with Wallace from the beginning, singing at the Philadelphia convention where he was nominated (probably the singingest one in U.S. history). Through Alan Lomax, People's Songs contracted to provide music for the Progressive Party; Boots even had a desk at Wallace headquarters. The Progressive Party so frightened President Truman and his advisers that they set out to tar Wallace's Communist allies. Two days before a Wallace rally in Yankee Stadium (where Pete was scheduled to sing), a federal grand jury issued indictments against key leaders of the Communist Party under the Smith (Alien Registration) Act. Seeger and his friends sang that much louder:

> A VISIT WITH HARRY
> (*to the tune of "Oh, Susannah"*)
> *I went up to the president*
> *And this is what he said,*
> *"This fellow Henry Wallace*
> *Is a rantin' Rooshian Red!*
> *We've got to jail the communists*
> *To keep this country free,*
> *And everyone's a communist*
> *Who doesn't vote for me. . . ."*

> THE SAME MERRY-GO-ROUND
> *The donkey is tired and thin,*
> *The elephant thinks he'll move in.*
> *They yell and they fuss, but they*
> *Ain't fooling us,*
> *'Cause they're brothers right under the skin.*
>
> *It's the same, same Merry-go-round,*
> *Which one will you ride this year.*
> *The donkey and elephant bob up and down*
> *On the same Merry-go-round.*

WALLACE MAN
(*by Woody Guthrie*)

*I like the way your face lights up,
I like your cornfield smile
Franklin D. had that same light
There, sparkling in his eyes
I don't like Hoover's lemony puss,
Nor Truman's bitter bark smile,
I'm betting my vote on the cornfield grin
Of this Henry Wallace Man.*

Pete Seeger and Paul Robeson were asked to tour with Wallace. Sometimes Toshi came along, bringing Mika (their new baby) in a bassinet. The campaign made a clean test of the power of song. "There were times when a song lightened the atmosphere," Seeger later reflected. "I think it probably helped prevent people from getting killed. It was a very touch and go proposition, that tour. A number of people thought Wallace was going to be assassinated. . . . The police allowed some of the Ku Klux Klan to get away with throwing things. Once they found out they could get away with that, then they really descended.

"I remember a courthouse in Mississippi, where an absolutely livid white Southerner stood in front of me and said, 'Bet you can't sing Dixie!' I said, 'Sure I can, if you'll sing it with me.' " The Dixiecrat stood there furious, unsure whether to sing or not, while Seeger sang not one, but three verses he had learned in the army.

By the end of August, the campaign was clearly sinking. HUAC had just finished a brutal attack on the Progressive Party; Harry Dexter White, a former Wallace aide, had a heart attack and died from the strain. Most of the CIO unions had fled the campaign, leaving the CP virtually alone in its support. Then Wallace decided, against his advisers' pleas, to campaign through the South, bringing Seeger to warm up the crowds and a black woman as his secretary.

Monday morning, August 30, 1948, fifteen cars in Wallace's contingent brought Seeger and the candidate to the textile town of Burlington, North Carolina. A grim mood hung over the entourage: The night before, a supporter had been stabbed twice by anti-Wallace crowds. A hostile throng of 2,500 awaited the caravan. It took four policemen to clear the road for the automobiles to reach the public square. One of them said, "Mr. Wallace, I hope you're planning to leave soon. I don't think we can handle this crowd." A Klan truck had preceded Wallace, passing out eggs and tomatoes.

The driver of the lead car, Marge Frantz, was an immediate target. The sight of blacks and whites in the same convertible (the top fortunately rolled up) sent a shock wave through the already excited crowd. A few cars back, Pete sat guarding his banjo and guitar. The angry Southerners crawled onto the hood of his car and peered down inside as it slowed to a halt. The mob started banging on the car doors, and the shell of metal must have seemed awfully thin.

He waited coolly as the crowd pressed in, yelling obscenities and "Go back to Russia." No one seemed to be in the mood for a sing-along. According to the plan, Seeger was supposed to leave the car, wait while a mike was positioned, and lead the crowd in group singing. But when he stuck his head out, the eggs started to fly. One hit Wallace, spattering his white shirt. It was clear no mike would be set up. Seeger hurriedly introduced Henry Wallace.

"Whenever Wallace attempted to speak, he was greeted by an un-friendly roar and had no chance to make himself heard above it," historian Curtis Macdougall wrote. "He waited as an occasional egg or tomato splashed on the street near him. Then he suddenly committed an act which, in retrospect, seems comparable to putting one's head into a lion's mouth. He reached out and grabbed a bystander.

" 'Are you an American?' Wallace shouted, obviously enraged. 'Am I in America?' "

Seeger and Wallace shared this vision of an America of rustic virtue, where people helped strangers and their union brothers, where black and white sang in church together and sat down to Sunday dinner afterward. In a land of honest woodsmen, confrontations like this were foreign. "Am I in America?" Wallace had to ask, waves of hatred roiling around him and his allies.

What keeps a performer cool when the audience is climbing on his car and pounding in the doors? Obstinacy, perhaps, and conviction: Seeger trusted music so much he would stand before an angry crowd and try to connect. And, incredibly enough, sometimes he pulled it off, and a thousand strangers found themselves disarmed and singing the "Star-Spangled Banner" together. Then there were the other times, when the magic failed and there wasn't even time to tune up, when no amount of banjo picking was going to stop the cold war.

Seeger wasn't alone in going all out for Wallace; People's Songs had invested heavily. For almost six weeks, the campaign became its principal activity; no one noticed how the stipend from Wallace headquarters had taken the place of members' dues.

"We knew the price we would pay," Irwin said. "We were losing out with the unions. If some of our friends who saw us as a folklore outfit were unhappy, well that was too bad." Pete might have been irritated at Irwin's comments; he had fought both right-wingers and the Party for his right to sing folk music. On tour with Wallace, while the candidate's advisers clustered in hotel rooms writing speeches, Pete had sat in his room writing an instruction manual for the five-string banjo, probably the first of its kind. He could work on it only in snatches, but he carried the sheets with him everywhere, stuffing them into his banjo case; after an evening dodging missiles from the crowd, he would return to his hotel and polish off a few pages. The book and his campaigning represented two instincts, side by side: his need for political engagement and his belief that music itself had social curative powers.

Downstairs in the bar, his fellow campaigners thought Peter a queer duck; but he kept to his room, intent on publishing the book himself. He turned the mimeo by hand, collating and stapling until his hands had calluses and just looking at the pages made him tired. The first year he sold only a hundred copies. It didn't matter. He was proud of both, the book and his dangerous evenings with Henry Wallace.

As the months wore on, Seeger spent more time on Wallace's campaign than he expected. The singing flourished at Wallace rallies, but few unions were leading the chorus. In the end, Wallace could joke as satirist Tom Lehrer did about the Spanish Civil War: "They may have won all the battles—but we had all the good songs." When the votes were counted in November, there were long faces at People's Songs. Wallace had not only lost, he'd received barely a million votes, finishing fourth behind segregationist Strom Thurmond.

Coming back to the office, Pete discovered what he should have known for months. While he was out on tour, PSI had slipped to the edge of bankruptcy. The problem was back salaries. Seeger estimated they'd fallen two thousand dollars behind in the first year, eight thousand in the second, and now their debt approached twelve thousand dollars. Desperate, the group tried a go-for-broke concert, but few supporters had the money or courage to attend. Their debts soared. The office remained glum, except for one officiously cheerful fellow who had wandered in—Harvey Matt, who offered to set up a book-and-record-buying club. He already had a reputation for selling the *Worker* in record time, and everyone figured fine, let him help People's Songs. It turned out Harvey wasn't much of a businessman. He ordered huge stocks of records, which disappeared, leaving a pile of bills. In December 1948, Lee Hays finally admitted to Seeger: "The times which led the Almanacs to live and make good songs are no longer here."

When the inevitable happened, and Seeger notified members of bankruptcy, he tried to strike an optimistic note: "We filled a great need and filled it well." The gala third anniversary edition shrunk to four pages when the printers wouldn't extend their credit. PSI ended so fast board members on the West Coast never even had a chance to vote. On March 6, 1949, the *Daily Worker* ran a special feature on PSI foresightedly calling it "a lusty baby of three with a long future." On March 11, the group disbanded. One of the last songs published was "Swinging on a Scab":

> *A stool is an animal with long hairy ears,*
> *He runs back with everything he knows.*
> *He's no bargain though he can be bought,*
> *Though he's slippery he still gets caught.*
> *But if your bargains are like the rear end of a mule,*
> *Go right ahead and be a stool.*

Opposite this was a birthday greeting from Harvey Matt.

"Thus ended a chapter of my life," Seeger wrote, but the full realization of the failure of PSI was months and years away. One thing was settled; that was the last office job he ever wanted for the rest of his life. His dreams of being a music organizer persisted, but he made an unwritten decision to leave the desk work to the Irwin Silbers—or perhaps to the Toshi Seegers—of the world. "In these years, the biggest pressure on Pete," said Irwin Silber, "was his proximity to People's Songs—we counted on him to be a full-time participant in organizational affairs." Pete, on the other hand, felt his contribution should be in making music. As far as Seeger's hopes of becoming an organizer, Silber continued, "His basis in Marxism was so sketchy I couldn't imagine Pete as a Party organizer. . . . What Pete does on stage is a marvelous act of communication, but there are very few people he can sit and communicate with—very difficult for him. There are times when you feel that the man's real life is in public life."

The ideal Seeger struggled for in People's Songs was captured in a song he and Woody had written on their first trip west: "Union Maid," a hymn to women in the labor movement. They wrote the song together—

though Pete copyrighted it in Woody's name: "Pete and me was fagged out when we got to Oklahoma City, but not too fagged to plow up a Union Song. Pete flopped out acrost a bed, and I set over at a Writing Machine, and he could think of one line and me another'n until we woke up with a great big fifteen pound blue-eyed Union Song, I mean Union, named 'Union Maid' " (to the tune of "Redwing"):

> *There once was a Union Maid who never was afraid*   ©
> *Of goons and ginks and company finks*
> *And deputy sheriffs who made the raids.*
> *She went to the Union hall when a meeting it was*
> *   called*
> *And when the Legion boys came 'round she always*
> *   stood her ground.*
>
> *This union maid was wise to the tricks of company*
> *   spies;*
> *She couldn't be fooled by a company stool,*
> *She'd always organize the guys,*
> *She'd always get her way when she struck for better*
> *   pay;*
> *She'd show her card to the national guard,*
> *And this is what she'd say:*
>
> *Oh you can't scare me*
> *I'm sticking to the Union*
> *I'm sticking to the Union. . . .*

At first, Pete didn't think much of the song; the lyrics were sappy. But the chorus was good-spirited and catchy ("sticking to the union" had a percussive effect when sung quickly). When the Almanacs recorded the song, they wanted another verse; Mill went off for an hour and came up with one that feminists later criticized:

> *Now you gals that want to be free,*
> *   take a tip from me:*
> *Get you a man with a union card,*
> *   and join the ladies' auxiliary*
> *Married life ain't hard when*
> *   you got a union card*
> *And a union man leads a happy life*
> *   when he's got a union wife.*

After People's Songs folded, the song took on a bitter irony; Seeger hadn't meant to be the unions' maid, but that's what PSI was reduced to, as they begged for labor audiences. The lyrics belonged to another era, when unions *were* more maidenly; by the late 1940s, many felt the Union Maid had developed myopia, and "company stools" looked like friends. The anti-Communist Left underscored this in a parody:

> *There once was a Union Maid who always was afraid*
> *Of Socialists and Anarchists*
> *And the games the C.P. factions played. . . .*
> *You gals who want to be free, just take a tip from me;*
> *Don't marry a man who's a union man,*
> *Might as well buy stock in the company.*

The reason "Union Maid" and PSI didn't ignite a singing labor movement was not mysterious: "When we went on the picket line to sing," commented PSI's San Francisco director, "we became aware that we were looked at as entertainment. The message we were singing was being tolerated or not listened to. We were under the illusion that somehow we were educating them. We *weren't* educating them, because we didn't talk to them in their language. . . . Their main interest was economic." Most working folks sang together in churches or bars, not in union halls.

People's Songs had been born too late. The scheme Seeger and his friends dreamed up on Saipan *might* have worked in the Almanacs' days; unions had different needs then: to garner publicity and to persuade members to join a labor organization for the first time. This is what the Almanacs had done; but after the war, when unions had a good foothold in the plants, picket lines largely disappeared in favor of contract bargaining—and picket singers vanished as well. Industrial workers wanted refrigerators and washers, not armed conflict. Seeger naturally resisted these tendencies, for they jeopardized not only his ideals of unions but his profession. He persisted at consciousness-raising—even after unions spurned this—because this was where his talents had the greatest importance.

These were blue times for a song agitator. Seeger searched for an explanation, but as People's Songs faded from view, he saw only its minor failings. In an April 1949 letter to Earl Robinson, about the end of People's Songs, Pete blamed musical arrangements: "P.S.I. banked too goddamned much on soloists." In the same note, he offhandedly mentioned receiving a songbook "of the Viet-Nam rebels."

Pete slowly reached a long-resisted conclusion: Not only were unions uninterested in a singing country or reviving folk music, they might not produce the social change he had expected since he was a teenager. Later he would comment: "Even unions with left-wing leadership felt they had to concentrate on pork chops to the exclusion of songbooks and choruses."

The six months after Wallace's defeat and the bankruptcy of People's Songs took a terrible toll on Seeger. "Shortly after the election, I was hired to sing at a birthday party by a wealthy person. I didn't really want to do it, but she said, "Oh Pete, I've just been married and it's my birthday party. My husband knows I'm a great fan of yours . . . come sing, and show him what I mean when I talk about folk songs.'

"So I went, and her husband had a whole lot of conservative friends there. One was about as insulting as she could be to Henry Wallace. She didn't know I'd ever been a Wallace supporter. I demurred a bit, but she kept going. Finally I just lost my temper. My hand was shaking in front of me, and I threw a whole glass of Coca-Cola up and down her entire dress. I walked out of the room shaking all over. The host brought me my banjo and mailed my hat back the following week."

This violent streak burst out only in his most trying times. Pete had now lost the self-confidence that had propelled PSI through its early days. Wally Hille remembered one unhappy evening at a "wingding" in Pete's basement, where his friends had gathered. Time after time, Pete was passed over as the crowd called for "Huddie" and "We want Huddie" (Leadbelly). Finally, Pete stood up and looked around. Competition hung awkwardly in the room. "I guess you don't need me around here," he told the gathering and huffed upstairs, two steps at a time. By the time Toshi calmed him down, the party had ended. There's nothing harder for an idealist than losing his vision: Take away his career and he feels martyred; take away his livelihood, and he takes up art. But take away his dreams, and you have his heart.

Pete's enthusiasm for New York City had died: "By 1949, I could see the disadvantages of city life. My health wasn't any good. I got no exercise except by running up and down stairs. Each day was a list of phone calls a foot long. We had a pay phone in our house and I did a sneaky trick of pinching two needles together to avoid paying the nickel for the call. . . . In those days, I didn't quibble about stealing money from Bell Telephone."

In a few months, Pete would turn thirty. He had two young children and no job. He would have to start over, with a strike against him: his red reputation. Pete didn't want to live off Toshi's parents; he was tired of the city, of his broken-down furniture, tired of bowls of salad for supper. He wanted to figure out what to do with his life. All he managed was to get by: teaching music at private schools and taking any booking that came in. (One of the strangest of these was on April 13 at the Thursday Evening Club, where Pete sang to a group of executives, including the forty-one-year-old Nelson Rockefeller.)

Nineteen forty-nine, when much of the Left stopped whistling in the dark and ran for cover, was a poor time to begin a second career. Casting about for work, he considered folklore; after all, Alan made a good living at it. Seeger wrote the Library of Congress proposing they film his banjo techniques in slow motion for the Archive of American Folksong. Unbeknownst to Seeger, Duncan Emrich (then head of the Archive) was collaborating with the FBI: as soon as People's Songs ended, he offered the Bureau his file of complimentary copies of the *Bulletin*. He told the FBI of his alarm "at the efforts of Communists and Communist sympathizers to infiltrate and gain control of Folksinging." Emrich worried that these singers "might be unpatriotic"; he eventually wrote Seeger "regretting" that he had no resources to spare.

Everywhere he turned, Pete found roadblocks in the way of his career. It wasn't until the afternoon of his first commercial television job, a children's program, that he realized how much he had given up for People's Songs and the Wallace campaign: "A sharp-faced man glanced at me as I waited in the lobby. In a few minutes, the director came out and said he was sorry, but plans had been changed and there was no room for me on the program. I found out later that the sharp-faced man had been the owner of the station. 'What's that young fellow doing in the lobby? He's the son-of-a-bitch who was singing at the Wallace convention. Get him out of here.' " This was the first of Seeger's many problems with television; his balancing act between commercial and people's music had collapsed.

One day a friend stopped by and found Pete sprawled across a couch and despondent: "I guess I ought to think about getting a job in a factory." He had reached a turning point where he had to pick himself up and go out and get himself a job, anything to put groceries on the table. With his career falling apart and PSI dissolved with a string of bad debts, such a move was overdue. Yet in the middle of his slump, Seeger did something peculiar. He wrote songs. Just when things looked bleakest, he turned to music to remind himself of the better times ahead, if only he could hold on. Afternoons, he would sit by himself at the piano, his oversize heron legs pushing out the sides of the upright. Lee would leave a set of lyrics taped to the piano's mantel and Pete would work out tunes. In the background, sounds of shoppers would distract him, and long shadows flickered across the basement as he worked on "If I Had a Hammer" and another lesser known Hays-Seeger collaboration, "Tomorrow Is a Highway." An underground spring nourished his hopes for a new and brighter dawn:

> *Come let us build a way for all mankind*   ©
> *A way to leave these evil years behind*
> *To travel onward to a better year*
> *Where love is and there will be no fear,*
> *Where love is and no fear.*
>
> *Tomorrow is a highway broad and fair*
> *And we are the many who'll travel there*
> *Tomorrow is a highway broad and fair*
> *And we are the many who'll build it there*
> *And we will build it there.*

Seeger realized his life needed a major change; Toshi agreed. His wartime dreams of a handmade kitchen and tool shop beckoned. His children deserved better than the city streets. Pete hadn't forgotten his own childhood: stalking the woods at Patterson, playing barn squash, and eating garden-fresh vegetables. In a time of crisis, the musician went back to the woods and the self-sufficiency of Seton's world: Chop wood yourself, and you'll never be cold; learn to plant and build a house, Pete now reasoned, and we'll survive. He decided to build a log cabin. In the spring of 1949, the Seegers used the last of their savings for a down payment on a few hardy acres overlooking the Hudson River. Youthful admirers in the Young Progressives bought him a pick and an ax, and he was ready to begin.

If I Had a Hammer /7

SEEGER began his house with the eagerness he brought to all new projects. With an ax he cleared two acres and chopped down enough trees to produce a view of the river and space for a garden. Then he went to the New York Public Library and looked up "log cabin" and took careful notes. Using wood from his land he began to construct the foundations of his new home.

If he thought the pressures of the city were behind him, though, he was mistaken; he had barely dug out his first trench when he sang at the bloody concert in Peekskill. The cold war had come up from the city for a visit and proved an intransigent guest.

Two months later, in November 1949, the blood and beatings at Peekskill still fresh in mind, Pete met with a quartet he had informally sung with for the last year, the Weavers. It was a dark period, with people still in the hospital from right-wing attacks: a friend of one of the group had his skull cracked open; another woman had her finger sliced off; the rock that smashed in Seeger's window, showering his son with glass, also tore open the eyebrow of their friend Greta.

For Pete and the others, the last months had been a round of hospital visits and committee meetings. Veterans' groups threatened more anti-Communist violence, and a roundup of leftists might begin any day.

The prospects for a left-wing musical ensemble were grim. The violence at Peekskill had hobbled the Weavers' career, for the progressives who made up their audience hesitated to gather in public. Dispirited, the group wanted to cut their losses and disband. Pete wanted them to continue. He had begun refusing solo bookings in hopes of finding the group spirit of the prewar period. "No," people told him, "we'll take you, but not the Weavers."

Pete hadn't yet moved from the Ohtas' house in Greenwich Village, and the basement where they talked was long and damp, with rotting floorboards. In one corner stood Pete's upright piano. Despite efforts to brighten up the place, the room had a gloomy, grottolike air that matched their moods—Why rehearse when no one dared come hear them?

Going around the room, there was Ronnie Gilbert, a voice student who had never sounded the same since she had discovered folk music. Ronnie was a brassy, attractive woman from Brooklyn in her early twenties, with dramatically arched eyebrows and stylish black hair. Next to her sat Freddy Hellerman, who, with Ronnie, had been a frequent visitor to the People's Songs office. He was twenty-two, and like Irwin Silber, fresh out of Brooklyn College. Freddy had a quick smile, and his receding hairline and prominent nose made him look like a jaunty rabbinical student. As a teenager he had hung around the Almanac house, eventually learning the guitar in the coast guard during the war. He and Ronnie had met at a left-wing summer camp, Wo-Chi-Ca (*Wo*rkers' *Chi*ldren's *Ca*mp). The senior members of the quartet were Seeger and Lee Hays, whom nature had endowed with the bass (and physique) of a tuba.

Hays and Seeger had the greatest stake in keeping the group together; the others, almost ten years younger, had alternate plans: Ronnie was ready for a family, and Fred wanted an M.A. in English. Even Lee was casting his eyes at a new career as a short-story writer.

The Weavers had a small following from the rallies and benefits where they sang. They also had a record out, produced by Pete's old friend Boots Cassetta: "If I Had a Hammer," a song first performed at a benefit for the eleven Communist Party leaders now on trial. The song's lyrics and majestic, rising melody characterized many of their collaborations:

> *If I had a hammer* ©
> *I'd hammer in the morning,*
> *I'd hammer in the evening,*
> *All over this land.*
> *I'd hammer out a danger,*
> *I'd hammer out a warning,*
> *I'd hammer out of love between*
> *All of my brothers*
> *All over this land.*
>
> *If I had a bell . . .*
>
> *If I had a song . . .*
>
> *Now I have a hammer*
> *And I have a bell*
> *And I have a song to sing*

All over this land.
It's the hammer of justice,
It's the bell of freedom,
And a song about love between
All of my brothers
All over this land.

"We wrought better than we thought," Seeger said later; neither had any idea how far the song would travel. *Sing out a danger, sing out a warning*—it was not surprising the Weavers considered breaking up; the beatings at Peekskill seemed only the beginning. Tolerance was in short supply, and the Weavers found themselves surrounded not only by anti-Communism, but by growing anti-Catholic, anti-Semitic, and anti-foreign emotions of the sort Pete had met on a recent trip.

Pete's family had been visiting Constance in Florida, where they basked in the sun and ate their fill of fresh fish. They left with dark tans, especially Toshi and Mika, their nine-month-old baby. The trip home had started out pleasantly, as the family roamed back roads with a trailer, chugging slowly up the hills. They rolled north through the flat coastal marshes of Florida and Georgia, lush and green with fall rains; then they drove the Blue Ridge Highway through North Carolina.

Pete threaded through his past; Constance and Charles had traveled this way twenty-seven years before, also in a trailer, also carrying their young children. Approaching the foothills of Appalachia, the Seegers passed near Asheville, where Pete had first met the five-string banjo in the crisp mountain air of the Piedmont. Pete and Toshi were in no hurry. They wanted to show their kids America and camp with them, letting matters at home slide out of mind. The last thing Pete expected was trouble with the police. In Salem, Virginia (near Roanoke), they were eating lunch at what they thought was a public picnic ground when a policeman came over, waving his pistol.

" 'You folks gotta get out of here,' he said.

" 'What's wrong?' I said.

" 'This park's for Americans only,' the policeman said.

" 'We're all Americans,' I told him. 'Not them,' he said, pointing at Pete's tanned and Oriental wife and child. 'Them's gypsies.' " The family drove off, furious, wondering how anyone could *look* un-American. There was no escaping the cold war in America.

In the Seegers' musty basement, the Weavers' discussions continued. Pete suggested again, more forcefully, that if they didn't find new audiences—even trying nightclubs, like professional singers—they might as well quit. Lee disagreed: "Our main job is not in nightclubs."

Pete had been stewing on this issue for months, and he wouldn't give up easily. He explained their duty, as he saw it: to reach out to the faces behind the rocks at Peekskill. Then he tossed out an idea Toshi had suggested.

"Look, I think Max Gordon would have me back at the Village Vanguard. Rather than go there by myself, let's go in as a group. If we split my salary four ways, we'd each get fifty dollars a week." Lee was still opposed, and Ronnie and Fred remained undecided. The gathering broke up as they agreed to think matters through.

Actually another incident motivated Seeger, a personally wrenching one he later spoke of as a crossroads in his life. One afternoon in 1949, Irwin Silber had been called by the left-wing American Labor Party, who wanted to set up a benefit concert with Richard Dyer-Bennett, a singer of traditional ballads.

"Perhaps I can help you get him," Irwin had answered. "But in case he can't make it, how about getting Pete to do the concert?"

"Oh, we know Pete," the caller from the ALP had replied. "He's sung on our sound truck for years. We need someone who can bring a mass audience. We need to raise money."

On hearing this, Pete's blood churned. He remembered long winter nights when he had sung outside for the ALP: "Here I was, trying to follow what I thought was a tactical, strategic course, and yet Dick Dyer-Bennett—who was making a career in a traditional fashion—was more use than me." This was a key, embittering insight. For years he had avoided commercial bookings, content with local, progressive audiences. If it takes a "name" to bring in a large crowd, Seeger figured, that's what I'll have: "I decided to stop congratulating myself on not going commercial."

The idea of trying their talent in the marketplace tempted Ronnie and Fred; furthermore, Pete's point about political isolation was brutally driven home while the Weavers campaigned for an ALP candidate, Vito Marcantonio. They went out on an open sound truck through neighborhoods of poor blacks, the traditional supporters of Marcantonio (probably the closest to an advocate the CP had in the U.S. House of Representatives). Gordon Friesen from Almanac days ran the affair well, but the crowds didn't respond. The Weavers sang their left-wing repertoire and a couple of songs made up for the occasion. From a nearby window, tomatoes started splattering the unprotected truck. Pete looked up anxiously and asked what they should do. "Be glad they're not bricks," Gordon answered with a grim smile.

The Weavers' nightclub premiere was set for late December. Toshi volunteered to be the group's first (temporary) manager. In her levelheaded way, she understood the changes necessary to sing in nightclubs: She marched them all down to an army-navy store to buy blue corduroy jackets (for fifty dollars a week, they weren't shopping Brooks Brothers). Then she negotiated the contract with Max Gordon, the Vanguard's owner. "Part of our agreement was two hundred dollars a week plus free hamburgers," Seeger laughed. "Max once came in and saw the size of the hamburgers I was making—I'd put half a pound of meat in, and eat three or four a night. He said, 'Let's rewrite the contract; two hundred fifty dollars a week, but no free hamburgers.' "

Singing carols, the Weavers opened in Christmas week, 1949. After the novelty wore off and their friends had visited, business dropped. One night in February, only a half-dozen customers visited the once-bustling club. Max Gordon liked the music, though, and he carried them. Every night was a rehearsal. By reworking and rearranging, they wove the songs into a dense harmonic tapestry, trading parts midsong. Alan Lomax brought Carl Sandburg to hear the group, and the poet's praises led newspaper editors to listen: "The Weavers are out of the grass roots of America. I salute them . . . when I hear America singing, the Weavers are there." Before the Weavers understood what had happened, crowds were packing the Vanguard.

It was at this point that two short, heavyset men introduced themselves: Harold Leventhal and Pete Kameron. They shook hands all around and told the Weavers they needed a manager. Kameron, the more sharply dressed of the two, volunteered for the job; soon the man Ronnie tartly called "a breath of old show business" was handling their business matters, including their soon-to-be lucrative song publishing. Despite Kameron's head start, it was Harold, the "silent partner" of this arrangement, who eventually represented Seeger for over twenty-five years.

At a typical Weavers show, Lee Hays told the story of a preacher who thought music was the devil's invention:

"Preacher," I argued, "how can you not like music? Music is the language of the soul: It expresses the inexpressible, satisfies the insatiable. . . ."

"I don't care if it unscrews the inscrutable," he declared, "it's sinful, and I'm against it."

Next Ronnie sang a love song, "I Know Where I'm Going," with Pete's recorder coloring the melody and Fred doubling up the bass notes on his guitar. Ronnie's intense, clear voice sent a shiver through the crowd. Finally, Pete stepped up to the microphone:

"We'd like to sing a song from South Africa . . . about the lost king of the Zulus, Chaka the Lion. The legend arose that he didn't die, he simply went to sleep. Someday he would wake up and lead his people again. The African people, slaves in their own land, sing that the lion is not dead but sleeping. Well, all you lions there. . . ." Pete strummed the banjo, "Way-up boy, Wimoweh, Wimoweh."

The Weavers closed with "Goodnight Irene," with Fred striking up a waltz rhythm. They hedged on the more controversial lyrics, dropping a verse about taking morphine, and changing the chorus from (Leadbelly's version): "I'll *get* you in my dreams" to "I'll see you in my dreams." No matter: In 1950, singing a song by a black ex-convict made an unmistakable political statement.

After a show like this one, a trim fellow walked up and introduced himself. "Gee, you guys are wonderful," he said. "My name is Gordon Jenkins and I work for Decca Records. We're exactly the company you ought to be with."

Seeger said yes, not really believing him. He'd heard of bandleader Jenkins, who worked with Louis Armstrong and Frank Sinatra: He had at least one record in the top forty every week. Most singers would have treated Jenkins like visiting royalty, but Pete more or less shrugged him off. He couldn't bring himself to care about pop music, as anxious as he was to be accepted in that world. Jenkins, on the other hand, was insistent. He invited them to visit Decca, where he would introduce them around.

What interested Decca in an unsexy folk-song quartet? The Weavers had musical verve and the genius of simplicity. In every era, a few musicians simplify the art of their time, producing a sound often called refreshing. This streamlining instinct, similar to Seeger's extending his banjo, underlay the Weavers' better arrangements. Quartets classically feature a tenor, bass, alto, and soprano. The Weavers had a baritone, a bass, a brilliant alto, and Seeger—who, because of his falsetto, described himself as a split-tenor. The group profited by being everything pop singers were not; they had spontaneous arrangements and untrained voices (except for Ronnie), and they downplayed vocal effects in favor of content. "They sang straight out, straight ahead," recalled the young Arlo Guthrie, whose father carried him to Weavers' concerts. "A few embellishments here and there to make things funny, but basically it was songs and stories—communication, not hype. . . . They interpreted the Leadbellys and Guthries, who were too foreign for mass tastes."

According to Seeger, the Weavers' audition was a failure: "Dave Kapp was head of Decca. He took one look at me and said, 'Oh, I know these guys, they're not commercial.' He knew I was a lefty." But on the way out Jenkins whispered, 'I'll get you in on my next recording date.' Kapp had to swallow his words when the songs became some of the biggest hits Decca ever had." The Weavers visited the renowned William Morris Agency, but when they walked in for an audition, Pete was greeted by the same man who had booked the Almanacs: "I felt like I'd been here before."

Seeger hoped to do things better this time, telling Lee: "Performing commercially is something that makes you want to see if you can do it as well as the next fellow." It might sound strange for Seeger to champion freedom of the marketplace; but if the Weavers were going to compete, he wanted to win. Deep down, he believed in very American symbols: log cabins, the nuclear family, the Bill of Rights. By venturing into the music industry's arena, Pete was saying, in effect, let the best song win, just as folk songs are themselves products of a musical Darwinism.

He need not have worried, for the Weavers had no competition: Outside the larger cities, few had heard anything resembling their music. In 1950 rhythm and blues was just spreading from New Orleans, where Fats Domino pounded out boogie-woogie on his piano; in Memphis, Howlin' Wolf and Sonny Boy Williamson played on KWEM radio, and B. B. King sang in bars. The Weavers ignored these trends; while young Elvis Presley stayed up nights listening to R & B on his radio, Pete Seeger sang South African freedom songs.

On May 4, 1950—a day after his thirty-first birthday—Seeger and the Weavers recorded "Tzena, Tzena," a catchy Israeli soldiers' tune. After years of drifting from one left-wing cause to another, Seeger had the beginnings of a career any commercial singer would have envied. He had turned thirty at a bleak time, a month after People's Songs' bankruptcy, but a year later he had landed on his feet.

Within weeks, the Decca recordings made the Weavers stars. Their first mention in the trade journals came in the *Downbeat* of May 1950. The article focused on Decca's difficulties in slotting the Weavers: Were they country, pop, or what? Three weeks later, *Variety* first reviewed their act at the Vanguard; by June 28 the Weavers were mentioned in five articles in the same issue. The Weavers suddenly had their choice of the country's top nightclubs; and crowning it all, they were offered a weekly national TV spot on NBC.

Starting in June, the Weavers' first record climbed so far so fast that disc jockeys didn't know which side to play. They turned over the exotic "Tzena, Tzena" and found "Goodnight Irene"; soon that was played more than "Tzena." Frank Sinatra launched a comeback with his cover version of "Goodnight Irene" in July. Lawyers argued over who owned the copyright to "Tzena," and Decca couldn't press the records fast enough.

Technological developments again favored Seeger's career. The Weavers were radio stars, coming along at a time when the medium was more concerned with ratings than the blacklist. Sponsors looked forward to increased TV programming, "ready to abandon radio like bones at a banquet," as Fred Allen put it. Challenged by TV shows like *Kukla, Fran and Ollie,* and Milton Berle's *Texaco Star Theater,* radio producers turned to the new, folk-style music for a competitive edge.

Success surprised the Weavers almost as much as it had the Almanacs, in the few glorious weeks before the blacklist in 1942. "It was too unexpected," Pete said. "I remember laughing when I walked down the street and heard my own voice coming out of a record store. Once I was up in a publisher's office and speaking about some other musician, Don Cherry, and I said, 'Well, he's one of those Decca stars.' And they looked at me funny and said, 'Don't you realize that you're one of those Decca stars?'

"I'd never thought of it. People came up to me and asked, 'How does it feel to be a success?' I felt kind of silly. To me, I was a bigger success nine years before, when the Almanacs sang for the Transport Workers' Union in Madison Square Garden." Peekskill and a Greenwich Village nightclub were only fifty miles away from each other, but worlds apart: Pete suddenly found himself a pop entertainer, complete with late-night temptations.

The Weavers headlined at Ciro's in Hollywood, the Shamrock in Houston, and the flashy nightclubs of Reno. In Reno the maniacal bustle and metallic clanking of the slots proved too tempting, and the group decided to try their luck. Only Pete refused to play: "My Puritan background was just revolted. Some of the Weavers got in over their heads, began to get nervous; instead of winning back what they'd lost, they lost more." Pete began acting like a prig. He had a silver dollar in his hand and said, "I don't mind wasting my money" and tossed the dollar into the pool.

The Weavers tasted success without understanding it; the drug fame affects each user differently. Hays, initially hesitant about playing nightclubs, now reveled in the experience. In Nevada he discovered room service; when he found out that as a performer he could get anything he wanted, he ordered the works. Looking at the pile of half-eaten dishes, Pete was nauseated. *His* problem was finding some useful way of passing his days. In L.A. he located a craftsman who taught him to hammer silver; in Houston, he collected songs at a black prison; in Chicago, to the dismay of the hotel management, the hypercreative musician turned his room into a studio and made plaster casts of Eskimo sculpture.

The group used to tease Pete and Toshi about their beat-up jeep wagon, the same one they'd driven through the barrage at Peekskill. When they were at Ciro's in Hollywood, an impish idea struck Pete. The Seegers were staying with a friend who owned a beautiful Cadillac, and one night they borrowed it. They drove out to the club, and Toshi told the others: "Peter finally gave in. He's decided you're right. Look what we've got!" Ronnie, Fred, and Lee sat in amazement as Seeger wheeled them out for a drive. "We don't believe it," one said. "Oh, Pete! Are you really not kidding us?" "No, great car, isn't it?" Pete said.

Success also had its sobering side, and after the excitement paled, Seeger considered how long this would last, and what their new fame meant. The Weavers began throwing in radical material, Spanish Civil War songs. To his horror, Pete discovered that no one noticed. In fact, the wealthy patrons liked the Spanish tunes so well, they would ask for them as encores. The Weavers' music operated on two levels: commercial pop songs, accessible to all listeners; and a symbolic, encoded music (available only at live concerts) that reminded the Left of its existence: calypso, peace, topical songs.

The tours, the television appearances on Milton Berle, the write-ups in *Variety,* all these showed that Seeger was winning his competition with success, but he often wondered if he was changing anything. Gradually he and Lee traded places, and Pete's initial enthusiasm faded. Though more experienced at touring than Ronnie or Fred, Pete had the most family responsibilities. When he was away too long, he missed his kids and felt stabs of guilt at leaving home.

Toshi, in her late twenties, took care of their two children, aged four and two. She built a house while living in it: fixing the gaps between the logs where the wind whistled in, chopping the firewood, and running errands for her parents. In addition, she took Pete's messages; the phone rang from the first day it was installed, even before they had a proper floor on the cabin.

When Pete would come home from being on the road for a month at a time, there were moments of stiffness, when he seemed practically a stranger to his family. The homecomings had their warm and tender moments, too, such as one Pete sketched in his notebook. Toshi sat across from Pete in one of their few chairs, rocking and staring into the fire with their two-year-old daughter Mika in her lap. The child slept in the warmth, her arms around her mother's neck. Across the room, his instruments put aside, Pete sketched with a thick lead pencil: the daughter drowsing, Toshi rocking gently in the candlelit darkness, the logs from their backyard sputtering in the fire.

This tranquillity vanished on the road, where people kept pressing drinks in his hand and offering him after-hours revels. Pete still had a bit of hermit in him; he preferred to sit around the hotel and doodle on his banjo. Once the Weavers shared a program with a man named Tiny Hill. Tiny weighed over three hundred pounds; he made even Lee look skinny. Backstage after a show, fans clustered around Tiny and the Weavers, plying them with booze. "Aw, Pete," they wheedled, "have a drink."

"They just didn't know how serious I felt about liquor," Pete later said, shaking his head. "I don't like to be forced to drink. If I don't want to drink, I don't want to drink! I'm not a very sociable person anyway, and their urging was making me a lot less sociable.

"'C'mon Pete,' they said, 'unbend, unwind, have a little drink.'

"I picked up my banjo and I said, 'You know how I feel about this?' and WHAM, there went one good banjo. I slammed it down on the table, broke it in half." Seeger broke the very tools he had worked so hard to develop.

Despite his misgivings, the Weavers continued, doing four and five short sets a day and commanding $2,250 a week at the Beacon Theater on Broadway. They played the Blue Angel, an extremely chic nightclub; the audience loved them. Among the listeners was New York's flourishing young district attorney, Thomas Murphy, who would face Seeger in court within the decade.

Not everyone was pleased with the Weavers' triumphs. Hidden in the applauding crowd, toward the back of the room, stood an FBI informant, Harvey Matusow, who later helped shatter the Weavers' career. On June 16, 1950, he suggested that though the Weavers weren't actually doing anything *wrong*, the FBI should keep an eye on them. It wouldn't be the first time the FBI had investigated cultural workers; the Bureau was chasing groups of anarchist writers as far back as 1919, even before the left wing of the Socialist Party gave its name to American radicals.

In this case the Bureau needed no prompting. They already had a file on the Weavers, complete with army intelligence reports; all that was necessary for an FBI file was a mention in the anti-Communist magazines the Bureau religiously clipped, like *Counterattack,* an ardent enemy of the Weavers.

Founded by three ex-FBI agents who hinted of access to "confidential" files, *Counterattack* was half gossip, half conspiracy newsletter—the FBI's unofficial leak. In the 1950s anti-Communism was a big business. Senate and House committees flew in ex-Communist "consultants," paying by the day to stretch out testimony. At twenty-four dollars per subscriber, *Counterattack* netted a hundred thousand dollars yearly. The editors operated a "clearing house," American Business Consultants (ABC), which specialized in internal investigations of large corporations at five thousand dollars yearly. In his book *The Golden Web,* Erik Barnouw, historian of radio and television, uncovered how these investigations worked.

The editors of *Counterattack* would call a company, telling them they had heard actress Y, of questionable background, was employed on their television series. As a public service, they would study her loyalty, and that of the supporting cast—for one thousand dollars. If the offer was refused, three weeks later the editors would run a story about how actress Y was not a Communist, but a "fellow traveler"—almost as bad. Using these tactics, *Counterattack* drew in General Motors, Du Pont, Woolworth's, Reynolds Tobacco, and many other patrons. Criticized for employing "pink" entertainers on his new variety show, Ed Sullivan invited the Counterattackers up to his living room to meet "performers eager to secure a certification of loyalty," as he wrote in the *New York Post.*

The Weavers were favorite targets for those investigating the entertainment and broadcasting industry; their visibility (and that of most entertainers) made them extremely vulnerable to attacks and provided blacklisters with headlines. Lawrence Johnson was one of these red-hunters; in 1951 he led an unsuccessful effort to stop the Weavers' records from being broadcast. A supermarket owner from Syracuse, New York, Johnson claimed to represent the National Association of Supermarkets. He labeled as "Communist" any soap advertised on shows mentioned in *Counterattack.* "Let the people choose," he apparently reasoned, "whether they want to wash with tainted soap." Because broadcasters received sixty percent of their ad revenue from household consumables, Johnson became one of the networks' excuses for blacklisting.

As the Weavers grew more popular, former friends also attacked them. This was the period of the Communist Party's "white chauvinism" campaign against racial prejudice, and Irwin Silber took the Weavers to task in a column entitled "CAN AN ALL-WHITE GROUP SING SONGS FROM NEGRO CUL-

TURE?" Using now-familiar terms, Silber criticized the Weavers' lyrics as "male supremacist." At one concert, women from a new group, People's Artists, told the Weavers to change the chorus of "If I Had a Hammer" from "love between all of my brothers" to "love between my brothers and my sisters."

"We don't have to," Seeger said. "You can sing it anyway you want. Anybody can change a folk song."

"No! *You* change it."

He argued a bit, saying, "Well, 'My brothers and my sisters' doesn't flow off the tongue quite as nice as 'All of my brothers.' "

"No, there's just been too much of this," they insisted.

Lee joked about it on stage: "All of my siblings, how about that?" They didn't think that was funny.

People's Artists was the CP-oriented successor to People's Songs. Seeger kept his distance from People's Artists, run largely by Irwin Silber and Betty Sanders. The spirit of People's Songs was there, but after years of redbaiting, the body was weak. Initially the group had only a few dozen members, a far cry from the two thousand that PSI boasted at its height. People's Artists booked left-wing performers and started a topical song magazine, *Sing Out!*, which took its name from the chorus of the song on its first cover, "If I Had a Hammer."

Since People's Songs, Pete had been changing his focus: "As the labor movement kicked out the radicals, I settled for 'Let's get America singing'; maybe the basic democratic philosophy in these folk songs will filter out subliminally to the American people." His allegiance to song proved stronger than his union ties, for after the labor movement shut out People's Songs, he had followed the singing and not the unions.

He also left the Communist Party in this period, more from an instinct for self-preservation than any political differences. By 1950 the Party was slipping into an isolation that Seeger could not accept; its membership had plummeted and its ties to unions all but vanished. A paramilitary spirit emerged, which made the organization less appealing than the high-spirited bunch Pete had met in New York in the mid-Thirties. All these factors—combined with the paucity of Party members in the Beacon area and the Party's halfhearted support of People's Songs—caused Seeger to drift away, though friends remained in the Party.

When he did run into former comrades from People's Songs, he'd occasionally see a strange mix of envy and scorn in their eyes. The rumor went around that "Seeger's got a fifty-thousand-dollar estate up the Hudson now!" Meanwhile, Toshi was feeding the family on beans because none of the royalties had come in. Some radicals openly attacked the Weavers' success, taking on names like "The Greivers" and "The Unravellers."

Irwin regularly carped at the Weavers. He even published an article in *Sing Out*! accusing the group of abusing Leadbelly's music, and then had the poor grace to run this soon after Huddie's death from sclerosis at the end of 1949. (Leadbelly died in neglect and on relief; his widow had to take a job as a laundress.)

Irwin's charges depressed Seeger, who had hoped to sing for both left-wing friends and wider audiences. It was on this very point that Pete had his first censorship wrangles with Kameron, the Weavers' manager, who sought to keep his valuable clients free of controversy. A soft-spoken fellow, Kameron managed to talk and dress up to the limits of the latest style, without ever overdoing it.

"Pete," Kameron said in his office after a booking was cancelled, "you can't sing at [those left-wing] hootenannies right now. A few years from now, you'll be in a position to do anything you want. Right now we've got a real problem to get you cleared and give you a *good* reputation. A brand new one. Your old reputation has got to go."

Kameron's nerves must have been strong. That was his talent: The manager always talked softly, as if he didn't want to insist.

"I don't see what's wrong," Seeger answered plaintively. "I've always sung at hoots." He couldn't believe he'd have to give up such an innocent pleasure.

"Now isn't the time," Kameron repeated. "You don't want to jeopardize the position you're in."

Seeger let himself be convinced, as he had at Avon when the headmaster chewed him out for his article critical of the school administration. "Well, all right," he told himself. "If I'm going to do this, I might as well do a commercial job," "Don't push it," his more loyal (and optimistic) friends urged, "you're in a position where you can get on the air." Yet his situation was a pathetic one. At last Pete *had* his hammer—his songs were on the radio and on people's lips—but he could do little with it. Now that his name could draw the audiences his left-wing friends desired, he was prevented from doing benefits. Like it or not, Seeger had become a "property" under contract. He had no more freedom to sing WITH fame than he had without it.

In negotiating with success, he also lost control over his music. Some of the Decca recordings sound cheesy: At the beginning of "Rock Island

Line," for instance, trumpets go "toot-toot." Decca liked Gordon Jenkins's sound; the company seemingly forgot that it was the Weavers, not Jenkins, that topped the charts.

All in all, Pete (and the other Weavers) were fish in strange waters. To reach the audiences he wanted, Seeger often had to dress up and sing the same harmonies, night after night. This sort of compromise was never his strong suit; one evening he insisted on wearing one green and one red sock underneath his tuxedo.

On June 25, 1950, just as the Weavers' first records appeared in the shops, the Korean War erupted. The casualty lists made Communists into America's mortal enemies and jeopardized the tenuous east-west division of Europe. Julius Rosenberg was about to be arrested for allegedly selling atomic secrets to the Soviet Union. And at the end of June, *Red Channels*: *Communist Influence on Radio and Television* appeared, from the publishers of *Counterattack.*

Bound in red with no authors listed, *Red Channels* destroyed hundreds of careers in a single edition. On the cover, below the title, a microphone leaned left as a crimson hand seized control. In phrases like "Where there's red smoke there's usually Communist fire," the book listed artists and entertainers with alleged "Communist-front" associations: Lee J. Cobb, Lillian Hellman, Dorothy Parker, Louis Untermeyer, and 147 others. Much of the material came from *Daily Worker* clippings similar to those in FBI files; the "associations" were as incriminating as signing a petition to support Henry Wallace for President. In the name of Americanism, the book damned writers for writing and musicians for playing for the wrong audiences.

As a result of *Red Channels* mentions, many musicians, including folk-song performers Burl Ives and Josh White, were pressured to testify before HUAC and clear their names. Oscar Brand, a long-time programmer of folk music on WNYC radio in New York, was called by one of HUAC's counsel. Brand had known Seeger for over a decade; he had included the Weavers on his show before they had a name. With his job shaky, he visited the Seegers' half-finished cabin for advice. "You know they're after me to try and cooperate with HUAC," Oscar told them. "What do you think I should do?" When Seeger answered, he must have realized he might some day have to make the same decision: He told Oscar that he had more to lose by cooperating than he could ever gain. Brand, however, "suspected" the Party's interest in folk songs, and in October 1951, at a speech at Cooper Union in New York, he broke with the left-wing folk-music world. He then met with a representative from HUAC, but refused a request that he testify; fortunately for him, he was never subpoenaed. Burl Ives *did* testify eventually on subversion in folk music circles.

The only Weaver listed was Pete Seeger—with thirteen citations he placed somewhere between Aaron Copland and Lillian Hellman. *Red Channels* reached a lot of important desks. The contract for the Weavers' TV series was canceled within a week; the timid sponsor was Van Camp's Pork and Beans. A less controversial group played opposite *The Lone Ranger*, and Lee Hays ate his way through the Weavers' only payment: twenty-four cans of pork and beans.

Yet despite the best efforts of the editors of *Counterattack*, the Weavers recorded hit after hit. In September 1950, when the Internal Security (McCarran) Act was passed into law—including provisions for "detention camps" for leftists—"Goodnight Irene" was number one on the jukebox, and "Tzena" fourth. In November, as Douglas MacArthur's troops reached North Korea and Congressman Nixon became Senator Nixon, "Irene" was the best-selling record in Britain. During 1951 the Counterattackers couldn't turn on the radio without thinking of millions duped by the Weavers' licentious "Kisses Sweeter Than Wine" or the sinister "So Long, It's Been Good to Know Yuh." The record-buying public never read the blacklists that spoke in their name.

In the summer of 1951 the FBI stepped up its activity against the Weavers. The Rosenbergs had been sentenced to death, and Americans were in a frenzy about subversion. HUAC had successfully blackballed most of the New Deal radicals; now conservatives turned outward with a "cold clinical but deadly bureaucratic repression": throwing radicals out of public housing and civil service; barring suspect organizations from public meeting rooms or from receiving critical tax exemptions; even denying Communists old-age pensions.

With the help of *Conterattack*, the Bureau scored direct hits on the Weavers. First a scheduled spot on the Dave Garroway show melted away; a month later Garroway had Connie Russell and the Songsmiths on to sing what *Variety* called "a rousing version" of "Tzena, Tzena." Garroway soon forgot the incident; "I was talent," he claimed, "and talent had no control over anything. Ask my producer."

Then, on August 9, 1951, the governor of Ohio, Frank Lausche, wrote the FBI for confidential information on the Weavers, who were scheduled to appear at the Ohio State Fair. His request put J. Edgar Hoover on the spot. The files requested were clearly "confidential"; no private individual, not even a governor, could legally examine them. Hoover's zeal got the best of him, however, and he passed along the information. The Weavers were canceled so fast there wasn't time to take their names out of the programs. They had no idea what had happened. When they reached Ohio, they were tailed everywhere they went. When they rehearsed in their hotel rooms, they were warned not to close their doors, or the vice squad might burst in. Governor Lausche promised Hoover not to reveal where he got his facts; he also offered to circulate the materials to reporters, if needed. A week later, Frederick Woltman of the New York World-Telegram published an "exposé" of the Weavers, using much of the same information in the FBI files. At this point, Senator Pat McCarran (D-Nevada) joined the hunt. The FBI turned over a basketful of informer reports and clippings to his Senate Internal Security Subcommittee, which decided the Weavers' "Rock Island Line" paralleled the Communist Party's. The McCarran Committee actually investigated whether the Weavers had violated Title 18 of the U.S. Code, sections 2383–85: Rebellion, Insurrection, Advocating the Overthrow of the Government, and Seditious Conspiracy. The Weavers may have been the first musicians in American history formally investigated for sedition.

Perhaps what disturbed McCarran and the FBI was that the Weavers—or any such menace—survived efforts to subdue them. In itself, the Weavers' music wasn't threatening (especially compared with later New Wave and reggae songs). But by their persistence the Weavers had become a rallying point for beleaguered radicals. They kept their heads high, slowly pushing the Bill of Rights toward freedom of song.

Amazingly enough, the Weavers' former colleagues chose this moment to criticize the Weavers for their formal attire and stage patter. Left-wing censorship joined right-wing efforts; only a handful of leftists publicly supported the Weavers' attempted bridge-building. People's Artists set up their own quartet as an alternative to the Weavers: two men, two women, two black, two white—a singing socialist version of Noah's Ark.

Haggard from legal battles, and sensing—perhaps rightly—a new belligerence toward social change, the Communist Left sought political purity over the mass support of its Popular Front days. Pete didn't—or wouldn't —get the message. Fortunately for his psyche, Pete received word that the Party supported the Weavers: "Keep working, put away as much money as you can, and sooner or later you'll end up singing for progressive audiences." Once Pete had compartmentalized his ideological and performing lives, the Party, ironically, accorded him more respect.

Other left-wing groups were less understanding. In Detroit, the Weavers had a job in a nightclub no black had ever entered. Asked to explain this, Pete limply quoted Paul Robeson's statement that a reputation as an opera singer let him be a more effective spokesman. The younger radicals walked out of the meeting, insisting: "Robeson would never do what you're doing. You are appearing in a lily-white club; now you know it's lily-white—are you going to refuse to appear?" Seeger swallowed his principles, and the quartet went ahead with the show.

The Weavers' blacklisting began to emerge in the press. *Variety* awarded them the distinction of "the first group canceled out of a New York cafe because of alleged left-wing affiliations," an honor the Weavers could not refuse. *Downbeat* acknowledged their ban, dryly suggesting, "If the Communists happen to come out in favor of milk for babies, go on record immediately as being squarely opposed to it." The Weavers' manager, Pete Kameron, visited *Counterattack,* pleading with the editors to call off their dogs. In his enthusiasm, the manager wishfully claimed the Weavers "were filling engagements with the American Legion and Daughters of the American Revolution." Kameron even staged a press conference where, according to *Variety,* Seeger hedged about his past, claiming he was not "sponsored" by People's Songs—"I was playing with words," he later admitted, "*I* sponsored *them*"—but "he did know members of the organization and sang with them." "Singing is all the Weavers do," said Lee Hays, in a superficially accurate statement. The publicity photos of this time show Pete stiff-necked and ill at ease with this posturing.

All this commotion made Seeger's life chaotic. Every day, his home grew less like the quiet homestead he had pictured during the war. It had been hard enough to find land—they had searched on weekends, looking at four or five plots they couldn't afford, before buying seventeen acres at a bargain price (one hundred dollars an acre) in the township of Beacon, an hour and a half's drive from New York. Improving it wasn't much easier; Pete had waited impatiently for the spring thaw: "I dragged Toshi up there just to hike up the hill, sleep in a freezing cold trailer, and then walked around the next day and realized there wasn't any work to do. Everything was frozen solid. . . . But in March, as soon as the snow was gone, we moved into a better tent, and we had a better fireplace. Toshi's brother helped us start putting in a little driveway. The walls went up. By September or October 1950, we had the walls and the roof on, and windows and doors in. It wasn't much fixed up, but we'd built a house."

Toshi found a job nearby for her parents, and when the Weavers went on their first tour, Pete and Toshi left the kids with them. Toshi hadn't wanted to leave Mika and Danny; she said they were too young. Pete needed her organizational skills, however, and couldn't bear to part with her for six months. She hadn't meant to be a road manager, but no one would let her stop. Toshi agreed, against her wishes. Throughout the trip she worried, as mothers will: Six months is a long time for a four-year-old. "We drove back to Beacon and there, by the road, was Toshi's father and the two babies. Her father said, 'There they are!' We stopped the car and got out and Danny says, 'You know, I didn't recognize you when you got out. Ta-papa said, "These are my mother and father," but I didn't recognize you.' " Toshi never forgave her husband; she had always before supported his career, but this was the last tour *she* made with the Weavers.

Partly in penance, Pete refused bookings for a while and poured his energy into their house. "Now I built the bed and the shelves. We got a cook stove. The following winter, Danny and Mika slept out on a little porch outside. I took a photograph of the snow all over them when they woke up once. Our heat came from two stone fireplaces, and when we wanted a hot bath, we went to Toshi's parents' place, two miles away."

Pete wanted the respect of his new community; he wanted to prove they were not some young couple from the city who'd last only a few months. His chance came when Danny began school. The local fathers were out clearing land by the school, when Pete came down and surprised them by holding his own. He made his reputation on his ax, like one of Seton's characters. Seeger must have been an odd addition, with his Japanese wife and foreign friends, but the citizens of Beacon grudgingly accepted him as a usable member of their community.

In a loft on Forty-second Street a meeting was taking place that would disturb Seeger's retreat. In their efforts to defeat the Weavers, the editors of *Counterattack* had found a trump card: Harvey Matt, the man who saddled People's Songs with bills for records they never sold. A short, pudgy fellow whom schoolmates nicknamed "Kid Nickels" because he hunted small change, Matt turned out to be Harvey Matusow, an ambitious informer. When the FBI couldn't satisfy his material needs, the young anti-Communist moonlighted as a loyalty consultant to New York's Board of Education and Police Department. He was a lonely, frustrated guy, delighted by headlines with his name, and visiting *Counterattack* was a step up for his career.

"It was there that I got my first training in how to use the names of well-known people in the theatrical world to my advantage as a money-making witness," Matusow later wrote. "We discussed the careers of the well-known quartet who, at the time, had the top-selling record in the U.S. One of its members [Pete Seeger] was listed in *Red Channels*, but there was nothing that could be pinned on the group specifically. . . . Having known all four of them, not as Communists, but as friends, I triumphantly said, 'I know them, and they are Communists.'

"Both [editors] gave me rewarding glances, as if saying, 'Keep that up and you'll make out all right.' "

"I think I remember Harvey," Ronnie Gilbert recently reminisced. "He was always walking up to people in a cafeteria and selling *Daily Workers*. We didn't take him seriously." They should have, for in the next months the brash Mr. Matusow wreaked havoc on their careers.

After leaving the city and the Party, Seeger had extra time to practice; he no longer had trouble coordinating voice and banjo as in his first, shaky recordings with the Almanacs, a decade before. He knew more now about holding audiences, but in the Weavers he learned show business, arranging, and group performance. From his years of solo performing since the Almanacs, Pete tended to listen to his own meter, beat out by his foot. On his own, he managed fine; with the Weavers, he couldn't be depended on to keep time.

The Weavers' talent for breathing life into a song distinguished the quartet *Time* called "the most imitated group in the business." When the group first rehearsed a song from a book, the song wouldn't come alive. After they went through it a second and third time, Pete's banjo picked up subtle syncopations and elisions that filled in the tune. Lee's song "Lonesome Traveller," for example, "just sort of lay there," he remembered, "until Pete changed one chord, from the minor to the major. It just popped out of Seeger's hands and gave the tune new character altogether."

Pete couldn't have explained what he did any more than a jazz improvisationist could. He was so steeped in folk music that he acted as a filter between the folklorist's field recordings and mass audiences. Never before had a folk song moved so quickly from a dusty volume to AM radio. Folklorists complained that once Seeger "filtered" a song, his version tended to be *the* version millions sang. Before electronic recordings and broadcasting, scholars could tell where a singer came from by the verses and tunes he sang; versions could be mapped like highways. When Seeger processed a song like "The Midnight Special," his ear for easily sung chords and harmonies produced a version that wiped out more complex variants, which had taken many years to evolve.

On February 6 and 7, 1952—after meeting with Joe McCarthy's aide, Roy Cohn, and coaching in the *Counterattack* office—Harvey Matusow testified before HUAC, under oath, that three of the Weavers were members of the Communist Party (Lee, he reported, had quit). Carried away by the lights and the attention, he almost buried the Weavers' story by adding that Communists were preying on the "sexual weaknesses" of America's youth to lure them into the Party. His testimony came at a particularly bad time for the Weavers. The day before in Cleveland, they had volunteered to sing on television for the Heart Fund, but several politicians and fellow entertainers had abruptly canceled appearances or developed "car trouble." The group had no way of knowing that the FBI was at work again, supplying confidential information to the telethon organizers. The few politicians who joined the Weavers apologized for their courage, telling *Variety*, "Fighting heart disease is not a left-wing act."

The morning of Matusow's testimony, a minor commotion broke out at People's Artists: No one could remember who the informer was. In one of those ironies that plagued the Left, Silber sent a new assistant to find Harvey's picture; but *he* turned out to be an FBI informer and reported to the Bureau. That afternoon the Associated Press called the Yankee Inn in Akron, Ohio, where the Weavers were performing. Taken aback by the testimony, the manager canceled the Weavers' contract, effective immediately.

Matusow's appearance "burst like a bombshell." The Weavers became untouchables. "We had started off singing in some very flossy nightclubs,"Seeger said wistfully. "Then we went lower and lower as the blacklist crowded us in. Finally, we were down to places like Daffy's Bar and Grill on the outskirts of Cleveland." Even there, the American Legion tried to get Daffy to cancel. "Hell no," dauntless Daffy replied. "It's just music. Quit hassling me or I'll get my boys on you." Though their single record sales now amounted to an incredible four million discs, the Weavers could barely find a hall to book them. On May Day 1952 Pete Seeger marched down New York's Fifth Avenue with a placard: THE CENSORED MIKE.

In his later autobiography, *False Witness*, Matusow recanted; in the grittiest detail, he admitted committing perjury and conspiring with U.S. attorneys to give false testimony. His conscience had caught up with him, but the price was that no one, right or left, trusted him. For his scruples, Harvey the ex-ex-Communist received five years in Lewisburg Federal Penitentiary.

The Weavers struggled through 1952, but by the following spring they realized they had lost the battle. After their last session under the Decca contract, the group took a sabbatical, which, as Lee Hays joked, "turned into a Mondayical and Tuesdayical." Yet in the left-wing community where they had started, their reputation remained high; when the Rosenbergs were executed a few months later, Lee Hays was told that they asked to hear the Weavers' "Goodnight Irene" on their way to the electric chair.

Counterattack and the FBI succeeded in blacklisting the Weavers, but "If I Had a Hammer" was unconquerable. The song had a specific radical message in 1952; when Seeger suggested the Weavers perform it on bookings, one of them answered, "Oh, no. We can't get away with anything like that."

"Why was it controversial?" Pete reflected. "In 1949 only 'Commies' used words like 'peace' and 'freedom.'. . . The message was that we have got tools and we are going to succeed. This is what a lot of spirituals say. We will overcome. I *have* a hammer. The last verse didn't say 'But there ain't no hammer, there ain't no bell, there ain't no song but honey, I got you.' We could have said that! The last verse says 'I *have* a hammer, I *have* a bell, I *have* a song.' Here it is. 'It's the hammer of justice, it's the bell of freedom, the song of love.' " No one could take these away.

The Weavers never had the opportunity to make a hit of "If I Had a Hammer"—that honor fell to Peter, Paul and Mary—but they had the satisfaction of seeing that no edict and no committee could kill a song. Songs, like revolutions, must often outlive their creators to take root. The great ones—whether commercialized, lost, or rediscovered—have a life of their own.

With the Weavers disbanded, Pete Seeger was on his own. He could sing for whomever he pleased, and one of the first engagements he accepted was a People's Artists hootenanny. Thousands of people jammed into a hall and sang their heads off. "I haven't been as far away as you might think," he told the cheering crowd.

Pete's love-hate relationship with Irwin reemerged when he stepped back into the sectarian world of People's Artists. He respected Irwin's commitment, for Silber had adopted the organizer's life Pete fantasized about, eventually entering the third circle of Party leadership. For now, Seeger made his peace with the idealogue, overlooking his priggish attacks on the Weavers. The journalist in Seeger itched to start a column for *Sing Out!*

This wouldn't bring in any money, however, and Seeger's finances hadn't materially improved since the end of People's Songs; he was one of America's best-known unemployable musicians. Thousands of less famous people suffered the same pressures and gave up their professions: Journalists went into advertising, professors drove cabs. He might have taken the road his friends Earl Robinson and Mill Lampell had: dividing himself between commercial work in Hollywood and more private progressive activities. Pete preferred to keep singing his own tunes, even if he starved. Construction on the house slowed as their savings went for food and gas; with cement at $1.25 a bag, they could afford only one bag at a time.

If no jobs were open to him, he would create his own: People always want entertainment, and a few places still knew him as a singer rather than the Red Menace of American Music. Toshi and Pete decided he should try barnstorming the country, playing in small colleges and churches; he made up a brochure, which he laid out with Toshi's help. She licked the stamps, and they sent out hundreds of them.

"Pete went underground," singer Don McLean explained. "He started doing fifty-dollar bookings, then twenty-five-dollar dates at schoolhouses, auditoriums, and eventually college campuses. He definitely pioneered what we know today as the college circuit. . . . He persevered and went out like Kilroy, sowing seeds at a grass-roots level for many, many years. The blacklist was the best thing that ever happened to him; it forced him into a situation of struggle, which he thrived on."

"Thrived" may be too optimistic. Seeger survived the early fifties, but only as a man forced to trudge across America, carrying his banjo into forty states. He eventually found an audience for his music where none previously existed. He had his hammer and his song; and these peripatetic years steeped Seeger in the life of America's small towns and bustling cities. From this point on, his career had a never-say-die glamour which only increased with each further setback.

Seeger found a new hero for his travels, a Yankee who attended Harvard and adopted Indian ways: Johnny Appleseed (John Chapman, 1774–1845). Pete named a new column in *Sing Out!* after this folk legend. As a boy, Chapman loved to hike through the rocky forests of Massachusetts and western Pennsylvania. At Harvard, he (like Seeger) was moved by the Swedish writer Swedenborg's antimaterialism. He earned his living by an invented profession—supplying farmers with apple orchards; Chapman would trade a night's lodging for apple seeds, just as Seeger had traded his paintings—though Chapman, unlike Pete, had a head for business. "Many thought him eccentric, thousands loved him," Seeger wrote, "but all recognized the practicality of his system." In his later years, Chapman helped slaves escape along the Underground Railroad. Leading a spartan personal life, he never married, and early sold the only home he ever had. Johnny Appleseed was, in short, a social worker at large, a man responsible only to his principles, the sort of American Seeger could admire.

In the early fifties, Seeger began what he called his "cultural guerrilla tactics." With no possibility of arranging formal radio or TV appearances, he turned to the surprise attack.

"I'd call up a local TV or radio station, and say, 'Is there a TV show I can come on?'

" 'Who are you?' they'd ask.

" 'Pete Seeger.'

" 'Well, what do you do?'

" 'I sing folk songs.'

" 'Oh, you were with the Weavers. Sure, I remember, "Goodnight Irene." Come on up, we'll chat a moment. I'll play your record—singing at the local college tonight? Good.'

"I'd go up there and we'd talk for five or ten minutes. Then he'd play some songs, and I'd be away before the American Legion could mobilize itself to protest this Communist fellow on the air."

Seeger worked effectively, but "guerrilla tactics" are a grandiose name for his efforts. In the 1950s, an underground *did* exist in the U.S., including Seeger's former comrades. The Communist Party, expecting its leaders to be assassinated in an armed fascist uprising, had set up a clandestine network of cadres "in deep freeze." These tactics unfortunately reinforced the impression created by anti-Communist "I Spy" films and television programs. In June 1954, a Harvard poll found that fifty-two percent of Americans favored imprisonment for Party members. Previously, the government had only charged Party leaders with advocating—not organizing—revolution; now it appeared that all who were Party members in 1948 would be eligible for prosecution and ten years in prison—including Pete Seeger.

For an entertainer, the gravest worry was keeping an audience. Seeger had been driven first from nightclubs, then from the music industry into his own circuit of schools and summer camps. Even to children, he sang subversive songs: "Be Kind to Your Parents" ("though they don't deserve it") and the "Children's Declaration of Independence" ("I will just do nothing at all, I will not eat my vegetables. . . .").

Children and adults both found Seeger's concerts a novelty. Not only did he sing totally different music from what they heard on the radio, he had this way—others might have made it a gimmick—of getting crowds singing. For the unprepared, it could be a startling experience. "The concert was like none I've ever seen," said a writer for the *Providence Journal* in 1953. "He let us sing the ballads with him."

Despite his growing popularity, Pete's media blacklist lumbered on.

Apparently his only nationally syndicated TV appearance in the 1950s was on Hugh Hefner's Playboy series, where Pete did his best to play banjo surrounded by bouncing "bunnies." His steady work came from teaching; folklorist and camp director Norman Studer hired him for music assemblies at Camp Woodland and the Downtown Community School, a liberal humanist school in Greenwich Village. Seeger earned twenty-two dollars a week, and he was glad to get it. One summer in the early fifties, he sang regularly at a summer camp in Lenox, Massachusetts; he and Toshi were jubilant when they discovered a nearby hotel that would pay him an additional twenty-five dollars a night. "Those were his bookings for the summer," Toshi said dryly. "Forty-five dollars a week." To earn this sum, he had to drive two hundred miles, round trip.

He had an alternative to this one-bag-at-a-time life style, even if he abhorred it: He might have done commercials and jingles; he might have worked a job at the nearby textile mill to support his songwriting. Or, with his Harvard pedigree and family connections, he could have taken up insurance (as Charles Ives did) or a profession. Except for his unquenchable need to sing with people, he might have become an executive, who serenaded the family on holidays with an old-but-treasured guitar.

Fortunately, Seeger found a patron in Folkways Records and his old friend Moe Asch, the visionary of the folk-song set. Despite mikes falling off rickety stands, and people opening the studio door and spoiling his recordings, Moe Asch and his assistant Marian Distler documented an American folk song revival long before anyone cared to buy the records.

"He was always the same old reliable sweet Moe," Bess Lomax said. "He went bankrupt and started back in again. He never paid us a cent of royalties, but if you were really flat—and most of us were—you could always drop by to see Moe, and he would invite you to lunch. Always the perfect gentleman, Moe would give you a couple of dollars, saying, with a twinkle in his eyes, 'Just so you can take a taxi home.' "

Others called Moe paternalistic; when Earl Robinson complained about not receiving royalties, Moe threatened to drop his records from the catalog. Asch had a violent, explosive temper and was not above manipulating his artists; depending on where one stood in his hierarchy, he was a benevolent or callous godfather.

To Pete, Moe was sweetness and light; he actually kept the Seegers eating throughout the fifties, by paying a fixed weekly sum—in the beginning, twenty-five dollars—"in lieu of royalties." Asch's generosity proved a bonanza for him in later years.

From time to time, Seeger would visit Moe's cluttered studio, with tapes spilling out of boxes and papers heaped in a corner with unanswered mail. There he would record an album in two days. On the first, Seeger brought in his instruments and a list of songs. He'd play one through, and if Moe liked the take, they went on to the next. The following day, they listened to the tapes. Pete never knew which songs would come out; Moe issued them as he saw fit. By 1955 Folkways had released twenty-nine Seeger albums, including the little-known "Darling Corey" and "The Goofing Off Suite," which show his mastery of traditional Appalachian banjo and his experiments in fusing classical and folk styles—on one record, Seeger rescored for banjo a duet from Beethoven's Seventh Symphony; the Chorale from his Ninth Symphony; and "Jesu, Joy of Man's Desiring" from Bach's Cantata 147 (a selection that must have pleased Pete's mother).

The short, affable son of the great Yiddish writer Sholem Asch, Moe was flexible and completely loyal; he didn't care what anybody said about Seeger or Communist-front politics. He didn't even care about making money. Moe allowed Seeger his own projects, such as the impractical idea of reissuing the Almanacs' "Talking Union" at a time when no more than a half dozen unions would purchase a copy.

In his recordings of this period, Seeger sought a cleaner, purer sound, closer to the original folk tunes than his big band numbers with the Weavers. This coincided with a new interest in folklore, dormant since his collecting trips in Alabama and Saipan. To begin the transition from performer to researcher, he applied for a Guggenheim fellowship in 1953 to make a "Survey of Instrumental Techniques in American Folk music." The grant was to underwrite expenses for field trips to film guitar, banjo, dulcimer, fiddle, and harmonica styles. The films were for "composers of the future"; the musician foresaw "a whole generation of young amateur musicians turning to folk music," to produce "handrolled, homemade music." Though Pete lacked a university degree, he clearly knew his field. Why shouldn't he receive the recognition that Alan Lomax had? Alan received *his* Guggenheim in 1947, before leaving the U.S. for Great Britain, where he maintained unofficial residence until blacklisting abated in the late fifties.

If the Guggenheim Foundation hadn't rejected Seeger's application following Matusow's testimony, he might have become a folk-song collector rather than a folk-song performer. The decision was probably a lucky one for American music.

Despite this turndown Seeger stubbornly pursued his new career, publishing articles in *Music Library Association Notes* and the *Journal of American*

Folklore. In 1955 he wrote a pamphlet on the chalil, an Israeli shepherd's flute. But no matter how scholarly his work, his singing and politics remained too controversial for the universities. No foundation came forth to sponsor his research. When Irwin Silber received a commendation from the Soviet Union calling him "the great American musicologist," Pete laughed, but with an edge of bitterness at the recognition denied him.

Following her return from the Weavers' tour, Toshi worked long hours to strengthen the family's ties to the Beacon community. While her husband was out chopping wood for the school, Toshi had joined the PTA; in 1952, she had been elected president. Despite her efforts, acceptance came only gradually, in part because of the city people who visited the Seeger place.

These visitors took part in what Lee Hays wryly called, "Seeger's Slave Gangs." Each summer anywhere from five to thirty-five people would camp on their land, helping to build the cabin (and later a barn). Peggy Seeger, who spent her teenage summers there, remembered it as one long folk festival: "You'd have all the New York types coming up. They'd forsake Washington Square for the weekend to come scrape logs or run up and down the hill for water." Occasionally someone would sit and play the banjo all weekend, in which case they'd put him in front of a mike with speakers all over the hill. There was music every evening: "How Pete had the energy to do it, I don't know. The man is *inexhaustible.*"

When Pete was not out on tour, he labored alongside his friends under the cooling shade of the birch and maple trees. Music filled their days, and even the long, warm nights could barely contain the singing. When the last songs were sung, the bodies wriggled down in their sleeping bags. In the morning the work and songs resumed.

A then eight-year-old visitor later remembered the scene as mysterious, compared to life in the city: "There was no electricity or running water." Everyone ate dinner outdoors, around an open fire, and they sang away the last of the daylight. Instead of chasing down MacDougal Street to a Party caucus, Pete dug up the garden on his hill overlooking the Hudson. His life had a lulling calm; for once no one seemed to be investigating him. He had more time to be a father, and to notice the first leaves turn color in the woods. Yet even the most peaceful days would change, as the river darkened suddenly and a gray cloud swept down, the wind striking roughly at the sailboats in the water. Thunder rattled the cliffs as a storm shook and tore at the river's glossy surface. Towlines of lightning flickered toward the hillside where Seeger and his guests worked. The rain came in drops, then sheets, until visibility fell to a few feet, and the soil drained in streams of clay-colored water.

For that short time, the group huddled inside, singing rain songs or tending a fire. Seeger would gaze out the window at his drenched foundations; he was so far from seeing his building complete.

Nineteen fifty-five brought a storm of a different kind into Seeger's life, as controversy overshadowed his performances. In January he sang at Pennsylvania's Bucknell University and chatted with a reporter from the *Sunbury Daily Item*. When the interviewer pressed Seeger to explain Matusow's allegations, the exchange grew strained. Then Pete pulled a guitar onto his lap and strummed as they talked—"and the tenseness left the conversation."

"I am a loyal American." Seeger sighed. "It's a terrible thing to be accused of being a Communist. You can never prove that it is not true, and it follows you everywhere." Pete won over the reporter by being disingenuous. Obviously he could never disprove charges of Party membership, but for reasons other than he let on—because he *had* been a member. Woody also dodged questions like these, insisting: "I'm not a Communist, but I've been in the red all my life."

Seeger had hundreds of similar discussions, where only the details of his affiliation was raised, and never its meaning: Was Party membership supposed to make him a worse singer? Did political involvement turn his austere moralism to hypocrisy, as driving a Jaguar might? Seeger often considered revealing his Party relationship, but feared that this would invite legal (and physical) attacks—perhaps on his family. Yet evading questions produced an increasing internal pressure: He felt he ought to speak out, but at the same time he sensed he shouldn't.

Matusow's allegations preceded Seeger everywhere, but often he booby-trapped his would-be censors. In April 1955, Pete was scheduled into the Chicago Art Institute, which asked him for an advance list of his songs. Seeger was an old hand at these challenges; he answered that his feeling for an audience determined what he sang, but he would send them a list of possible songs. The Art Institute then rejected three as too controversial: "UAW-CIO" (an Almanac tune from 1942); "Lincoln and Liberty" (an 1860 campaign song used not only by Lincoln, but by Horace Greeley and Henry Clay); and another campaign song, "Rejoice, Columbia's Sons," whose chorus goes:

> *Rejoice, Columbia's sons, rejoice*
> *To tyrants never bend a knee*
> *But join with heart and soul and voice*
> *For Jefferson and liberty.*

Seeger didn't sing the offending songs. On the other hand, he had never promised not to *talk about* singing them. He treated the audience to a blistering recital of his correspondence with the Art Institute.

At least he no longer had left-wing censors; once the Weavers disbanded, Irwin Silber and *Sing Out*! praised them profusely, calling Pete "an outstanding people's artist of the generation" and pointing out that he had sung for more people "in the flesh" than any other singer of folk songs in the history of the United States. "Self-appointed vigilantes of our time began to attack the Weavers," Irwin commented innocently, excluding himself. These tributes were no doubt welcome; but they were also a reminder that radicals sometimes embrace failure more easily than success, that losing for the right cause can seem superior to winning.

At last summer came. Schools were on vacation, and Pete spent more time at home, where visitors were already camped and erecting a barn/office where Pete could plunk away in peace. In the first week in August 1955 Seeger and his helpers prepared to raise the barn's walls. He was so engrossed in his work that at first he didn't notice the shiny black car that bounced up his driveway in a cloud of dust. The car stopped and a man in a suit got out. He walked straight toward Pete.

"Are you Pete Seeger?" the man asked. Pete said he was.

"I've got something for you," he said, handing him an envelope and turning on his heel. Pete's eye caught the seal of the U.S. House of Representatives: It was a subpoena from the House Committee on Un-American Activities to testify in two weeks.

Pete stood motionless at the top of the driveway. He heard the activity all around him: saws stripping trees of bark, hammering, the sounds of teenagers laughing as they hauled water up from the brook. For five years he'd been expecting this, his turn before the congressional committee that specialized in harassing left-wing artists and professionals. Many who were called to testify lost their jobs or ended up with jail terms and fines for refusing to cooperate; the resulting chaos broke up families, even caused suicides. He turned back toward the house, where he'd have to tell Toshi, and braced himself for the next weeks.

It wasn't so long ago that he had talked with Oscar Brand about testifying; that had been relatively painless. When Josh White, a close friend from the Almanac days, had actually testified, it had cut Seeger to the quick.

"I wanted to write Josh and let him know what I felt. . . . He'd hated [HUAC's John] Rankin so much! The Josh White I know would literally rather have died than go and crawl before that committee. I found out he had called Robeson the night before and said, 'Paul, I just have to let you know that tomorrow I have to go and make a heel of myself.'

" 'Well, why do you have to?' Robeson said.

" 'I can't tell you why, but I just have to, I don't have any choice.' "

Seeger shuddered at the memory. He had never mailed the letter he'd written Josh. He still had it in his desk: a picture of a guitar, broken in two.

Now it was his turn to testify—just when he was back on his feet financially. In the last two years he had regained his audience, tromping from one school to another like a singing salesman. The concerts weren't much, but they were all he had. If only HUAC had subpoenaed him following Matusow's testimony; at least he wouldn't have had to go through this all another time. Now, if liberal schools and camps continued hiring him, they might face a subpoena of their own and possible bankruptcy from legal expenses. Counting the blacklists of the Almanacs and the Weavers, this made a third round of right-wing attacks.

As usual, Toshi took care of practical arrangements. She found a lawyer—Paul Ross of the Madison Avenue firm of Wolf, Popper, Wolf, Ross & Jones—and arranged to meet with previously subpoenaed friends to find out what to expect. The situation didn't look good, Ross told them. Apparently if the witness didn't plan to cooperate—which Pete didn't—the most common choice was to invoke the Fifth Amendment (and refuse to testify against yourself) or the "modified Fifth," the position Lillian Hellman described in *Scoundrel Time*: testifying about one's own life, but not about one's friends; the third alternative was the First Amendment. Challenging the Committee on First Amendment grounds, however, meant years of court battle, with no assurance of avoiding jail at the end. The Hollywood Ten had tried this and received a year in prison. Think it over carefully, the lawyer advised.

None of these options appealed to Seeger. "Unfriendly" witnesses always had a hard time, as Frank Donner wrote in *The Un-Americans*: "He knows that the Committee demands his physical presence in the hearing room for no reason other than to make him a target of its hostility, to have him photographed, exhibited and branded. . . . He knows that the vandalism, ostracism, insults, crank calls and hate letters that he and his family have already suffered are but the opening stages of a continuing ordeal . . . that his family faces a kind of community outlawry. Most of all—and here the tension arose between Seeger's extreme moralism and the laws that confronted him—"he is tormented by the awareness that he is being punished without valid cause, and deprived, by manipulated prejudice, of his fundamental rights as an American."

From HUAC, Seeger could expect none of the privileges guaranteed citizens in a court of law. He had no right to be informed in advance of the charges against him; no right to cross-examine accusing witnesses or present his own evidence; and no right to be represented by counsel, except in an advisory role.

Pete had expected a subpoena years ago and talked over his situation with Charles Seeger.

"Father," Pete said, "I sometimes wonder if it wouldn't be more sensible just to give up and go to prison. It'd be one or two years. Friend of mine is there now and I went to visit him—it's not so bad."

"I begged him not to do it," Charles remembered, bringing up parental concerns: He was not a boy now, he had a family to support; he could do more good outside prison than by rotting away inside.

Pete's father had his own reasons for wanting him to stay out of trouble; Charles was himself under surveillance by the FBI. He had only two years to go before retirement and a pension (barely enough to support Ruth and their four children), but each year the red-hunters' nets drew tighter around him. As one of the founders of the International Folk Music Council, he had enjoyed a diplomatic passport in 1950. In 1951 he was downgraded to a regular passport, without explanation. In 1952 his passport was suddenly limited to official travel. And in 1953, though he was now a member of a UNESCO conference on world music, Charles's passport was revoked; no one would say why. On top of his other troubles, Ruth had fallen ill. He went to the head of the passport division and volunteered to quit his job at the Pan American Union—where he'd worked since 1940—to "keep things down."

His sacrifice didn't help. The FBI visited the elderly Seeger in his home—arriving almost the same day doctors discovered Ruth had incurable cancer. "They really grilled me. I confessed to being a member of the Composers' Collective." The Bureau brought up his days in Berkeley and his refusal to buy war bonds; everything was in the files. Charles Seeger eventually got his passport, but the price meant humiliation by the FBI. Soon afterward, Ruth died of cancer.

The year Pete received his subpoena, Charles had moved the family to Cambridge, where his eldest daughter Peggy attended Radcliffe. Charles didn't tell the children how he'd been forced from his job. His ex-wife Constance, now in her sixties, was more upset by Pete's subpoena. In her retirement in Florida she had grown more conservative. She didn't know what to make of her youngest boy. Not only was he moving further from the virtuoso she had hoped for, now he was in trouble with the law. Pete remembered her acting "pretty brave, all considered," comforting herself that "I'm not responsible for what my son does." If Pete landed himself in jail for contempt of Congress, it would be that stubborn streak of his that got him there.

Aunt Elsie was more supportive. Pete wrote to Charles's sister, the kindly woman who had taught him to draw at Patterson and now was a recognized historian, her *Pageant of Russian History* having recently appeared. "No, I am not troubled or embarrassed," she wrote back, "I am disgusted at the demand that people inform on their former associates and hope that both you and Arthur Miller [scheduled to testify later] will refuse."

Discussions about Pete's legal alternatives continued nonstop with lawyers and friends. Whatever he and Toshi decided, advisers warned, the decision would haunt them. He already knew he wouldn't cooperate with HUAC. Once he'd decided to fight, however, the next step was neither obvious nor easy. A number of options lay before him, some more dangerous than others.

One of the most infuriating parts of Seeger's situation was the shadiness of HUAC's legal authority. The U.S. Constitution has no provision for government by exposure; Congress may only enact laws. From this beginning, Congress assumed the power to hold investigative hearings to inform their lawmaking—but HUAC's showy interrogations did not produce much legislation. By 1955 the Committee was seventeen years old; having long ago exhausted or jailed its most headline-worthy witnesses, the Committee now played reruns and the also-featured. HUAC's goal was not gathering information so much as impugning the reputations of witnesses unwilling to provide names HUAC already knew. Obviously Seeger was not alone in opposing this virtual character assassination. The year of his subpoena, HUAC called 529 witnesses; and an incredible 464 (88 percent) remained silent.

Seeger had to decide which draught to swallow: a short, bitter drink of gall, as he took the Fifth; or the nettle cup of litigating his First Amendment right to free speech—in his case, free song. Though sweeter, this second drink cost far more time, money, and was not without unpleasant after-effects.

Pete plowed this ground repeatedly with Toshi and Paul Ross: "The expected move would have been to take the Fifth. That was the easiest thing, and the case would have been dismissed. On the other hand, everywhere I went, I would have had to face 'Oh, you're one of those Fifth Amendment Communists . . .' I didn't want to run down my friends who did use the Fifth Amendment, but I didn't choose to use it." The presumption of guilt was more than Pete could stomach.

Seeger also felt a duty to defy HUAC because "I was peculiarly able to do it—after all, there was no job I could be fired from." In 1953 I. F. Stone had written: "Great faiths can only be preserved by men willing to live by them. . . . [HUAC's violation of the First Amendment] cannot be tested until someone dares invite prosecution for contempt." Seeger was precisely the person to take up such a dare.

Scheduled to testify at the same session, Lee Hays had already made up *his* mind: "I wanted to take the Fifth and be done with the whole thing. I never did think much of the 'Hurrah!' side of the First Amendment." According to Lee, Harold Leventhal, now acting as Pete's manager, also argued him toward the simple route. How, Pete was asked, did he intend to pay for a First Amendment battle? He had to admit he had no idea.

As the days ticked by, he grew more and more disturbed. From his window, he looked out at the wood for the barn. In the last stormy days, all work had stopped; his tools and siding sat forlornly by the side of the cabin. Seeger hiked off by himself with a notebook, jotting down answers to as many of HUAC's probes as he could anticipate: "That question's like 'When did you stop beating you wife?'" He couldn't help his outrage—men he considered a national disgrace would question *his* patriotism, and his right to sing where and when he pleased. "You are the un-Americans," he wanted to shout at them.

"Not only have I not done anything criminal or subversive," Seeger planned to state, "but no one I know has, or would. Immoral or sinful, perhaps, but not criminal or subversive—why I'm often accused by family and friends of being an old New England Puritan." Seeger's anger finally led him to immodesty. "(Are you a radical?) Why, yes, you know, like Jesus Christ was. And a number of my ancestors were."

These jottings were Seeger's rehearsals for inquisition. He tried to clear his mind of pressure, but for this he needed more than a notebook.

Where Have All the Flowers Gone

8

A FEW DAYS before his HUAC testimony, in mid-August 1955, Pete Seeger was strumming banjo for summer campers at Camp Woodland, nestled in the green Catskill Mountains of New York. Singing was his tonic and private remedy for law books, and Pete indulged himself, stealing time from his worries.

His stage was a wooded amphitheater cut into a hillside, with gray shale covering the brown, loamy soil. The sun dried the dew from the moss, which gave off the smell of warm woods and shadow. Kids crowded in to hear the man adults whispered about: "What's so dangerous about *him*?" an eight-year-old asked disappointedly. To the children, his banjo seemed as long as a canoe. The metal pegs shone and the strings glinted like taut metal hairs. He swiped the strings gently, barely touching them with his nails. The children absorbed his music; a few of the words passed them by, but others caught in their memory, where the songs lay like broken pottery until patched together at the next singing.

Naturally, the children knew nothing about Pete's legal trouble, and he didn't force it on them. He wanted a morning of good singing, an excuse to be outside in the woods, playing banjo instead of writing out statements and pondering appeals. Once HUAC finished with him, there was no telling when he'd get another chance. He sang "Die Gedanken Sind Frei" ("Thoughts Are Free") that morning, and his voice nearly cracked. Then he sang his Bantu story-song, 'Abiyoyo," about a wicked giant in the days before congressional investigations.

"In a little town there were two outcasts: a boy who played the ukulele incessantly and his father, a magician, who loved to make things disappear. The boy's constant plunking and the father's practical joking were not popular. The father would wave his wand and make glasses of soda disappear on hot afternoons" (boos from the under-eights in the audience). "Chairs disappeared just as people would sit down in them" (roars of laughter, as Pete sat in midair).

"One day the town's much-feared giant, Abiyoyo, appeared. Strong men fainted! He had long matted hair, because he never combed it" (oooooh). "Long scary fingernails, 'cause he never cut them (ooooooooh). "And green slobbery teeth 'cause he never brushed them" (children inched down to the stage, looking for an adult hand to hold). "The townspeople cried 'Run for your lives, Abiyoyo's coming.'

"The father said to the son, 'God, if I could just find a way to make him lie down, I could make him disappear, and we'd save the town.' The boy thought about it for a moment and started strumming his ukulele. He began to play a song. 'Abiyoyo, Abiyoyo, Abiyoyo, Abiyoyo, Abiyoyo, Abiyoyo, Abiyoyo.' " (Pete pranced around, strumming his banjo like a ukulele.) "Well, the giant had never heard a song about himself, and he got mighty proud. A foolish grin spread across Abiyoyo's hairy face." (Pete produced a slobbery monster grin.) "He began to sing the song. Soon he started to dance. 'Abiyoyo, Abiyoyo, Abiyoyo, Abiyoyo.' Well, he danced some more and he began to get tired. 'Abioyoy-puff-Abipuff-yo-yo-puff-puff.' He fell on the ground." (Pete staggered and stopped.) " 'Zip-zip' went the father's magic wand and Abiyoyo was gone.

"Well, the townspeople poured in and the boy and his father were great heroes. 'Come on back, bring your damn ukulele, we don't even mind the practical jokes.' And the whole town began to sing" (the banjo pointed into the crowd, and eighty squeaky voices sang at the top of their lungs), " 'Abiyoyo, Abiyoyo' " (kids slid off their seats), " 'Abiyoyo, Abiyoyo, Abiyoyo.' "

At the end of the song, Pete, still huffing, said, "Some good stories have a moral: here, one good song beat a giant. Next week, I'll be questioned by some men who want me to stop singing. Maybe they've talked to your parents." A few of the older children looked around knowingly. Pete quietly strummed the chords to "Abiyoyo," captivating an audience that would stick by him for decades, through Bo Diddley and the Beatles.

"Even though the townspeople scoffed at the boy's music," he continued, "it helped solve their troubles. It's not what *I* sing, but how *you* sing. A good song reminds us what we're fighting for. Help me with this one:"

> *We'll sing out a danger* ©
> *We'll sing out a warning*
> *We'll sing out love between*
> *My brothers and my sisters*
> *All over this land.*

Anti-Communists didn't bother about Pete's singing for kids; and so when the Weavers disbanded, he made his young audiences his singing group. This long march through the summer camps and schools was an unexpected by-product of the blacklist. It started from necessity, but like many of Seeger's enthusiasms, he soon made it a creed. In *Sing Out!* he praised "the thousands of boys and girls who today are using their guitars and their songs to plant the seeds of a better tomorrow." Seeger became a gardener of song, fertilizing and breaking ground at every stop. But if Ted Kirkpatrick, editor of *Counterattack,* rejoiced that the former nightclub star earned twenty dollars a show in summer camps, he underestimated Seeger and his determination to be heard.

Before Pete headed home from camp, he stopped at the mess hall to eat a mammoth dinner. The good food could not dull the metallic taste of apprehension, however; "You could tell Pete was upset by the way he'd talk about it," Bess remembered. "He was very serious about the hearing; this was no joke." Seeger's choice between the First and Fifth Amendments might today seem academic, but this same decision had brought bitter fights and recriminations to a generation of radicals. If he acted according to his material circumstances, the Fifth would be the logical choice; then he could have walked out the hearing doors a free man with a smallish blot on his moral armor. If he chose by character, he would storm at HUAC head-on, proclaiming for free speech.

Pete's discussions about HUAC with Paul Ross had now degenerated into arguments decidedly not Ross's fault. The attorney, formerly Mayor Fiorello La Guardia's right-hand man, had more patience than his client. One afternoon, stretched out in Paul's comfortable Madison Avenue office, Pete told Ross of his plans to get on the witness stand and tell the committee off.

"No, if I'm going to represent you, Pete, you have to take my advice. Don't argue with them. Be polite, and politely decline to answer."

"I want to get up there," Pete insisted, "and attack these guys for what they are, the worst of America, the rich hunters."

"Don't try and be a smartass," Paul repeated. "Don't be clever. Be polite and answer the question; if you're not going to answer it, say why." Each time the committee found him in contempt, Paul soberly reminded him, he was liable to a year in jail. Pete agreed to do his best, but he couldn't make any promises.

Former radicals continued to fill Pete's concerts, even as many tried to bury their political pasts. His performances provided an excuse for old friends to mingle and to pass on left-wing culture to their kids. In this way, Seeger helped preserve a community under siege. Children thought him a martyr and an adult who wasn't afraid of looking silly. He would squeal like a barn hinge at the top of his voice and croak like a frog. Such qualities made Seeger a new generation of fans in the 1950s, including the "red-diaper" babies who later sat in and marched their way through the 1960s. If a novelist is studied through the characters he devises, and the politician by the key votes and sudden reverses of his policies, the test of an entertainer such as Seeger is his audience.

As he vanished from public view on television and radio, Pete became the flag-bearer of the Left. He fit an American mold, the underdog seeking justice, a patriot whose peculiar heroism lay in acts of conscience; they called him the "Karl Marx of the Teenagers." Including progressive social clubs, summer communities, and unions, nearly 75,000 children grew up listening to Pete Seeger—not a large number in a country of 160 million. Pop stars like Little Richard or Fats Domino probably had twenty times as many fans. But Seeger's followers were more than record buyers; and he was more than an entertainer. He had become, in the broadest sense of the term, a music educator.

A growing number of nonradical young people also turned to Seeger as the authority on the five-string banjo; his children's records and traditional folk songs had a wholesome cult following. In person, his musical imagination was inspiring. One teenager who took banjo lessons from Seeger in 1954 remembered sitting with him on a bus one rainy afternoon. Pete stared off into space as they rode, then turned to the boy and said, "You know, we could do something to the rhythm of those wipers." "Pete's Eager," two Glasgow girls called him later, and earnestness wins the hearts of youth.

"Pete kept joking that all these kids would be adults someday," Moe Asch said. "*Then* he'd be popular—and that's just what happened. Seeger's vast audience in the 1960s would come from those same kids—who now ran the campus folk music club. They would bear any kind of controversy to get Seeger there."

On the evening of August 14, 1955, the House Committee on Un-American Activities arrived in New York for hearings on Communist infiltration of the entertainment industry. Three members of the committee, Gordon Scherer (D-Ohio), Edwin Willis (D-Louisiana), and Francis Walter, chairman (D-Pennsylvania) conducted the four-day hearings. They were welcomed to New York by anti-Communist notables Victor Lasky and Vince

Hartnett (who had allegedly supplied HUAC with documents to identify Seeger). Someone joked that the committee was hunting musicians overthrowing the government by "force and violins." Actually, the congressmen had not chosen Seeger or any of the twenty-two other witnesses testifying before them. The selection had been made months in advance under the previous chairman, Harold Velde, a man famous for the number (rather than quality) of his public hearings. Velde had even subpoenaed Harry Truman after the ex-President called HUAC "more un-American than the activities it is investigating."

The first day of the hearings, August 15, brought few surprises. Most of the witnesses were excused after taking the Fifth Amendment. That night, chairman Walter was the guest of honor at an anti-Communist rally where he claimed that ninety-nine percent of his witnesses had been reds. In Washington, I. F. Stone published a report on soldiers decommissioned because their families had left-liberal leanings; one soldier was accused of being "closely associated with your mother . . . a reported CP member, whom you continue to correspond with."

On the second day, Lee Hays testified. The actor Eliot Sullivan preceded him in the morning sessions, accompanied by his attorney, Bella Abzug. Sullivan refused to cite any amendment and attacked the committee. This put chairman Walter in a dour mood; he told his fellow congressmen that "it doesn't seem to matter" to the witness that he would be charged with contempt. "Of course it makes a difference to me!" Sullivan replied heatedly. "I have a wife and two children and I am anxious to work." Committee members promised he would pay for his speeches in jail. After lunch, Lee came to the stand; *The New York Times* dismissed him as "a burly sandy-haired folksinger." The first order of business was straightening out Hays's identity; it turned out another Lee Hays—a television actor greatly preoccupied for his reputation—had been subpoenaed by mistake. Asked about People's Songs, Lee invoked the Fifth Amendment; after another half-dozen questions brought the same response, Hays was excused. The audience, including Pete and his family, saw how effortless testifying could be—if the witness uncombatively took the Fifth.

The morning of Seeger's hearing, over breakfast, he read *The New York Times's* praise of chairman Walter for running HUAC's hearings with "decorum." "It is a duly constituted committee of Congress," the editorial commented, "and, as such, witnesses who fail to give it their cooperation must bear the onus of public suspicion that they have something to conceal."

A couple of hours later, Pete entered the hearing room in the imposing U.S. Court House on Foley Square, site of the Smith Act trials six years earlier. Toshi carried his banjo: She knew it would relax him to have it nearby. Pete quietly listened to Tony Kraber, a friend from People's Songs, cite both the First and Fifth Amendments in his defense. Then he watched Congressman Scherer needle the witness like a picador, until Kraber lost his temper.

Finally, Seeger's name was called, and he stepped forward, "amid the popping of flash bulbs . . . the clicking of still cameras, and the bustle of the press table." The high ceilings made the room echo, reducing all sounds to a dull clatter, over which the chairman's gavel was barely heard. Facing Seeger and his "silent" counsel—lawyers could not officially address the hearing—sat the three members of the committee and its chief counsel, Frank Tavenner, who did most of the questioning.

Of those interrogating Seeger, Francis Walter was by far the most imposing. His thick black-framed glasses and his thin gray hair, combed straight back, made him look perpetually sour, the sort who sues at the smallest dent in his car. Walter also headed two other committees, as a colleague pointed out: "One is the House Patronage Committee; if you cross him, you can't get an appointment through. The other is the House Immigration Committee; if you cross him there, you have no chance of getting some poor fellow into the U.S. through a private immigration bill." Spite and anger ruled Walter's emotions to the extent that *The Washington Post* once termed him "unfit" for public office; he continually conjured up a "terroristic Marxist Criminal Conspiracy."

Gordon Scherer was HUAC's "ideological sergeant-at-arms," a sponsor of the John Birch Society. Fond of phrases like "It is significant that . . . ," he specialized in carving innuendos out of coincidences, and glaring at witnesses to unsettle them. Scherer always made sure, in the heat of exchanges with witnesses, that the hearing record had everything necessary for quick and efficient contempt citations.

Representative Willis wasn't as vocal as his two colleagues. A newcomer to the committee, he was best known for his comment, "If you can't trust the FBI, whom are you going to trust?"

The first questions concerned Seeger's residence and occupation—with these, local vigilantes could take matters into their own hands. Seeger answered willingly: "I make my living as a banjo picker—sort of damning in some people's opinion." The committee ignored this veiled antagonism; Pete had promised Ross to behave himself, but it wouldn't be easy.

Though music hadn't been his intended profession, Seeger declared, "I continued singing and I guess I always will." Pete kept his anger in check, anticipating that his transcript would one day be published. On their side, the investigators had already chosen parts—Walters lorded his authority, Scherer scowled, and Willis watched silently.

Trouble began with the first substantive question. Tavenner asked Seeger about singing for the Communist Party, quoting an ad from the *Daily Worker.* The musician answered icily, "I refuse to answer that question whether it was a quote from *The New York Times* or the *Vegetarian Journal.*" The investigators now knew—if they hadn't guessed—that Seeger wasn't "friendly."

As an "unfriendly" witness, Seeger would be forbidden to sell liquor, collect unemployment, tend bar, or perform as a wrestler, if he was cited for contempt. Each state had different restrictions; in Washington, D.C., he couldn't legally tune a piano. To HUAC, he was just another unrepentant subversive, and they gave him no quarter:

> MR. SCHERER: He hasn't answered the question, and he merely said he wouldn't answer whether the article appeared in *The New York Times* or some other magazine. I ask you to direct the witness to answer the question.
>
> CHAIRMAN WALTER: I direct you to answer.
>
> MR. SEEGER: Sir, the whole line of questioning—
>
> CHAIRMAN WALTER: You have only been asked one question, so far.
>
> MR. SEEGER: I am not going to answer any questions as to my association, my philosophical or religious beliefs or my political beliefs, or how I voted in any election or any of these private affairs. I think these are very improper questions for any American to be asked, especially under such compulsion as this. . . .

The first round went to Seeger, for confounding his questioners; instead of citing an amendment to justify not answering, he dismissed their questions as improper. He sat before them, but he stared into the future. Seeger no longer spoke to anyone in the room; they had vanished, and his words were addressed to history.

Yet if Pete thought, as he sat there in his plaid shirt, checked suit jacket, and garish yellow tie, that the Committee would simply accept his statement and be done with him, he was mistaken.

Tavenner pulled out a clipping advertising Pete Seeger at a May Day rally in 1948. Had Mr. Seeger sung on that occasion? Seeger consulted with Paul Ross before answering:

MR. SEEGER: I feel that in my whole life I have never done anything of any conspiratorial nature and I resent very much
and very deeply the implication of being called before this
Committee that in some way because my opinions may be different from yours, or yours, Mr. Willis, or yours, Mr. Scherer,
that I am any less of an American than anybody else. I love
my country very deeply, sir.

CHAIRMAN WALTER: Why don't you make a little contribution toward preserving its institutions?

MR. SEEGER: I feel that my whole life is a contribution. That is why
I would like to tell you about it.

CHAIRMAN WALTER: I don't want to hear about it. . . .

MR. SCHERER: Let me understand. You are not relying on the Fifth
Amendment, are you?

MR. SEEGER: No, sir, although I do not want to in any way discredit
or depreciate the witnesses that have used the Fifth Amendment. . . .

As Pete waived his Fifth Amendment protection, his responses shrank
to one-liners such as: "I have given you my answer." He knew what he was
doing; he needed no reminders of the legal battles to come, where court
costs alone would amount to more than he earned in a year. He was mildly
awed at his courage: "I realized that I was fitting into a necessary role. . . .
This particular time, there was a job that had to be done, I was there to do
it. A soldier goes into training. You find yourself in battle and you know the
role you're supposed to fulfill. And similarly a musician trains to find himself on the stage." Seeger knew his duty and how to follow it through,
regardless of consequences.

In the hot, airless courtroom, Seeger and the committee implicitly
battled over patriotism: Who passed the loyalty oath—those who took it or
those who refused? Who was more American: Francis Walter, goading
witnesses to testify, or Pete Seeger, claiming no one should be questioned on
his beliefs? After questions on "Wasn't That a Time," a song they thought
subversive but which he considered deeply patriotic, Pete offered to perform the song for the committee.

The congressmen didn't know what to think. The request sounded like
a joke, but Pete wasn't kidding. He had a physical need to make his voice
heard, to demonstrate what he did with his life. Leadbelly had *his* chance to
sing his way out of trouble and succeeded. Perhaps Seeger hoped his song
might slay the giant.

Walter would hear none of it. The committee was accustomed to making people pay in full for disobedience: sending them to jail, ruining their personal lives and reputations. The fact that Seeger did not seem to care about HUAC's power probably disturbed the congressmen more than where or what he sang. When defied politely—and Seeger kept using "sir" in his answers, to his lawyer's delight—the committee became powerless. Their threats of contempt were real, as Seeger would discover, but if a witness would not play victim and soil himself, the committee became a Wizard of Oz confronted by a determined twelve-year-old.

Tavenner grimly pulled out more folders with clippings from the *Daily Worker,* and Seeger kept declaring his belief in the power of song—"My songs seem to cut across and find perhaps a unifying thing, basic humanity, and that is why I would love to be able to tell you about these songs, because I feel that you would agree with me more, sir."

Either Seeger was satirizing the committee (unlikely) or, like an early Christian, he genuinely believed in his power—and that of a song—to turn away wrath. Finally the Committee moved toward the Big Question—was he paid by the CP?

> MR. SEEGER: The answer is the same, and I take it that you are not interested in *all* of the different places that I have sung. Why don't you ask me about the churches and schools and other places?
>
> MR. TAVENNER: That is very laudable, indeed. . . . If you were acting for the Communist Party at these functions, we want to know it.

Seeger was continually tempted to open up his involvement with the Party. But if he, like Lillian Hellman, had been willing to testify on his own membership, the second question put to him would be "who else?" If he refused to answer this, he would be as much in contempt as if he had refused to answer at all. If he answered the second question, he would be confronted with others: "Who are your relatives? Your friends? Your business associates? Your acquaintances?" If he complied with these questions, wrote Dalton Trumbo of the Hollywood Ten, "he is involved in such a nauseous quagmire of betrayal that no man, however sympathetic to his predicament, can view him without loathing."

Despite Pete's efforts to control his temper, Tavenner finally provoked him.

> MR. TAVENNER: I hand you a photograph which was taken of the May Day parade in New York City in 1952, which shows the front rank of a group of individuals, and one is in a uniform

with military cap and insignia, and carrying a placard entitled
CENSORED. Will you examine it please and state whether or not
that is a photograph of you?

(*A document was handed to the witness.*)

MR. SEEGER: It is like Jesus Christ when asked by Pontius Pilate,
"Are you king of the Jews?"

CHAIRMAN WALTER: Stop that.

MR. SEEGER: Let someone else identify that picture.

Seeger was clearly shaken, and Scherer leaped in to press the advantage
home.

MR. SCHERER: Again, I understand that you are not invoking the
Fifth Amendment?

MR. SEEGER: That is correct.

MR. SCHERER: We are not accepting the answers or the reasons you
gave.

MR. SEEGER: That is your prerogative, sir.

Except for calling one of Pete's summer camps "slimy," Willis remained
silent. The others kept pushing Seeger: Did he understand he was in contempt? Didn't he want to save himself and name names?

MR. SEEGER: I am saying voluntarily that I have sung for almost
every religious group in the country, from Jewish and
Catholic, and Presbyterian and Holy Rollers and Revival
Churches. . . . I love my country very dearly, and I greatly
resent this implication that some of the places that I have sung
and some of the people that I have known, and some of my
opinions, whether they are religious or philosophical, or I
might be a vegetarian, make me any less of an American.

After nearly an hour under the lights, Seeger walked unsteadily from
the courtroom. The next day the committee adjourned the hearings, claiming they had succeeded "in alerting people to the situation in the theater."
The committee returned to prepare its contempt citations—back to Washington, "a city of whispers, of tapped phones and cautious meetings," as
Dalton Trumbo called it, "a city whose very air is polluted with the smell of
the secret police."

After the scorching day in New York, the return home to Beacon must
have been soothing. A creek ran behind the Seeger property, the perfect
place to sit and dangle his feet in the water or look up into the canopy of
blue sky and trees, thick with summer leaves. Home from school, the children splashed in the creek and shouted in the woods, where only the owls

and robins heard them. Toshi was digging up the garden for the fall plant-
ing and the weeding needed to be done. The view along the Hudson was
as restful as ever; in the distance, New York City resembled a ball of dust.

Here he passed the next few weeks, as he slowly faced the extreme
seriousness of his situation. Others had received a year in jail for refusing to
answer one question; he'd brushed off nearly two dozen. Having hobbled
the giant, he must now pay for his pleasure. Seeger busied himself with
simple tasks and for a while felt protected, far from legal harassment and
commotion.

Contempt of Congress citations proceeded routinely, and Seeger had
the dubious pleasure of knowing what lay ahead. First, the House would
vote to cite, then a federal grand jury would hand down an indictment. He
would appear in court and await his trial. Since the government won most
of these trials, Seeger could look forward to an expensive appeal in Circuit
Court and, if that was unsuccessful, to the U.S. Supreme Court. Then came
a fine and jail, perhaps for as much as ten years. By then the forest would all
have changed; his children would be teenagers.

The strain twisted inside Pete; "He never allowed himself to speak
out," Bess recalled, "and he resisted a lot of cheap shots he could have
gotten off at people who *didn't* behave so well." Yet he had worries enough
to cause a breakdown; all he owned was his cabin and his land, and bankruptcy from court costs could take these away.

From this point on, Pete's life was punctuated by a succession of court
dates which only people who have had serious legal trouble can appreciate.
He could count on Toshi, Moe Asch, Harold Leventhal, and his friends to
help him through the next years; but his prospects were poor. His life had
fallen into a pattern: initial success, attacks and censorship, and finally
privation. This had happened when the Almanacs rode the patriotic,
beat-Hitler sentiment, then lost their jobs and reputation to the blacklist.
Then there had been the Weavers' sudden rise, their painful fall, and his
long search to find an audience. Now, beginning anew, he had been slug-
ged again—just in time to lose a round of bookings as the school year
began. Any professor or administrator who hired Pete Seeger after that
testimony had to be willing to pay with his job for the privilege.

Not long after this, Pete began quoting a fragment of Walt Whitman's
poetry in his performances:

> *Have you heard that it was good to gain the day?*
> *I also say it is good to fall.*
> *Battles are lost in the same spirit they are won.*

Another part of this cycle of Seeger's was a burst of musical creativity which followed his personal disasters. In 1949, after People's Songs had fallen in shambles, he had turned inward for his most lasting tunes; his music was his hope. Now Seeger again looked to music for solace, and it did not desert him. Locked out of the clubs, he went into the recording studio, turning out discs at the astonishing rate of six per year from 1954 to 1958. (This level of production was due to Pete and Moe's complete disregard for normal recording procedures—Asch never even kept a list of Seeger's sessions.)

Many of the records were for children, and they introduced songs Americans now take for granted: "Frog Went A-Courtin'," "The Keeper and the Doe," "This Old Man." Probably a hundred thousand children first heard American folk music through these recordings.

In 1956 Folkways released *American Industrial Ballads,* one of the most comprehensive collections of American labor songs recorded. By playing fast, brief versions, Pete managed to squeeze twenty-four cuts on a single album, rescuing songs from obscure volumes. In 1957 Seeger's *America's Favorite Ballads* record was a best-selling LP.

Perhaps because of the pressures he kept inside, Seeger sang and played with a fervor he rarely matched before or after. Records had become his only outlet. He performed where he could, but since few heard him live, he visited Moe Asch's studio—where he was always welcome—to record for posterity.

While he shuttled between Beacon and New York to make records, most of the stay-at-home business fell to Toshi, who also bore the hostility Seeger's testimony had created locally.

In the Fifties, Beacon remained a bustling upstate town of ten thousand or so, with a hospital for the criminally insane and a textile factory. The people were of conservative Dutch, Irish, or northern European immigrant stock; passersby on Main Street sometimes stared at Pete and Toshi—imagine that, an interracial couple! Following the headlines about HUAC, "the family was scared, to say the least," Pete said. "I had been singing with the PTA, and they asked that we discontinue the group. They couldn't stand the controversy." The local principal called in his teachers and said, "I want you to let me know if anyone makes it hard on the Seeger children." By this time Danny was eight and Mika six; they had a new sister: a blonde, Asiatic-looking baby named Tinya. The Klansmen who had stoned the Seegers at Peekskill continued to live in the area, and when HUAC singled Seeger out, their suspicions grew. From time to time, Pete's kids would come home in tears after a name-calling session at school.

Toshi put aside her pottery to manage her husband's defense campaign, but at the price of her own career. Previously, she had launched the Weavers, kept track of Pete's bookings, and managed the family. Now, in addition to finishing a house lacking plumbing and privacy, where loads of itinerant folk singers trooped in at all hours, she coordinated meetings with lawyers and fellow defendants. The weight was almost too much for her to pull. Her socks were more hole than cloth, and carrying gallons of water up from the stream strained her back to a stoop; she paid a hard price for her husband's principle.

While Toshi ran Pete's affairs, he kept to the top of his hill, practicing and writing. Mornings, he'd drive down, pick up his mail and the groceries, and come home. Rarely did he find a friendly smile in town, though once a gray-haired hardware merchant looked Pete right in the eye and said, "I don't know what your politics are, young fellow, but this is America, you got a right to your opinion."

As if his troubles in Beacon weren't enough, more arrived by mail. Two weeks after the hearings, a letter came from a family in Pittsburgh: "Because of the recent adverse publicity, my family and security responsibilities force elimination of your plans to stop over with us on September 8. Though our acquaintanceship with you has never had any political under- or overtones, I'm afraid the times and temper will not understand." The letter sounded like its author sent a carbon to the FBI. "Save to show to his grandchildren," Pete penciled sadly in the margin. Somehow Seeger knew exactly what this note would mean twenty-five years later; he knew the world would change.

If the FBI didn't see that letter, they certainly read a lot of other mail on Seeger and his circle. A month before Seeger's HUAC testimony, the Bureau began a report to classify People's Artists as subversive under the Internal Security Act. In October their informants removed and duplicated the group's correspondence. The FBI monitored the group's mail and even its trash. J. Edgar Hoover wrote Assistant Attorney General William F. Tompkins discussing "technical installations" for gathering "data." Then, just as the FBI completed their investigation, the group dissolved for lack of funds.

The FBI's interest in folk music did not stop here. Throughout the fifties the Bureau actively recruited informants, including some who went on to small and large careers in folk music. The Bureau would approach a singer known to be on the outs with the Silber-Seeger axis, someone who wouldn't do benefits, for instance, or who mistook political criticism for censorship. The agent would appeal to the individual's patriotism, to his "good reputation," and occasionally to private information at their disposal. The FBI filed everything—the date the subject's father Americanized his name, the informer's fear that his name would be made public. Even more common was placing "volunteers" in People's Songs or People's Artists. If they played the guitar, so much the better; customarily, as in the case of Harvey Matt, their function was nonmusical—to report on meetings and copy documents. Once the Bureau sent a phony typewriter repairman up to the PA office; he managed to spend the entire morning tinkering with the keyboard while eavesdropping on the organizers of a benefit.

While FBI agents stole into People's Artists, Seeger worried about a vaster theft—of his audience. The Folkways recordings kept him singing, but Seeger was no studio musician; without an audience life paled. He thirsted for a crowd the way a wilting plant seeks nourishment. He looked for work as far away as California. To cover his travel and lodging, he was forced to perform four times a day there—twenty-five dollars was the maximum he could get. "So I sang at a school in the morning, another school in the afternoon, and a little playground later in the afternoon. In the evening, I did a party." At the end of a grinding day like this—four separate performances, with transportation required from one place to another—Seeger slept soundly.

His blacklisting not only exhausted him, it filed away at his soul. Pete was particularly demoralized when his union, Local 802 of the American Federation of Musicians, almost expelled him following his HUAC appearance. Getting kicked out of the union would have further barred Seeger from stages in New York, where union membership is often required by contract. The union actually held a preliminary hearing on Seeger; but Paul Ross reminded the executive board that the singer wasn't even accused of a crime—and it would take a pretty poor union to oust a member on hearsay. The board stopped short of lodging charges, but the devastating irony of the situation was not lost on him: The man who had done the most to spread labor songs in the U.S. was asked by his own union if he was loyal enough to be a musician.

Then organizations he had counted on for support began to hedge, and Seeger's sadness turned to cold sarcasm. The head of California's Idylwild Folk Music Workshop, Max Krone, asked him for a "forthright statement about present membership in any party advocating force or violence." "Come to think of it," Pete replied, "I am a registered Democrat. I rather think some of the Southern members of this group do believe in force and violence . . . if your board will overlook this, I will be glad to."

"Dear Mr. Seeger: We regret that we have to cancel your concert," began a January 1957 letter from the New York Historical Society. "We did not know until the last minute that there was any political unpleasantness . . . we have to be careful to avoid criticism and unpleasant publicity." Seeger crammed files full of correspondence with trustees who deeply regretted, sincerely apologized, and under-the-circumstances-sought-to-avoid having Seeger play in their communities.

Underlying these battles (and the hundreds that followed) was one critical factor which even his defenders rarely knew—that Seeger *had* been a member of the Communist Party. Though his participation was insignificant—over the years he had attended a few dozen meetings—at the point when his membership became a public issue, he did not step forward.

Suppose Pete had been blacklisted for actually belonging to the Communist Party, rather than for helping or associating with Communists—would Seeger have seemed less of a hero? Would there have been a feeling of: "Well, he got what he deserved"?

"This would have meant I'd have had to argue politics ninety percent of my time," Pete said defensively. "Let the songs carry it. It's misleading to get into all those arguments about words. I didn't want to do that. I wanted to sing songs." Seeger often preferred the complications of politics to vanish, leaving issues as sharply defined as a ship's mast against a clear sky, as uncompromised as a woodsman's lair.

In the mid-Fifties, public debate on Seeger centered on issues of free speech. Instead of asserting that Pete Seeger (and his music) was revolutionary, his partisans battled over his right of dissent, a battle liberals wage more comfortably. The public heard "Pete Seeger has a right to sing," not "Revolutionaries have a right to organize," or "Communists, too, have a right to free speech." Midway through his career, attention shifted from Seeger's musicianship to his symbolic role as a censored voice of the time.

Though he ultimately benefited from this shift, Seeger, preoccupied with truth, yearned to make his CP ties public. This tension had surfaced as early as 1950, when the Weavers first made their way out of Greenwich Village and into the fancy nightclubs. He had a dream then of stripping off his clothes in public and proclaiming himself "a nudist at heart." Lee's interpretation revealed his deep understanding of his friend: "Your great urge to unveil yourself for what you are is constantly thwarted, and you are in a turmoil of frustration and suspense."

Pete's discontent would have been far easier to bear if not for critical changes in the Communist Party U.S.A., which worsened his situation as an ex-Communist facing jail: Khrushchev's denunciation of Stalin and the invasion of Hungary by Soviet troops. Separately, each was momentous;

together and in quick succession, they marked that phase of an organization when its core shatters. The fallout affected even fellow travelers and lapsed members like Seeger.

In the spring of 1956, following release of its leaders jailed under the Smith Act, the CP reached the conclusion Pete had after Peekskill: that the Left must be heard more widely. But before the Party could consider any changes, Nikita Khrushchev gave his famous speech denouncing Stalin's crimes at the Party's Twentieth Congress. This came as a bombshell to members who had defended his excesses for decades—including Seeger, who had considered Stalin only "a hard driver."

Khrushchev's speech drove thousands from the already shrunken organization. Then, before the disbelief had waned, Hungary was invaded by Soviet troops. The *Daily Worker* dispatched a senior correspondent, but when he sent in reports sympathetic to the Hungarian rebels, the paper killed his stories.

Soon after these shifts, Seeger was singing in Canada when a Party member remarked how his world had changed. "Well, I don't think much has changed," Seeger snapped, leaving the other open-jawed. Refusing to take the Fifth Amendment was only the most recent evidence of Pete's individualism; the Party favored taking the Fifth to give comrades more time to work on the outside. Pete had been warned about this tendency. Earlier he had visited San Francisco and received a caution about a Berkeley friend—better not visit her any more. "Why not?" Pete had complained. "Simply because she *associates* with Trotskyites?"

He did not criticize the Party, however. Criticizing automatically made one a renegade, for the organization refused to distinguish the ex- from the anti-Communist. Members either followed Party discipline or they were out in the cold and suspect. An anti-Communist bard like Burl Ives could have a Hollywood career, but Pete would not break ranks. Newspapers promoted only the god-that-failed ex-Communist, but people actually took different routes on leaving the Party. The Paul Robesons or Pete Seegers did not find fault; to do so would have challenged not merely their pasts, but their dreams. To date, Seeger has never publicly criticized Soviet intervention in Hungary or Czechoslovakia.

As usual, the Trotskyite singers had a few sharp choruses to needle the Communists, this time a revision of "Talking Union."

> . . . *So he joined the Party, he was doing fine*
> *Parroting out that old Party Line.*
> *He'd carry an umbrella if the weather was fair*

> *'Cause if it rained in Moscow that's all he'd care*
>   *He was loyal,*
>   *True blue,*
> *Just like His Master's Voice.*

The Hungarian invasion and the denunciation of Stalin left Seeger in an awkward position. To risk jail for refusing to discuss his CP membership was bad enough; to go through this while doubting the Party must have been agony. Al Richmond, editor of *People's World*, called the situation "absolutely tragic."

Fortunately Seeger had something to fall back on: The Weavers were back together. Harold Leventhal had orchestrated a Weavers reunion concert at the end of 1955, bypassing the usual ifs-and-buts of a decision by renting Carnegie Hall and *then* telling the singers. Harold, born the same year as Seeger and like him a progressive, had given up garment manufacturing to move into the folk music field; he kept in touch with the Weavers. In the two-and-a-half-year lull, Ronnie Gilbert had married and had a child. Fred Hellerman had become a producer-arranger-publisher, and Lee Hays was writing mystery stories for *Ellery Queen's Magazine*. After a few rehearsals, the old harmonies fell into place. Old friends turned out and the concert was sold out months in advance. Life was picking up for Seeger; at least he had a group to perform with, as long as he could stay out of jail.

At a folk festival in Louisiana a few weeks after the Weavers' reunion, Pete had an amusing shock. After a performance, he accepted an invitation to sing Cajun songs at a private house outside of town: "They met me at the door, saying, 'Mr. Seeger, meet Congressman Willis.'

"You could have knocked me over with a feather. Willis [one of his interrogators from HUAC] didn't bat an eyelash, but there I was sitting in his house; we were singing songs, having a good time, and I could see him growing more and more uncomfortable, watching me sip his liquor. . . . He took me out in the kitchen and said, 'Mr. Seeger, small world, isn't it? How did you get here?'

"I told him I was invited down, and he said, 'Well, you're not welcome.' " Pete's first reaction was embarrassment for his hostess, but he relished the chance to sing; not only did the company find his songs innocent of subversion, the congressman's wife had been singing along gaily. "The local people tried their best for me to stay. I was due to sing in the public school and so on, but Willis said he'd raise a holy fuss. Well, they didn't want to embarrass him, and *I* didn't want to embarrass him—it wasn't his fault I got invited—so I said goodbye to my friends and went off to Houston." The incident showed that Seeger had been correct in his testimony. His songs did "cut across and find a unifying thing, basic humanity."

Soon after this, on July 26, 1956, the House of Representatives voted 373 to 9 to cite Pete Seeger and seven others (including playwright Arthur Miller) for contempt.

After the citation came an indictment, and then a trial. Seeger carried on as best he could, singing for young people at liberal colleges like Oberlin and Reed. En route to one of these concerts, Seeger had the inspiration for "Where Have All the Flowers Gone?"

On the plane, he pulled out his pocket-size song notebook: "Leafing through it, I came across three lines I'd written down, oh, at least a year or two before: 'Where are the flowers, the girls have plucked them. Where are the girls, they've all taken husbands. Where are the men, they're all in the army.' "

He'd read this in a novel by Mikhail Sholokhov, *And Quiet Flows the Don*; the three lines came from a Ukrainian folk song. For a year he had searched around for the original song, then given up, jotting down this fragment in hopes of using it some day. This time he glanced at the words, and "things just slipped into place."

For four or five years, Pete had also carried a musical phrase in his head, like an old man saving string: "long time passing." He had been struck by its melodic beauty: the four vowel sounds are sequential, opening up the mouth as they are sung. "All I knew was that those were three words I wanted to use in a song; I wasn't quite sure how, where, or when. Suddenly it fit with this 'Where have all the flowers gone—long time passing.' And, five minutes later, I had 'Long time ago.' Then without realizing it, I took a tune, a lumberjack version of "Drill Ye Tarriers Drill': it was as unconscious as Woody using 'Goodnight Irene' as the tune for 'Roll on Columbia.' "

> *Where have all the flowers gone?* ©
> *Long time passing.*
> *Where have all the flowers gone?*
> *Long time ago.*
> *Where have all the flowers gone?*
> *The girls have picked them, ev'ry one.*
> *Oh, when will you ever learn?*
> *Oh, when will you ever learn?*
>
> *Where have all the young girls gone?*
> *Long time passing.*

Where have all the young girls gone?
Long time ago.
Where have all the young girls gone?
They've taken husbands, every one.
Oh, when will you ever learn?
Oh, when will you ever learn?

Where have all the young men gone?
Long time passing.
Where have all the young men gone?
Long time ago.
Where have all the young men gone?
They're all in uniform.
Oh, when will you ever learn?
Oh, when will you ever learn?

At first, the song seemed too short to be serviceable, with only three verses. Pete sang it once in a medley of short tunes (released on a fascinating though obscure disc, "Rainbow Quest") and forgot about it.

But a song is like a child; once it gets out into the world on its own, it often surprises the parent. About three years later, around 1959 or 1960, Harold asked Pete whether he wrote "Where Have All the Flowers Gone?"—the Kingston Trio had recorded and claimed the song. When Pete called them up, they said, "We didn't know you'd recorded it; we'll take our name off."

The song traveled around the world. In Germany, Marlene Dietrich's daughter insisted she record it; both Peggy Seeger and Dominic Behan, the Irish singer, told Pete that it was his best song.

"When I came out to Camp Woodland the next time," Seeger continued, "I gave the words to a counselor, Joe Hickerson, and he sang it with his kids. That gave it more rhythm." Hickerson sang the first verse at the end, giving it a cyclical feel, and added two verses. After Peter, Paul and Mary recorded the song, it reached the hit parade.

A dark period had again produced one of Seeger's universal songs. The musician who thrives on poverty and despair has become a cliché; yet in Seeger's case, when everything tipped against him, when his liberty, career, and safety were in jeopardy, a spark inside ignited a song.

Pete Seeger, as Alan Lomax has pointed out, planned his life in five-year blocks, and in the mid-Fifties he set out to revive an interest in American folk music. His only chance for breaking the blacklist lay in preparing a new, widespread audience for his music. His survival depended on it. "I am glad to report partial success in my campaign to lead the younger generation astray," Seeger wrote in *Sing Out!*, "by persuading them to spend their college vacations hitch-hiking around the country, learning about people and regions." Seeger wrote this at a time when *Life* reported college students swallowing goldfish and crowding into phone booths. Pete had a different constituency. A friend suggested he owed his success to "an underlying sprightly militance, which youth, for good or bad, has admired."

In fact, he hoped not only for a folk-song revival, but a youth rebellion in the 1960s. He rarely left a young audience without tossing in songs like the antiestablishment "Poisoning the Students' Minds." Spreading folk music (both for his ideals and his career) was uppermost in his mind: "There's a big folk-singing revival going on," he told *Labor's Daily*. "I'm trying to do my part. I sure wish more unions would get interested."

In *Sing Out!*, Pete introduced songs he hoped would catch on, including one from the Georgia Sea Islands, "Michael Row Your Boat Ashore." He suggested people set up singing groups in each other's houses: Hold pot-lucks and sing! If Pete had run the land, these clubs might have been a unit of government.

He did inspire a singing club in his father's house, including Peggy and Mike, the eldest children of Charles and Ruth. The singing Seegers even recorded a little-known family album for Folkways, with Barbara and Penny, Peggy's sisters.

Mike, twelve years younger than Pete and a tall weedy fellow in blue jeans, always avoided music. "My parents would offer him these tests," Peggy remembered. "Empty the garbage or play a musical instrument. Mike preferred to take out the garbage."

Then, around the age of eighteen, Mike came down with shingles in his eyes, and he had to lie in darkness for six weeks. Pete had just sent Peggy and Mike a copy of his banjo manual, and Mike hooted: "You can't teach the banjo by a book!" "Prove it," Ruth said cagily. "You try it and see if you can."

"So there was Mike on his back," Peggy recalled. "This banjo appeared. I'd sit up there and read the passage, 'you've got to go plunk—di-de, plunk—di-de' and Mike practiced in the dark. That's how he started playing banjo, and he never looked back after that. Once he discovered he could do 'plunk—di-de,' he went on to 'bump—ditty, bump—ditty.'

"Then, *I* wanted to try it, and Mike said, 'The banjo's a boy's instrument.' So of course me, wearing jeans and climbing trees and playing football, I thought, 'If it's a boy's instrument, that's for me!' " Mike and two friends formed an old-time string band, The New Lost City Ramblers, in 1958. Peggy dropped out of Radcliffe to see the world.

In resurrecting the left-wing folk-song movement of the Thirties, Seeger had set himself an enormous task. The era of "Talking Union" had passed, along with the songs asserting the Left had a hammer and could use it. Seeger's music had a new function: reminding radicals of a better world to come and recalling past glories—where *had* all the flowers gone? Pete often repeated one of Woody's stories about two rabbits chased by hounds. They ran until they couldn't stand it any more; finally they holed up in a hollow log. The hounds bayed, but the little rabbits nestled inside, out of reach. The boy rabbit turned to the girl rabbit: "What do we do now?"

"Stay here till we outnumber them," she answered. In the Fifties that log—where the old Left often snuggled with itself—had just enough room for a skinny banjo picker.

In this period, Seeger faced the dilemma pointed out by poet Stephen Spender—those writing revolutionary songs or poetry must confront the antimaterialist form of their own art. The most moving political songs actually distract listeners from social reality, as the music and the performance spellbind their audience. "Music is the most powerful of all the idealist drugs except religion," Spender wrote. Thus, Pete's best political songs evoked not the bitterness of repression but the glory of its solution, the potential beauty of a world remade. His music couldn't overthrow a government, he had come to realize, but the children he sang for might begin the process. He wasn't inspiring direct political action, he was inspiring *people*.

More than anyone else, Pete encouraged young people; he'd become a modern Pied Piper as he traveled among the children, "leading them astray" with his music. Signs of his new revival appeared. A generation of folklorists had now grown up with his music, though none had the power to step forward and offer him formal recognition. The Vega Company, one of the oldest American banjo makers, named their new, extra-long model the "Pete Seeger."

From where he stood, looking back on the decades of isolated work by the Lomaxes and the Seegers, he saw that the seedlings of a folk-song revival had begun to sprout. The music was no longer exclusively left-wing; other folk-song performers followed the college trail that Pete had pioneered: Jean Ritchie, the exquisite Appalachian dulcimer player; Richard Dyer-Bennett; Jack Elliot, Woody's protégé; and many others. Guitar sales hit the half-million mark in 1956; his banjo manual had entered its second edition; and royalties from Folkways were increasing by fifty percent yearly.

The best part of his new success was honoring his old friends. Pete performed in *Bound for Glory,* a stage adaptation of Guthrie's autobiography. Woody sat in the balcony, smiling. Huntington's Disease had tied Woody to his hospital bed, but he came out for occasions like this. Seventeen years had passed since Woody and Pete had first sung together. Tears rolled down the faces of some old-timers as a thousand voices, mostly Pete's teenage audience, sang "This Land Is Your Land."

On March 26, 1957, Seeger moved one step closer to jail, with an indictment from a federal grand jury on ten counts of contempt of Congress. The indictment branded Seeger; he stood in court before a judge, accused of a crime. On March 29 he pleaded not guilty and was released on one thousand dollars' bail, having no prior offenses. Pete expected the trial within three to eight months, telling his friends: "I still feel I committed no wrong, and that my children will not feel ashamed of me in future years. If only we could look down like the Gods upon the scene, it might even appear funny, if it were not also tragic."

His friend Bess remembered a doctor in Pete's position: "After he had testified he said, 'It's funny, but when you get into it, you damn well have to behave well. . . . Unless you want to break with everybody you've ever known in your life, you've got to go through with it. If you asked me if I would do this again, I'd say, "hell no!" ' You are forced into being good whether you want to be or not," Bess pointed out. "Maybe a lot of famous people are led kicking and screaming to do these noble things."

Whether or not Seeger had to be led, the indictment threw an abrupt check on his career. The judge forbade Seeger to travel outside the Southern District of New York without permission. He couldn't take the subway to Brooklyn without the court's consent, much less cross the Hudson to New Jersey. Eventually Paul Ross negotiated this to notification. Every time Pete traveled—practically daily—he sent the District Attorney a telegram stating where he was going, when, and by what transportation. This left him with a paradox: As publicity of his court proceedings made bookings scarce, Pete had to travel farther afield to find jobs—but the court limited his travel. Forced out on the road for long stretches of time, Pete became a lonely figure carrying his banjo and his duffle along bus station corridors. When he arrived at a hotel, he had to check the closets, for fear of a right-wing frame-up. Crank calls pulled him out of bed at all hours of the night. As if this wasn't enough trouble, his family life deteriorated. From 1956 to 1958 he toured by himself and with the Weavers to nearly every state and Canada. His kids had a hard time forgiving him for missing their birthdays time after time. "This [Canada] trip is the hardest one I ever took, from the standpoint of being away from the family," he wrote Moe Asch. "I hope never to be away so long for any reason whatsoever."

Somehow, though folk music had increased its popularity, Seeger was having as hard a time as ever. He had become the oddest sort of celebrity. Bobby-soxers did not wail for him, and only the tiniest sliver of the population knew his music; yet he had started a growing cultural movement. He began to take right-wing attacks as a perverse tribute to his effectiveness. When the world praised the inflated or the shrill, he had his own standards, and no amount of neglect (or attention) from the world threw him off course. In some ways, the HUAC ordeal was the making of Seeger, rather than his undoing. Until challenged, his puritan habits had a boy-scout leader's blandness, and his music seemed too wholesome and rural for mass audiences. Under HUAC's attack, however, he became a warrior of song.

Still, few in the world of music took him seriously. When folklorist John Greenway published *American Folksongs of Protest,* he gave Seeger only two footnotes; and when Burl Ives published his second songbook in 1957, Pete couldn't help noticing that no Pete Seeger songbook had appeared.

Burl Ives had everything Pete didn't; skilled at commercializing folk music, he had amassed both popular acclaim and wealth. In reviewing Ives's book for *Sing Out!* , Seeger made sure readers understood the different paths he and Burl had taken; Pete savaged Burl in the most scathing article he ever published.

He hadn't forgiven Burl's "fingering, like any common stool pigeon, some of his radical associates" before HUAC. Ives had done this, according to Seeger, "because he felt it was the only way to preserve his lucrative contracts; and that makes his action all the more despicable." Pete compared him to Falstaff, "gross, gargantuan, talented, and clever; he was also not quite intelligent enough to be honorable." Seeger ended on an affectedly pious note: "When he comes up before the bar of judgment, let us be generous enough to allow him to present his positive contributions, which have been many, before his sins are weighed on the other balance." A few readers exploded: who did Seeger think he was—Saint Peter?

By this time, Pete knew who he was: "a master musician with music in his bones, nerves, and fingers," as his former hero Mike Gold called him in 1958. In "A Paean to Pete Seeger and American Music," the writer who had chided Pete's father for ignoring folk music now lauded the son. By making his voice heard in difficult times, Pete had become the opposition's singing patriot.

In July 1958 a U.S. Circuit Court judge faced a decision on Seeger's music, which effectively summed up his situation in the 1950s. The case began when the Detroit Labor Forum wanted to present Seeger at the Institute of Arts auditorium. The Detroit Arts Commission banned Seeger on the grounds that the auditorium "may not be rented for programs of a political or controversial nature." The Labor Forum took this ruling to court, insisting "Mr. Seeger was being presented not as a political figure but as a singer."

Right-wingers seemed to have stumbled on a whole new method of attacking Seeger: He was not a musician, but a politician, and hence should be kept out of theaters. (A similar argument had gotten a student group, the Labor Youth League, thrown off campus at the University of Wisconsin for sponsoring Seeger a few years before.) If this reasoning prevailed, anyone with a controversial opinion lost his or her right to sing in public.

The case was heard by Wade McCree—later U.S. Solicitor General—and Thomas J. Murphy, ruling on an issue that would puzzle even a professional critic. Was what Seeger did with an audience musical or political? According to the Art Institute, singing was allowed in the auditorium; politics were not.

Judge Murphy adopted the easy way out. Seeger would be singing; ergo, he was a singer, and the concert could proceed. "Judge Murphy's position was that singing songs isn't likely to start a riot," the *Detroit Free Press* wrote. Seeger must not have enjoyed hearing he was so harmless. Underlying this legal attack were fundamental, unexamined questions of whether Seeger was a politician or whether governments have the right to suppress a singer. In Seeger's case, the answers were not yet in. During the next decade, the naked-hearted singer became the most picketed, blacklisted entertainer in American history.

John Henry  9

THROUGHOUT the late Fifties, Seeger's legal troubles shadowed his career. The Justice Department agreed to hearings, then postponed them, awaiting the best moment for a conviction. Instead of the three to eight months Pete had expected, the proceedings stretched out for years. No one knew what would emerge at his trial. Seeger was set to challenge HUAC publicly; the Committee had Seeger's FBI files, including potentially damaging information about his Party membership. "Don't be in a hurry," Paul Ross told his client. "A trial next year will be better than one this year."

Pete and Toshi tried to enjoy what tranquillity they had. In 1958, for the first time in twenty years of singing, Pete turned down work to drive Toshi and the kids across the country. For one brief vacation the Seegers toured Yellowstone and the Grand Tetons like any other American family. For once they met no pickets, no police moving them on. Pete threaded through the enormous plains and miles of wheat and corn that Woody had first shown him back in 1940. The family camped out and father chopped yard-high stacks of wood for campfires. At dusk he played quiet tunes on his recorder, and the notes floated out across the mountainsides and forests. Driving the western highways, he was proud of the American land. At the end of a long afternoon behind the wheel, he pulled over to watch the mountains color at sunset. He couldn't help himself. He actually burst out with "America the Beautiful."

Pete had more time, now that he was drifting away from the Weavers. He no longer needed a performing group, he found a new one at every stop. And because of the blacklist, the Weavers never regained their earlier popularity; when they finally had a chance to return to the airwaves, it was a mixed blessing: a commercial for Lucky Strike cigarettes. Pete remembered the moment sadly, "the most commercial thing I'd ever been asked to do." None of the others were enthusiastic about the idea, but they needed commercial jobs and access to radio and TV. The Weavers voted, and Pete was in the minority.

"Why couldn't it be for yogurt," Pete reportedly muttered. "At least I like yogurt!"

He asked his father for advice. He couldn't refuse the group's wishes, but he couldn't stomach making the commercial. "Peter," Charles answered, "you ought not to try and sing with the Weavers forever." Pete went back to the group, did the commercial, and left the group the next day. He suggested the Weavers hire Erik Darling, his former student; they did, and Pete soloed, nursing his hopes of a folk music revival.

"In dreams begin responsibilities," wrote the poet Delmore Schwartz; Seeger's dreams only made him severe. If he had been born in his father's time, Pete might have become a Kodály, a Grieg, or a Bartok: a symphonic composer who wrote nationalistic music based on folk tunes. Instead, as a child of the Popular Front, Pete had set out to fuse America's folk and popular musics. A vision of Americans playing their own music— instead of hearing professionals perform it on radio or discs—captured Seeger as few other goals in his life did. To him, folk songs had a patriotic undercurrent; the music had been carved from the rhythm of daily lives, the curves of the American land, the outline of its architecture, and its climate. For generations, the stream of folk music had flowed underground, beneath America's pop and high culture: Indian dance tunes, Irish airs, Afro-American shouts and blues. Pete wanted to bring these traditions close to the musical surface, so Americans could reclaim the riches. Nothing excited him more. He had endured and kept his hands cupped around the flame till others were ready to receive it.

In the fall of 1958 the Kingston Trio's recording "Tom Dooley" publicized folk music as dramatically as the Weavers had—the record sold 2.6 million copies. The song echoed from radio to radio, saturating an urban nation with nostalgia for country roots. Groups like the Chad Mitchell Trio, the Brothers Four, the Tarriers, and the Limelighters mined folk treasuries for similar hits.

By 1961 the editors of *Webster's Third New International Dictionary* included *hootenanny*: "a gathering at which folk singers entertain." The term Pete and Woody had brought back from Seattle now adorned pot holders and pencil cups. *Look* printed a column on what to wear to a hoot: "Fashion is stylishly singing along: bulky knits and . . . a vaguely beat but neat look."

Charles Seeger had predicted this revival back in 1949, once again anticipating his son's career. Peter had been raised as a citybilly; folk songs were his window into rural life in America. He associated folk music with a life style uncomplicated by materialism; and he convinced many of his association. Folk songs came to represent campfire sing-alongs instead of TV bandstands, hiking boots and flannel shirts instead of penny loafers or button-down collars.

Finally an industry emerged from Seeger's enthusiasms, and he was in the position of a master painter whose work is discovered. He not only had a warehouse full of records, but he had taught most of America's younger folk performers. At a single 1954 concert in Palo Alto, for instance, Seeger inspired the careers of both Joan Baez and Dave Guard (of the Kingston Trio). All this would have mattered little, however, if not for the work of Toshi and Harold, who had formed a phalanx to promote Seeger and folk music.

Leventhal had come a long way since he introduced himself to the Weavers at the Vanguard. Leaving behind his garment business (but not his sofa stuffed with padding from the brassieres he manufactured), Harold had prospered. He had put on weight and taken to wearing suits, but he still cut a boyish figure compared to his peers in the music industry who talked only gross and net. Harold often entered his office with a smile on his round face, as if humming a lovely tune which he couldn't quite remember. At times his soft-spokenness led performers to wonder if he represented them forcefully. He did. Seeger was his Number One, though; Harold saw a long career for him.

One of the factors cementing Harold and Pete's relationship was their shared political philosophy; the manager was, according to Joe Klein, the author of *Woody Guthrie,* "a Communist, which meant he could be trusted." He served as an informal confidant for progressive musicians, becoming one of the only managers to handle both the mercantile and the philo-sophical problems of a politically oriented performer. Leventhal under-stood why Seeger enjoyed benefits, and Pete used Harold as a sounding board for his eccentric ideas; if he suddenly decided to write a dance based on a Chopin étude (which he once did), Harold would have a say (but not the final word) on whether to publish it. Harold kept track of Pete's friends and pet concerns—and learned to call Toshi if he needed Pete to sign anything.

After years of practice, Toshi had become the organizer Seeger always hoped to be. While her husband practiced banjo in the barn, Toshi would take a notebook and fill in his schedule, and "God help Pete Seeger if he lost that book," a family friend laughed. When he left the house on a booking, Toshi stuck a few dollars in his pocket. "When she forgot—and it didn't happen often—Seeger ended up bumming money for coffee."

Despite the sudden, widespread interest in folk music, Seeger fared no better with his old enemies—*Counterattack,* HUAC, and the American Legion. As the red hunt subsided in America and the "Impeach Earl Warren" billboards yellowed, anti-Communists increased their fire on "Khrushchev's Songbird," as Seeger's hunters fondly called him. If these groups weren't up to many new targets, at least they weren't letting the old ones slide.

By now Pete took the harassment for granted; on a 1959 tour of England with Jack Elliot, he found to his surprise that his approaching trial had created a stir in Europe. He had to convince people that he was *not* fleeing America to avoid jail—"It never even occurred to me." Given the seriousness of the charges against him, the expectation was a reasonable one. The attacks worsened in the year following his return. In December 1959 an appearance in Great Neck, Long Island, had the community in an uproar. A few months later, the San Diego Board of Education demanded Seeger sign a loyalty oath before singing in a high school auditorium. He refused. The usual drama unfolded. The San Diego branch of the American Legion insisted Seeger was criminally subversive: He was, after all, under indictment. Liberal sponsors of the concert called for freedom of speech. One school-board member actually listened to Seeger's music before passing judgment. William Elser checked out "Cindy," "Froggy Went A-courtin'" and other tunes from the school library: "I couldn't see anything wrong with them," Elser said; "There's nothing communistic about these songs."

Seeger's right-wing critics failed to realize that these challenges only brought him more listeners. When he finally sang in San Diego, the pickets carried signs reading "Ban the Bum"; but Pete had his triumph. Halfway through the concert, as he was building up steam, he peeled off his sweater, showing the audience a bright scarlet shirt. He smiled sweetly at their laughter and casually bent over to expose matching red socks.

A similar incident occurred a few miles downriver from Beacon, when the American Legion tried to cancel Seeger's performance in Nyack. They held a press conference with one of HUAC's staff, who traveled three hundred miles for the occasion. Rockland County papers praised the local citizens who opposed the "beards, berets, and beat-up attire" of visitors from New York City. Seeger eventually sang to a small crowd, but his neighbors' hostility was chillingly clear. A local official discovered the theater had an out-of-date license and ordered the place shut before Pete could sing a second night. If the theater was to stay open, a special licensing fee had to be paid immediately; in a gesture of creative skulduggery, municipal offices yanked down their shades, and the town clerk and mayor arranged to be out of town for the day.

Seeger's troubles stretched on and on. He could barely hold on to his past, much less the present; a right-wing group, Texans for America, actually managed to convince textbook publishers to delete all references to Seeger's career. He tended to underestimate his attackers, in hopes that the rising interest in folk music would carry him ahead. But a letter-writing campaign could still frighten a network; a woman who had Pete sing at a barbecue in her backyard in Ohio received a HUAC subpoena. No matter how popular Seeger became, a few would always hear a Communist plot in his songs.

Just as Pete often performed "All My Trials" at the time of his HUAC appearance, he now sang "John Henry." All his life, he found inspiration in the story:

> *The captain said to John Henry*
> *"I'm gonna bring that steam drill around,*
> *I'm gonna bring that steel drill out on the job,*
> *I'm gonna whup that steel on down."*
>
> *Now the man that invented the steam drill,*
> *He thought he was mighty fine;*
> *But John Henry drove fifteen feet,*
> *The steam drill only made nine.*
>
> *John Henry hammered in the mountains,*
> *His hammer was striking fire,*
> *But he worked so hard, it broke his poor heart,*
> *And he laid down his hammer and he died.*
>
> *John Henry had a little baby,*
> *You could hold him in the palm of your hand;*
> *And the last words I heard that poor boy say,*
> *"My daddy was a steel driving man."*

"It's a good example of how a folk song means as much as you want it to mean," said Seeger. "When I was fourteen, it was simply a Paul Bunyan-type extravaganza, a tall tale like 'Jack and the Beanstalk,' with a strong man exaggerated beyond belief. Then Alan Lomax told me of the bawdy significance: a man sitting holding the drill between his legs and coming down with a big hammer on top of it. . . . Later on, I think I understood more of the tragedy of the song, and at the age of sixty, the verse I would never leave out is 'John Henry had a little baby.' "

Seeger believed the John Henry myth: that a person of good intentions who gave his all could defeat any opponent. As a symbol, John Henry aroused his class sympathy: a working man, relying on strength and tools to resist dehumanizing progress and profits. Seeger appreciated a fight worth laying down a life for; his own struggles pitted him against an equally impersonal machine: televison.

One afternoon in December 1960 Pete sat in his drafty office in the barn. Huddled by the old-fashioned space heater in his office, he typed unevenly, with more determination than accuracy. In the pale winter light he looked frail and bony, though his arms showed a wiry strength from chopping wood. His face had the first lines of middle age, and his nose had a reddish hue. His trial had finally been set for March, three months hence; Harold had begun organizing his legal defense, but it was not on this that Pete typed. He had a new hope: televising folk music. Over the last five years he had concluded that television would shape cultural movements of the future. Seeger was ready to approach (and eventually assault) the medium. That he had been kept off network TV for a decade only increased his estimate of its power.

Television could be a new beginning for his career. Singers were now telling audiences: "Here's a song I learned off an old Pete Seeger record." Pete was only forty-one, but thanks to the blacklist, he might have been dead and buried. He wanted America to hear its folk songs—and he wouldn't mind being the guy who sang them on TV.

Throughout December 1960, Pete sat at his desk, laboring over drafts of "Pete Seeger, Banjo Traveller," for the Canadian Broadcasting Corporation. The scope was enormous—twenty-six half-hour documentaries, with locations in French Canada, the Caribbean, and throughout the U.S.—an ambitious project for a man who might be in jail before the first filming began.

Downstairs, Toshi spurred on guests adding a new room to the barn; eventually, after they cleared away the debris, her pottery studio would be installed. When the phone rang in the cabin across the yard, Pete would ignore it—and the unanswered mail Toshi piled on his desk. With the first snows, their driveway grew icy slick, and visitors departed. Unfortunately, the mail increased proportionately, until the only time he had to practice was early in the morning and late at night, when he was too drowsy to answer letters. The mail had become a major ritual: Toshi would pick it up and screen it. Then Pete would write answers while Toshi pulled the paper out from under his pen and addressed them. They could get through seventy-five letters a day this way, each brief but handwritten, with a banjo sketched beneath his signature (a Japanese custom from Toshi's family).

Pete was in a bind; he disliked dictated letters for their impersonality, but mail days left him cranky and tired.

As his trial neared, Toshi's support became more and more critical. Under similar circumstances, other spouses had fought bitterly for a more "reasonable" stance, even using the children as a threat that charity begins at home. Seeger could have reconsidered; he could have told the judge he wanted to make a clean breast of it. No one would have blamed him, and he might finally have received the TV audience he desired.

Pete held on. If Toshi had wavered, if in protest she had stopped answering phone calls and fending off reporters, her husband might have caved in. She did not flinch; she was Seeger's full-time partner. At concerts, everyone looked around for Pete, but it was Toshi who examined the crowd: a short, unstylish, intensely quiet woman in her late thirties, leaning against the wall, smoking a cigarette. Her hair was shiny and dark, its color suggesting Indian or oriental blood; her eyes flicked around the room, staring through people. She got things done, always the last to leave—"Staying after every concert," a young admirer recalled, "in dark auditoriums to pick up papers and trash long after the audience and performers had left." It was no secret to fellow performers that Seeger's career was as much hers as his. Their partnership didn't always run smoothly, however. When Toshi showed her temper, her voice took on a cutting, brittle tone. She knew Pete's weaknesses the way he knew his instruments.

Toshi wasn't the only one under pressure from Pete's trial and blacklist; Pete's eldest brother, Charles III, had trouble obtaining government clearances. After Pete's indictment, both Mike and Peggy also suffered. In 1958 Mike had quit one of his first jobs, with the Social Security office in Washington, because of a security check. "The government later sent me a dossier on my father, brother, and sister, asking me to comment on it. . . . They told me that if I didn't answer and tell them yes or no, I would never get another government job again." To test this blacklist, Mike got himself hired on a radio show sponsored by the Social Security Administration. When it came time for the musicians to get their checks, Mike stepped forward and gave his name. The producer refused to write him a check, making it out instead to Mike's friend, folklorist Ralph Rinzler.

Mike staked out a territory where he could be recognized as more than Pete's kid brother. If Pete was a popularizer, Mike became a preservationist, duplicating tunes note for note from the original sources. Radical songs and audience singing did not inspire him; he would rather teach four reverent people country mandolin than get four thousand singing.

Peggy Seeger also had a specialty: ballads, many of them learned from her mother's transcriptions. She also sang folk songs in a feminist vein, frailing and double-thumbing the banjo better than Pete. In the late Fifties she left Radcliffe for Europe and China; she found herself harassed by customs officials, who tried to take away her passport. On returning from England to visit her family, she had a thick dossier labeled "Seeger" slapped in front of her. "In 1957 you said this," they told her, and "Would you say this is a likeness of you?" British immigration officials later peered into a similar file and put Peggy on a ferry back to France.

On March 27, 1961, Pete Seeger went on trial for contempt of Congress in New York City. Thomas Murphy, formerly the prominent young D.A. who had applauded the Weavers at the Blue Angel, presided; since then, he had made his career as the prosecutor of Alger Hiss. Arriving on the first day, the government's lawyer, Irving Younger, had never seen so many people in a court before—five hundred spectators, mostly of college age, and more lined up at the door. Younger had inherited the case; "as a lawyer," he commented, "I speak for whoever retains me; I didn't think twice about prosecuting Seeger. I'd never heard of him." Younger told the jury that the case concerned contempt, not Seeger's involvement in the Communist Party. Paul Ross attacked HUAC head on, insisting the members had no right to question Seeger: "In no instance in this committee's investigation was the matter of national security, espionage, sabotage, or the advocating of the violent overthrow of the government involved."

Seeger watched this spectacle in bad temper; he had received the depressing news that Canadian television had rejected his project. If the liberal Canadian Broadcasting Corporation wasn't interested, no American network would touch it.

For his trial, Seeger had subpoenaed the subpoenaer: Francis Walter, former HUAC chairman, was the key defense witness, testifying on HUAC's purpose in investigating Seeger. Paul Ross had a rough day: Judge Murphy didn't intend to have the congressman harassed, and he excluded 102 of Ross's questions. During the challenge to HUAC's authority Murphy ordered the jury from the room. "Seeger will be lucky if he gets off with the electric chair at this rate," gibed one reporter.

One of the factors prejudicing Judge Murphy was Seeger's FBI files, which made yet another appearance—this time in closed session, when Irving Younger used them to cross-examine Seeger's character witnesses, inserting into the trial record allegations of three informants (among them the notorious Louis Budenz) on Seeger.

A reporter from *The New York Times* attended the trial each day, an indication of the importance Seeger now had in the music industry and the public eye. The best trial coverage came from the *Harvard Crimson,* which did not miss the irony of Irving Younger (class of '53) prosecuting Seeger (whom they flatteringly called class of '40). Murray Kempton of the *New York Post* noted Walter's "expression of dyspepsia" as he left the courtroom. "The menace Seeger," Kempton wrote, "sat through the proceedings slouched and far away over the distant hills," quietly doodling snails with fancy tails.

Harold Leventhal appeared at every session, despite the fact that he was now the best-known manager in folk music. He'd sit and chew on an unlit cigar, more nervous than Pete himself. "For Pete's Sake," the newsletter of the Friends of Pete Seeger, was his idea.

On the final day of the trial, Pete's lawyer urged the jury to find him not guilty: His answers were in good faith, even if they didn't satisfy the committee. Younger insisted he was guilty of refusing to cooperate. When the judge gave the jury its charge, Seeger knew he was in trouble. Murphy "determined as a matter of law" that HUAC's questions were pertinent to the committee's legitimate investigations. Seeger's case for freedom of song wilted.

The jury began deliberating at 3:30 P.M. One hour and twenty minutes later, they returned the verdict: guilty.

The ruling didn't hit him at once. It took time to realize that jail was no longer an abstraction, that he would be sentenced in six days. The part of him that fundamentally believed in justice in America was disappointed. Toshi, Mika, and Danny sat in the courtroom with him. Shaken, Pete gathered up his family and left for home.

"DANGEROUS MINSTREL NABBED HERE," wrote the *New York Post* on March 31, 1961: "Amid our larger tribulations, the Justice Department has moved fearlessly and decisively against ballad singer Pete Seeger. . . . That the combined powers of the House committee and the Justice Department should be rallied to imprison him is a bitter burlesque. Some jail will be a more joyous place if he lands there, and things will be bleaker on the outside."

Seeger's public reaction was steely cold, as if he saw his situation from a distance of centuries. He was only doing his duty; in 1955, that had meant speaking his mind, at the risk of jail.

Seeger's anger came out in other matters. He fumed when Canadian Immigration wouldn't admit him on a concert tour without guarantees that he would return to the U.S. for imprisonment—they didn't want the minstrel loose in *their* country. He watched grimly as "John Henry" was turned into hoked-up parodies by crew-cut singers and their packager-producer-arrangers: John Henry the street cleaner, John Henry the idiot or math whiz. Worse, songs not destroyed were often stolen; attaching the words "adapted and arranged by" gave two cents extra royalties per disc to the singer.

Commercialism in folk music wasn't new, but the contradictions of copyright had sharpened as "Tom Dooley" made thirty thousand dollars a week for the Kingston Trio, while Frank Proffitt, the song's collector, barely earned enough for gas. Pete's most painful copyright problems had begun in the late Fifties, when Alan Lomax had asked Pete to acknowledge him as the owner of folk songs he and his father collected—many unearthed while they were on the federal payroll. Pete had been furious. How could Alan, who knew better, claim royalties from songs that belonged in the public domain? Alan had received foundation grants and had earned a respectable wage from the Library of Congress, CBS, and Decca Records while Pete was barely surviving.

The topic sickened him, though Pete did not entirely renounce the commercial success of folk music. A few months before his trial, Columbia Records had asked him to sign with them. Moe Asch had agreed, provided Folkways could release its previous recordings. But before producer John Hammond could get final permission, he had to consult senior CBS executives. Hammond met with Columbia Records' president, Goddard Lieberson, in his plushly appointed office; Lieberson called Richard Salant, a corporate V.P.

"I've got a question in a delicate area. It's Pete Seeger. Can we use him?"

"We don't need him, and he's not welcome on CBS television," Salant said flatly.

"We want to sign him to Columbia Records."

Salant asked if he thought Seeger would sell.

"I wouldn't be calling you if I didn't," Goddard replied. "Well, we're big boys now," Salant decided. "Do what you want." They signed Seeger, but they didn't completely trust him; Pete didn't hear about this conversation until fifteen years later.

Pete Seeger regretted leaving Moe, but he bartered an affection for Folkways for a mass audience; Columbia promised to put his records in stores across the country. Malvina Reynolds, who also signed with Columbia, understood Seeger's decision: "The only reason Pete and I are interested in whether records sell is that people get to hear our voices. . . . It's not as simple as commercial or noncommercial. You become surrounded by this complex of grabbing people and wonder, as you become a big commercial property, if you'll be cut off from the very thing that made you special."

Three days after his conviction Seeger walked on the annual Easter peace march, sponsored by the Committee for a Sane Nuclear Policy. The weather blew cold and rainy, but the marchers kept their spirits up by marveling how their numbers had grown. In the Fifties, hundreds had turned out; now, with papers discussing the Ban the Bomb movement, 3,500 marched. Pete and his family trudged along, keeping out of the public eye. He appeared remote; a hardness in his face kept people from asking his feelings.

Twelve blocks long and the width of Broadway, the march crossed midtown Manhattan to the United Nations with petitions for nuclear disarmament. Easter paraders watched from the sidewalk, their lacy hats flopping in the wind. Families pushed baby carriages with picnic baskets tucked inside, and young progressives marched in the footsteps of the old Left. "Peace in the world or the world in pieces" read a six-year-old's sign.

From socialist summer camps to peace marches, the children that Seeger sang for had now reached adolescence. Their progressive world had its own rules: *Time* and *Newsweek* were unwelcome guests in these homes, as were authors Graham Greene (for converting to Catholicism) and George Orwell (for criticizing Communists in Spain). Folk songs were well loved, but not Josh White or Burl Ives. To these teenagers, Seeger remained a mythic, John Henry-like figure, the man who fought the machinery of blacklisting.

When the march arrived at UN Plaza, literature tables greeted demonstrators with dime pamphlets; the Communist Party sold enameled doves for "committed" Christmas-Hanukkah gifts. As the rally ended, a speaker noticed Seeger in the throng. The last thing Pete wanted now was celebrity, but "the demostrators throbbed the chant 'We Want Seeger,' " according to the *Journal-American*. The sound must have rung in Pete's ears like a fire alarm to a man with a hangover.

"Pete Seeger" (applause). "Let's bring him up here, what do you say?" (The applause swelled to an ovation.) "Pete's been through hard times recently. For fighting HUAC, the government wants to lock him away for ten years. Ten years! Let's give him our support." Seeger reluctantly climbed atop the platform, but instead of speaking, he nodded to the crowd like an old friend. He sang a peace song, asked everyone to work hard for disarmament, and began to climb down. "What about your case?" someone called.

He looked around in protest. He rarely talked about himself in public, but his feelings swelled almost out of control. Pete hesitated, embarrassed that people thought him a hero, yet frustrated at his unjust conviction. In the end, he shook his head and stepped down, unable to shed his optimist's garb: "I don't think I did much talking that day. One of the hardest things I learned to do was to smile and acknowledge the applause."

Later he discovered that when the crowd had called out his name, the sponsors of the march were more distressed than he. A disagreement had taken place backstage—was a convicted felon to address *their* crowd? The liberals of SANE wrote Seeger: "Unless we ask you to be on the platform, please don't." Fear of controversy knows no Left or Right.

Tuesday, April 3, arrived, and Pete drove to New York for sentencing. He walked into the courtroom wearing a suit with his banjo slung over one shoulder. Photographs show him looking chipper, more like a man headed for vacation than jail. Before passing sentence, Judge Murphy asked Seeger if he had anything to tell the court.

"Thank you, your honor. After hearing myself talked about, pro and con, for three days, I am grateful to say a few unrestricted words." Pete thanked his lawyer and again declared he hadn't "sung anything in any way subversive to my country." Just as in his testimony, he addressed an audience beyond the courtroom.

"Some of my ancestors were religious dissenters who came to America over three hundred years ago. Others were abolitionists in New England in the eighteen forties and fifties. I believe that in choosing my present course I do no dishonor to them, or to those who may come after me."

"Don't forget, Peter—you come from good stock!" grandmother had said. Though his notion of quality differed from hers, Pete was true to her spirit.

"I am forty-two years old, and count myself a very lucky man. I have a wife and three healthy children, and we live in a house we built with our own hands, on the banks of the beautiful Hudson River. For twenty years I have been singing the folk songs of America and other lands to people everywhere. . . . The specific song whose title was mentioned in this trial, 'Wasn't That a Time,' is one of my favorites. The song is apropos to this case. I wonder if I might have your permission to sing it here before I close?"

"You may not," Judge Murphy said firmly.

"Perhaps you will hear it some other time. . . . Do I have a right to sing these songs? Do I have the right to sing them anywhere?"

The judge brushed aside Seeger's concerns and sentenced him to a year in jail for every count—ten years. The sentences could be served concurrently, however, leaving him a year and a day in federal prison. To this, the judge gruffly added the costs of prosecution; Pete had to pay for the government's expenses in trying him, even Francis Walter's lunch.

Seeger was still standing, facing the judge, when Paul Ross stood up and said: "Your honor, I want to see about bail."

"There is no bail. Bailiff, take him away."

There was a gasp in the courtroom. Pete didn't have time to turn around before the bailiff clamped the handcuffs on. Toshi walked up from behind and lifted his banjo from his arms.

He was led through a door and down a flight of stairs to the basement of the courthouse; there they locked him in a cell with three or four men awaiting trial.

Upstairs, Seeger's lawyer ran over to the Court of Appeals. The Circuit Court could set bail; if they didn't, Seeger might stay inside for quite a while. Harold had to find cash in a hurry; he hopped in a cab and started visiting friends who worked near banks.

A hundred demonstrators had assembled outside the courtroom, chanting that Seeger be set free. Pete could barely make out what they were saying. From the next cell a man looked out and said, "Hey, there's a big crowd outside for somebody. Some Commie." He came over and looked in at Pete. "Oh, you're the guy," he said, slightly disappointed.

"We'd been talking before," Pete said, "and now I was just sitting there. The guy was so surprised; I was mildly eating a sandwich, and he was expecting to see some real revolutionary-type person."

Somewhere, Pete knew, Toshi and his friends were doing their best to get him out. He almost enjoyed himself, mildly exhilarated to find that being in jail for the right reasons wasn't so terrible. He felt "momentarily speechless," but he had a warm glow: He'd held on to his principles. He would go down fighting, like John Henry or Uncle Alan, who would have been proud, he who had charged gallantly to his death in the Foreign Legion.

"The funny thing is . . . ," Pete explained, stumbling for words to describe the sensation of righteousness. "You see, it's a hard thing to explain, but when you're following what you think is the right course, it may not be fun, but you feel a certain satisfaction in doing it."

Paul Ross got the petition for appeal approved, though it took hours. He rushed back to the courtroom to find Harold: Seeger's freedom could be had for two thousand dollars. Toshi and Harold and Paul together counted out the bills to the clerk.

Downstairs, a black man next to Seeger was singing: "If that judge believes what I say, I'll be leaving for home today." The guy next to him said, "Not if he sees your record, you won't." In his few hours behind bars, Pete Seeger learned a folk song.

In New York, Seeger's situation sent a tremor through the folk-music community. The recently arrived Bob Dylan—pressured by his friends to become the next Pete Seeger—expressed the feelings of many Greenwich Village folkies: "They're framing him—they just want to shut him up."

His conviction added to an antiestablishment atmosphere in the Village. Six days after his sentencing, a small-scale riot broke out, the Battle of Washington Square. For fifteen years, singers and guitar players had gathered on Sunday afternoons in the park at the foot of Fifth Avenue. Then, in April 1961, Parks Commissioner Newbold Morris made the mistake of trying to ban singing in the park, at the request of the Greenwich Village Chamber of Commerce. Commissioner Morris based his order on an all-but-forgotten law forbidding minstrels in public parks.

On April 9 singers gathered in the Square to test the ruling. The police duly instructed them to sing *a cappella*: If they played instruments, they would be arrested as minstrels. The singers laughed and displayed signs reading: MUSIC TAMES THE SAVAGE BEAST. This was the kind of symbolic battle Seeger relished; if he had been less weary of publicity, he probably would have attended.

Inspired by the nonviolent civil-rights demonstrations in the South, the singers held their ground. At four o'clock, the police decided to clear the park: Anyone caught playing an instrument would be arrested. A crowd sat down in the fountain (fortunately, it was dry) and sang "We Shall Not Be Moved." Using their nightsticks, New York's finest cleared the park, leaving behind a crowd of baffled tourists.

News of the demonstration appeared in *Time* and as far west as the *San Francisco Chronicle*. The Greenwich Village Right to Sing Committee formed. After a month, Parks Commissioner Morris rescinded the order, and freedom of song returned to Greenwich Village. Columnist Walter Winchell wrote of an officer who stopped a stroller near the Square: "Whatcha doin' here?" the law demanded. "I'm looking for someone to mug," admitted the man. "Sorry," the law apologized, "I thought you were a folksinger."

When Pete visited the Village Gate at his first session for Columbia three weeks later, he taped the lyrics to a brand-new "Ballad of Washington Square" to the mike. He looked "shy and a bit nervous," according to Peter Bogdanovich (later a prominent filmmaker); in the audience were Columbia executives and ex-members of the Almanacs and Weavers. As usual, Pete wore bright colors (aqua and tangerine) to give himself visibility; a half-hour into the concert, he asked the audience to join him in a yodel.

Waiters rushed about the room, taking orders and spilling drinks. No one noticed; even the clink of ashtrays and glasses had stopped. The audience hadn't come to yodel, but Pete demonstrated with a smile; he knew they'd go along. Sure enough, a few minutes later the room sounded like a convention of drunken alpinists, the high-pitched falsettos bouncing off the rafters.

"It's amazing how Pete does it," his sister Peggy once said. "He's perfected certain motions and things you say to an audience until it seems spontaneous. He'll pick out one person in the crowd and address something to them. This helps the singer look on the audience as an aggregate of individuals, rather than a blurry mass. Sometimes he brings up someone from the audience to play. It's not a ruse, it's a way of putting yourself in the audience's shoes, and putting them in yours.

"I'm letting you in on trade secrets now," Peggy continued: "If you appear night after night, you have to keep yourself fresh. . . . You know what you're going to say for the next song, but you stop, and you have a silence of about three or four seconds. This makes it look as if you're thinking, groping for something new. The audience is waiting, you know what you're going to say, but you can relax your shoulders, take a breath and think 'I don't have to push anything out.' The boxer gets a minute between rounds, you get four seconds."

On stage, Seeger told a story of two cats: Male cat says to the female, "neeow," and the female answers "not neeow." The audience laughed; the musician warmed the audience like a fire on a starless night. He led them through a tricky song, then took an intermission.

"Pete makes it all look easy," fellow singer Mike Cooney pointed out. "Don't believe it. All great art looks simple, but Pete's professional reputation was built on musicianship. His appearance of ease is deliberate. 'Look at me,' he seems to say, 'I don't have a voice as smooth as dewdrops rolling off rose petals—you can sing this too.'"

After the break, he did "John Henry," allowing himself some virtuoso banjo work. By its utter simplicity, the song represented an aesthetic challenge: taking three chords (and a story everyone knew) and dramatizing them. To accomplish this, he leaned on his vocal delivery, calling to John Henry as if he stood in earshot. On the line, "Hear John Henry's hammer *ring*," Pete brushed the strings so smartly the steel seemed to sing.

"Two more songs, then I have to go home." He started "Bells of Rhymney," where the bells of Welsh coal towns toll on his guitar. In Seeger's setting of a poem by Idris Davies, each phrase was repeated in a high, fast tempo; they blended into one another with a hint of dissonance. Only on the last phrase did the sound soften; the effect was like walking on a country road when two sets of bells pealed together. The musical tension rose until the last cadence resolved, and an enormous sigh swept the room. After Woody's "So Long," Seeger stepped off the stage with material for two albums. He bowed and applauded the audience as they applauded him.

Evenings like these raised Pete's spirits. Jail seemed distant, unbelievable; if he was scared of anything it was his own success. When Moe Asch publicized Seeger as "America's Greatest Folksinger," even his long friendship didn't spare him Pete's wrath: "If 'America's Greatest Folksinger' were true," he wrote Moe, "it wouldn't be necessary to say it. The puffier the publicity gets the more embarrassing the collapse later on, no?" This was a shrewd and stoic assessment from a man famous for optimism.

"An artist like Pete Seeger starts off with twenty, thirty years of experience before he surfaces," Don McLean said. "He's drawn to this, he's drawn to that. He develops a line of communication with people and his inner self. He refines that line of communication until the feedback starts. Then everything happens. When his experience is put through the recording industry, through the television screen and radio, that is when the enormous return comes from the audience. It's also when all the external, meaningless pressures start to box you in—when people who haven't the slightest clue what you're about try to mold you.

"It's those years you spent in the tunnel with the light on your hat that determine whether you will stay true to your goals as an artist, or whether you'll sell out for money. Money is the key to it all; Pete prefers the light on his helmet."

Now that Seeger was in great demand, money entered his life in embarrassing quantities; song royalties pushed his income into six figures for the first time. But the more money he had, the less he wanted to know about it. In the decades since Pete had served as the Almanacs' accountant, he had stopped handling accounts; he made people shelter him from his own finances. One of his rare fights with Harold occurred when a concert producer mistakenly handed Pete his check; looking into the envelope he was horrified to find several thousand dollars. Pete demanded that Harold lower his price immediately, an anecdote Harold told with relish.

Success seemed less righteous than failure. Part of him still yearned for his adolescent hermit's den; he didn't want to be the first musical revolutionary tycoon. Soon after his tiff with Harold, he wrote a poem on his wealth: "My son and daughters, if I had three million dollars, I would not will them to you, for I would not want you to be hated . . . by the determined poor people of this our world."

His predicament would not have bothered many. He might have traded in his battered old VW bug or built a swimming pool, but his puritan instincts balked. Money only made him uncomfortable, and he took out his discomfort on the wrong people. When the publishers of his songbook *Goofing Off Suite* advertised PETE SEEGER on the cover, Pete tore off a bitter note, complaining his name was blown up like a "goddamned star." An offended editor pointed out that Seeger had chosen a commercial profession: "Accepting the benefits of commercialism on the one hand, you should not damn it on the other."

In the fall of 1961 Seeger obtained the court's permission to tour England. In the two years since his trip with Jack Elliot, he had developed a large following; four thousand turned out at London's Royal Albert Hall. England had its own "Pete Seeger Committee" with Paul Robeson as president, the great ballad singer Ewan MacColl (now Peggy's husband) as chairman, and Benjamin Britten, Doris Lessing, and Sean O'Casey as sponsors.

The five weeks in Britain were precious, tender times, the vacation Pete and Toshi sorely needed. No Un-English Committee stalked him; no FBI monitored his singing. In a rented car, the couple and their six-year-old girl, Tinya, visited the cozy inns that dot the English countryside. On a whim they would stop at a pub unannounced, then rest the night in a country bed-and-breakfast, awakening to the smell of home-cured ham and broiled tomatoes.

The chill English winter had not yet begun. They motored through the heath country of Yorkshire on their way north, savoring the end of an Indian summer. Some days the clouds would break and the country lanes would be flooded with sunshine. The enormous golden fields and ancient stone fences appealed to the folklorist in Pete. Here, on the fog-covered moors of the Scottish border, great crimes and wars had launched a hundred ballads. Driving the deserted country roads, Seeger could almost hear the songs of false knights and castles. Sometimes, through a tip at a local pub, they visited a traditional singer and heard songs as they were sung centuries ago. Music, not tour books, guided them through what Seeger described as the "crowded midlands, to the smoky valleys of Wales, through the high, windswept moorlands, to the rocky coasts of Scotland."

The political songwriting of Great Britain revitalized Seeger, and he returned and talked with Sis Cunningham (of the Almanacs) about starting a magazine of topical song, *Broadside*. The songs of Bob Dylan, Phil Ochs, Tom Paxton, Eric Andersen, and others soon filled its pages.

On May 18, 1962, the Court of Appeals ruled that Seeger's indictment was faulty and dismissed his case. The judges disappointed him by side-stepping questions of his freedom to sing when and where he pleased, without having to answer to his government. Instead, the court found that HUAC's authority hadn't been clearly explained. Seeger thought this absurd; he had hoped to attack the whole edifice of Un-Americanism; but all he won was an instruction for the government to draft better documents.

In closing, the court couldn't resist a subtle insult: "We are not inclined to dismiss lightly claims of Constitutional stature because they are asserted by one who may appear unworthy of sympathy." Seeger did not receive his vindication, but an acquittal is an acquittal, and he was now free, unless the government appealed or retried him. The *New York Post* called the decision a "return to reason," and "a big day for Miss Liberty."

"Hooray for us all and for Tom Jefferson," Seeger told *Sing Out!*. In one of those happy coincidences fate periodically offers, "Where Have All The Flowers Gone?" hit the top forty charts the week of his acquittal. The Kingston Trio had recorded the song two months earlier, and now Peter, Paul and Mary (Travers, his former student) had a success with this and a streamlined version of "If I Had A Hammer." To Pete's delight, the two versions of "Hammer" harmonized. At his concerts people sang in unplanned harmony; he couldn't stop talking about this, insisting politicians could learn from it.

With Leadbelly gone and Woody in the hospital, Seeger saw himself as a link in a chain tying these two to new audiences. Guthrie could not longer play or sing, but he did recognize visitors, and Pete and Toshi often stopped by, sometimes with young Arlo. After Woody was transferred to Brooklyn State Hospital, Pete and Arlo visited to sing one of his favorite songs, "Hobo's Lullaby," and the hospital odor and bare walls dropped away. Woody no longer had the muscular control to speak or applaud, but he heard. A light shone from his eyes, and he blinked tears.

All that was left of Leadbelly was a rough film clip, and Pete spent the next summer at an editing table, synchronizing Leadbelly's image and voice. His mind wandered to the world outside the cool, darkened room. Now that he had survived his seven-year legal battle, new possibilities shimmered before him in the silvery light of the editing machine. Americans sang his songs; a generation of folk musicians idolized him. Next he would introduce America to folk music via television, and as he peered into the tiny screen where Leadbelly capered and sang about the invincible "Gray Goose," Pete believed he could do it.

> *The fork couldn't stick him.*
> *And the knife wouldn't cut him.*
> *They throwed him in the hog pen,*
> *And the hogs couldn't eat him,*
> *And he broke the hogs' teeth out.*
> *They put him in the saw mill,*
> *And the saw couldn't cut him,*
> *And he broke all the teeth out. . . .*

The goose and John Henry had a lot in common with Seeger; he, too, had broken the saw's teeth.

Bleary-eyed from editing, he began to imagine his own television show. By August, the idea had taken shape: a musical fantasy, "The Magic Thinner." A girl invents a solution that makes everything paper thin. To restore the objects, she plays a tune on an accordion, and POP!, everything returns to normal. Here was a parable from Pete's heart: song was the amulet, the magic restorer of balance. Ideas like this one inhabited the imagination of the man who brought a banjo to his trial. If someone spilled magic thinner on the judges and prosecutors, Pete Seeger would have the songs to restore them—if he chose.

Typical of his high spirits that summer was one of his finest recording sessions, which Columbia released as *The Bitter and the Sweet*. The album included "Where Have All the Flowers Gone?" and a superb performance of "False Knight on the Road," where Seeger's banjo brought a new tension to the ballad, subtly punctuating it with strums and arpeggios.

Then in July, Pete stumbled on a terrific new song: "Guantanamera." At the same camp where he had performed before his HUAC appearance, a Cuban counselor, Hector Angulo, stood up and sang Pete a poem of José Martí set to a Cuban folk tune. Seeger translated and rearranged the song, giving the counselor proper credit. Eventually, the song traveled across Europe, Japan, and South America.

To his joy, Seeger realized that his compositions had begun to enter the American repertoire, perhaps to reemerge as folk songs.

"My essential purpose in singing is to help the listener understand reality," Pete wrote in a telling letter to friend and music critic Henrietta Yurchencho. "And the path to understanding the reality of any age lies through the 'here and now' and thence to the 'faraway and beyond.'" Others sought this distant, harmonious land through religion or mysticism; Seeger reached for it in music.

Capacity audiences now turned out wherever he went. Anti-Seeger pickets at campuses like Chapel Hill were outnumbered a hundred to one by students eager to hear him. Folkways calculated that they had sold a million of Seeger's records since World War II. Slick magazines ran flattering profiles of him. Pete found he could make thousands of dollars doing what paid him twenty-five dollars in the Fifties. Yet if history had been his guide, Seeger might have suspected his good fortune; when all went well, he could expect a disaster.

The boom in folk music was now so prominent that *Time* placed photogenic Joan Baez on their 1962 Thanksgiving cover: "Guitars and banjo akimbo, folk singers inhabit smoky metropolitan crawl space; they sprawl on the floors of college rooms; near the foot of ski trails, they keep time to the wheeze and sputter of burning logs." Pete had hoped folk music could avoid this sort of attention; his pain at reading Leadbelly described as "a whooping primitive" can be imagined.

Nor did *Time* forget the man they called the "current patriarch of folk singing": "Seeger commands so much respect among folk singers that the only criticism leveled against him is that he can't carry a tune. But that gives him the seal of authenticity. His voice sounds as if a cornhusk were stuck in his throat."

Seeger's audience at New York's P.S. 84, five hundred third- through sixth-graders, disagreed. Reaching these squirmy kids was a challenge; their music teacher had barely managed to finish "America the Beautiful" without being booed off the stage. Seeger always considered young audiences far tougher than adults, ". . . especially with children of different ages. Their attention span is short. And they have their own prejudices: A kid of ten wouldn't be caught dead liking a song that he liked when he was six or eight—why, he's grown up now."

"Seeger walked down the aisle," journalist Peter Lyons wrote, "wearing a fuzzy sweater, a shirt of firehouse red, rough worsted trousers and heavy thick-soled shoes." Until he started playing he looked like a gaudy scarecrow: "But when he unlimbered his banjo and gave the children a warm, inclusive smile, something magical happened in the room. He sang:

Lou, Lou, skip to my Lou . . .

"At the second line, fifty voices were singing with him. At the third, a hundred had joined in, and scandalized teachers were shushing all over the hall. To no avail: Seeger and the children understood each other perfectly. . . . This routine miracle achieved, Seeger walked back up the aisle, submitted to an interview by three small shrewd reporters for the school paper, signed several autographs, rescued his instrument from a group of eager experimenters and made his way to the street.

" 'Can I,' he asked his wife Toshi, 'have some breakfast now?' "

In January 1963 Seeger had his long-awaited break: CBS-TV called Harold Leventhal about having Pete and the Weavers perform on a "Dinner with the President," sponsored by the Anti-Defamation League of the B'nai B'rith. Pete was ecstatic; he'd *known* his time would come. With his old classmate, John F. Kennedy, he would break bread and the blacklist.

His chance might never have come but for Harold, who had fought Seeger's censorship as if it were his own. The manager seemed to be everywhere at once; from his midtown office high above Broadway, he could book (and fill) virtually any auditorium in the country with Judy Collins, Don McLean, the Weavers, Odetta, and Theodore Bikel, among others. Harold increasingly worked as a unit with Toshi, including on her new project, the Newport Folk Festival, where performers ran the festival themselves and paid everyone equally.

One afternoon, soon after Harold had received word that CBS wanted the Weavers and Pete Seeger, his phone rang. A spokesman for the Anti-Defamation League had the unpleasant job of telling Harold he had made a mistake. The caller referred obliquely to a blacklist: Did Harold know some people wouldn't televise Seeger? According to Nat Hentoff, the man "had the chutzpah to ask Leventhal if he would try to get Joan Baez for the program. To his credit, Leventhal explosively refused." Harold was too good a friend not to know how this would disappoint Pete.

The show went on as scheduled, but without Pete. For decades he had been preparing a feast of folk songs for the American public; now that the fare was ready, blacklisters at the networks told him he wasn't loyal enough to serve it.

What was CBS afraid of? What could Seeger and the Weavers have sung that made them dangerous enough to censor? Perhaps the networks didn't care what they sang, the "Internationale" or "Jingle Bells"; Seeger's reputation was at least as dangerous as his songs. "I'm not afraid of him,"

Pete imagined network executives saying, "but I'll be damned if I want to put him on *my* program. Let somebody else hire Seeger. Let them stick *their* neck out."

He might have been more devastated by this news had he not heard that ABC-TV was planning a weekly folk music series, *Hootenanny*, and that he would be included. Since nobody at ABC knew much about folk music, they relied heavily on talent consultants, all of whom knew Pete Seeger. It's an old story: Stay in one place long enough, and a city grows up around you.

Some thought the show's title a bad omen; since folk music had become popular, the word hootenanny had been tarnished. Nevertheless the chief adviser to *Hootenanny*, Fred Weintraub, called Seeger to encourage him: "Pete, I'll try to get you on. First, we have to get the show on a firm basis commercially, so we're in a strong position." From the first show, there was something bogus about *Hootenanny*, like a half-dollar without enough silver. Seeger, starved for a chance to see folk music on TV, overlooked this. Besides, with Weintraub intimating he could sing—no loyalty oath required—the American public, fifteen million at a time, would finally hear his voice.

His troubles at Columbia Records temporarily spoiled this good news. Seeger had signed on in hopes of a broader audience, but their enthusiasm had dipped. His records didn't turn up in the shops. From time to time he would mention his concerns to Harold or to his producer, John Hammond; there was nothing Pete could put his finger on. Hammond was loyal and pleasant to work with, though Pete felt folk music never captured his attention the way jazz did. It dawned on Seeger that Columbia wanted his name more than his music: "If somebody accused Columbia of not recording folk music, they could say, 'Look, we have Pete Seeger.' " He had left Folkways willingly, helping Columbia attract Bob Dylan and others, but he felt used.

Toward the end of February 1963 Pete worried why he hadn't heard from *Hootenanny*, which had already filmed its first shows. He had Harold check matters out.

Weintraub called backed to reassure him. Everything was fine, he said: "We're going to get you on this show somehow. Can't do it in the first shows, but I'm going to get you on somehow."

On March 6 attorney William Kunstler received a letter from one of Pete's young fans at Brown University, where two of the ten *Hootenanny* shows were being taped. When the camera crew arrived at Brown, this junior detective grew chummy with an associate producer and asked about

Seeger and the Weavers. No, the answer came, they wouldn't be on because of "pressure from advertising agencies, sponsors, and stations." Kunstler passed the note along to Harold, asking if he wanted to do anything about it. Harold told Pete and Nat Hentoff, columnist for *The Village Voice* (and a veteran campaigner for freedom of speech).

Hentoff tracked down the rumor. To his dismay, he found Seeger wasn't scheduled. A little publicity, however, might change the producers' minds. Hentoff broke the story on March 14, in an article prickly with indignation: "That Ole McCarthy Hoot!" Keeping Pete Seeger off *Hootenanny*, a word he had brought to national circulation, was like barring Charlie Parker from Birdland. "At least we'll be getting folk music to a lot more people," Weintraub told Hentoff apologetically. "It's tough on Pete, but after all, he's been turned down on all three networks. Why pick on us?" Hentoff challenged performers to follow Joan Baez, who had refused to appear where Seeger was unwelcome: "What are you exposing when you go out there and leave Mr. Seeger behind?"

Hootenanny also turned down the Tarriers, an interracial folk group; but under pressure, the show's producers gave them a spot, making them one of the first integrated ensembles on TV. There was one problem. The Tarriers had to perform at a Village cafe on the night scheduled, and who could they ask, on short notice, to stand in so they could appear on *Hootenanny*? Pete Seeger, of course—when he heard their situation he agreed, chuckling to himself at the irony.

The folk community chose up sides. "I can't blame Mother Maybelle Carter for going on *Hootenanny*," Joan Baez said. "But it's disgusting that there are city folksingers—including some who don't need the bread or the exposure—who perform on those programs. They should know what it's about." Fifty performers formed a *Hootenanny* boycott committee, among them Barbara Dane, Mary Travers, and Bob Dylan. Rumors circulated that Peter, Paul and Mary had turned down twenty-five thousand dollars for one *Hootenanny* show. A *Hootenanny* appearance became a dividing line—which side were you on? Joan Baez refused, Judy Collins accepted; Tommy Makem boycotted, but the Clancy Brothers appeared; Dave Van Ronk wasn't interested, but Theo Bikel agreed, telling *Billboard* if everyone acted like "sane responsible people" and avoided "ineffectual public protest," the situation would resolve itself.

On April 14 in the *San Francisco Chronicle* Ralph Gleason reported a *Hootenanny* producer as saying Seeger was "too slow and thoughtful" for the show. Two days later, *The Nation* warned: "The blacklist syndrome could soon regain its earlier virulence." Seeger had become—for the umpteenth time—a test case. He bided his time; controversy-fearing advertisers might still arrange an appearance.

"I'm outraged," he told Ralph Gleason. "I actually get hot and flushed just thinking about it. We have all this richness and variety in our country but a bunch of schmoes, out to sell soap, keep the whole country seeing the same dreary things night after night."

Meanwhile, behind-the-scenes negotiations continued. The American Civil Liberties Union offered legal help; Pete asked them to wait and see how things turned out. Seeger's fans called for an audience boycott. Fifty angry pickets carrying END THE BLACKLIST signs paced the street outside ABC-TV's Manhattan studios. Late on a Saturday afternoon, the place looked deserted. The network had decided its position on Seeger: If asked, the show's producers could claim that they wanted Pete, but the sponsor (Procter & Gamble) wouldn't agree. The sponsor was to say that *they* wanted Pete, but the public didn't. ABC Public Relations ran off copies of critical letters they had received and stacked them on polished mahogany tables, ready for distribution.

When no one came out to meet the pickets, they grew angrier. Who did ABC think it was, keeping Seeger off TV? Nobody was throwing bricks, but the crowd was irate. Folksinger Hedy West (daughter of Appalachian poet and singer Don West) played the banjo and led Seeger's supporters in improvised lyrics insulting ABC. Strange, this picket *for* Pete, after the hundreds of right-wing picket lines he'd braved to perform.

Hootenanny offered unparalleled audiences, fees, and exposure, and for a singer who had been scraping by for a decade, the offer looked overwhelmingly attractive. Political and personal resentments broke out like a rash; Izzy Young at the Folklore Center couldn't stand Bob Shelton, the *New York Times's* folk-music writer; the *Times's* skimpy coverage of the *Hootenanny* affair didn't make matters better. The situation reminded insiders of the film industry infighting during HUAC's hearing on the Hollywood Ten.

Seeger couldn't bring himself to attack *Hootenanny*; it would seem self-serving. In fact, when he met with the boycott committee, he told fellow performers: "You can't *not* go on the show. The fact they've blacklisted me attracts more attention to the folk-song movement."

"Call it 'Pete Seeger's logic,'" explained Howie Richmond, Seeger's supportive music publisher. "Pete only sees the life of the songs."

"Harold and Pete both encouraged me to do the show," Judy Collins said. According to Bob Shelton of *The New York Times* she appeared three times and she quickly discovered that "their taste was, shall I say, not impeccable." Midway through her rendition of "John Riley," the producers cut two verses to "speed things up."

In May 1963 executive producer Richard Lewine held a press conference. There *was* no blacklist on *Hootenanny,* he explained. With limited space on the show, he couldn't hire everyone. After considering Pete, listening to his records and all, it boiled down to one thing: "Pete Seeger just can't hold an audience."

After it became clear *Hootenanny* would not have him, Seeger let loose: "This story needs to be told now, not next year, or even next month," he wrote in *Sing Out!* "The ABC network, the talent agency (Ashley), the sponsor (Procter & Gamble) are all charging ahead with the idea of making a fast-paced show, 26 minutes of screaming kids in the studio audience." Seeger pointed out how long Alan Lomax and others—he didn't mention himself—had proposed a series on folk music, to no avail.

"When will the TV producers learn that some of the best music in our country is made by unlettered farmers, miners, housewives," Pete asked sadly, "people with generations of folk traditions in their veins." He offered the Newport Folk Festival as an alternative; readers could write and let ABC know their feelings: "These hucksters have no minds of their own, you know."

That was as much bitterness as Seeger allowed himself in print. He had been taken for a ride, but his rage turned inward, to sadness and futility.

Pete and Toshi decided to leave the country for a year. They told the press they wanted to travel as a family before the kids grew too old. Interestingly enough, the bulk of their baggage turned out to be movie equipment. They were determined to film folk music in authentic settings, not in front of screaming college kids. Just before he left, *Hootenanny* offered him a spot if he would sign a loyalty oath. "Dear ABC," he replied brusquely: "I just finished a seven-year court battle to prove the principle that such oaths are unconstitutional, and I was acquitted and vindicated." Next to this he noted: "Release after departure" and "Leave country without a stir."

He had let his hopes carry him away. His songs were on the hit parade, *Variety* recognized him as the leader of the folk-music movement, and the courts had cleared him of wrongdoing. Then came *Hootenanny,* grinding in his vulnerability. If Seeger had been made of soft wood instead of oak, he would have cracked and split.

We Shall Overcome 10

THE SEEGERS' departure was set for August 18, 1963, three months hence. Plans for the trip grew more and more elaborate, until they were to visit thirty countries and carry several cameras plus suitcases of film and accessories, all to be priced and purchased before departure.

Before he could begin assembling equipment, however, Pete's attention turned to another of his interests: civil rights. During the past year, he had heard about freedom rides, sit-ins, and the music blacks sang as they were dragged off to jail. When Pete finally had an invitation to sing in the South, he had agreed excitedly, and in October 1962 he found himself bumping along the back roads of rural Georgia. He was headed into the thick of the street fighting and civil disobedience sweeping this once quiet corner of the Black Belt, visiting a black church which had asked him to sing.

For the past two months Albany, Georgia, had been on the brink of a race riot. A thousand black demonstrators had already been jailed, and white vigilante gangs burned crosses on hot summer nights. A pray-in at the city hall had brought a young preacher down from Atlanta, Martin Luther King, Jr., who was arrested along with seventy-five other clergy. The nearby Mount Olive church was burned to the ground when a sheriff discovered a civil-rights meeting there. Another organizer had been shot and paralyzed when a bullet tore through the wall of a home she was visiting.

These were minor skirmishes in a war for racial equality that had been spreading since the mid-Fifties, when Rosa Parks's refusal to sit in the back of a bus sparked the now famous bus boycott in Montgomery, Alabama. Sit-ins, jail-ins, even swim-ins, broke out in dozens of southern cities. On the evening Seeger drove into Albany, a convoy of two hundred National Guard trucks and jeeps guarded James Meredith as he registered to be the first black student at the University of Mississippi.

Pete's car jolted over the hard-packed earth with an uncertain clatter. This was *not* the place for a breakdown; the local White Citizens' Council had promised to take revenge on every outside agitator who fell into their hands. He crossed a lonely stretch of country with the smell of horses at pasture and freshly plowed dirt, a reminder of how far away he was from home. Years before, Pete had read W. E. B. Du Bois's *The Souls of Black Folk*, with its stories of Georgia sharecroppers and slave violence. The one-room cabins still dotted the horizon, marking the boundaries of the old plantations. It was close to harvest time, and now, as in Du Bois's time, the fields of cotton were "like a silver cloud edged with dark green." Pecan trees rattled in the wind, and the unpaved roads rolled across reddish clay soil.

Albany had a singing movement. The black community used the old hymns for their battles, and they sang so loud and so long, they were ready for any enemy when they finished. They had invited Seeger so they could see what they could learn from a veteran songster; he looked forward to singing on the battle lines.

When he pulled up at the church, the building was packed. From the back entrance, Seeger could already hear singing:

> *Oh, Freedom, Oh, Freedom*
> *Oh, Freedom over me*
> *And before I'll be a slave*
> *I'll be buried in my grave*
> *And go home to my lord*
> *And be free.*

The Georgia Patrol circled the neighborhood in their sleek sedans, ready for trouble. Off to one side a crowd of whites gathered to jeer at the churchgoers; three or four carried lead pipes. Seeger hurriedly unloaded his instruments and stepped inside.

Few onlookers would have suspected this erect forty-three-year-old in blue jeans was one of the country's top songwriters. ("If I Had a Hammer" now topped the hit parade.) Yet here he stood in Dougherty County, where "nigger lovers" were welcomed with buckshot and beatings. Pete had been raised on slogans like "Black and white unite," and now it looked as if it were coming true.

Inside the church, six fans provided little relief in the soupy heat. The room was overcrowded; if someone had shouted "fire," people would have been trampled to death. An eighteen-year-old girl, Bertha Gober, led a

traditional hymn with new words, and the congregation sang verse after
verse in slow, surging meter.

> *We been 'buked*
> *And we been scorned*
> *We been lied to,*
> *Sure's you're born*
> *But we'll never,*
> *No we'll never turn back.*

Their singing moved Seeger more than any speech could. The community had sung these tunes for generations, and the harmonies floated
down like the echoes of a summer rain. Between songs, the congregation
told of beatings and harassment at the courthouse; anger mixed with amens
until another song began to rise. The pastor stood up to introduce Seeger,
who hurried to the pulpit.

He was an odd choice to address a mass meeting of blacks in Georgia.
Not until he left Harvard for New York did he meet blacks for the first time
and learn of lynchings and segregation. (The only ones he had seen at Avon
played on a nearby football team.)

In later years, he had known Paul Robeson well and counted many
blacks among his circle. In 1956 Pete had flown to Birmingham to sing for
Dr. Martin Luther King, Jr., and the Montgomery Improvement Association. Afterward, King wrote him a flowery note, praising his "moral support
and Christian generosity." Seeger had promised to return if needed, and
now he volunteered his time, paying his own expenses.

In an unusual move, Pete had already decided what he would sing. He
wanted to explain how in the 1930s white labor organizers had also adopted
hymns; he wanted to give "a wide picture" of organizing through music and
the Old Left. Unfortunately, Seeger's timing was off, as it had been in
People's Songs.

Standing in the minister's place, Seeger picked up his banjo. It might
have been wiser to leave the instrument at home. Among black churchgoers, the banjo usually meant minstrel shows and loose dancing; this was
not church music. Unaware of this, Seeger kept right on picking. He did
notice that the audience seemed surprisingly restrained as he began "If I
Had a Hammer." He discovered later that the audience liked to sing the
song with different lyrics.

When he started the union hymn "Hold On" he found himself singing
not only different words, but out of rhythm and out of tune with the

audience, who generally sang it in a minor key. People began to stir in their seats, asking each other how this guy was supposed to help *them* sing. Something had gone wrong, Pete realized; they sang better with their own songleaders. Perhaps they were tired. Seeger decided to sing a long ballad and give them a rest.

It was the wrong move. He had half finished an old English tune when someone whispered, "If this is white folks' music, I don't think much of it."

"Shush," another replied. "If we expect white folks to understand us, we've got to try and understand them."

If he had known that Guy Carawan (from the leftist Highlander Folk School) had earlier run into the same problems trying to teach labor songs here, Pete might have avoided all this pain. Carawan had stayed in the community long enough to build up trust, however, and eventually won acceptance. Seeger rushed in and attempted his customary miracle in two hours.

Minute by minute Pete grew more self-conscious. "There I was, repeating the same unrhythmic melody over and over with little or no variation. . . . The story was so ancient and so unfamiliar as to have little meaning for the listeners. I sang with a deadpan expression purposely not to detract from the words, and this only made the melody seem more boring to them." The situation drifted from bad to worse, until the only song that roused the crowd was "We Shall Overcome."

Pete had first heard "We Shall Overcome" in 1947, when Zilphia Horton (one of the founders of Highlander) had taught him a version from striking tobacco workers in North Carolina. The song was originally an old gospel tune, "I'll Overcome" or "I'll Be All Right"; Zilphia sang it "We Will Overcome." Pete made a few key alterations: "I changed it to 'We shall.' Toshi kids me that it was my Harvard grammar, but I think I liked a more open sound; "We will' has alliteration to it, but 'We shall' opens the mouth wider; the 'i' in 'will' is not an easy vowel to sing well. . . ."

He also added new verses: "We'll walk hand in hand" and "The whole wide world around." In the Fifties Pete taught the song to Frank Hamilton, a singer in California, who in turn taught it to Guy Carawan, a lean-looking sociology M.A. from Los Angeles who ended up at Highlander in 1959. Carawan had reintroduced the song to the community which had started it—black labor and civil-rights workers. Since then, without a recording, "We Shall Overcome" had traveled orally across the south, a widely known non-hit.

"The song was different than in union days," one organizer for the Student Nonviolent Coordinating Committee (SNCC) remembered. "We put more soul in, a sort of rocking quality, to stir one's inner feeling. When you got through singing it, you could walk over a bed of hot coals, and you wouldn't notice."

By the time Peter performed it in Albany, "We Shall Overcome" had evolved from a song to a ritual, where the audience stood and swayed, crossing hands. Seeger kept the song in his armory for tense situations like this one. Here in Georgia, its meaning reinforced by distant police sirens, the song brought hope and community. Pete gave up on educating his audience and let them sing. This mollified the crowd, and they thanked him politely as he left the church.

Fifteen years later, Seeger would look back on the Albany concert and shake his head, calling it one of his great failures at reaching an audience. Many professionals would have chalked it up to a bad night and moved on; Seeger could not: Misreading an audience threatened his self-confidence. Two summers before the Albany concert, he had brashly written in *Sing Out!*: "There are plenty of young people who can play rings around me on guitar or banjo. But I'm proud that I hardly ever met an audience I couldn't get singing."

In Albany he confronted a new situation, where songs really *were* at the center of change, when the community itself sang. Civil rights was a genuine mass movement, not one born of left-wingers in New York, and Seeger's radical traditions seemed remote to blacks facing police with cattle prods. Perhaps no one needed a middle-aged New England radical in a black church in Georgia.

Since the Almanacs in the Forties, Seeger had faithfully maintained that music would transform society; he was virtually the last of his crowd to do so. Alan Lomax had drifted into editing records and then to grant-getting and his study of world song styles, cantometrics. He had no patience with demonstrations. Lee Hays still sang with the Weavers (who had replaced tenor Erik Darling with Frank Hamilton); Lee willingly performed the new freedom songs, but he did not follow them into towns where he could have his head blown off. Burl Ives continued his acting career; Josh White had arthritis in his hands, which made playing painful. Mill Lampell had finally fought his way out from under the blacklist with his first Hollywood film writing credit. In many ways, Pete stood alone. Duty and good causes beckoned him long after his friends decided to let someone else sing up a storm.

Pete's debacle in Albany made his world tour even more urgent—it became a quest to see how far his music could reach: "to test myself," as he wrote in his journal, "by the toughest means possible that my chosen work has a basic, universal validity." By setting his standards so high, however, he made the trip an ordeal; he could not afford to fail.

In the next few months Seeger—as if trying to prove his powers— labored mightily for civil rights. As he changed planes in Atlanta the day following his Albany concert, he stopped to sing at a benefit for SNCC, a group of young organizers, mostly black and southern. Afterward, the singers gathered at the house of Dr. King's aide, Andrew Young (later U.S. ambassador to the UN), where Seeger met a young singer from Albany, Bernice Johnson. A short stocky woman with tightly curled hair, Bernice had a voice like a cannon; when she sang the largest room filled with her rich, resonant tones.

When Pete met her in the fall of 1962, nineteen-year-old Bernice already had a reputation as a civil rights singer. The daughter of a minister, Bernice had a deceptively quiet air and large gentle eyes. Her temper could be peppery, however, and she had been suspended from Albany State College for demonstrating. Pete encouraged her to start an ensemble of SNCC singers who could spread freedom songs the way the Almanacs had stumped for the CIO. Bernice took Seeger's advice literally; the day after he flew to New York, she quit Spelman College, packed her bags, and left the South. She called Toshi Seeger long distance and asked her to arrange a tour for the Freedom Singers, as she called them. Toshi became the group's unpaid manager and Bernice a member of the Seeger family.

The civil rights movement quickly became a major priority in Pete and Toshi's lives. Pete's work had suddenly doubled, for Toshi and Harold had overbooked him, assuming that he might soon be in jail and need the extra money. By the time his conviction had been overturned, he was committed to appear. Seeger turned these dates into a musical forum for civil rights, carrying the freedom songs like a gardener bringing in flats of vegetables. He stirred up interest, but the marathon schedule nearly flattened him.

The first week in April he performed in Newark; a week later he sang at a sold-out Civic Opera House in Chicago. A few days later it was Winnipeg, Canada, and the day after, New York's Town Hall, standing room only. Six days after that, Joan Baez and he filled the Washington, D.C., Coliseum, after which he returned to New York to perform at Carnegie Hall, two nights in a row, for the Weavers' fifteenth anniversary concert. His voice sounds tired on those recordings, and it must have gotten worse the next day in Los Angeles, when he sang at the UCLA Folk Festival, before flying off to Minnesota for a concert.

Judy Collins visited the Newport Festival office in New York and found Pete asleep on the floor, too tired to drive back to Beacon. Toshi finally told her husband, "Look, you have to ease up—you're going to drop dead if you don't."

He managed all this travel without road crew or manager for company; often Seeger marched by himself from one airport cafe to another, his banjo strapped to his shoulder. He hadn't moved his audience in Albany, but these penitential travels produced converts across the country.

Of course Pete wasn't the only one busy—booking the Freedom Singers proved a full-time job. At one point Toshi told them, "You better go to the bathroom now, because next month's schedule's so busy, you might not get another chance." Toshi knew what she was doing; for fifteen years, she'd done the same work for Pete. That receipt he had sent home from the army had joined thousands of others and file cabinets of correspondence. Toshi knew which auditoriums sounded best, who would accept a low down payment for a hall, even which reporters to contact. For once she threw herself into a cause independent of her husband's career. A fellow organizer called her labor "a perfect meeting of the Old and New Left. No one went off without instructions, follow-up calls, food after the show, and airplane tickets for the next date. All those Old Left/union organizing skills began to flow through SNCC."

The Freedom Singers (originally Bernice, Charles Neblet, Cordell Reagon, and Rutha Harris) often visited Beacon, rubbing shoulders with the conservatives who had tried to kill Paul Robeson at Peekskill, fifteen years before. Bernice had now married Cordell Reagon, but she remained close to the Seegers, even naming her first baby Toshi. One Christmas she spent the holidays at Beacon, gaining a new insight into Pete.

Winter had piled the autumn leaves into snow-covered banks, and the cold wind off the Hudson resembled nothing Bernice knew from her childhood in Georgia. Christmas at the Seegers' was a busy time, with relatives stopping in, blankets passed around, kids cooking and making their own wrapping paper. Toshi was friendly but occupied and Pete remote, chopping wood until he was red in the face or off by himself practicing. On a walk one wintry afternoon, Bernice stooped to pick up a chestnut. Returning to the Seegers' cabin, she asked her host what it was.

Pete raised his head. "You know . . ." he began, staring over her shoulder, and launched into a parable until Bernice broke in, astonished.

"I told him, 'Thanks, but I'd just like to know a little something about chestnuts.' He didn't know how to handle a real, down-to-earth exchange.

Before you get his answer to a question, he's removed it so far from himself!"

All the time she had managed the Freedom Singers, Toshi had kept preparations for the trip on a back burner. Now that Pete had finished most of his bookings, their departure neared. The *Hootenanny* affair still galled Pete, and he and Harold concentrated on arranging appearances on foreign television. Among the other preparations for leaving was a farewell concert at Carnegie Hall, where Seeger could sing the freedom songs he had practiced. Harold persuaded Columbia Records to make a live recording.

As this concert and their departure neared, the Seegers confronted the intricacies of transporting a family, baggage, and instruments around the world. The teenager who wouldn't even carry a sleeping bag now had a caravan of equipment. Toshi, exploring a new career, made sure they had all the equipment for lighting, recording, and shooting movies. The next few weeks passed in securing visas and getting injected with a bewildering array of shots.

If Seeger and the Freedom Singers were busy, civil-rights workers were equally pressed in that spring of 1963. Veterans of the Albany movement now gathered in Birmingham, Alabama, a die-hard city that preferred to close public parks rather than integrate them. In April, Birmingham's notorious sheriff, Bull Connor, had slapped Dr. King into solitary. In May, 969 children, six to sixteen, were arrested in one day, a minor record for civil disobedience in America. The next day, as crowds of blacks gathered in prayer outside a church, police sealed off the exits and unleashed their dogs.

Like millions of Americans, Seeger watched the dogs attack on TV. A fire hose sprayed into the crowd, and a slender teenage girl jerked along the ground in its blast. As the TV crews panned the scene, they picked up the nonviolent demonstrators singing Seeger's arrangement of "We Shall Overcome." Violence against blacks filled the news, but the cause paid in blood for the privilege of seeing itself on TV.

Leaving this battle for a world tour made Pete self-conscious, and he wrote Chico Neblett, Bob Moses, and Sam Block of SNCC's Mississippi office: ". . . I promise you I'll sing songs that tell of the great freedom fight you are putting up."

His farewell concert turned out as much of a test as his tour, but of a different sort. Columbia Records was getting impatient with him; his records weren't selling well. Two talented producers had tried, but no one had captured Seeger in the studio; he was the classic "live" performer, whose electricity came from the crowd. Unless matters changed, Columbia might have to drop him. Seeger determined to "do as good a job as I can" on this record, and rehearsed an informal chorus to sit on stage, where the mikes would pick up a balance of voices. The concert took place on June 8, 1963, just as John F. Kennedy was preparing a major civil-rights speech.

"If you want to get out of a pessimistic mood yourself, I've got one *sure* remedy. Go help those people in Birmingham or Mississippi." The words rolled smoothly through Carnegie Hall's plush triple balconies. College kids in rumpled workshirts cheered as Pete struck up "Oh, Freedom." They wanted to do their part, a thousand miles north of the fray, and Pete was at his most persuasive. By the end of the evening, his audience embraced civil rights the way Seeger had revered Republican Spain, twenty-five years before:

> The only thing that we did wrong
> Stayed in the wilderness a day too long
>
> Keep your eyes on the prize, hold on
> Hold on, hold on . . .
>
> The one thing that we did right
> Was the day we begun to fight.

The biblical images of the song had withstood the long transition from hymn to song of action. Seeger sang the news, as his predecessors, the troubadors, had hundreds of years before. For a few short hours the audience had the illusion that by singing they, too, were fighting.

On evenings like this Seeger reached for two emotional centers in the audience: One touched off a physical reaction—whistling, hollering, clapping; another lay further inside, accessible only to art. "Pete aims deep," commented banjoist Mike Cooney. "Most of the time he doesn't want whistles or applause; he reaches for the audience's core."

> If you miss me on the back of the bus,
> And you can't find me nowhere,
> Come on up to the front of the bus,
> I'll be riding right there.
>
> If you miss me from the Mississippi River,
> And you can't find me nowhere,
> Come on down to the city pool,
> I'll be swimming right there.

Spain had Hemingway, Malraux, and Orwell; the civil rights movement had its chroniclers, who worked in song—Malvina Reynolds, Phil Ochs, Len Chandler, and Bob Dylan.

"Let me sing a song by a young songwriter, twenty-two years old"— here Carnegie Hall kindled with applause for the voice of youth—"Bob Dylan." Seeger sang "Who Killed Davey Moore," and then his favorite Dylan song, "Hard Rain." Playing over the applause, he did Reynolds's "Little Boxes." Finally he strummed "We Shall Overcome": "They're all kinds of jobs that need to be done. Takes hands, hearts, and heads to do it—human beings. Then we'll see this song come true."

Pete's song introductions combined oratory and exhortation. "In other days, Pete Seeger would have been a politican or an evangelist," a reviewer wrote in 1963. "He has some sort of inborn sensitivity to crowd techniques." Seeger worked in the tradition of great American stump speakers, like William Jennings Bryan, the Great Commoner, attacking the gold standard, or Frederick Douglass assailing slavery.

". . . We shall live in peace, the whole wide world around." "We Shall Overcome" rose on its own power and crescendoed in layers of harmony. Seeger used his broad range to carry two harmonies at once, catapulting his voice from a rolling bass to his upper tenor. The desire to overcome tightened in chests filled with song. "We are not afraid," Dr. King had sung in Montgomery in 1955; eight years later in Carnegie Hall, the walls seemed to buckle with sound.

By sharing the singing, Seeger convinced people that they, "his great audience," did all the work; *they* were the stars. Like a concave mirror, he focused his listeners' admiration back out into the balconies, inspiring people with an image of themselves as better (more tolerant, compassionate, international) than they were. He kindled their hopes.

If someone had walked into that hall recruiting kids to fight racism in the South, they'd have filled their quota in minutes. Yet in the finale, as the audience stood and linked arms, friends and strangers singing "We shall overcome someday," the first discords echoed. The young and irreverent got carried away. To sustain the mood, to carry the song home and out into the streets, a few started singing "overcome today." A small difference, perhaps, but within three years the militant minority would outnumber the old guard. "We shall overcome *today*," they sang, "right NOW!"

If Pete noticed the substitution, the crowd couldn't tell. Head tilted back, he rocked on his heels and drummed the bass strings of his guitar. The audience closed their eyes and swayed. When Seeger slowed to his finish, a suppressed sigh whooshed through the hall.

Released as *We Shall Overcome*, the concert was a triumph, but not the kind he most sought. His mind continued to dwell on his tour: "What happens on this trip will tell me much, I think, about my work, and about myself. . . . I really do feel like a man headed, with faltering step, straight toward the moment of truth." At forty-four, Seeger had three kids, fine health, and more wealth than he could spend. Yet something was missing from his life; he couldn't tell what his art accomplished, and this Pete had to find out.

Answers were hard to come by. The change Pete hoped to inspire was near impossible to measure, for the effect of a song is subtle, and often separate in time and space from the original singer. Audience response is not always audience change.

Singing for social change and actually making that change happen have always been different activities. Much as Seeger tried to collap e the distance between singing and organizing, songs were not the same as votes or bullets. Music *has* encouraged and even inspired revolutions; thus, governments tortured musicians like Victor Jara or Mikos Theodorakis, hoping to destroy a song by silencing its composer. But a song is made of unbreakable stuff, words and music that need only breath and spirit to live. Torture might have been easier than neglect for Seeger. In the United States, there were no thumbscrews to prove his valor; the government relied on a repressive tolerance. Crude censorship creates partisans rather than vassals. Songs, even in the most socially explosive moments in history, must butt against authority to be subversive. Sanctioned or subsidized, they pose little danger.

As he entered middle age, Seeger realized his talent shone most brightly when TV executives or school administrators blundered into censorship. He had a gnawing feeling that if he had been really successful, the government would have tried harder to silence him. Pete did not enjoy being lauded; he did not want to be a millionaire or an institution. He often felt like Woody at that tryout in the Rainbow Room—that in his success, he had enough freedom to hang himself.

The family left the country in August, after introducing the Freedom Singers to the West Coast and to the Newport Folk Festival. In October, having stopped in Samoa, Australia, and Indonesia, they landed in Japan, where the Seegers (or the Ohtas, as they were called there) had a busy visit. Toshi whisked the children off to visit her father's birthplace. Pete joked around with some kids as he filmed playground songs in a Tokyo schoolyard. The footage wouldn't impress a film critic, but he seemed to be having a second childhood.

He had already run into his first problems: English was not widely enough known for audiences to follow his songs. He played instrumentals and resigned himself to strumming along with an interpreter.

From Japanese television he received a warm welcome. Though he was still barred from *"Hootenanny"*—which struggled along despite a performer boycott—the Japanese knew him as a songwriter, not a subversive. Singing "Where Have All the Flowers Gone?" on prime-time TV so perked up his mood that he didn't mind the translator. Enough TV broadcasts around the world, and he might finally get a spot in the U.S.

Seeger particularly looked forward to visiting India. The language and cultural barriers were as severe as in Japan, but there were parallels between the civil rights movement he had left behind and Gandhi's Satyagraha ("holding to the truth"). Both used nonviolence and inspiring songs. Gandhi, like Seeger, fought in symbols, reviving the spinning wheel and living sparsely. He would have felt at home in Pete's log cabin.

Seeger's reception in India buoyed his spirits; he seemed to be passing his own test. One hundred thousand people—including the U.S. ambassador—turned out to hear him in Calcutta, and the *New Delhi Statesman* reported his singing had "a fervour that is almost evangelical." On All-India Radio, his listening audience was estimated to be as large as the entire population of the U.S.

Yet departing for Africa, Seeger was still not satisfied: "Nowhere on this whole adventure," he wrote, "have I had quite the same feeling . . . the wish—more than a wish or a hope, the ache—to carry out my purpose where the odds against it seem large but the stakes high. . . . I don't delude myself that what I know of the American Negro is going to help me here."

From the moment they landed in Kenya, mistaken schedules and minor illnesses disturbed the trip. The Seegers were expected either two weeks earlier or a month later. Pete, whose fair skin burnt easily, nearly passed out from the sun. Once the family spent hours setting up their equipment—with Mika, fifteen, taking a light reading, Danny, seventeen, hunched over the tape recorder in earphones, and little Tinya squinting into the camera eyepiece—only to discover, after they finished shooting, that a pin had rattled loose from the camera, ruining their film.

Pete finally took the safari he had imagined as a boy, poring over travel brochures. From Nairobi the family drove south to Dar es Salaam in a rented car. With the city a few miles behind, they approached a vast plain and distant peaks overhung by clouds. Soon they were driving through herds of zebra, hartebeest, and antelope. Seven-year-old Tinya squealed at the giraffes and wild buffalo. They were in the country of the Masai, tall herdsmen who carried twelve-foot spears to drive cattle to the fields. As they neared the awesome Mount Kilimanjaro, rising steeply to nineteen thousand feet, Pete had to remind himself this was real, not something he had dreamed in Beacon.

Before descending into Dar, a sun-baked city on the Indian Ocean, they hit a stretch of road so bumpy the strings on Seeger's banjo snapped. Driving a Mercedes—all they could find—didn't exactly make them feel at one with the natives; and when the jars of peanut butter and jelly opened up all over their food and clothing, they almost gave up.

Had Seeger not had such high expectations, he might have seen the delight of strangers hearing a banjo for the first time. But because of the heat, the missed meals and sleep, the interminable paper shuffling at borders, Pete overlooked his own success. Instead of relaxing, he pushed himself harder, even when his concertizing made life difficult for his road-weary family.

Pictures from that trip show Pete happier than the others. Danny looked bored; Mika cast her eyes slightly down, impatient. Tinya shyly held her mother's hand, while Toshi, in a sari, looked as if she had a clipboard of details on her mind. There seemed a centrifugal force at work in the family, each member edging away from its axis, Pete Seeger: "As soon as we possibly could," Toshi recalled with a wry smile, "we'd get away from one another to different sides of the plane or hotel room." Inconvenient and uncomfortable as the trip had become, Pete had sung about living in peace, "the whole wide world around," and he was determined to live that verse through.

A few days before Christmas 1963, matters began to improve. Pete sang at a graduation ceremony in Dar es Salaam; jubilant to be performing again after the trip across Kenya, he walked on stage—and discovered there was no microphone: "And all those faces, turned eagerly to me, waiting, with no notion I'm in trouble." He banged out a few loud square dance numbers on his banjo. Then he tried freedom songs, hoping his voice would hold out. He sang one that caught their attention, and as he wrote in his journal: "That does it. I can always tell, to the split second, when that marvelous moment comes—the 'click' of singer and listener—when I have really found my audience and it has really found me." The song was "We Shall Overcome."

It wasn't easy to stand up without a mike in a ballroom in Africa and teach black teenagers the meaning—and how to sing—"We Shall Overcome." Yet he had traveled halfway around the world for this interchange. "Wimoweh" was another hit, particularly among exiled South Africans: "It goes so well, I don't want to stop it. Some of the South Africans start a dancing line. So long as they keep it up, I've got to sing. But now I'm getting hoarse. Finally, breathless, I hold up a hand, take a last bow. Did it! What a feeling!"

He had three miserable days of laryngitis afterward, but he was fulfilled. Pete had represented America and its music in a new way: "One wonders why this image of America is never promoted here," a paper in India had commented after one of his concerts. "There was not even a suggestion of the loud gawkiness one associates with American pop music in his program." This was one of the unalloyed triumphs of Seeger's life. He had overcome barriers of language, race, and culture; words were limited, but his music universal. Success was costly—tour expenses amounted to over thirty thousand dollars beyond his concert fees—but there was no price tag for this affirmation.

Pete's mood improved still further when he learned that in his absence, with Harold placing weekly ads in *Variety*—"Seeger in Indonesia," "Seeger in Japan"—he had the first solo hit of his life, "Little Boxes," which Columbia had excerpted from *We Shall Overcome*. For the first time in twelve years, his voice was heard on radio.

In Africa, Seeger had regained confidence in his craft. When a government folklorist led them to a remote village in Tanzania, Pete performed as an equal. The tribes would dance and drum; then his turn came, and Pete would amaze them with a banjo tune like "Old Joe Clark." He had to rely on his musicianship, and he relearned how music can say what words cannot.

As Seeger triumphantly flew from Ghana to Europe and Russia on the last leg of his tour, he felt a rising impatience to get home. He had heard of a massive education and voting rights project planned for the next summer in Mississippi, and he wanted to be htere; if he could get Africans harmonizing, he would not again fail in the South.

Fatigued by travel, having visited thirty countries, the Seegers boarded a flight to New York on June 2, 1964. "The U.S. seems very big, very rich, the cars huge," Pete wrote with the shock of reentry. "The Hudson Valley still seems one of the most beautiful spots on earth, even if it does stink with sewage." He returned even more firmly committed to world citizenship and to integration, but a few matters stood between him and Mississippi: the Newport Folk Festival and the two hundred thousand feet of film they'd shot. Toshi foresaw lonely months at the editing table, with Pete off singing; she insisted that if he didn't edit *now*, he would never find the time.

The first time Pete was able to travel south was in August 1964, with the summer almost over.

In the ten months he had been out of the country, Pete had missed a great deal. The March on Washington for Jobs and Freedom had brought a quarter of a million people together, with many of Pete's friends singing. JFK had been shot in Dallas. Racial violence escalated; four young girls had been killed in an explosion at a church in Birmingham. SNCC workers now called themselves "guerrilla fighters," and the white youngsters Seeger had recruited to civil rights looked for some way to live up to their ideals. The Mississippi Summer Project, sponsored by SNCC, Dr. King's Southern Christian Leadership Conference, and others, seemed like an answer, a Huck Finn attempt to end racial injustice in one intense summer. Many of the most dedicated teenagers Pete knew were involved; if they could risk their hides in Mississippi, he could at least provide musical support.

One volunteer who partly credited Seeger with his moral awakening, Paul Cowan, described the motivations for going to Mississippi: "The project seemed to be a turning point in America's history. We were an army of love, and if we integrated Mississippi, we would conquer hate's capital."

Mississippi welcomed Seeger and his young initiates with rifles and clubs; in those days, SNCC organizers were Negro, not black, and mixed marriages not merely taboo, but illegal. Before the summer ended, eighty volunteers would be beaten, thirty-five black churches bombed or burnt, and dozens of shootings reported. "We've been told over and over about brutality and beatings and murder," a volunteer wrote home. "They say none of us believe it inside. We probably feel we have a lucky charm which will give us a halo of sanctity."

Others cold-bloodedly talked of the volunteers as decoys. "It was high time for the U.S. as a whole, a white-dominated country, to feel the consequences of its own racism," wrote James Forman, SNCC's executive secretary.

On August 2, 1964, Pete visited voter registration projects in Mississippi. Though part of a caravan of entertainers, he traveled alone. At the last minute, Toshi's father worriedly asked them not to go; news reports of three missing civil rights workers disturbed him. Pete wouldn't be dissuaded. He had thought the decision through, and his mind was made up. After much back-and-forthing, Toshi stayed in Beacon and Pete departed.

Trouble started before Seeger could get out of the airport in Jackson. A man followed him off the plane, a Mississippian who had overheard Pete talking with a reporter from *Life* during the flight.

"He accosted me with blood in his eye," Seeger wrote his father. " 'Are you coming down here to sing for the niggers?'

" 'I've been asked down here by some friends to sing,' says I, trying to be at my most gracious. 'I hope that anyone who wants to hear me can come, negro or white.'

" 'Well, you just better watch your step. If we hadn't been on the plane when I heard you talking I would have knocked the shit out of you.'

"I tried to mollify him, but he wasn't interested in listening."

As Pete sped from this Mississippi welcome, he rode into an even more tense situation. The volunteers had brought unexpected problems, such as black-white extramarital sex (as welcome as bubonic plague in small southern towns). SNCC's southern black staff felt displaced as the earnest young whites moved in and ran the offices.

Seeger would have understood this conflict better if he had stayed longer. He hadn't yet learned the lesson of his Albany failure: that he couldn't always zoom in and reach people in the middle of a crisis. He was willing to visit, but not to commit himself to months of knocking on doors under the Mississippi sun.

On a drenchingly hot August afternoon, Seeger pulled into Hattiesburg, Mississippi, where blacks had a one percent of the vote in a county that was sixty-seven percent black. Walking through town, he met an old friend: the woman known as Calamity Jane, who had put him and Woody up in Duluth, back in 1941.

"Pete arrived with his guitar over his shoulder, playing," the white schoolteacher recalled. "He was sweating, and the shirt clung to his back." A black minister guided him to a seat in the shade and sent his daughter for ice water. Soon not only civil-rights workers but townspeople wandered over to what sounded, with clapping and amens, like a revival meeting. Calamity Jane was amazed—days before, black and white SNCC workers had been yelling at each other.

"Get off our backs," Seeger's friend had finally told one of her local black critics. "If we weren't for you, we wouldn't be here. Since when are *we* the enemy?"

"Listen," a black organizer had answered. "It would be nice if we could give you all big badges: 'I WAS IN MISSISSIPPI. I'M A GOOD WHITE.' Our people are angry and you may be killed or hurt with the rest. We can't say these are innocent and those are guilty."

Into this situation—complicated by white racists trying to scare off the civil rights workers—Seeger brought a truce. Everyone sat down together. The heat, the ever-present threat of violence melted, and, for a moment, they sang in a cool meadow. No one wanted to stir, for fear of waking. They sang "We Shall Overcome" and again had one cause, one enemy. Then, too soon, the songs ended. Ragged from the heat and from holding within him the group's tensions, the singer limped off to the next town.

On August 3, Pete performed in Meridian. "We sang a lot of freedom songs," remembered one volunteer, "and every time a verse like 'No more lynchings' was sung, or 'Before I'd be a slave I'd be buried in my grave,' I had the flash of understanding that sometimes comes when you think about the meaning of a familiar song. . . . I wanted to stand up and shout: Think about what you are singing—people really *have* died to keep us all from being slaves."

In the middle of the concert, someone handed Seeger a note: SNCC workers Andrew Goodman, Michael Schwerner, and James Chaney had been found buried in a swamp.

A damp feeling, first of terror, then sorrow, swept through the crowd; Goodman had been in Mississippi less than twenty-four hours before he disappeared. Seeger quietly sang:

> *O healing river*
> *Send down your water*
> *Send down your water*
> *Upon this land*
>
> *O healing river*
> *Send down your water*
> *And wash the blood*
> *From off our sand*

Amid the crying and shock, Seeger closed by saying "We must sing 'We Shall Overcome' now. The three boys would not have wanted us to weep, but to sing and understand this song." He didn't rage, or stir up an assault on the Klan. In difficult moments, his religious streak surfaced, as Christian as the inscription on his banjo: "This machine surrounds hate and forces it to surrender."

Seeger felt a need to explain to friends why he had gone, and ended up sounding moralistic. "What am I accomplishing, some may ask. Well, I know I'm just one more grain of sand in this world, but I'd rather throw my weight, however small, on the side of what I think is right, than selfishly look after my own fortunes and have to live with a bad conscience."

If Pete Seeger salved his conscience in Mississippi, his prescription soon lost effect. The Summer of Freedom had been a peak in the brief alliance between white and black liberals. On the journey down to earth, as the racial gradualists fell behind and those for justice *today* took command, fellow travelers like Seeger would be left behind.

The musician returned from his brief trip with a lightness to his step and a notebook full of songs. He had used his talents as the movement asked, not taking sides, floating above factionalism to a high harmony.

His career rose faster than he could follow. Countries he had visited now requested return engagements; had he wanted, he could have taken another world tour. *Life* published a feature story on him, but otherwise he remained a grass-roots celebrity, widely recognized as an important American musician but never appearing on TV and rarely on radio. He was as well known as he had ever been in his life, but fame touched off a peculiar need to deprecate his achievements. Pete wrote a self-criticism in *Sing Out!* which he signed with Toshi's name; he called his sixty or seventy records "one of the most uneven bodies of recorded music that any performer could boast of, or perhaps be ashamed of. . . . If one could dub onto a tape a few songs from here and there on his many LPs, one might have quite a good one-hour tape of Pete Seeger. The trouble is, no two people would make the same selections. Therein lies his defense."

Pete's uneasiness with success led him to urge his fans *not* to buy his records. He wanted to make the songs available, but he preferred people to sing them rather than play the records.

His association in the public eye with the civil rights movement also made him uneasy; he hadn't spent that much time with SNCC. Once, when Seeger was performing at Martha's Vineyard, Lillian Hellman invited him to a reception at her house. No sooner had he sat down when she complained to him about "We Shall Overcome." Pete squirmed.

"You call that a revolutionary song? What kind of namby-pamby, wishy-washy song is that?" Hellman browbeat him. "Mooning, always 'Some day, So-o-me-day!' That's been said for two thousand years." Pete was at a loss to answer. Her remarks troubled him so much that he wrote them to Bernice, who answered, "Well, if we said we were going to overcome next week, it would be a little unrealistic. What would we sing the week after next?"

On March 24, 1965, Pete and Toshi joined a march from Selma to Montgomery, Alabama, at the personal invitation of Dr. King. Marveling at the line of demonstrators trudging under the hot Alabama sun, the Seegers had no idea of the danger of the next few days, or that this would be their last march for SNCC.

"It was Pete Seeger's thing come true," a fellow marcher remembered. "He went nuts trying to take down all the songs." Pete had walked into a song agitator's dream: poor people singing together, black and white, well organized and in high spirits.

The march had its origins in demonstrations led by Dr. King in February, when Selma's sheriff, Jim Clark, had locked up 1,150 people. A young voter-registration worker, Jimmie Lee Jackson, had died after being shot in the stomach by police. Martin Luther King and his staff called for a massive march to Alabama's capital, which SNCC, fearing bloodshed, joined reluctantly. On March 7, two thousand people started for Montgomery, but Jim Clark's posse on horseback turned them back with cattle prods and clubs. Then the call went out to Seeger and other celebrities.

The events in Selma echoed across the country. In Washington, a week after the first march, Lyndon Johnson addressed Congress in support of the Voting Rights Act of 1965. "We have already waited a hundred years and more, and the time for waiting is gone. . . . We *shall* overcome!"

On March 21, the march began again. Clergymen and nuns were at the head of the line, and the contingent grew by the hour as chartered planes landed from all over. When the Seegers arrived on the fourth day, they found five thousand sweating and determined people. To protect the marchers from attacks, President Johnson posted two thousand armed national guardsmen along Route 80.

The crowd stretched six abreast for over a mile. The sun beat down, but the line flowed like an army on the move, with food and latrine trucks bringing up the rear. Pete noticed a one-legged man walking along on crutches. As the march twisted between cotton fields and dirt farms, Seeger heard three or four freedom songs drifting up from different places along the line: "They were creating one great song after another—before our very eyes! . . . Imagine—they were singing 'I Love Everybody' ":

> *I love everybody in my heart*
> *I love everybody in my heart . . .*
> *You can't make me doubt it in my heart,*
> *You can't make me doubt it in my heart,*
> *I love Governor Wallace in my heart. . . .*

But the Ku Klux Klan didn't love the marchers. The organization had promised someone would pay for inviting these agitators to make trouble for "their nigras." The threats were so public, Johnny Carson joked: "Some troops were shipped out and they didn't know where they were going. When they got to Vietnam, they were so relieved—they thought they were headed for Selma!"

The sky was hot and clear. Asphalt oozed onto the marchers' shoes, but no one cared. The Alabama State Troopers—the Dixie Dandies—flashed by in air-conditioned cars on the lanes open for traffic. Behind them passed cars with signs reading: "White Citizens' Council—HELP MAINTAIN SEGRE-GATION." Sheriff Jim Clark sported a new hat, dark glasses, and a button that read "NEVER."

The tension did nothing to dim Seeger's enthusiasm. Topical songs, the folk-song revival, integration—everything came together at once. Blacks and whites were clapping, eating, singing together. In recordings made by New York's WNEW-FM, youngsters improvised words to rock 'n' roll tunes:

> Well, I read in the papers (dadat dadat dat)
> Just the other day,
> That the Freedom Fighters
> Are on their way.
>
> Oh, Wallace
> You never can jail us all
> Oh, Wallace,
> Segregation's bound to fall.

Seeger picked up the next verse:

> I don't want no mess
> Don't want no jive
> And I want my freedom
> In sixty-five.

Pete loosened up. The scion of a family that crossed on the *Mayflower* raised his head back and hollered out "Don't want no jive," his tight Yankee tenor left at home.

A flash shower turned into a downpour, and soon the road was caked with mud. It was another burden, but the rain cooled the air and somehow lifted spirits. Teenagers poured out of school to join the march, adding a carnival air. Feet were a major topic of conversation; the blacktop had heated people's shoes until they felt like twin ovens. When the march turned into camp for the night, Dick Gregory mused, "I'm sure Dr. Scholl's underwrote this march."

After receiving armbands, everyone learned the security precautions and settled in. Seeger wandered from campfire to campfire, picking up songs. He'd appear at the edge of the light, jotting down lyrics like an anthropologist. The New Englander stood out, but he was simply one among many singers, accepted not because he was famous but because he could sing.

"There was no time for celebrity adulation," said a march organizer. "You have to understand: People didn't know whether they'd be shot or whether the Alabama National Guard would suddenly start dropping bombs from the helicopters which kept circling the camp. This was for real, and we had *total* security in the camps at night. Guards on all-night shifts. Lighting systems. Evacuation plans. All in all, the place was like a huge caravan with giant tents, everyone huddled together."

Fears of attack made the darkness eerie. "People were scared, really scared," the organizer continued. "But they carried on. People sang like they might never get another chance." Old-time hymns, new songs—the marchers sang to keep back the night.

Next morning, March 25, 1965, the demonstrators started toward downtown Montgomery. The last day of the march was the hottest yet. Many marchers had faces white with sunburn ointment. The line paused near the Montgomery airport, where thousands joined the demonstration for the final stretch to Alabama's state capitol. Pete and Toshi pulled out lunch and shared it with two black friends, the talented songwriter Len Chandler and Jimmy Collier.

Pete had met Jimmy as a teenager a few years before at the University of Chicago folk festival. Now Collier worked as a songleader and organizer with Dr. King's organization. Short, square-chested, with an infectious grin, Jimmy always seemed to be moving, like a child with new sneakers. He walked up and down the line with his guitar, picking behind people as they sang, tossing in words. Seeger admired his ease, and Jimmy, like Bernice, became a family intimate; he was the same age as Seeger's eldest child, Danny.

Pete had his little notebook out, writing down lyrics. "Excuse me, ma'am," he said to one woman, "could you tell me the words to 'Oh, Wallace?' "

"The words? Why there are no words!"

Seeger tried again. "Well, do you know any of the verses?"

"Why sure. You just make 'em up. Here's a few . . ." She smiled as he earnestly wrote them down. "Don't you know you can't write down freedom songs?"

Right on schedule, the celebrities walked out of the Montgomery airport to join the march: Harry Belafonte, Tony Bennett, Anthony Perkins. The TV cameras began to roll. In its final hours the march numbered thirty thousand. The long night was over and the day looked clear and unthreatening. Pete remained as excited as ever, hopping from group to group like a nervous journalist. Toshi walked alongside, photographing the marchers.

Seeger probed for the source of the singers' vitality, as if he could bottle it and bring it north. He marveled how hymns that he'd sung for years, songs like "Jacob's Ladder" and "Lonesome Valley," had blossomed into freedom songs. Back in 1955, during the Montgomery bus boycotts, Dr. King's group had sung hymns in traditional versions, but everyone understood a new urgency:

> We are soldiers in the army
> We have to fight, although we have to die
> We got to hold up the (freedom) banner
> We got to hold it up until we die.

In 1960 and 1961, through song organizers like Guy Carawan, the civil-rights movement readapted union songs, such as "We Shall Not Be Moved." Then, to Pete's joy, the demonstrators themselves made the adaptations. Long nights in jail had given activists plenty of opportunity to break in the new songs.

Entering Montgomery, the marchers turned up Dexter Avenue toward the state capitol. Pete and Toshi had to leave and catch a plane home. As the day was turning dark, a woman volunteered to drive them back along Route 80 to the Montgomery airport. They were surprised to find no protection for the marchers returning to Selma. A few hours earlier, the road had been filled with demonstrators; now the highway was deserted.

Bernice Reagon understood why the Seegers traveled without protection: "If you walk from Selma to Montgomery, you may think you can walk or hitch all the way back. You get real loose. . . . You think you can do anything you want with that space—including being blown away."

Later, Len Chandler was driving along the Selma road when he saw a car smashed through a barbed wire fence. "There were about thirty or forty troopers with lights turning. I thought it was an accident. We'd marched right past the spot."

The car had been driven by a middle-aged woman from Detroit, Viola Liuzzo. In the dark stretch of Alabama highway, a car came up behind her carrying three Klansmen, one of them an FBI informant. Someone had a gun. Two shots traveled through her brain, and the driverless car screeched across the road, out of control.

The Seegers were a few hours ahead of her on the same road. The Montgomery airport loomed ahead. Unlike Liuzzo, they arrived in safety; but as soon as they got out of the car, they felt the hostile stares. Their plane had not yet arrived, police protection was gone, and the couple began to get extremely nervous. "We had obviously slept with the marchers the night before," Toshi remembered. "We were covered with mud. Finally we found some bathrooms and scrubbed off what we could. Anything could have happened to us that night."

Pete returned from the Selma march glad to have gone and glad to have survived. His time there had been too short. For two glorious days, he had found the singing movement he had hoped for since he was twenty-one. He seemed as excited about the singing as at the movement's more concrete achievements.

But no sooner had he found his place in this movement than it began to slip from him. The Selma march was more of a turning point than the participants could have imagined. A highway through the Alabama Black Belt might be far from Eden, but a year later, amid cries of "Black Power" and separatism, the march seemed innocent, even blissful.

Perhaps Seeger felt the change coming. In the next few months, he increasingly sang for the new anti-Vietnam-war groups. He helped plan the 1965 Newport Folk Festival, never dreaming of the havoc Bob Dylan would create there. The Freedom Singers had separated, but Pete and Bernice continued to perform together. But all this paled before Pete's memories of the Selma march; the joy and anxiety there had lit a fuse that had nowhere to burn.

Separated from the day-to-day workings of SNCC, Pete knew little of its silent evolution. Toward the end of 1965, a purge of "northern middle-class elements" began as chairman John Lewis called for a "Black-led, Black-dominated" organization. The word went out: Whites rode in the caboose or dropped off. SNCC cancelled plans to extend a Summer of Freedom-type program throughout the Deep South; whites could organize in their own communities. "If we are to proceed toward liberation," a SNCC position paper read, "we must cut ourselves off from the white people."

The eruption did not occur at once. That summer Pete was still discussing the best way to build a local power base with Myles Horton of Highlander and black SNCC activist Stokely Carmichael. Stokely had by this time been jailed twenty-five times; born in Trinidad and raised in Harlem, Carmichael had a street-tough manner that belied his high-school days in Greenwich Village and at the Bronx High School of Science. As he explored nationalist and separatist programs, SNCC's white benefactors became "white liberals."

One afternoon Stokely and Jim Forman paid Harold Leventhal a visit in his office. In the past few years, Leventhal had gone out of his way to help set up benefits; his influence in the folk-music world was well known, and he had a nodding acquaintance with SNCC's leadership. Stokely arrived in Harold's office fresh from backwoods organizing, however, and he was anything but cordial. As Harold later reconstructed the talk, Stokely began calmly, pointing out how much publicity Leventhal's performers had received for their brief time in the South; SNCC wasn't sure they needed any more folk performers flying in for a weekend of struggle. A lot of work went into setting up those concerts, Harold answered. They raised a lot of money—was he saying he didn't want any more benefits? Carmichael turned on him with a snarl, and "anti-Semitic, anti-white charges crackled in the room. It was a terrible time, and we were wrongly the victims," Leventhal recalled painfully. Seeger, the traveling organizer, heard nothing about this scene.

Yet an unsettling mood hung in the air, and sensing it, Pete held tightly to his friendships with Jimmy Collier and Bernice Reagon, who came up for the holidays and helped out in light construction work. "It was during this time," Jimmy pointed out, "that we became good friends. Bernice and I represented idealistic kids. I know Theodore Bikel—and a lot of others—felt hurt and angry at what was happening to SNCC. Pete didn't. Maybe he wasn't as sensitive. Maybe he wouldn't know if someone was insulting him."

To Pete's dismay, civil-rights singing had begun to disappear. As in People's Songs, the music faded once its morale-building and media-gathering functions diminished. Len Chandler stopped singing "Black, White, Christian, Jew, we must keep marching through." In its place he performed:

> You conspire to keep us silent in the field and in the   ©
>   slum
> You promise us the vote and sing us, "We Shall
>   Overcome"
> But John Brown knew what freedom was and died to
>   win us some
> That's why we keep marching on. . . .
>
> Move on over or we'll move on over you
> And the movement's moving on.

"We Shall Overcome" fell out of vogue.

Yet as American blacks gave up "We Shall Overcome," South Africans picked it up. On April 1, the song was sung on the gallows of the Pretoria Central Prison by one John Harris, just before the freedom fighter was hanged for having planted a bomb in Johannesburg. Agents of the South African security police searched record stores in Johannesburg, according to *The New York Times:* "They were especially interested in one version of 'We Shall Overcome' recorded by the American folk singer Pete Seeger." It contained the last words the hanged man sung: "We shall all be free." Soon "We Shall Overcome" ceased to be heard in public, and Pete's recording disappeared under the counter. But the song had a new life, in South African prisons.

Less than a year after Selma, one of Pete's friends, black songwriter Julius Lester, wrote *Sing Out!* a biting letter that could have been aimed straight at Pete's heart—a funeral speech for the civil rights movement as Seeger knew it:

"Those northern protest rallies where Freedom songs were sung . . . began to look more and more like moral exercises: 'See, my hands are clean.' Now it is over: the days of singing freedom songs and the days of combating bullets and billy clubs with love. 'We Shall Overcome' (and we have overcome our blindness) sounds old, out-dated, and can enter the pantheon of the greats along with IWW songs and the union songs.

"As one SNCC worker put it after the Mississippi March, 'Man, the workers are too busy getting ready to fight to bother with singing anymore.' They used to sing 'I Love Everybody' as they ducked bricks and bottles. Now they sing:

> *Too much love,*
> *Too much love,*
> *Nothing kills a nigger like*
> *Too much love."*

Here was a protest song Pete was unlikely to perform.

Seeger had faced abrupt changes in his repertoire before, and he knew how to ease the pain. Instead of growing bitter, he redoubled his efforts and moved on. But as he traveled into the anti-war movement, he left a piece of himself behind. An integrated society seemed more distant than ever. Though outwardly confident, there were undertones of frenzy in Pete Seeger, at first faint, but growing louder, as a mass audience continued to elude him; as his godchildren moved off in unpredictable directions.

Seeger's banjo, whose legend reads,
"This machine surrounds hate and forces it to surrender"

Pete Seeger testifies before the HUAC, 1955 (*New York Post photo* by Calvacca. ©
1955, New York Post Corporation)

Seeger and Henry Wallace, 1948 (*Phil Schultz*)

With Lightning Hopkins and Bill McAdoo (*David Gahr*)

ABOVE With Irwin Silber at *Sing Out!* office, early 1960s (*David Gahr*)

TOP RIGHT Alan Lomax (*David Gahr*)

RIGHT Early publicity photo: the Weavers (*Jules Kreigsman*)

ABOVE Pete and Toshi Seeger
(*David Gahr*)

INSET The Seeger cabin near Beacon,
NY, 1962 (*David Gahr*)

The Seeger family at home, 1958;
from left: Mike, Toshi, Tinya, Danny, Pete See
(*David Gahr*)

Woodcut by Leona Pierce Frasconi, 1958

LOWER RIGHT Peace march, late 1950s
(*Sing Out!* archives)

BELOW Right-wing pamphlet, late 1950s

IDENTIFIED

COMMUNIST

seeger

SINGS

With Malvina Reynolds (*David Gahr*)

RIGHT Peggy Seeger (Pete's half-sister) at Newport Folk Festival, mid-1960s (*David Gahr*)

Crowd at Newport Folk Festival, 1966 (*David Gahr*)

ABOVE Pete Seeger and Jimmy Collier, 1977 (© *Pat Goudvis 1981*)

ABOVE Woody Guthrie Memorial Concert, 1968:
Pete, Judy Collins, Bob Dylan, Arlo Guthrie (*David Gahr*)

INSET With half-brother, Mike Seeger, at
Newport, 1966 (*David Gahr*)

ABOVE The first crew of *Clearwater,* including Lou Killen and Don McLean (left); Reverend Fredrick Douglass Kilpatrick, Jimmy Collier, Len Chandler (to Seeger's right), and Rambling Jack Elliot (extreme right), 1969 (*Sing Out!* archives)

ABOVE Civil rights at Newport: Peter, Paul, and Mary; Joan Baez; Bob Dylan; the Freedom Singers; Pete, 1963 (*David Gahr*)

TOP The *Clearwater* viewed from the
east bank of the Hudson (*Patrick
Whitaker*)

INSET Sloop *Clearwater*
on the Hudson River (*Charles Porter*)

(*Emilio Rodriguez*)

Waist Deep in the Big Muddy 11

FOUR MONTHS to the day after Pete Seeger left the Selma march, he stepped out on the stage of the Newport Folk Festival with a newborn child. "Tonight let's sing for this child. Let's show her a world of peace," he said.

Black separatists might purge whites from the civil rights movement, but at Newport, Pete assumed he was among friends. The festival was his home-away-from-home, where commercialism and rock 'n' roll never entered. Here, folk music devotees savored the quiet fire of mountain singers like Roscoe Holcomb and Jean Ritchie, alongside citybillies like Seeger and Dylan. Pete needed a refuge from "fakelore" and electrified, imitation folk music of the *"Hootenanny"* variety. Electrification had come to symbolize demon pop music; it led to the harder stuff, like rock 'n' roll. Pete enjoyed telling a story about a fellow who walked into an English folk club and plugged in an electric guitar.

"What in the name of God is that?" the cafe owner asked.

"It's an electric guitar," said the musician.

"And whose electricity are you using?"

"I'm just plugging it into the wall."

"If you can't play it yourself, you're not going to play it with my electricity," the club owner said firmly.

"And out he went," Pete finished, with a touch of smugness.

At the 1965 festival, people parked ungrumblingly in the vast lots and carried in instruments and picnic coolers. The camp grounds filled with teenagers singing and carrying sleeping bags. When a downpour threatened an outdoor concert, performers and audience laughed and sang rain songs.

The Sunday night concert which Pete had opened featured the best-known artists: Bob Dylan, Peter, Paul and Mary, and Fannie Lou Hamer—fresh from civil-rights work in Mississippi. Dylan, the preeminent songwriter of the day, stood out; his songs were on everyone's lips. No stranger to

Newport audiences, at twenty-four he was already an accomplished guitar player and lyricist. Seeger had introduced him at Newport two years before; Joan Baez had brought him out of the wings at her concerts. By 1965, Dylan needed no introductions—he had left Joan and Pete behind in a cloud of publicity. His latest album with electric backup, *Bringing It All Back Home*, had surprised folkies; its high-pitched single "Subterranean Homesick Blues" played on AM radio. His earlier enthusiasts were appalled; "a sellout," some murmured in Washington Square. Newport audiences were a pipe-smoking, flannel-shirt-and-denim crowd. Teeny-boppers weren't supposed to like folk music, and Dylan should no more succeed on AM radio than Pete Seeger should replace Johnny Carson on TV. The press at Newport awaited the confrontation between Dylan and the traditionalists.

Late Sunday evening, the stage darkened and the stagehands prepared for Bob Dylan. Pete sat backstage; he didn't notice the long setup time as desk-size electric amplifiers were carried out. A new, stylish Dylan darted on stage. Black leather jacket and black slacks set off his yellow dress shirt and pointed boots. He walked out in night-black square shades—carrying a shiny electric Fender guitar. The electrically amplified Paul Butterfield Blues Band positioned themselves around him like bodyguards. The little red lights on top of the speaker-amplifiers glowed eerily behind Dylan.

"Louder," Bob called to the sound man as he tuned up. "More guitar."

No one can say for certain what happened in the next forty-five minutes. Al Kooper, who was playing organ, told one story and Bernice Reagon, backstage, remembered it completely differently. Pete insisted he didn't hear anything unusual until Dylan's first chords.

Pete had virtually adopted Dylan, taking him to Mississippi in 1963 and proclaiming him a genius. He offered this sponsorship to others, but Pete was "Hovering over some young songwriters (like Bob Dylan) like a father," said writer Jon Pankake. When Dylan had arrived in the New York folk circuit, he had referred to Seeger as "a saint." In Pete's presence, Bobby had been engagingly humble: "My songs were there before I came along. . . . I just sort of took 'em down with a pencil." Intensely ambitious, Dylan understood that at Newport, the electric guitar meant a declaration of war. He had smuggled rock into the citadel of folk music.

After the first "Let's go" to the band, Dylan's "Maggie's Farm" staggered and crashed over an astonished audience. The music was too loud to be heard.

Was this deliberate? Dylan thought so: "They didn't like what I was going to play and they twisted the sound on me before I began." Even pianissimo, some decided they had heard too much. Halfway through the first song, the crowd started yelling. Dylan played over them, letting the band set up the rhythm while he concentrated on singing, pounding out the words to "Like a Rolling Stone" in his best make-a-point diction.

"It was one of the rare occasions that Pete 'flipped out,' " said Leventhal. "Pete would have liked to cut the cables." Pacing the wings, Seeger watched his folk-topical song movement unravel, before what he later called "some of the most destructive music this side of hell."

"The sound's too high," Pete shouted at Albert Grossman, Dylan's manager. "Turn it *down*!"

"Bobby wants it that way, Pete." Grossman moved in front of the sound board.

"Damn it, you can't hear the words," Pete said frantically.

"We were sitting in the press section, maybe thirty yards back," guitarist Eric von Schmidt remembered, "and yelling, 'Can't hear ya!' and 'Cut the band down!' In the beginning, only about four or five people were hollering. Then they went into the next song and no one had changed any dials. It was the same thing, no voice coming through at all, just the band doing a solo. After that more people began shouting, 'We want Bobby.' "

In the middle of the third song, someone shouted, "Go back to the Ed Sullivan show!" The audience laughed. Dylan finished and yelled over his shoulder at the band, "Let's go now, that's all." Bob may have made the right music at the right time, but only he could have made it in such a wrong place.

Dylan plunged backstage as Peter Yarrow of Peter, Paul and Mary covered the mike. He pushed right past Pete; the man he had once called "a living saint" stood crying in the wings.

"Was it to be marshmallows and cotton candy or meat and potatoes?" wrote Paul Nelson about Seeger and Dylan. "Rose-colored glasses or a magnifying glass? A nice guy who has subjugated and weakened his art through constant insistence on a world that never was and never can be; or an angry, passionate poet who demands his art to be all, who demands not to be owned, not to be restricted or predicted. . . ."

Bobby returned to perform "It's All Over Now, Baby Blue" with his old guitar and harmonica. The audience gave him a standing ovation—applauding themselves for beating back the electric spectre. While Dylan played his acoustic set, Pete went from musician to musician, gathering people for a unifying finale.

"Does anyone have an E harmonica? *Anyone?* Just toss them up here," Dylan continued, charming a half-dozen onto the stage. His acoustic version of "Mr. Tambourine Man" quelled the storm, but Dylan ran off stage faster than he had entered. He left Newport's stage for good, taking with him most of the folk revival's audience.

Irwin Silber criticized Seeger's finale as "a tasteless exhibition of frenzied incest." Pete had grown a bit tired of these diatribes from Irwin, who later became one of Dylan's (and Newport's) harshest critics. But a grain of truth underlay Silber's gibe; as Newport ended, performers had tried to present a united front, but the harmony rang false.

Dylan's departure might have affected Pete less had it not opened a floodgate of recriminations within the folk-music community. A *Sing Out!* forum on topical song produced unexpectedly bitter responses: Pete's brother-in-law, Ewan MacColl, wrote, "The folk magazines seem to compete with each other in the hunt for superlatives with which to describe Bobby and Phil and Tom and Peter and all the rest of the mostest, bestest, youngest and newest." Poet Don West chided Seeger as a publicity-seeking hero.

The brickbats continued. Jon Pankake, a writer who grew up listening to Seeger, attacked his "blithely slipshod musicianship, occasional tastelessness in presentation of topical material, and a kind of eager-beaver naïveté." A new generation of folk song enthusiasts preferred the less citified picking of Mike Seeger to Pete's smooth, spellbinding concerts. Jazz critic Robert Reisner pushed this tide of criticism to ridicule: "Folk music is the shortcut to becoming an 'entertainer' these days. Express yourselves! Make girls! Get a record contract. You buy a guitar, learn three chords, and you are set. The society is the easiest in the world to make. There are no standards of wit or intelligence or financial income. All you need are some dirty clothes."

Dylan's defection shocked Seeger into reevaluating his life. Many blacks had given up freedom songs; now the leading political songwriter had rung down his own curtain. Pete wrote out his feelings about Dylan in a memo, to keep the anger from churning in his thoughts. He blamed Albert Grossman for Bob's "commercial" orientation and referred to Dylan as a corpse.

If not for the implied rejection, Seeger might have seen himself in Dylan's rebelliousness; after all, Pete's decision to experiment with pop music and to take the Weavers into nightclubs had met similar criticisms—

especially from Irwin, who had the Jeremiah-like distinction of denouncing both developments.

In the weeks following Newport, this perspective escaped Seeger. He blamed himself (and everyone else with hopes for Dylan) for pushing the young singer too hard too fast, and ended his note on Dylan by paraphrasing a poem he'd written about cancer, "The Beast with a Hundred Claws":

> *The fangs and claws sink swiftly deeper now*
> *First the muscles, then the brain*
> *The fangs reach for the heart, and*
> *   victory is won*
> *And when we reach for him, we have*
> *   only the shrivelled corpse.*

Having sorted out his feelings, Pete withdrew, as he had following the bankruptcy of People's Songs. His disappointment with Bob Dylan was only partly to blame; in a few months' span he had watched the decline of the freedom and topical song movements he had hoped for all his adult life. In August he wrote his father and friends that he was giving up all his projects. He resigned from the Newport board of directors, despite pleas that he remain. He quit his position as a director of the Woody Guthrie Trust Fund, and even dropped his column in *Sing Out!*, his last tie to his boyhood journalistic dreams. "I am resigning as many things as I can," he wrote Don West.

Nothing turned out right for him. Pete visited Russia that fall, taking great care to make sure what he said and sang would not be misconstrued by right-wingers at home. The concerts went well until one momentous night, when he sang to some Moscow students who asked him about the mood on American campuses. Pete couldn't resist trying out a new song, "King Henry," whose last verse contained these lines:

> *The year it is now nineteen sixty-five*   ©
> *It's easier far to stay half alive*
> *Just keep your mouth shut while*
> *   the planes zoom and dive*
> *Ten thousand miles over the ocean.*

A *New York Times* reporter recognized what Seeger had in mind: the conflict—few Americans yet called it a war—in the tiny country of Vietnam, where American "military advisers" had died. The reporter, who had asked

Pete to escort him into the meeting, dashed off an uncomplimentary story, which the *Times* picked up the following day. A headline writer captioned the article: SEEGER SONG IN MOSCOW IS ANTI-U.S. Subsequent editions appeared with a toned-down heading, but Pete was furious. A *New York Times* editor eventually apologized for the headline, but it was too late—the damage had been done.

Pessimism was not Pete's native state, and gradually during the next year, he picked up the pieces of his life. He renewed his ties with those black organizers willing to work with whites. Learning from their criticisms, he turned to a movement closer to home, one he had understood instinctively as a child: environmentalism. Inspired by Rachel Carson's *Silent Spring,* Seeger poured his heart into a new album of conservationist songs, a lyrical call to resist the asphaltization of America. The title song, "God Bless the Grass," could refer to Seeger; it tells of a hardy grass that grows up through the cracks in the cement: "The concrete covers it, but the grass grows back."

Soon after Pete's disappointment at Newport, a neighbor lent him a book that fired his imagination, *Sloops of the Hudson.* Written in 1908, the book contained beautiful drawings of old-time sailing ships—the name derived from the Dutch *sloep*, the boats that once plied the Hudson. The descriptions of the boats (sixty to ninety feet long, with masts a hundred feet tall) thrilled him: "It wasn't great literature, but I loved it."

Probably only a project that touched his naturalist side could have pulled Pete out of his slump. He remembered building wooden sailboats in his father's tool shop in Patterson. After Jack Elliot had showed Pete a children's book, *We Really Didn't Mean to Go to Sea,* in 1959, Pete had caught the sailing bug. He had even bought a small fiberglass boat of his own.

He was no expert sailor; often he would capsize and paddle for shore. But he enjoyed skimming along the water and hearing the slap of wind-filled canvas as the boat lurched forward. Seeger sailed the Hudson because it was convenient, but he could scarcely stand to look in the water. Raw sewage floated by, and grisly chemical residues discolored the water; he did his best to keep the boat upright.

Sailing and working on *God Bless the Grass* simultaneously, he began to speculate on a tie between the two. His film and TV work distracted him, however, and sailing remained only a way to lose his cares in the wind.

Television had never ceased to entice him. Seeger now decided to put his *Banjo Traveler* series on the screen, even if he had to finance it himself out of song royalties. He found a producer, Sholom Rubinstein; a name,

Rainbow Quest; and counting on educational stations to pick up his expenses, he plunged ahead. Initially broadcast on a UHF channel in the New York area, the show seemed a success. *New York Times* critic Jack Gould called the series "Channel 47's first certain Emmy award." The format was extremely folksy. On the first show Tommy Makem, the Clancy Brothers, and Tom Paxton strummed and chatted around a picnic table. Only seven stations aired the series at the start, however, and Seeger ran out of funds. The budget limitations frustrated him, particularly since the money had to be taken from house and family expenses.

Seeger remained determined to chip his way into network broadcasting, even though the decisions to keep him off the air were made at the highest levels; when Richard Salant told his colleagues at CBS Records that the network did not want Seeger on TV, he was not kidding around.

To gain access to prime-time air, Seeger had four options. The first was to sing what he was told; but Pete had never learned to tailor his ideals to convenience. Second, he could have decided not to try at all, and left the medium to its antiperspirant and fast food ads; at least he could have congratulated himself on not having soiled himself. His third option was to set up a grand confrontation and beat his breast in public, a temptation he had narrowly resisted with *"Hootenanny."* Seeger was at heart a confrontationist, and did not back away from dramatic stands, shy though he was one-to-one. In the end, however, he would have no better luck than he had had with *"Hootenanny."*

To succeed, he needed a strategy every bit as elaborate as his HUAC defense. He would begin with his UHF series and appearances on a few local programs; then he might get occasional spots on non-network syndicated shows. His first network appearance would be on the one spot not vulnerable to pressure from sponsors—the religious talk shows, the Sunday Morning Ghetto, as it was called. At this point, surely, the stars of a Big Show would throw their weight (and, as it turned out, their careers) behind Seeger.

But what a path of rejections and embarrassed lies, what a personal torment for a man who hated to argue—trying to pin down directors whose careers had been spent dodging commitment, lobbying an industry addicted to mirrors. Even playing the entire hit parade, first to last, might have been easier for Seeger.

And to what end was all this struggle? He didn't need the money. In itself, he had no use for publicity. Seeger revealed his motivation in a one-shot broadcast on Canadian television: "Folk music's the kind you can make yourself. It doesn't have to come out of a loudspeaker. What a tyrant that little box can be [outlines TV frame with his fingers]. . . . How sad to think, in millions of homes, of a husband and wife sitting back woodenly on the sofa staring at the screen while an expert lover pretends to make love to another expert lover." Seeger ultimately wanted to use television to dissuade people from watching it; no wonder the networks were unenthusiastic.

One of the things that got Seeger through the initial stages of his television campaign was a new song, "Waist Deep in the Big Muddy"; he called it a love song.

The story is a simple one: Back in 1942, a platoon of soldiers is ordered to ford a river. The sergeant and soldiers tell the captain the river is too deep, but he pushes them on, leading them into the water: waist deep, neck deep . . . until the captain drowns. The last verse, the one that later gave Seeger so much trouble, went:

> Now I'm not gonna point any moral   ©
> I'll leave that for yourself
> Maybe you're still walking, and
>   you're still talking
> You'd like to keep your health.
> But every time I read the papers
> That old feeling comes on
> We're waist deep in the Big Muddy
> And the big fool says to push on.

"I was thinking of Vietnam. On the other hand, I purposely decided I would just let it be an allegory on its own, like the political nursery rhymes. As the years go by, the song may make another appearance and be sung in another context."

He began the song in the spring of 1966, tentatively naming it "General Fathead," starting with only the last line: "Waist deep in the Big Muddy, and the damn fool wants to push on." The words and a short tune arrived together, and he wrote it down in his pocket notebook. He kept pulling it out and telling himself: "Well, I really should finish that, it's a good idea for a song." He worked on it intensively for three or four weeks until he got it. "I sang it in Wisconsin one time, where I was staying at a professor's house. I had lunch with him the next day, and he said: 'Guess what! This morning in my class, I opened up the textbook and said, "Well, let's get cracking on page 183." And from the back of the lecture hall, two hundred people, there comes, "The Big Fool says to push on." The whole place just cracked up. I had to laugh too.' "

Meanwhile, Pete's strategy was beginning to work. In the summer of 1966 he had his first network appearance on the nondenominational *Lamp Unto My Feet.* A producer, a gentle, middle-aged Englishwoman, had approached him. She had heard about the blacklist, she told him sweetly, and she wanted to have him on anyway. Seeger came in, and after a few quick run-throughs two shows were taped. It was a beginning, but the experience didn't satisfy him; the show was unsponsored, and "I didn't really think of it as prime-time network TV." Soon afterward, he appeared on *The David Susskind Show,* a popular (non-network) talk show.

That fall Pete visited Columbia for his next album, *Waist Deep in the Big Muddy.* In the studio, he pulled up the mike as far as it would go on its stand and adjusted another for his banjo. Headphones covered his ears and his army-short hair. His Adam's apple danced as he sang, and his tall, bony frame made him look like Ichabod Crane, wired for sound.

Much had changed in the past year: Seeger now had an electric bass, drums, and a second guitar backing him up, the first session he recorded with electric accompaniment. Following Dylan's lead, Joan Baez, Arlo Guthrie, and Judy Collins had all experimented with folk-rock, as the style was called. On this session, Seeger's voice had an odd, straining sound, as if trying not to sound like the singer his fans knew; the ensemble, the Blues Project led by Danny Kalb, sounded as if they were playing along behind a Pete Seeger record as best they could. Pete's first attempt at folk-rock proved a disappointment, and he abandoned the idea for a number of years.

Outwardly, Seeger seemed a success. In the past year, not only had he appeared on TV again, but he received a sympathetic profile in *The New York Times. Who's Who* listed him, confusing him with his brother Mike. Seeger had successfully challenged the cancellation of his concert in East Meadow, Long Island, setting an important legal precedent: Neither he—nor anyone else—could be denied use of a school auditorium because of "controversy." When he finally sang in East Meadow, six hundred pickets stood outside, the largest number he had seen since Peekskill.

Internally, something had gone awry. The rivers of enthusiasm that had carried him through so many movements had dried up. The imperturbable singer, the optimist who inspired the crowds, showed fissures in his personality. As America became more and more involved in the faraway and sordid conflict in Vietnam, Pete's insides soured. The folk song revival—what was left of it—had taken off in a direction he hadn't intended. He told *The New York Times*:

> When I feel pessimistic, as I sometimes do, I feel like the man who loved to go out in the woods and track animals. He wanted other people to know what it was like, so he wrote a book about nature.
>
> It was a simple book, but it became a best seller . . . and then there were organized tours . . . and LPs of bird calls, and all the rest. And the man said, "But that isn't what I was talking about at all."

Pete had suffered a relapse of his post-Newport, post-Selma blues. Paying taxes to support the war disgusted him, but after talking with Joan Baez, he found withholding wouldn't make any difference; the IRS visited the box office. He began doing more benefits—what he didn't earn, the government couldn't take away.

Pete still couldn't accept success and notoriety; he winced every time he saw his name in large letters. In 1966 he toured with Bernice Reagon. A friend of Bernice handled the promotion, and she worried that her basic poster wasn't good enough. So she prepared one with Pete's name in banner headlines and sent it off to beef up the old one.

"When Pete got to town and he saw that [second] poster," Bernice remembered, "he ripped it off the wall. He said, 'Who did this!' She said, 'Well, I did.' 'You!' Pete said and went into a rage, crumpled it up, and threw it on the floor." Bernice calmed him by showing the first poster, which he liked. Pete pulled himself together and apologized. "He had this thing about not being a star, and somehow, he went off at that point," Bernice said. Seeger grew steadily more irritable, particularly toward groupies. Though a crowd-pleaser, he rarely attracted sexual propositions; his persona was more grandfatherly than rakish. Nevertheless, he had his opportunities, such as the time he sang at a wealthy psychiatric hospital, a very informal place: "After I finished singing, a woman says, 'Where are you going,' and I said 'I'm due over at somebody's house for supper to-night.' She says 'Come on up and have a drink.' Well, I went up to her room and had a beer, and I suddenly realized she was hoping we'd have a good time together. As soon as I realized that, I eased myself out of the room. It's an old joke in the family, I'm the New England puritan. Matter of fact, I was singing in Dublin once and somebody said, 'Do you want to go hear Seeger?' His friend said, 'Oh, no, who wants to hear that old clergyman.' "

Another time, a singer kept coming up and letting Pete know she was available. Seeger edged off politely, but finally he got furious; instead of rejecting the woman, he tore apart her singing. "It's a Jesus mentality," Bernice smiled. "Like the sage of the community, who has to maintain a certain kind of position."

"That isn't what I meant at all," Seeger said to the world that lionized him. The more people praised him, the more he tried to set the record straight, at least in his journal: "The man is a singer, but he obviously hasn't much voice . . . he tries to talk simply, but obviously has a good education and reads widely. He sings about poor people, though I doubt he is poor himself." In his pocket notebooks, eerie interior monologues appeared: "I have no employer to fire me, so I will speak my mind. If the day—or night—should come when I am assassinated or put behind bars, you will know that you cannot trust the land of Lincoln any more, and the claws will come unsheathed." Pete quoted one of his favorite playwrights, G. B. Shaw: "Assassination is the extreme form of censorship."

One stark clipping in his notebook lay bare Seeger's affliction: a *New York Times* article about a U.S. Air Force cluster bomb that accidentally crushed a school in Tanuyen, South Vietnam. In apology, Air Force lawyers paid families thirty-three dollars in crisp new bills for each child killed.

Though he never publicly vented his reaction to atrocities like these, his private response was grim: "How do you kill a savage beast? Poison its waterholes," he scrawled. He felt the conscience of his country dying around him, deaf to attempts to awaken it. Violence outside bred violence within. "Within me are two opposing forces," he wrote:

> *One says kill*
> *The other says create.*
> *Which will win?*
> *Which will win?*
> *Which will win?*
>
> *If the one, then my neighbors had best beware.*
> *If the other, then we can learn to share.*

Amid his daily rounds of concerts and fund-raisers, these feelings slowly pushed up inside him like hot lava.

In December Pete finally resumed his *Sing Out!* column, but his tone was stern, and the photo at the top of the page had changed; Pete wasn't smiling any more. He gave his readers an unusually candid picture of new strains in his life.

"Sitting at a desk while the sun is shining bright outside is bad enough. Standing at a set of rewinds editing film in a dark room is worse. OK; somebody has to do it. But I'm getting too old for it."

I was grumbling thus to my wife while we drove into the city, through Bear Mountain State Park. We passed three or four park service employees raking near the highway.

"Now there's a good job. Lots of fresh air," says I.

"I can give you that any time you like," answers my wife. "You can start in on our lawn as soon as we get home." . . .

"No, that isn't the same. The men there looked so carefree. But I can't get my mind off Vietnam."

These lines contained a broad hint of family tensions. Like many couples in the sixties, Pete and Toshi argued over feminism and sex roles. Their friend Don McLean noticed a "tremendous frustration" in Toshi. "She's paid a heavier price than anyone for all this cultural history that Pete has lived through. She never had a chance to use her enormous expressive capabilities for herself." She hadn't forgiven Pete's taking her away from her children when they were infants, or her unending nights alone with the kids, while he trudged from one college to another—once for nine months straight. Toshi hectored Pete and insisted he begin cleaning and cooking. She knew she was indispensable to Pete Seeger as the world knew him. "To be able to be Pete Seeger, you've got to have Toshi," Judy Collins said wistfully; women in the arts or professions rarely receive such tireless support from their mates.

New York's radical folk music community was not as free of sex-role stereotyping as their rhetoric suggested. In the Weavers, Ronnie Gilbert had struggled mightily to make herself heard over the convincing words of her three male colleagues. She had to raise the roof more than once to get them to take her seriously. Sis Cunningham had similar problems back in the Almanac house; she and Bess Lomax had done much of the cleaning around those most bohemian quarters.

Toshi, who had never set out to be a performer, had a different experience from these two; nevertheless by the end of the 1960s, Pete had stopped joking that Toshi had earned her managerial ten percent when she suggested a song to sing or a benefit to avoid. His words had left a bitter taste, and Pete finally understood why: "She felt that she has spent all of her life working on somebody else's career, when she would have liked to have done pottery or a number of things herself. Like many women, she found it easier to put it off. They say, 'No, I can't do it now, I've got to help the children.' Then, too late, they realize they shouldn't have done it, they should have disciplined themselves and said, "No, I *will* do this in spite of them.' "

In the next years, Toshi would vacillate between chiding her husband for his dependency and taking on as much of his career as she could. Even if few knew it, his triumphs were hers as well.

If Toshi had her scores to settle, the children had theirs as well. "I don't guess it was much fun having Pete Seeger for a father," said Jimmy Collier, who often stayed over at the house. When Pete was home—which wasn't often—he could be loyal and occasionally tender, but he had a way of disappearing into himself, even in the same room with his family. With Jimmy Collier, Pete had a special intimacy, which both treasured: "He was not distant from me, not off on a mission. I felt comfortable enough to tell him 'Hey Peter, let's get a beer. Stop being so serious.' . . . I was black too, at a time when he didn't have that much real contact with blacks."

At the beginning of 1967 Seeger set off on another series of overseas concerts. He performed in Germany for the first time, having avoided the country for fear of seeing people his age and wondering what they had done in World War II. "This was silly," he now decided. "In future years an American will receive the same glances—what was he doing in 1967." Seeger sang "We Shall Overcome" in East Berlin, creating a headache for leaders who assumed protest songs only applied to capitalist countries. For years afterward young East Germans sang the song.

In late spring he visited first Lebanon, then Israel. Visiting the Lebanese refugee camps did not lighten his mood; meeting Harold in Israel afterward, he burst into tears as he described the camps, and refused to enter the Israeli section of Jerusalem. He wasn't anti-Israel; he just felt each group shared in the problem. He tried bringing the two sides into harmony—literally—by throwing a concert at his expense at the Tel Aviv Hilton, busing in refugees and kibbutzniks to sing together; he dedicated a verse of "Guantanamera" "to exiles of two thousand years and exiles of nineteen years." Seeger was out of his depth. The tension in the hall so unnerved him he stopped in the middle of his singing, close to tears, and walked off the stage. It was like singing before the anti-Wallace mob in North Carolina; music didn't have a chance. He left Israel early, three days before the Six Day War broke out.

Pete arrived home just as *Waist Deep in the Big Muddy and Other Love Songs* left Columbia's factories. Seeger hoped the controversial song might finally win him a prime-time TV appearance. "Oh, don't I wish it would sell a million," he wrote in *Sing Out!*, wondering when American TV networks would allow songs like his on the air.

Opinion had been changing about the war in Vietnam, particularly as films of the carnage entered living rooms via TV. Few Americans understood why the U.S. fought in this distant country. When the draft threatened college-age sons of the middle class, the country split along age lines. "Hell no! We won't go!" was heard on campuses from Berkeley to Kalamazoo. Underground papers printed photos of families burnt to death with Dow Chemical's napalm, their skin peeling off in layers. The government stopped pretending the soldiers in Vietnam were advisers; suddenly, flunking out meant the loss of a student deferment and a possible trip to fight "Cong" in the Mekong Delta.

Always attentive to his audiences, Pete sensed this growing opposition immediately. He would choose a judicious moment to sing "Big Muddy," deliberately letting pro-war hecklers interrupt him: "Our boys are dying in Vietnam, and that guy is singing a song like that. I'm not going to let him get away with it. Boo. Boooo." What Seeger knew (and his hecklers didn't) was that after the song ended, there would be thunderous applause. The booers found themselves outnumbered, and Pete relished their shock.

He could have dusted off the anti-war ballads he and the Almanacs had written twenty-five years before: "Get Out and Stay Out of War" and "The Ballad of John Doe." It was a tribute to his musical powers that the older songs were still singable, and that his newer songs, like "If You Love Your Uncle Sam, Bring 'Em Home," were much more fully developed.

> *There's one thing I must confess*
> *Bring 'em home, home, home.*
> *I'm not really a pacifist.*
> *Bring 'em home.*
> *If an army invaded this land of mine*
> *Bring 'em home, home, home*
> *You'd find me out on the firing line,*
> *Bring 'em home.*

"Bring 'Em Home" left audiences wondering about his rejection of pacifism—as Pete intended. Seeger had actually aligned himself with the enemy; in his song, the U.S. became the invader and the Vietnamese the patriots.

Ever since the days of the Popular Front, Pete had been proud to be an

American. His songs, stories, clothes, even his log cabin fostered his native-son image. For three decades, he'd harked back to American radicals for inspiration—even in his darkest moments with HUAC. But in Vietnam, Pete found no room for patriotism. "Pete's an incredible idealist," Bernice Reagon said, "an optimist throughout the period of the civil rights movement—the struggle was going to win, we're going to fix it. He ran into real trouble handling the United States and the war in Vietnam. He did not sail through it. He took a heavy glimpse of what was happening and got incredibly frustrated and depressed. . . .

"There was one period where I felt Pete was at some base level an American—you know, 'Our fathers bled at Valley Forge' [from "Wasn't That a Time?"] and 'This land is your land, this land is my land.' At some point in this Vietnamese war, those things became the issue and the problem—you were no longer working for the dreams of the founding fathers."

Seeger's patriotism was still at issue. *Counterattack* now harped on anti-war dissidents, complaining: "American fighting men have one hand tied behind them." Grass-roots anti-Communist groups popped out of the woodwork when Seeger came to town. The Citizens' Anti-Communist Committee of Connecticut called Seeger "Moscow's trained canary." The Committee to Combat Communist Propaganda handed out leaflets with pictures of wounded GIs captioned:

THE HORRIBLE TRUTH!
THROUGH THE ADMISSION CHARGE
YOU ARE FINANCING COMMUNISM
. . . THROUGH PETE SEEGER

A California school superintendent asked *Scholastic* for a statement that Seeger wasn't a Communist after the magazine published an interview with him. "Our respect for the dignity of an individual restrains us from asking anyone questions related to his personal convictions or beliefs," responded a brave editor. But these outside forces—including the American Legion pickets that continued through the sixties—threatened Pete less than the pressures within him.

Pete had marched, spoken politely, petitioned Congress, and nothing had changed; the bombers kept rolling out a carpet of death. Pete was himself stuck in the Big Muddy; he could not avoid his responsibility as an American in the Vietnam War era. His internal conflict surfaced explosively after his return from the Middle East, when he performed for a group of Arab professionals in Dutchess County, New York. Midway through the evening, Pete made the mistake of asking one man why he hadn't gone back: "He smirked and said, 'Well, there's a lot more money here, after all.' And I said, 'But don't the people there need you?'" The man made a derisive remark. Pete got so mad he lost control. He grabbed the nearest tablecloth, from a table set with fine crystal, and before he knew what he was doing he had wrenched it from the table, causing an awful crash. The Arab sat down astonished. The whole room stopped talking and stared. Toshi hustled him out the door, furious at his making a scene.

Seeger had no more control than in 1949, after he discovered PSI was going bankrupt and he threw a glass of Coke at a woman who had baited him about Henry Wallace. His anger came from the peculiar passion that makes a performer. "If you are very hot all the time, you have to be able to control it one way or another," Bess Lomax reflected. "In performance, you can pour out your emotion on the stage. Another way is by finding ways to keep yourself very cool in normal human interaction. I've seen Pete just walk away and then put his fist through something."

Pete's frustration was also directed at Columbia Records. He had hoped "Big Muddy" would be a breakthrough for him; after all, Robert Shelton of *The New York Times* had called it a potential smash hit. Throughout the summer of 1967 he waited to see if "Big Muddy" would take off as a single. A few progressive FM stations played it once or twice and the free-spirited Pacifica stations wore their copies out, but commercial stations ignored the song. Without radio play, sales lagged. Still, Pete reasoned, he should have word-of-mouth success; at concerts the crowd wouldn't stop applauding. Something funny was going on at Columbia.

Of course, Pete Seeger had never been a record executive's dream. He had as many records as any singer alive, but only one "hit": "Little Boxes." He toured constantly, and anyone who gave as many concerts as Pete should have sold a lot of records. Yet his first four record companies had gone out of business or fallen to conglomerates. The record business had now become the record industry, with multinational companies controlling publishing, distribution, and TV and radio stations; gross album sales had surpassed a billion dollars annually.

Pete was the animal that zoologists of the record world had failed to classify. He didn't know a Buying Power Index from a Weekly Sales Net. No half-ton of amplifiers, instruments, and road managers arrived with The Pete Seeger Show. He had no private bus with wraparound stereo and hot and cold running drugs. He refused to plug his records. In fact, he rarely listened to them or to the radio; he owned one of those hi-fis advertised for ten dollars down, ten dollars a week.

Seeger inhabited a world of song that record companies occasionally visited. They came looking for folk tunes as if on a French country picnic, bringing their own cutlery and tablecloth, to make sure the fare was served to their taste. Then, at a hint of controversy or gravity, they fled; Seeger—and his friends—were left to tend folk music until the next visit.

In 1965, Columbia Records had let his option drop. Pete had quietly returned to Folkways until John Hammond demanded CBS renew Seeger. He had optimistically re-signed, waiting to use Columbia's well-oiled distribution system for something he really cared about. Now, with "Big Muddy," he had his chance—but nothing had come of it. "Columbia dropped the ball," Judy Collins reflected. "I just don't think they put enough money, time, and effort into Pete's records."

Midway through the summer after "Big Muddy" came out, Pete met a man working in Columbia's distribution agency in Denver. "Pete, I have to tell you that record of yours arrived a few months ago. My boss just laughed: 'They expect me to get this sold? They're nuts.' He didn't even ship them out of the delivery room, they just stayed on the shelves." Pete was distraught. After going along with Columbia for so long, he'd expected better.

Seeger could do nothing; he irritatedly set off on tour with Bernice, traveling to Texas, where he visited his brother Charles. The five-day tour began in a poor mood. Pete finished writing one of his only original blues, "False from True," an extraordinarily personal song for him.

> When my song turns to ashes on my tongue   ©
> And I look in the mirror and see I'm no longer young
> Then I got to start the job of separating false from
>   true
> And then I know I need the love of you.

The lyrics so disturbed Charles's wife Inez that she told a reporter that she hoped "everybody who loved Pete would come and tell him that the world was not hopeless"; and that "False from True" was a symbol of his depressed mood. The newspaper printed her comments. "She shouldn't have said that," Pete angrily told Bernice.

"That song seemed a very internal and personal statement," Bernice remembered. "He was saying that stuff was not working out the way he thought it should. . . . I remember feeling he must really be in bad shape now."

He was. Married to an Asian-American, his children a mix of Japanese and American, Pete took the destruction of Asian children personally. Pictures of burned children haunted him; in page after page of his journal, he searched for a solution. He wrote a poem about a baby in North Vietnam whose mother delivered her during an American air raid. The child, Bao Ngac, was wounded before she was born, when shrapnel pierced the mother and tore into the baby's cheek.

> *You will bear the scar all your life long*
> *And I, whose only scars are mental ones,*
> *Must stagger out and tell my countrymen*
> *What happened. . . .*

The weeks passed and with them an endless stream of concerts: short intermissions and long encores. At first, it was his fans who noticed a change in Pete, the ones who came to every concert, who knew by his introductions what the song would be. Then, gradually, the casual listener sensed the difference. Had Seeger been quite so somber the last time? As strained and stark?

His columns in *Sing Out!* had a new grimness, and he needed more and more space for what he had to say. He talked endlessly of television, which came as no surprise to anyone reading the papers, for his television career had suddenly become a national conversation topic.

Pete's long-range planning had succeeded. In August the producers of *The Smothers Brothers Comedy Hour* received word that Seeger could appear in prime time on CBS. The *Los Angeles Times* broke the story, calling it an "important event," and "the glimmer of light at the end of what must seem to Seeger like an endless black tunnel." Pete agreed, warning that he would do "Big Muddy," or another anti-war song. Tom and Dick Smothers wanted him on, but after a while they started to get nervous and asked Pete for a list of songs.

Many agreed that Seeger's break was overdue. *The New York Times* and the *Delaware County Daily Times* ran editorials praising CBS's heroism. The network received more publicity for breaking its blacklist than they did for maintaining it for seventeen years. Among the Smothers Brothers' sponsors were Procter & Gamble, a major advertiser on *Hootenanny.* "Presenting Seeger," said the Smothers Brothers' producers, "is the most significant thing we'll do all year."

On September 1 Pete flew to Hollywood with Harold, in a quietly jubilant mood: "Pete's not the kind of guy to jump up in the air," Harold laughed. "He was reserved, but plenty glad to be back." All summer he had been talking about buying time on TV to sing "Big Muddy"; now he wouldn't have to take out ads, or underwrite a TV series to be heard.

"I was on my mettle as much as I've ever been in my life," Seeger said in recalling the taping. "I felt history was being made. And when you stop to realize—it was. The more President Johnson got into the war, the more opposition there was, far beyond the narrow left or pacifist wing. . . . All of a sudden here was a breach in the wall of prime time, a very dangerous thing as far as the establishment was concerned." If Seeger exaggerated the importance of "Big Muddy" and TV's power, this only indicated how seriously he took his opportunity.

Yet excited as he was, Pete had a hard time singing. The television studio inadvertently robbed him of his sounding board: the audience. The acoustically deadened walls kept the crowd from hearing themselves sing and frustrated Pete. Lights, boom stands, cameras—they all got in the way of the songs; no one paid any attention to the audience. His twenty-minute segment didn't give him time to build up momentum. Despite these problems, however, he left feeling victorious.

Afterward, when the editor of a small folk-song magazine criticized him for lending his talent to TV, Pete hotly defended himself: "I am no expert at stractics and tategy [sic]. I think all of us who love music and love America and the world must figure out how we are going to take the next steps. Unless we prefer to get off in a corner by ourselves and congratulate each other on our exclusiveness."

On September 10, 1967, Tommy Smothers smiled nervously and introduced Pete Seeger to millions of American households. Pete began with "Wimoweh"; then Tommy asked Pete, who was holding a twelve-string guitar and fingering the strings, if he was going to sing "that song." The camera closed in on Seeger's face for a moment. When it moved back, Pete was holding a banjo and "Big Muddy" had vanished into the ether.

Watching at home, Pete practically smashed in the TV set. They'd been had.

"It's perfectly possible that some clever person at CBS said 'No, don't let him sing his song now,' " Pete speculated later. " 'Let's build up publicity and let him sing it in January.' It's theoretically possible. On the other hand I think more likely they said, 'That's just the kind of goddamn song we knew he'd try and sing. Well, we've got to stop it somehow—scissor it out.' The editor said 'How do I do it?' 'Oh,' they said, 'find a way.' So the poor editor might have said, 'Well, I'll do it the most awkward way, so everybody knows it's been scissored out.' "

Censoring Seeger provoked even more attention than the original decision to broadcast him; once again censorship bolstered his career. On September 13, *Variety* ran one of its inimitable front-page headlines: "BIG MUDDY" IN CBS-TV'S EYE: SLIP SEEGER'S NUMBER FOR ANTI-LBJ SLANT. The network weakly replied that they didn't want "political controversy on entertainment programs." Exercising mammoth self-restraint—perhaps in hopes of a second chance—Pete refused public comment. *The New York Times* headlined SEEGER ACCUSES CBS OVER SONG, asserting Pete had been told he could sing "Big Muddy" if he dropped the last verse ("Every time I read the papers . . ."). Pete telegramed Michael Dann, a CBS vice-president, that he hadn't "accused" CBS of anything; he denied leaking the story, but concluded: "Do feel strongly that radio and TV communications should allow audiences to judge for themselves. The best censor is that little knob on the set."

The *Honolulu Star-Bulletin* asked: "Is the presidency so teetery that it cannot withstand the musical barbs of a folk singer? And is our democracy so fragile that songs of social protest must be stricken from the public airwaves? We think not." *Newsweek* pointed out that CBS records featured the song on Pete's current album. The September issue of the *National Catholic Reporter*—with its premature praise of CBS's "courage"—remained on the stands for two weeks after CBS censored Seeger.

As usual, Pete left the public indignation to others; Tommy Smothers told the press, "We definitely plan to have Seeger back and he's probably gonna want to sing 'Big Muddy' again. Maybe we'll sing it with him." Only Pennsylvania's *York Gazette* grasped how uncomfortable and out of place Seeger appeared. He might *never* be content on soap-selling, mass-merchandising shows ("which are products of inhibition, repression, and fearful calculations."). Television was not fit for Seeger, the *Gazette* concluded, rather than the other way around.

Two weeks later, after all the flutter had died down, Pete performed in San Jose, California; a writer there noted he sang "Big Muddy" "with an aggressiveness that was out of character."

Throughout the crisis of what Pete could or could not sing on TV, one of his favorite causes had floundered. *Sing Out!*'s circulation dropped with each issue, and the magazine was mired in infighting, with bitter attacks both by and against Pete Seeger. From three hundred in 1950, the circulation of *Sing Out!* had risen to a thousand in 1955; by 1965, they were mailing almost twenty thousand copies. The folk song boom had seemed unending and, as editor of *Sing Out!*, Irwin Silber willingly took credit for the magazine's success. Then, in 1966, the magazine's attempt at newsstand sales proved a disaster—they printed truckloads of copies that went unsold and lost twelve thousand dollars. Circulation ebbed as the commercial folk song revival faded, but *Sing Out!* couldn't retrench fast enough. In 1966 Pete had worried that the magazine was too fat and slick; a year later, the magazine was bankrupt. The shrinking circulation opened the magazine to charges of irrelevancy, which came, strangely enough, from its editor of fifteen years.

Since Irwin had first become editor, Pete had tried to put aside his differences with Irwin and support his editorship. He appreciated Irwin's dedication, but he worried that the magazine was pandering to the star system. And Silber's self-righteousness had always bothered him; "When he thinks he's got the answer it doesn't bother him at all if he had a different opinion awhile before, or that he was illogical." Irwin somehow managed to be both the major critic of commercialism in folk music and co-owner of the largest folk music publishing house, Oak Publications. But when Irwin bitterly denounced the 1967 Newport Folk Festival in print, that was the final straw.

Silber had come back from a trip to Cuba re-revolutionized and ready to turn *Sing Out!* over to the class struggle. Despite a reorganization of the magazine as a cooperative, bitterness against Silber grew until the magazine rocked like an overloaded ship on an uneven keel. On November 13, 1967, Pete's nonpartisanship broke. He wrote Irwin a fierce and bitter letter: "I feel if you are trying to kill *Sing Out!* . . . you are doing a good job. For 15 years, I've defended you against all attacks. . . . If I have been a blind King Lear, I probably have been most blind about your own failings." Irwin eventually gave up his editorship, and the magazine has struggled along to the present on handouts from Moe Asch, the Seegers, and many friends.

On October 3, 1967, one of *Sing Out!*'s oldest friends, Woody Guthrie, died. He had been in the hospital for thirteen years, and, in the end, had little control over his body. Leadbelly and now Woody . . . Pete felt mortal and alone. He heard the news while on tour in Japan; *Life* asked him for a eulogy, and he obliged, asserting Woody would have been disgusted by the war in Vietnam. "Woody will never die," Pete wrote, "as long as there are people who like to sing his songs."

On the campuses where Woody was best known, frustration with the war grew daily. Some burned their draft cards or fled to Canada to avoid fighting. Many of Pete's followers felt pressured to do anything to shut down the machinery of war—throw rocks through windows, pour glue in the locks at the draft board. Declaring opposition wasn't enough; irrevocable acts were called for—going to jail or arming for guerrilla warfare. Black

Panthers talked of being "part of the solution or part of the problem." Local police forces, used to panty raids rather than sit-ins, overreacted and broke students' heads. Vietnam had become, as *The Washington Post* observed, "a generation-wide catastrophe." Pete privately thought street fighting and yelling "pig" at the police were self-fulfilling prophecies. "My own tactic was to isolate the potential fascist and see if I could turn him into a potential human being."

Everywhere he looked, a new culture spread among young people, one he barely understood. Why should anyone want to take LSD? Why had Abbie Hoffman left civil rights for *Revolution for the Hell of it?* When people came up to him at concerts and handed him flowers and beads, Pete didn't know what to say. The music changed so fast, he couldn't keep up: the Doors' "Light My Fire," Smokey Robinson's "Tracks of My Tears," and the Beatles' "Sergeant Pepper." The Monterey Pop Festival outdrew Newport five to one.

"All You Need Is Love" wasn't going to salvage America, that much Seeger knew—particularly in the long hot summers of the mid-1960s, when arson left Detroit and Newark looking like Bristol after the German bombings. And Jimmy Collier had written a song justifying the riots, "Burn Baby Burn."

Pete no longer recognized his "children," many of whom spent more time getting high and listening to the Cream and Jefferson Airplane than to Pete Seeger. Pete's music was "right on," but his records sounded dated and lacked the rhythmic release of the Rolling Stones. Pete kept his distance from marijuana, long hair, and talk of free sex. A dream he wrote down in his journal revealed how out of touch he felt: He was performing at a boys' school, similar to Avon, and the students wouldn't sing. In the middle of his concert, the audience filed out one by one to smoke grass on a darkened balcony—and Pete didn't even realize they had gone.

His moral imperatives were hard to swallow in an indulgent age. A young English journalist pronounced him "lamentably and typically middle-class" and "the reverse of hip." "Pete Seeger is getting old," wrote a student in the *Daily Pennsylvanian*. "His voice cracks and he is no longer the best five-string banjo man around." The same reviewer pointed out how Pete used to flourish a crimson bandanna, but now his shirt was dull red. "Times have passed him by, and he is now a respected member of society." Pete believed in learning from young people, but he was forty-eight, and communes and psychedelics were not for him.

At the end of 1967 the remnants of Pete's "children" gathered at Carnegie Hall for his annual Christmas concert—folkies, peaceniks, and war resisters. At the Fifty-seventh Street entrance, a woman in army fatigues and a "Dump Johnson" button passed out leaflets for a demonstration at next summer's Democratic convention in Chicago. Twenty-year-olds in first beards exchanged stories about Tim Leary's latest cross-country stump.

The crowd disagreed whether Pete was still a radical. He had clearly aged—considered a sign of decreasing radicalism in the Sixties. Pete symbolized the folk revival, peace, and civil rights movements; but symbols fade. The previous fall at the University of Wisconsin, students had hissed Joan Baez when she said she wouldn't fire a gun. Pete's most devoted audience was also the toughest one to please.

To many at this reunion, Pete represented their parents' generation, the bureaucratic "Old Left," as opposed to "Student Power." Instead of the CP's closet politics, the New Left invited the press to be-ins. Newspaper editors answered with slogans—"Send them back to Moscow" and "Our country, love it or leave it."

While the crowd milled outside, Pete considered what he would sing: "My main skill as a musician," he later said, "is in pacing a group of people I've never seen before—improvising a program which seems to make sense and having it flow from one song to another. And I've found I can do it better on stage than I can in advance.

"It's a chain of words and ideas as well as a chain of rhythm, melodies, harmonies, and feelings. Only after I've touched base with the kids out there, the women and the men, the old people, the discouraged people and the impatient people and so on, that we finally pull things together. . . . It's as though I've taken my golden thread and I'm weaving it through one person's buttonhole, and another person's, and another, and finally, we're all together. Then we can really sing some songs."

After the crowd filed into their seats and the lights dimmed in the gilded hall, Pete strode on stage with his banjo, wearing a turquoise shirt. He stood out even from the distant third balcony, a stick figure with his musical wand. "It's Christmas and Hanukkah. I've got a wish for the New Year. Let's get America to wade out of the Big Muddy." The audience laughed, relaxing in his resonant, sing-song voice. Genial, with no hint of the tension in his journals, he resembled a favorite uncle back from vacation. He played a nameless lick on the banjo and ended suddenly, catching the audience off guard, like a pitcher striking out two batters in the first inning.

Next came his banjo tunes: "Old Joe Clark" and "Darling Corey." Seeger paced them too fast. When people applauded, he played right over them. "We were really on edge the first part of the concert," Pete's friend Josh Dunson wrote afterward. "It seemed for the first twenty minutes or so, you were trying desperately to relax, to get absorbed in the music."

Then Pete played "Jacob's Ladder," and for one minute the clear arpeggios mounted in silver rungs. The sound spread like mortar, clean and solid, and he trimmed it into place before the ear could notice. Yet he seemed ready to break off at any time, unsure whether to release this perfection or cover it up, lest he be thought too much of a virtuoso.

Pete started a hymn adapted by the civil rights movement. People stirred uncomfortably—here comes the nostalgia. But Pete presented the songs as music, not solutions, and got the crowd singing without having to acknowledge that the black-and-white-together era had ended. In the balcony, a few freedom riders—blacks who rode in the front of southern buses to integrate them—began to rock and clap to "This Little Light of Mine." The rest of the audience followed.

"Pete steps out of the wings, walks on stage, and he takes it over," Judy Collins said. "It looks like that stage is too small for him. . . . What makes his voice so marvelous is really what makes all the greatest singers marvelous—you understand every word. He has a miraculous gift for phrasing. It wouldn't matter if he was singing *Rigoletto*; he would still mesmerize."

Next Pete did a somber song, his "Letter to Eve," and his voice colored with a personal distress. "If you want to have great love, you've got to have great anger. . . . If music could only bring peace, I'd only be a musician." The militant refrain suggested his private doubts about music.

At intermission, the balconies were awash with remembered causes. SNCC stories tumbled out so fast, a motion from the orchestra seats might have resurrected the moribund organization. "If music could only bring peace . . ." echoed in the halls. When the lights blinked, people streamed back for more.

"Say, those old Christmas songs sound fine when you sing them in harmony." Seeger's joviality rang false. The audience again shifted in their seats: Christmas songs weren't going to save the Vietnamese. Ignoring the mood, Pete divided the crowd in thirds for "We Wish You a Merry Christmas" and amazed the audience by fitting the pieces together like doweled pine. A few carols and environmental songs later, Seeger sang "False from True." "Musicians are supposed to cheer people up," Pete said in introduction, "but who's going to cheer up the musician?"

> When I found tarnish on some of my brightest ©
> dreams

*Yes, and when some people I trusted turned out to be
  not what they seemed
Then once more I have to start the job of separating
  false from true.
Then I know I need the love of you.*

He didn't ask the audience to come in on the chorus; his lyrics projected shadows instead of optimism. When Pete sang "No song I sing will change Governor Wallace's mind," the audience was as fascinated and shocked as if Pete had opened his shirt to show a wound; for the first time, he sang about his life, rather than serving the world. The crowd almost didn't want to see his anguish—it was too intense, like gazing in a teacher's face and seeing corruption there.

"I was most concerned by that song you sang—the new one with 'My dreams had been tarnished,' " a fan wrote after the concert. "There was so much real pain in that song. If you despair, what happens to the many, many people like myself who look to you constantly for hope and the bliss of spirit which you bring to our lives?"

Pete soon picked up the tempo with an anti-war song, but the crowd remained behind. A few moments ago he had made himself vulnerable; was that the performance, or this? He pounded out "Support our boys in Vietnam, bring 'em home," forcing the audience to drop their individual thoughts and share his anger. One by one they sang, overlooking his intimations of mortality. At the end of the song, he applauded the audience. With a quick "Thank you, Merry Christmas," he was offstage with his instruments. Restrained feeling broke out with a roar. The audience wanted its optimist back, but he could not oblige.

In the end, the crowd left warmhearted. Something in the group singing—a roomful of strangers reverberating together, their ears filled with a communal resonance—left a sense of community. He had broken down the barrier between performer and audience. Though *The New York Times* called his performance "distracted," Pete had held his audience— barely. As his belief in song wavered, his step became less sure. A handful of listeners left wondering how much longer Pete could keep up.

Throughout 1968, which Pete called "the year of revelations," images of Vietnam pursued him, robbing him of his moments of triumph, resisting his attempts to pound them out at the woodpile.

In February he had finally sung "Big Muddy" on the Smothers Brothers' program, but the triumph was anticlimactic. Only the CBS affiliate in Detroit had censored the song—and then only the pointed last verse. Citizens of Detroit didn't want to hear criticisms of the President, according to Lawrence Carino, an executive of Storer Broadcasting. The following year, CBS canceled *The Smothers Brothers Comedy Hour*. When the entertainers sued, this same Lawrence Carino testified that the show caused him "problems" in Detroit—citing Pete Seeger's appearance.

Carino's protectiveness was unnecessary, for on March 15, Lyndon Johnson announced a limited pullback of troops and his decision not to run for reelection. Pete took some of the credit for this, calling the Smothers Brothers appearance "one of the high points of my life; I probably reached seven million people all at once."

Pete always believed that the right song at the right moment could change history. He used to argue this point with Bess Hawes and her husband: "Butch felt art came out of events and didn't make them. Pete never thought that was true," Bess said. "There was a line from Engels we discussed: 'Art is the spume of history,' what flies off the top. Pete was convinced songs had helped start the civil rights and union movements; Butch felt songs appeared only when events provided the material."

"Big Muddy" was Pete's case in point, but in an electric age, songs didn't seem to have the punch they possessed earlier. In *Sing Out!*, Pete wrote his favorite story about how a song had stopped a war:

"In 1758, an English force attacked at Brittany. Local militia advancing to battle were astounded to hear a local song. It was Welsh mountaineers, singing an old Celtic melody, older than their estrangment. French officers commanded the militia to fire, but the troops would not."

A touching story, certainly, but in the 1960s, army bomber pilots couldn't hear the songs of the Vietnamese as they sighted the troops in infrared scopes. Pete nonetheless pushed his music toward his desired effect, just as he had in his world tour. "My songs must be so good that they reach out to 190 million Americans," he wrote the organizer of a festival in Japan. ". . . I have not succeeded yet, but I must keep trying, as long as I have breath in my body. I need songs with melodies so unforgettable that listeners will be humming them at their work. The words of some songs must be so well put together that even those who disagree will want to hear them again. Songs must be so funny that even the stony-faced will break into a grin. And we need songs with strength to make cowards stop fleeing, turn around, and face the future with a breath of courage."

On April 4 Martin Luther King, Jr., was assassinated, and Seeger received an emergency call from poet John Beecher.

"Pete, you've got to come down here. I've never seen anything like it on any southern campus. After King's assassination, about two hundred white students [at Duke University] decided they must *do* something, not just talk. They went to the million-dollar home of the president. . . . He refused to talk further with them. They refused to leave. After two days he went to the hospital with a breakdown. They moved their vigil to the quadrangle. Their numbers grew to five hundred, to a thousand, to fifteen hundred. I've been reading poems to them. Will you come down and sing for them?" Pete agreed to come, two days later, but his conjuring was in short supply. He was more in the mood for a public burning than reasoned discourse.

Duke University, in Durham, North Carolina, is set amid the rolling hills where Pete and his family had once been accosted as gypsies. When Seeger arrived, he found two thousand disturbed collegians waiting for someone to explain the America of 1968. They were seated on the grass at the center of the campus, listening to an improvised P.A. system; a lone light bulb hanging from a tree lit the stage. John Beecher read, and the president of the maintenance union of black workers spoke: "I have a vision that I'd like to pick up after black boys here, as well as white boys." Then Pete stood up to sing.

Facing the crowd that night, Pete's mood was dark and fiery. King's assassination, the end of the civil rights era, youth culture, and Vietnam— all these had pushed him to the edge of despair, judging from his journals. Graceful songs and witty quotations disappeared from his music notebooks, replaced by song fragments that slid off the staff lines. Phrases like "peace of the graveyard" kept returning to his thoughts; a few days before visiting Duke he had written:

> *Go tell White America*
> *If he wants his cities to burn*
> *Three hundred years is long enough*
> *Both cheeks have been well turned . . .*
>
> *Go tell every light-skinned face*
> *I'm not a violent person*
> *But there's one thing I've learned*
> *If you want freedom you got to fight for it.*

Despite these dark reflections, Pete remained a master performer, and his songs stirred hope in the students, a hope he could barely give himself. The crowd applauded appreciatively; student radicals cared more for his personal authenticity than anything else; Seeger's embodiment of his music had become his stock in trade. Before closing his part of the concert, Pete lined out a hymn or two and asked one of the students, "Why hasn't there been more publicity about this nationally?"

"Oh, the local papers have been full of it," he replied, "but the wire services hardly mention it. When we called up the TV networks they said they didn't have any cameramen to spare, 'but let us know if there is any violence—we'll send someone down.' "

"I felt a deep rage boil in me," Seeger wrote, "as though all the experiences with TV censorship and misrule had suddenly come to a head. When my turn came to sing again, I found myself speechifying—probably a dangerous thing for any singer.

" 'You read today about crime in the streets! I say there's crime in the New York offices of CBS and NBC! Crime! I'd like to make a pledge to you here tonight. . . . Before I leave Duke I'm going to take a stone with me, and put it in my banjo case, and if I ever meet a TV man up there who says he won't cover a story like this because there's no violence, some*thing* is going to get hurt.' "

Yet preoccupied as he was, one side of Seeger kept imagining ways life could be improved on a small scale. There was always something positive to be done. If teenagers burned up the cities in the summer, why not set up block parties to cool the tension, he wrote Thomas Hoving, New York's imaginative parks commissioner. On one page of his notebook he would speculate how to set up free outdoor movie showings—paint walls white in vacant lots and bring in mobile projectors; on the next, he would plan allegorical dramas of the end to the human race, such as the *500-Mile Bookshelf* where various creatures evolved and became extinct; it could happen to humans too. These zany ideas were Pete's way of reminding himself that too often we live our daily lives inside an immense wall, which cuts us off from any really different future, and which isolates us from our past. Pete wanted people to scale the wall, to address a better future. This was the vision behind "Tomorrow Is A Highway": Seeds of the future exist in the present, and children and other idealists must steel themselves for a battle to rebuild and purify, to keep the best stuff of humanity alive during troubled times. This Pete had done for decades, carrying radical traditions of the 1930s in songs. He had endured and persisted, even when his optimism weakened, for revolutionists have to say they will overcome, even when they know they may not.

Not everyone was ready to listen to such lofty sentiments. In the spring of 1968, Jerry Rubin and Abbie Hoffman—Hoffman had previously written Seeger signing himself "a devoted fan"—met with Pete and Harold to persuade them to participate in demonstrations at the Democratic National Convention in Chicago. Pete listened thoughtfully but urged them "to represent all the different kinds of human beings in the U.S.A. because there's all kinds of people that are against the war. It's all right if we have long hair there and pot smoking," Pete said magnanimously, "but if we don't include short-haired people as well, old people alongside the young people, we'd be making a mistake."

"You're not going to have a revolution with a bunch of short-haired older people!" said the two members of the Yippie Party, looking at him as if he were crazy.

An Oberlin College student sensed the distance Pete felt from his former audience: "The war had left him wounded and scarred, internally bleeding, like the abominably infected knife of an incompetent surgeon, poisoning by its touch what it did not cut entirely away. . . . His songs grew harder and more cutting. Perhaps something in his voice when he sang 'Letter to Eve' ['If music alone could change the world . . .'] gave subtle hints of a new urgency that had not been there before." Pete could remain youth's fellow traveler only so long.

Despite performing "Big Muddy" on TV—the best he could do—Pete's frustration with singing and marching rose steadily as the war dragged on. In *Sing Out!* he quoted Henry Thoreau: "Is there not a sort of bloodshed when the conscience is wounded? Through this wound a man's real manhood and immortality flow out and he bleeds to an everlasting death. I see this blood flowing now."

More then ever Seeger sounded like a preacher, disdainful of wealth and worldly vanities: "What is right and what is wrong in the world?" he wrote. "The most truthful answer I know comes from that hard-boiled section of the Bible, Ecclesiastes." Years before, Pete had turned a passage from Ecclesiastes into a song, adding a final couplet and a refrain that titled the song: "Turn, Turn, Turn." In this, Pete's favorite chapter of the Bible, a worldly preacher traveled with his gospel and, like Seeger, preached a moral life:

> Dead flies cause the ointment of the apothecary to send forth a stinking savor: so doth a little folly him that is in reputation for wisdom and honor.

In the Sixties, this puritanism seemed especially out of place; people wanted a little folly. Pete understood this no better now than when he had complained about Woody buying a pint on the sly. He demanded moral consistency in an inconsistent time; and his righteousness could be grating as he asked, in the words of an old country song: "Do you preach what you live/Would you live what you preach?"

Pete's thinking grew apolcalyptic. He borrowed a line from Uncle Alan's most famous poem, "I Have a Rendez-vous with Death" to express his own fantasies:

> At midnight in a flaming angry town   ©
> I saw my country's flag lying torn upon the ground
> I ran in and dodged among the crowd
> And scooped it up to safety.

> And then I took this striped old piece of cloth
> And tried my best to wash the garbage off,
> But I found it had been used for wrapping lies.
> It smelled and stank and attracted all the flies. . . .

Then, in May 1968, he confided a dreamlike parable to his journal and to his friend Bess: "I feel like I'm on a ship and we're going down the river. There's a big crew and we're having a party. Everybody is singing and dancing and having a marvelous time. And the word comes in that there is a huge waterfall ahead. I go up and try to tell everybody that we had better stop and get the ship turned around before we go over the falls. But everybody is so busy singing and dancing that they won't listen to me." The only way to make the crowd listen, Seeger concluded, was to drill holes and sink the ship.

A chilly rain drenched the ground outside the Seeger tent in Resurrection City in June 1968. Toshi and Pete had come to Washington to support the encampment that Martin Luther King had begun organizing before his death—gathering America's poor together in the nation's capital.

Cold wet weather had spread mud and mosquitos throughout the campsite. Rows of battered and hastily constructed plywood houses stood leaking and abandoned. Kids from the streets of Detroit and Chicago had just been sent home for harassing visitors and the whites in the campsite. As the Seegers arrived, police threatened to bulldoze the campsite; government bureaucracies ignored the demonstrators. People walked through the puddles of Resurrection City without shoes, because they'd worn out their only pair marching. Others sat in groups huddled under blankets and stared up at the gray sky.

The Poor People's Campaign hadn't started out this way in March, when Dr. King had sent out the call. Liberal presidential aspirants Robert

Kennedy and Eugene McCarthy had endorsed his plan. Candidate Nixon had responded that America couldn't afford to fight an all-out war on poverty at the same time it fought in Vietnam.

On dedicating Resurrection City—three weeks before Pete arrived— Reverend Ralph Abernathy had said the poor would "plague the Pharaohs of this nation. . . . We'll stay here until 'We Shall Overcome' becomes 'We Have Overcome.' " Andrew Young, one of the campaign leaders, declared: "If they close down the City, they have to close down America." Reading all this in the papers, Seeger had been glad to be going.

Before he left for Washington, he appeared on Steve Allen's TV show. He had started to sing "It Takes a Worried Man," and about two verses into the song had stopped, saying, "I can't sing this song." When Lee Hays later asked what happened, Pete said that the spirit just went out of him. "The idea of the spirit going out of that man is very, very unusual," Don McLean reflected soberly. Pete could not bear the America he saw, but he could not stop himself from looking. On June 6, Robert Kennedy had been assassinated in Los Angeles; the country seemed infected with violence. "Don't be afraid of death," Pete had written in his journal. "And when you finally take his hand, death will be no stranger."

The Seegers camped in the section where the Appalachian people had been, as Jimmy Collier remembered: "Everything was wet. The mud was two feet thick and for the whole camp, all we had was a couple of portable showers. Pete and Toshi and Tinya wandered around, going from one campfire to another. At nighttime, people sat down in the mud and sang. There was urgency and real seriousness in the atmosphere: King had been *killed!*"

The residents of the lean-to city were determined to stay, despite the nearby bulldozers. Their resolution was strengthened by a demonstration on June 19 of fifty thousand people from across the country. The crowd booed Vice President Humphrey and cheered Seeger and Gene McCarthy. *The New York Times* found a quiet desperation in the speeches. A little girl carried a sign: THIS IS THE LAST CHANCE FOR NONVIOLENCE. That night, when Pete and Toshi returned to their tent with Tinya, they found few white people left.

One of their last nights there, Pete helped out on a sing-along. By this time, the encampment was out of control. Police were using tear gas against gangs of black kids throwing firebombs at passing motorists. What had started as nonviolent was now semiviolent, and heating up by the hour. Garbage had become embedded in the mud, and the acrid smell hung in the tents. Everyone's nerves were on edge. Nobody knew what would happen next, and the people were too tired and too uncomfortable to care.

Pictures show Pete sitting in the mud, a hat covering his wispy hair. Gaunt with fatigue, he resembled a victim of an air crash after a day without food, skin pulled in at the cheeks. His angular New England features and his clean shirt gave him the air of a clergyman, unafraid in a roomful of black faces.

The encampment depended on music to keep up its spirits. Every night they had held programs in a cultural tent led by Jimmy Collier and Reverend Frederick Douglass Kirkpatrick ("Kirk"), a six-foot-three black with a gentle manner and a quick laugh. Kirk managed to be both angry and philosophic at the same time, a quality that later made him Pete's treasured friend. Kirk and Jimmy rounded everyone up for marathon music sessions. They called square dances while Pete played banjo. A man in his seventies stood up and "Africanized" a white hymn, dancing and shouting out in rhythm. To finish off the evening, Seeger asked Collier to lead "This Land Is Your Land." Jimmy hesitated before answering: "Pete, why don't you ask Henry Crow Dog first—ask him if it's all right to sing that song." Seeger was dumbfounded. How could it *not* be all right?

"You have to understand," Collier said later, "sitting with a couple Apaches in full dress I felt a little silly singing 'This Land Is Your Land.' "

"Reverend Kirkpatrick and Jimmy Collier were saying, 'This land belongs to the Indians! I'm going to sing "This Land," but I've asked Chief Crow Dog's permission,' " Bernice remembered. "That song was the basis of Pete's principles, him and good old Woody. And it's the basis of the American dream—coming in and building a country, freedom, blah, blah. I felt that in '67 and '68, all that got smashed to smithereens. . . . I remember Pete talking constantly about that exchange with Kirkpatrick and Collier around Chief Crow Dog, and how he then had a hard time doing 'This Land Is Your Land.' It felt like he didn't know *what* to sing . . . he was not sure what his function was."

The Seegers packed up and left soon afterward, before the bulldozers moved in and hundreds were arrested.

The gathering storm had hit, and Pete didn't know where to turn. Despite all his efforts to live a good life, he found himself part of a system beyond his control. His world looked corrupt, beyond redemption:

> *If my skin showed an African cast*
> *It would be easier for me to be honest*
> *But as I am I can walk upon the carpeted floor*

And only when they find out my name
And only when I won't deny the blame
Will I be finally shown the door.

Pete wrote these lines in his song notebook; but he could not craft a song from such thoughts.

He had lost the self-direction that had led him through hundreds of pickets and angry crowds, through seven years of fighting HUAC. He had succeeded in his profession, and successful song agitators put themselves out of work. Eventually, as Bernice said of Pete, "the people don't need you to sing their folk songs; they can sing themselves." His faith in his music faltered. On his next album, due to be recorded in a few weeks, he decided to have Bernice and Jimmy and Kirk with him.

The album issued as *Pete Seeger Now* was as openly incendiary as any he recorded. He sang "False from True," "Letter to Eve," and a bitter talking blues against the war. The record is a cry for help, to wake up America before her ship shattered in the falls.

"Pete invited Bernice and me to do this concert," Jimmy recalled. "I think it was in Westbury, Long Island [a largely white, upper-middle-class suburb]. Pete was becoming—and the times were creating a situation where he became—more radical. He was also at the end of his romance with Columbia Records. It didn't feel like an old man singing Burl Ives's songs. You hear that on the record.

"You see, Peter wasn't that much of an actual organizer. These moments were pretty meaningful for him. There was a war going on, and this was a battlefield and a sense of danger. It was an intense and personal time. People were having to make decisions. People were beginning to doubt that sweetness and goodness and light would win over. At that concert we were all angry—that was our stance. And Pete, spending that time in Resurrection City, caught that anger."

After finishing the record, Pete Seeger decided to give up singing.

Golden River  12

PETE had resolved to quit singing before; he made the threat when his life reached an impasse, musically or politically, when he couldn't "see how to grow." In the summer of 1968 he was looking back on his life with dark reflection. He had started singing to help organize unions—and wound up helping bloated, self-satisfied institutions that had no place for him. He had restocked America's repertoire with songs from the reservoir of folk tradition—and had produced *Hootenanny* which also had no place for him: "Maybe I felt I'd shot my wad, and there wasn't much more to do."

After the death of Dr. King and the debacle at Resurrection City, Pete's hopes for integration lay in ruins. His friend Julius Lester again tore holes in liberal ideals: "Yet while black anger increases, whites remain only concerned and deeply disturbed. . . . This is why the black radical reserves his greatest anger for the white who, to all appearances, is most sympathetic to him."

Then his daughter Mika was arrested and jailed during student demonstrations in Mexico at the time of the 1968 Olympic Games; ironically, Pete had been asked to write a song celebrating the games. There were rumors of CIA involvement in the arrest—police were waiting for her when she returned from a demonstration—and though Mika was eventually released, she had refused aid from her parents.

Paradoxically, his troubles once again led Seeger back to music. He had reached the final phase of a now-familiar cycle. After his success in the mid-Sixties and his censorship on TV, Pete again began composing songs of optimism, like "Old Devil Time" and "Quite Early Morning":

> *You know it's darkest before the dawn* ©
> *This thought keeps me moving on.*
> *If we could heed those early warnings,*
> *The time is now, quite early morning. . . .*

And so we keep on while we live,
Until we have no, no more to give.
And when these fingers can strum no longer
Hand the old guitar to young ones stronger.

This irrepressible optimism lay at the core of his art; the more defeats he suffered, the more resilient his music. Seeger didn't follow through on his decision to stop singing, at least not in 1968. Instead, in the last decades of his middle age, the forty-nine-year-old set out to find a cause worth singing about, something positive to inspire a people numbed by war. Pete became passionately involved in the environmental movement.

Actually, this interest had begun in self-defense in 1965 when, during a boycott of one of his concerts, Pete's neighbors nearly ran him and his family out of town. On September 20, 1965, at the invitation of the Beacon Teachers' Association, Pete had agreed to give a benefit to endow a scholarship at Beacon High School. For months students and teachers had wanted him to sing, but the principal kept refusing; finally, after threatening a suit, they had their way. On November 26, he would sing in the high school gym. "You may get some hassles," Seeger warned. "We don't care," his sponsors told him. "We want to go ahead."

Pete put the date out of his mind until that October. Returning from a tour of the Soviet Union, Pete and Toshi had read the *Times's* headline: SEEGER SONG IN MOSCOW IS ANTI-U.S. They guessed there would be trouble, and it surprised neither of them to reach home and find local conservatives attempting to cancel the concert.

The Right Reverend Monsignor Hubert Beller, pastor of St. John's Church in Beacon, objected to having Seeger perform on school property; recent headlines, he wrote the *Beacon Evening News,* "give positive proof of his [subversive] views." For the next two weeks, Beacon's papers headlined the controversy. The community was finally taking note of its most famous resident, though not in a way the Seegers liked. Another local conservative called Seeger "an American who bites the hand that feeds him."

Three weeks before the scheduled concert, Pastor Beller handed out anti-Seeger leaflets in church, based on information from HUAC and John Birch Society files. A Stop Pete Seeger Committee formed, sponsored by the Veterans of Foreign Wars, the Knights of Columbus, and the Catholic Daughters of America. Even the local fire department joined the boycott; luckily, nothing caught fire at the Seegers'.

At the ice-cream parlors and gas stations on Main Street, people passed petitions to deny Seeger the school gym. "Who's behind the Seeger show?" one letter in a local paper asked ominously. Neighbors asked each other who this guy was; few had ever met him in town. The liberals Pete counted on for support—Beacon's professionals—refused to speak out; one told him, "Pete, you know this is fascism. You know perfectly well what it is, and you are going to be run out of town if you don't cancel this."

At first, Pete hadn't known how seriously to take the challenge. It seemed absurd: He could sell out concert halls across the country, but in his home town, he wasn't considered patriotic enough to donate his services. Once his music was called anti-American, few in Beacon would listen long enough to judge for themselves. It was like fighting HUAC all over again. As the number of signatures mounted on the petitions, Pete realized the seriousness of his opposition. He told reporters: "Small businessmen have been threatened and forced to sign the petition."

Neighbors on the hill where he lived were asked to sign the petition—people who had known Pete and Toshi for over fifteen years. They signed. By challenging Seeger in his own town, right-wingers sought to humiliate Pete: keeping him from the high school he paid taxes to support, defaming and endangering his family.

If the Seeger family didn't build up support, if conservatives successfully barred Pete from singing in Beacon, there was no telling what the next attempt on him would be. Ten-year-old Tinya still attended the local public school.

His relations with his neighbors had barely improved since Peekskill. The trees he had chopped down for the nearby school were long forgotten; Toshi's PTA work had ended years ago. Seeger's HUAC appearance and trial, on the other hand, were still talked of in town. Ironically, the bulk of the opposition to Seeger came not from the town's wealthiest conservatives, but from the working-class community. While Pete toured or kept to his study, organizers went from home to home chatting over coffee about how to keep Seeger from singing.

At one boycott-Seeger meeting, Pete's supporters were ruled out of order. They had brought a record player and records, but no one wanted to listen. "Such things are not important," the Reverend Beller said. "I know enough about the man's background." At the next board of education meeting, Pete's opponents presented seven hundred signatures on their petition, nearly ten percent of the voting population. "He doesn't even deserve to live here," one shopkeeper said. "If he likes Russia so much, why doesn't he go there? Why don't the people in this town just ship him there?

"I don't know the man myself. They tell me he's a great artist—maybe he is . . . but that doesn't matter, I can tell about him. His wife's half-Jap, but I guess that doesn't matter either. But you should see the people who go to visit him. They look like queers and beatniks, you know. Why the other day there was a man going out there I could have sworn he was a spy. You could tell by the way he looked, with his shifty eyes. You can tell about Seeger from the way he lives, way off in Beacon like some crazy hermit."

Such talk upset Pete, but the community's antagonism had a basis in fact. Pete was an international, not a local citizen; he had used his home town as a hotel, as Paul Cowan pointed out in the *Village Voice*.

Seeger's first break came when a conservative doctor, one of the town's biggest taxpayers, decided to support him, writing in the *Beacon Evening News*: "It seems to me that American democracy is big enough to encompass all opinions. Why all this fuss about Mr. Seeger's singing?" Then the teachers' association renewed its invitation, and the school board finally voted to allow Seeger to sing. Some of the petitioners retreated. "All of a sudden the liberals realized they didn't need to be so scared. Every day there were more letters in favor of me and fewer against me."

When the concert took place, a few cars cruised past the sold-out gym, with people hollering and spitting at the concertgoers. The Beacon police expected trouble. They advised Pete and Harold to come in different cars, which the officers checked for bombs. Harold stood backstage through the whole concert, worried sick. Midway through the concert, he thought he saw a gun protrude from the curtains, pointed straight at Pete. Harold ran on stage and knocked over what must have been a very surprised photographer holding a telescopic lens.

The whole affair shook Pete badly. In 1968, as he contemplated quitting music, he mulled over the lesson of the incident in a letter to black entertainers Ossie Davis and Ruby Dee: "One of the weaknesses in my own work, and probably the work of many an intellectual, is that I may have friends all around the world, but in my own neighborhood, I am in a very weak position, and can be knocked down by anyone who wants to tell a few lies about me."

Pete began considering ways to end his local isolation; he might not get off so easily a second time. He also heeded the advice of former colleagues in the civil rights movement: "Work in your own community," whites were told. "Be effective."

Pete met with the neighbor who had lent him *Sloops of the Hudson* and borrowed more books. Before long he was telling Jack Elliot and other friends: "Wouldn't it be fun to build one of these sloops?" Why not build a community-boat, get to know people, and clean up the river? Clearly this was one of Pete's crazy ideas, an impractical one for someone who had just weathered an attack from his neighbors. Yet the more he heard of local history and sailing, the more excited he became.

In the days of the sloops, the Hudson River had been alive with commerce and marine life: "Ice cut near Kingston tinkled in the glasses of New York restaurants. Sturgeon were common; the packing of this fish was an important industry. They called them 'Albany Beef,' and America exported caviar to Europe," Seeger wrote in *Look*. Tourists came from all over to sail and even to drink the Hudson. "Said river water is far from being dirty," a nineteenth-century traveler wrote. "Rather remarkable for its purity, it is a pleasant, wholesome beverage." From Lake Tear of the Clouds high in the Adirondacks, Pete read, the river had once flowed through a densely wooded Hudson Valley. Shad, bass, clams, and oysters were abundant.

The Iroquois and Algonquin Indians had once inhabited the river's shore, and Pete discovered a local Indian legend that enchanted him, "of a river that went to hear a fountain sing. The song was so beautiful that the river decided to sing it to the ocean. All the way to the shores of the ocean, the river sang. Soon, the mountains heard of the river's song and came from all over the land to listen. And because the song was so beautiful the mountains settled down and stayed to listen forever. . . ."

When Pete started talking like this, Toshi could do little but throw up her hands. Anyone could see the river was filthy—coated with an oily slick and lined with old tires and junk. Every time they drove near the shore, they smelled chemical wastes. But Pete took to sailing more often, particularly in the months following Dylan's departure from the folk scene. One night Pete sailed off on his own; Toshi worried because of his inexperience: "You mean you're going out all by yourself, overnight?" she asked him.

On the water, he peered at the skies for signs of a summer storm, prepared to race the thunder that often crashed down the rugged alley made by the river's cliffs. Then he relaxed, savoring his first time out alone. He drifted silently with the current and had the river to himself. The sail flapped lightly, and the boat tipped to the water: "The sun was first golden, and a few minutes later it was orange and a few minutes later it was beet red, and then the sky was all purple and finally it got dark." As he floated across the rainbow-colored reflections, he imagined what the river would look like if it were clean. His mind slid from the present to the future, to what could be. He could see the beaches cleaned up and full of children wading in this golden river and fishermen hauling in nets of sturgeon.

Tacking his way through the glowing darkness, he made up "Golden River":

Sailing down my golden river   ©
Sun and water all my own
Yet I was never alone. . . .

Sunlight glancing on the water
Life and Death are all my own
Yet I was never alone.

Life to raise my sons and daughters
Golden sparkles in the foam
And I was not far from home.

Sailing down my winding highway
Travelers from near and far
Yet I was never alone.

Exploring all the little byways
Sighting all the distant stars
And I was not far from home.

"Like 'Where Have All the Flowers Gone?' I wrote it and didn't think it was such a good song. I never sang it. Then I was quite taken with surprise when Don McLean and another guy were singing it once in harmony, backstage. I said, 'Where did you learn that?' They said, 'We heard you sing it.' 'Well, gee,' I said, 'that's beautiful. . . . I was too embarrassed to sing it.' "

Building a giant sloop seemed to him a wonderful, dreamy symbol. The destruction of the river concerned everyone along the Hudson, conservative upstaters and the crowded millions who lived in New York City, at the river's mouth. He hoped the as-yet unnamed boat would unite "wealthy yachtsmen and kids from the ghettos, church members and atheists"—the new popular front he had hoped to reach on TV. He remained a coalitionist to his toes, and like the best of them, he experimented for the best mix. If song brought people together, a sailboat might too.

Among his friends, reactions were mixed. Jack Elliot called his plans totally impractical: "The boat would cost $100,000 at the minimum, and require a large crew. Where are you going to get that kind of money?" "You're out of your mind," Mary Travers told him flatly. Others pointed out—as if Seeger needed reminding—how conservative the townsfolk were, and how little success he would have in involving them. Within New York's folk-music community, people wondered if Seeger was off balance—was this a new hobby, playing with yachts?

Such talk forced him to think seriously about the project. His followers had high expectations; as Pete neared fifty, it grew harder to keep not only his performances, but his life in inspiring form. This was not just another good cause for him; the project would move his focus closer to home, into the community that had nearly spurned him. Over the years he had adopted many movements—racial and economic equality, freedom of speech—but none of these was rooted in his own experience the way reviving the Hudson was. It was the river near which he had been born, by which he had lived most of his adult life. Much as the word conjured up the leisure class and bird sanctuaries, conservationism was not foreign to Seeger. This was Seton's spirit, crunching through the snowy woods to sketch animal prints.

Implicit in his hopes for restoring the river was a notion of environmental memory. Each generation that allows the biosphere to decay risks having its sons and daughters forget the taste of woods-scented water, the sight of an emerald mountain lake, just as succeeding waves of people arriving at a lawn concert cannot imagine what it was like to be surrounded by empty space. As early as 1958, Pete had speculated about this to an interviewer, his voice rising with emotion: "Look at the waste we make of our rivers, beautiful clear streams like the Hudson which flows past my door—an open sewer! . . . A river which was once clean and clear—Indians speared fish twenty feet down—is now an open sore. Nobody swims in it; you go on a boating trip, you just don't look down." By 1965 Pete had begun writing songs about the Hudson, including "Sailing Down My Dirty Stream." For once he meant to do more than sing.

That had been three years ago; before the war in Vietnam had ravaged his conscience, before his battles with TV, before he felt the desperation of Resurrection City or considered giving up singing. In between were long years of fund-raising, as he built up funds as he had his house, one bag of cement at a time. In the midst of fighting the furies of his conscience over America's role in Vietnam, Pete had sung three and four times a day and raised a hundred thousand dollars; the *Clearwater,* as she was now called, had a 108-foot mast of Douglas fir and stood ready for her maiden voyage and the first bottle of Hudson Valley champagne on her hull.

To assemble this much cash, Toshi, Pete, and their friends in the Hudson Valley Sloop Restoration had canvassed wealthy sailors and local historians with estates on the Hudson. This wasn't Pete's favorite audience, but he had gritted his teeth and attended barbecues and cocktail parties. Once he had met with a Hudson Valley millionaire who had reservations about the *Clearwater*. "It's a beautiful boat all right," the millionaire had said, looking over the drawings. "But why do you want to sail the Hudson for? I do my sailing around the Virgin Islands."

Pete had scarcely contained himself: "I felt my fingers clenching in anger, but I didn't say anything. Unwittingly, he had given us our best reason for building the boat. . . . We had allowed some people to make a good profit along the Hudson, and then go somewhere else to enjoy clear water."

Having an enemy had made it easier to keep going. Local residents—who stood to benefit the most—had remained mostly hostile or indifferent, at least in the beginning. Conservatives among them had assumed Pete was up to his old tricks: Perhaps he planned to use the boat for something sinister, like ferrying in undesirable aliens.

Painful as this period of fund-raising had been, Pete had learned a great deal. Pete had watched in frank admiration as Jimmy Collier, who had now moved to the Beacon area, had driven around town with a big smile, waving to people on the sidewalks, and saying, "Hi. Come on down to the waterfront tomorrow night. Don't forget." Jimmy had excelled at what Pete had the hardest time doing: dropping in at the local pool hall to drink beer and shoot the breeze. "It was a real lesson," Pete said. "Here I thought of myself as somebody who knew political organizing, but I didn't know it at all. In the past, all I had to do was come in and sing a song. Other people had to do the dirty work." Toshi must have smiled to see her husband enroll in Organization 1 under Professor Collier, for Jimmy had learned much of what *he* knew from Toshi: "It was most assuredly Toshi who kept things together . . . calling on the phone, getting people together at night, knowing who the right people were and making sure they showed up." As with many husbands, Seeger had a hard time learning from his wife.

"Pete Seeger could make his dreams come true," Jimmy said. "The *Clearwater* project—so many times—was almost a failure. Through sheer guts and power—financial power and contacts—Pete kept it together with his spiritual ability to motivate people. . . . He goes into these projects with the same attitude you or I might have: frustrated, not knowing whether things will come out right. But somehow he could hold on long enough, till the tide turned."

Between fund-raising concerts, Pete had helped out at the shipyard in Maine. He'd enjoyed the manual labor, painting red lead on the boat's weights, thirty thousand pounds of iron. He had worked calmly and steadily, sweating as he exercised unused muscles. At the end of a day carrying weights into the bilge, Pete had ached, but the pain was a fulfillment, and the salty mists were bracing. The labor tightened his lean frame and tanned him evenly, as he worked shirtless alongside college-aged volunteers. To celebrate his fiftieth birthday, he had done something he had never dared before: He grew a beard. "It's hard to believe that a beard could be such a big thing," Jimmy said. "But for years Seeger kept promising himself he was going to do it."

Pete had always taken pains to appear sober and upstanding. "You're singing enough strange stuff," his manager in the Weavers had told him, "you might as well look conventional." While working on the ship, Pete had finally loosened up: " 'Now's my chance,' I said to myself, 'Nobody is around to say no, so I'll try it.' . . . I stopped shaving and the workers in the boat yard couldn't dig it. They said, 'These young people are one thing, but you!' I told them I was going up to the shop to pick up a wrench and one said, 'Better pick up a razor too.' "

Pete had expected problems in accommodating wealthy donors, but not the jeers of left-wing friends. "In my mind," one said, "the *Clearwater* is probably the closest thing in recent years to Don Quixote tilting at the windmills. It's a diversion. Pete's a playboy with a yacht." Bernice Reagon had told him what *she* thought: "Ecology is racism coming into your own front door."

Seeger had alienated many radicals by approaching the financiers who traditionally underwrote conservation. The American Left had never taken to conservationists like Laurence Rockefeller, who equated enviromental preservation with "efficient management," development, and high consumption; who called conservation "essential to any national defense program" at the same time he made a fortune selling uranium for nuclear reactors. Pete had found himself in strange company, working alongside yachtsmen bent on preserving a stretch of water for their pleasure.

Radical hostility to conservationism partly originated from the Soviet Union's struggle to industrialize in the 1920s, when belching smokestacks were associated with progress and an end to exploitation. In Marx's time, Progress seemed to require expanding industrial development; Marx apparently assumed that once the profit motive faded, people would minimize waste through social planning. Thus, orthodox Marxists had difficulty understanding arguments for a separate "ecology" movement. Environmentalists had a reputation as politically naïve, more given to speechifying and symbols than organizing. To some radicals, Pete was playing banjo while corporations burned up the land; the more he succeeded with this project, the more opposition he met.

On June 27, 1969, the *Clearwater* slid quietly toward the Atlantic Ocean, the first boat of its kind in thirty years. She floated 106 feet long from boom to bowspirit. The deck was twenty-four feet wide, and the boat had bunks for fifteen, plus a captain's cabin, storage, and the ship's mess. The *Clearwater* was outfitted ninety-five percent in the traditional manner; the major improvements from the twentieth century were invisible from a distance: Dacron sails, electricity, and an engine. She was a vision of the past, like something out of a science-fiction drama.

The crew was an odd bunch, all musicians, some of whom had never been on a boat before. All they had in common were good voices and excitement; even the captain, Alan Aunapu, played the guitar. In full complement, the crew included Len Chandler, Jimmy Collier, Reverend Frederick Douglass Kirkpatrick ("Kirk," Pete's friend from Resurrection City), Jack Elliot, Don McLean, and Lou Killen, who led chanteys and played the concertina like an old tar. First mate Gordon Bok, a singer of ballads from his native Maine, was the only true sailor in the lot. Sailing proved to be hard work and dangerous for amateurs. Strumming in the foredeck when the jib swung round could result in a musician's being pitched into the water before anyone noticed. Every day brought a new crisis. Fitting thirteen landlubbers into the small hold was pretty uncomfortable— particularly when it rained. "On top of everything, these were all musicians, with musicians' egos," Jimmy Collier chuckled.

As pleasant as it might sound to skip across the waves with a boatload of musicians, a seriousness hung over the voyage. The sloop was so far in debt that fund-raising concerts had been scheduled the length of their journey, each a day's sail from the next. The crew was expected to perform every night and sail all day. Seeger had the most at stake, having personally guaranteed some loans; he had to show radicals and doubters what the boat could accomplish.

The first night out, they sailed through forty miles of ocean fog: cold, clammy, and eerie. The first *Clearwater* concert took place in Portland, Maine. The great ship swooped into dock from the fog, and then, like the Magical Mystery Tour, out popped the musicians.

"They all came down to the water's edge," Pete wrote, in love with his creation, "to look at one of the world's most beautiful boats, a symphony of curves, especially under sail. In every town we held a sort of community festival, with homemade food, exhibits, and homemade music. The townspeople felt the damp breeze in their face, and heard the lapping of the waves." Sea gulls swooped overhead in the breeze. Pete's beard was stubbly and gray; he wore a watch cap, and a bright handkerchief often dangled from his jeans.

Wafted by the wind and the current, his mood expanded like a sail in good wind. His body toughened and his eyes grew bright from the sea air. On board the *Clearwater,* the woodsman in him joined the organizer and the musician. Raising the mainsail required hard tugging and heaving, but instead of cursing, Lou Killen would lead off "In South Australia I Was Born," and the crew would holler "To me heave away, to me haul away." Pete would pull until he was out of breath and the sail finally taut. He learned to keep a weather eye open for changing winds, and when to rig up the tiller tackle for better leverage.

There were quiet times, too, perfect for singing "Golden River" or for pausing to listen to the waves thump against the bow when everyone was below deck. In such moments an eerie stillness settled on the sea, and the water slid by like memories, under the sparkling velvet of night. Pete looked out in darkness: a New England salt steering his ship through the ocean.

Thirty-seven days after they had started, the *Clearwater* pulled into the murky East River, having earned twenty-seven thousand dollars on her first cruise. In New York Harbor, the *Clearwater* amazed traffic on the Triboro and Queensboro bridges. Tugboats jockeyed alongside, sounding their horns. Sailing by the Brooklyn Navy Yard, the sloop passed a giant sewage pipe spilling waste into the water. The crew motioned to people on shore, pointing at the pipe and holding their noses.

Mayor Lindsay welcomed the *Clearwater* to Manhattan Island and took a turn at the tiller. Helicopters swooped low and TV news crews appeared with shotgun microphones: high technology in an old-fashioned setting. Pete Seeger made the "Quote of the Day" in *The New York Times*: "The price of liberty is eternal publicity. And we're getting it."

It would have been easier on Seeger if he could have relaxed with his triumph, but his aims were so high that he spent his life tracking behind them. "I wish I could give [Pete] the gift of goofing off," Lee Hays once wrote. Pete was a bleeder; the tiny pricks of conscience were for him slow to heal. He continued to be haunted by battles in Asian towns with hard-to-pronounce names. He stayed in the Hudson Valley, but his thoughts traveled to world pollution and wars, as he noted in his journal: "As a U.S. taxpayer, I help support one of the biggest, most hypocritical, and certainly the most expensive murder machine in history." He started (but rarely finished) songs about the imprisonment of Angela Davis and overpopulation ("Stork, I thought you were mankind's friend"). He could not leave the world on shore behind. On May 4, 1970, the shootings at Kent State threw Pete into a black mood; for four days, he brooded in silence. Throughout the war in Southeast Asia and at home, he kept hunting for a bright spot, a phrase of music to lift the soul. This did not come easily; in the coming months, his hopes for the *Clearwater* were attacked not only by local conservatives, but by leftists and within the *Clearwater* organization.

Just as in the Weavers, some of Pete's severest criticisms came from former colleagues like the ubiquitous Irwin Silber, who called the *Clearwater* "antiseptic" in a letter to Seeger: "Being who you are, you have the ability to involve many others in your schemes—for a variety of reasons. And this means you are capable of wasting a huge amount of effort, energy, time, and funds on hare-brained, diversionary projects. . . . I wish I could believe that these undertakings and the philosophy behind them were leading us to fundamental change. . . . But I don't believe it. And if you think they are, I think you're kidding yourself. Perhaps it's easier that way."

It wasn't so much the political philosophy behind the *Clearwater* that disturbed radicals as the company Pete kept. When Allan Young, writing for the Liberation News Service, discovered that a conservative founder of *Reader's Digest* had contributed to the boat, he concluded the project was "hardly militant." Compared to Black Panther shoot-outs with the Oakland police or the bombing of Cambodia, Pete's talk of bringing people together at the waterfront seemed out of touch. Many who had followed him from disarmament to civil rights to anti-war demonstrations now questioned the *Clearwater*'s uncharacteristic tameness. "At some point around this time, I began to get the feeling Pete was no longer on the cutting edge of the movement," Bernice said.

"What can a song do?" Pete weakly answered his critics, reverting to his favorite passion. "What can a sailboat do? Some would say music exists just to soothe or distract people from their worries. Some say sailboats are just rich men's toys. Wrong, wrong. In the summer of 1969, they helped clean up a river."

"There's as much of a relation between the *Clearwater* and socialism as there is in putting out a book on how to play the banjo," Pete said another time. "[Both] are part of a continual struggle to oppose the inhumanity of the technology which capitalism foists on people: 'Don't do anything creative yourself, just do your job, and let the machine do the rest for you.' But you play a little music yourself, you start making up songs for yourself, and next thing you know, you'll be thinking for yourself. Maybe voting right."

Seeger had even worse problems with local conservatives, including a few he and Toshi had mistakenly recruited to the *Clearwater*'s governing board.

In 1970, midway through the *Clearwater*'s second season, the boat docked for a songfest at the town of Cold Springs, once a stronghold of Ku Klux Klan activities. A year before, the *Clearwater*'s first appearance had caught conservatives unawares, but afterward, they were outraged. "So when we came in 1970, they were prepared," Pete said. "The *Clearwater* had a nice show set up; there had been rumors somebody was going to cause trouble, but I said, 'Well, we got away with it last summer . . . let's not back out now." This particular evening featured classical music: The Mid-Hudson Philharmonic played a Haydn symphon᷉ for five hundred people. Then Pete appeared on stage before the last piece to thank the crowd for coming.

"At that moment," Pete continued, "fifteen or more drunken people stood up waving little American flags and saying 'Throw the Commies out.' They stood in front of the stage and unrolled a banner: STOP POLLUTION, GET RID OF PETE. The conductor decided to ignore it and started to play Mozart. They stayed there, waving the little flags. After the short piece was played, the conductor quickly said, 'Star-Spangled Banner in B-Flat.'

"They did the most rousing rendition I ever heard an orchestra do. . . . I stayed behind to see that everything was going okay. They came up to me and said, 'Seeger, why don't you sing some American songs?' I said, 'What songs do I sing that aren't American?' 'Oh, you know, all those songs you sing aren't *American.* Why don't you sing "In the Good Old Summertime"?' "

Finally one of the policemen suggested he leave. That night someone cut the sloop's mooring. There were threats to dump gasoline on deck and set the boat afire. While everyone agreed that none of this was Pete's fault, these incidents weren't the pleasant outings board members enjoyed, and a new tension broke out within the *Clearwater* organization.

"As the boat became more and more of a reality," explained Jimmy Collier, "problems of priorities came up—who was going to get the boat? Is it going to be allied with schools or with hippies?" After initially pulling together to fund the boat, the sailors, historians, and community activists each developed separate agendas. The tenuous coalition—based on Pete's charisma—floundered, and some of the five-person board wished the boat's reputation was less tied to Seeger's. His 1970 testimony on behalf of the Chicago Seven didn't make this group any happier. When the government tried to impugn Seeger by bringing up his experience with HUAC, he was ready. With a twinkle in his eye, he offered to sing "Wasn't That a Time," the song mentioned by the prosecution. Judge Hoffman refused. Pete recited the words, but at the last stanza, he couldn't help himself; he started singing. "It was just a lilt, your honor," said Bill Kunstler for the defense. "I'm afraid I'm a better musician than you," Hoffman told Kunstler in reprimanding Seeger; "that was no lilt."

However much Pete's conservative colleagues disapproved of his politics, they knew the *Clearwater* needed him badly. No one denied his ability to raise money; "Toshi and Peter know how to write grants," Jimmy Collier pointed out. "And they have many admirers. . . . The old rich people liked these replicas of boats that sail up and down. 'We can go have cocktail parties on it,' they thought, 'and invite our friends.' " Pete and Toshi, on the other hand, wanted the ship to stop at the Harlem docks. At one point, a conservative board member asked Pete not to sing "Big Muddy" at any *Clearwater*-sponsored event: "We're singing about the *water*. Can't you stay away from all that Vietnam stuff?"

"Look," Pete replied, "all these subjects are tied together. You know why we don't have money to clean up this river? Guess who takes the big bite out of the tax dollar?"

Pete had a hard time *not* offending conservationists. Once, singing for a well-to-do group, he performed "Garbage," a song about the root causes of pollution. A man came up afterward and asked, "Pete, tell me. Are you still a card-carrying member of the Communist party?"

"Nope," he answered, looking him right in the eye. "Nor do I still beat my wife. . . ."

"Don't you have any faith in America?" persisted the conservationist.

"If I didn't have any faith in America, I wouldn't be doing what I'm doing."

It dawned on his opponents that there was no changing Seeger; he intended to sing whatever and whenever he wanted. The disenchanted sailors and historians, anxious about their investment in the *Clearwater*, decided he had to go. Fights always left Pete with a bad taste in his mouth. This time he was particularly upset, sensing that if he won, he would owe his victory to Toshi's effective organizing rather than his own ability.

In the late Sixties, Toshi Ohta Seeger had found herself simultaneously managing her husband's life and complaining about it. Pete's domestic consciousness raising had now progressed to where he wrote, with that uneasy humor men often adopt in answering feminist challenges: "Most men only chain their wives to a sink. I've chained mine to a desk as well." Because Toshi was a woman, and because she disliked spotlights, she never received her due. As Pete's producer, she made sure he was in the right place at the right time in the right mood, and that he knew where to go next. When problems arose, she took the blame. At tax time, when her shy singer couldn't face how much money he earned—or worse, how much he gave the government for war—Toshi would place a blank page over the return when Pete signed it. The realization of this dependence pained him. He knew what Toshi did for him and the debt he owed her. "Is it really necessary to have a Personal Manager, Publicity Agent, a Road Manager, and an Accountant? [All roles Toshi occasionally filled.] Where is it all going to end? Perhaps what I should do is make seven carbon copies of myself . . . and thereby afford the vast organization, the Empire that revolves around me."

His words had a bitter ring; he had been hearing complaints of his "inaccessibility." As Seeger's gatekeepers, Toshi and Harold had become a combination one disgruntled associate called "the fist and the iron glove." If Toshi and Harold took this role, however, it was Pete who abdicated it. He needed them, but his dependence cut two ways, as a comment by Irwin Silber made clear: "I guess that all of us who have dealt with you over the years as publishers, editors, producers, managers are all participants in a similar kind of deception. . . . I'm sure you are aware how almost all the people in your life are constantly trying to manipulate you—just as I'm sure you're working on them in turn—yours perhaps with a 'larger' purpose, theirs for more mundane, private purposes."

While Pete digested comments like these, Toshi continued to be torn between absorbing and rejecting her husband's career. She rarely talked to reporters, but when she did, her remarks were certainly original. "I hate it when people romanticize him," she told a surprised reporter from the *Chicago Tribune*. "He's like anybody good at his craft, like a good bulldozer operator." Another time, asked why Seeger had remained popular over the years, she answered that his fans were "nuts." Did Pete ever give a bad concert? "When he talks too much—when he doesn't sing," she said. Discussing male chauvinism, she teased her husband, "I should write 'pig' on the back of your shirt"; the interviewer had obviously hit a sensitive moment.

Leaving aside her rare barbs, the partnership worked well; if Toshi had received recognition—which she shunned—the arrangement might have been perfect. "Toshi's been a partner, not a closet partner, but a real partner," Judy Collins said. "The fact that he's on the stage—and she isn't—doesn't make that much difference."

At times Toshi became Pete's overseer; yet in certain matters he was indomitably stubborn. When duty was involved, there was just no arguing with Peter. And he was not the easiest man to live with: He didn't drink coffee or liquor, he didn't smoke, and he disliked listening to records or going to the movies. Attending concerts with him could be aggravating; Pete grimaced when the performers' timing was off, or when they misread their audience. Despite all his hopes for TV, it was all he could do to sit silently for a half hour; he kept getting up to turn the set off. On the other hand, if you liked hearth-sitting and listening to the banjo at all hours of the night, he was just the fellow to have around.

In the fall of 1970 the confrontation between Pete and the *Clearwater*'s other directors finally came to a head. Pete persisted in defending Captain Aunapu's right to wear long hair: "They were convinced that the hippies and Seeger were all cut of the same cloth," Pete said. "Board meetings got very tense. Here my experience with the Young Communist League (at Harvard) stood me in good stead; I knew some of Robert's Rules of Order."

Jimmy Collier remembered people insulting Pete to his face in the meetings. "Toshi would sometimes organize another little meeting afterwards; Pete wouldn't get involved," Jimmy recalled. ". . . When we started to do our little caucusing, we'd never tell Peter; we just did it, because he always thought matters ought to go right. His attitude was: if you'd tell people about things, they'd do what was *right*."

On September 27, at the conclusion of a particularly acrimonious meeting, Seeger's opponents made their move. One stood up and said, "Pete, we can't clean up the river by ourselves. We need the establishment to do it. They are the ones with the power. If you antagonize them, we'll never clean up the river."

"They're never going to clean up the river, period," Pete answered. "You've got to get a new establishment before this river's going to be cleaned."

"As long as Seeger is connected with this organization, we'll never get far," board member Donald Presutti declared. He introduced a resolution calling for Pete to resign; it failed by only one vote. Then Presutti resigned, later telling a *New York Times* reporter that he no longer wanted to be associated with the "hippie types" attracted by Seeger's involvement with the boat.

Though he had won his battle, Pete gradually withdrew from the *Clearwater*. He had a right to stay and wouldn't be driven out, but he sailed less. The *Clearwater* hadn't satisfied him; besides, he was ready for the rank-and-file to take over their boat. He still longed for a chance to make his voice heard widely, and for this, Seeger looked to television. He stubbornly held onto his hopes for reforming television as his only chance for a new audience: "I used to be snobbish about TV; I am no longer. Anyone who says, 'Slobs can watch the boob tube, I prefer to read books,' is like someone who says, 'I don't care who swims in the polluted river; after all, I have a swimming pool.' "

Seeger still hadn't received many TV offers; the reasons for this were obvious, as one incident showed. Pete was invited on the *Today* show, one of the most popular morning programs on television.

"Pete," he was asked on arriving in the studio, "what do you have for us?"

"Well, I have two songs, but one's very short, so I'm sure there's time."

"You have five minutes."

"Fine," Pete answered. "The first is a nice cheerful banjo piece, the second is kind of a satire, in contrast." He played a banjo tune, then sang "Garbage," with a new verse about "financiers and other crooks. . . . Nukes and other knavery." He had expected a protest, and he got it.

"Pete! It's kind of early in the morning for that. Do you have anything else?" the producers asked.

"Well, how about this?" Pete said, singing "Walking Down Death Row."

"Do you have anything else?"

Pete sang "If a Revolution Comes to My Country."

"Well, I guess we better stick to 'Garbage,' " the producers agreed.

At that the whole studio broke up with laughter. The cameramen and directors agreed, "Yeah, we'll stick with 'Garbage!' "

Seeger wasn't as naïve as his critics made him out to be. No one had to tell him why he wasn't flooded with invitations; he would not sing what he was told. "Tell a man what he may not sing," Mary Renault has written, "and he is still half free; even all free, if he never wanted to sing it. But tell him what he *must* sing, take up his time with it so that his true voice cannot sound even in secret—there, I have seen, is slavery."

Pete had tried television, without much luck; he had tried folklore, but lacked the patience for scholarship. Now he decided to try his hand at writing: if he couldn't make himself heard on TV, he could publish his thoughts.

That Seeger chose, among his many interests, to write about aesthetics in his first article for *The New York Times* is instructive:

"The artist in ancient times inspired, entertained, educated his fellow citizens. Modern artists have an additional responsibility—to encourage others to be artists. Why? Because technology is going to destroy the human soul unless we realize that each of us must in some way be a creator as well as a spectator or consumer." "Make your own music, write your own books," he fairly shouted, "if you would keep your soul."

Of course, Pete had already been widely published, in *Saturday Review, Life, Look,* and scholarly journals. And in between contributing over two hundred pieces to *People's Songs Bulletin, Broadside,* and *Sing Out!* (and editing a half-dozen song and instruction books), he had composed over a hundred songs.

It wasn't enough. Pete had more to say, and in the early seventies, he worked on five books, completing two of them. The best known of these (and the most ambitious) was a collection of writings brought out as *The Incompleat Folksinger* in 1972. Publishing anything remotely autobiographical was a departure for Seeger, who, with Toshi's help, had always publicly downplayed his accomplishments. In his journals, however, Pete imagined the day when his biography would be written: "The cult of the personality needs to be fought every step of the way. It leads to a dead end trap. If, in the future, anyone pores through these notebooks with biography in mind, please be hard-headed. . . . Think of the really great artists and thinkers whose reputation has been well-nigh ruined by unthinking adulators."

A strange note for a man to leave historians, but true to character. This same distrust of individual achievement hamstrung *The Incompleat Folksinger,* where he summed up his career in twelve pages: he wanted to be known only as "a link in a chain" of singers. The book's title reflected his assuming modesty. He tried to persuade his publishers to display the name of the editor, Jo Metcalf Schwartz, in the same size type as his; he even tried to restrict the advertising, a request editors at Simon and Schuster rarely received from authors. The book that emerged from Pete's renunciations was an almanac, a disarming hodgepodge of favorite recipes (cheddar rarebit and strawberry shortcake), songs, and homespun philosophy. The perfect book for anyone who ever wondered how to carry a banjo, two guitars, and a recorder at the same time (answer: sew your own banjo case, instructions provided).

After *The Incompleat Folksinger,* he published *Henscratches and Flyspecks* ("How to read melodies from songbooks in twelve confusing lessons"), a guide to sight-reading for those who like to sing but distrust music teachers. Next he wrote down his favorite stories and anecdotes. He did this with reluctance, firmly convinced that good storytellers retell freely rather than read stories aloud. In 1973 Macmillan made a children's book out of his father's *Foolish Frog* story, but the bulk of Pete's stories lie buried in a fascinating typescript, "Stories for Retelling," a treasury of folksy American humor. If published, these tales might become exactly what Seeger hoped to avoid: literature, read aloud by rote.

Perhaps the most revealing work was his *Fantasies of a Revisionist,* the story of an invalid with crazy ideas for saving the world. In his isolation, the hero ruminates on opening a storefront "Freedom of the Press" reading room (featuring Pete's favorite quote from Jefferson, "We have nothing to fear from error as long as reason is free to oppose it") and on oxygen rations. (Since the poorest, nondeveloped nations supply oxygen for industrialized ones—an American consumes one hundred times as much as a Hindu—why not equalize society by a universal currency of air?) These writings provided an outlet for Pete's half-baked, half-visionary ideas.

Writing didn't fill the hole in Pete's life. He was basically bored by his successes, except small ones, like persuading a class of second-graders to make up verses to a song. Americans thought him a singing relic. The *Wall Street Journal* published a flattering profile, an honor the twenty-year-old singer of "Talking Union" could not have imagined.

Seeger wanted something more dynamic in his life than a typewriter; he needed a fight closer to the barricades. Pete decided to visit the countries forbidden to U.S. citizens: Cuba, North Vietnam, and China. A few months after the showdown with the *Clearwater*'s board, Pete flew to Cuba by way of Spain, accompanied by Mika and her Puerto Rican photographer friend, Emilio Rodriguez.

The Seeger party received VIP treatment, with a twenty-fourth-story suite in the former Havana Hilton and a chauffeured car taking them around the island—just what Pete didn't want. His greatest disappointment was his lack of contact with the Cuban people. He had looked forward to cutting cane, but his schedule allowed him only two hours in the field. Yet if the Cubans thought their lines and shortages might disappoint Pete, they need not have worried; he remained uncritical. Riding in a car with a former prosecutor of Batista's allies, he was told: "It was a pleasure to execute them." Pete listened silently. "I have reservations," he wrote in his journal. "What happened to their families? Should one shoot them too? Where did they draw the line?" Seeger would have made a mediocre Robespierre; this was a country surrounded by enemies, he rationalized, including CIA operatives.

Pete always had a blind spot to the excesses of socialism-in-the-making. Decades after quitting the Party, his harshest criticism of the Stalin era was "an awful lot of rough stuff." He refrained from criticizing the Soviet Union even when groups of musicians, such as the Czech "Plastic People" ensemble, were tried and jailed under Russian pressure. About the only thing Pete objected to in the U.S.S.R. was a few polluted lakes and the Siberian weather. Criticisms were still for renegades and right-wingers.

Returning to Spain on the way home from Cuba, the musician found himself with a censorship battle surpassing anything on American TV. Government censors forbade him to sing three songs: Country Joe McDonald's "1, 2, 3, What Are We Fighting For," "Bring 'em Home," and inexplicably, "Sally Racket," a chantey sung on the *Clearwater* (perhaps the chorus, "Haul 'em away," suggested street arrests). By knocking on enough doors, though, Pete received rulings that counteracted each other. He knew he couldn't sing—and didn't try—the songs of the Spanish Civil War, which he had recorded for Moe Asch back in 1944. As it was, he broke Spanish law by singing Basque separatist songs at a party.

His moods were mercurial. When Seeger failed to get an audience singing in Seville, he plunged into self-doubt, as confused about his art as he had been in 1963, on his world tour: "I seem to stagger about this agonized world as a clown, dressed in happiness, hoping to reach the hearts and minds of the young. When newspaper reporters ask me what effect my songs have, I try and make a brave reply, but I am really not so certain."

When he arrived in Barcelona the following week and discovered the police had canceled his concert at the university, fearing a left-wing riot. Pete's mood picked up. He decided to visit the campus anyway. As he drove up he could see a traffic jam near the theater, and thousands of students standing at a distance. Near the university building, mounted police patrolled. Pete decided to go around to the back door. The head of the engineering school met with him in the corridor, but as hundreds of students crowded around, they heard pounding feet. The police started to enter, and the director moved off in one direction and Seeger went the other way. Being back on the battle lines was a terrific tonic; the controversy reminded him of his purpose. The government genuinely feared his songs.

"I am sorry that the concert could not have been held," the dean told Seeger an hour later. "It is out of my hands. The governor of Barcelona says that he personally ordered the police to stop it, and he did so on orders from Madrid." Pete left, vowing to sing in Barcelona another time.

In the spring of 1972 he set out again on a marathon tour of the Soviet Union, North Vietnam, and China with Toshi and Tinya. He pushed himself restlessly, visiting not for scenic or musical interest, but as a remedy for internal pressures, traveling to the far corners of the socialist world.

Before he left, a documentary about him premiered at a New York cinema—*Pete Seeger: A Song and a Stone,* directed by the talented filmmaker

Robert Elfstrom. (The stone was the one Pete had carried in his banjo case since the 1968 incident at Duke.) The film turned out a minor disaster; Pete was disappointed at its hero worship, and *The New York Times* called it "perfectly dreadful, ranging from merely inept . . . to openly offensive." While *Cue* and *New York* were mildly impressed, the *Times*'s comparison with Leni Riefenstahl's pro-Hitler documentary *Triumph of the Will* sank the film.

Then the Seegers flew to Moscow for concerts and a tour of Russian Central Asia. He spoke with scientists on Soviet pollution and found them concerned, if not active. He stood on the banks of the Dnieper in Kiev, the river whose mighty dam he had read about in *New Russia's Primer,* forty years before. These childhood visions of five-year plans still colored his thinking: He compared the port before him to Kansas City—only the Soviets, he decided, had built nice parks.

In March he and his family arrived in North Vietnam. Their plane circled Hanoi, and below them lay the small land, about the size and population of New York State, that had held its own against Uncle Sam. Palm trees and rice fields stretched off on all sides. He had no idea how he or his music would be received here; the Vietnamese had good reason to hate Americans. At the airport, though, the Seegers were greeted with bouquets of flowers and hugs; Pete broke down and cried at feeling so welcome in "enemy" country.

His emotions continued at a peak throughout his stay. Preoccupied by his responsibility as an American, he watched the Vietnamese carrying fuel and live chickens on their bicycles, gardening, and rebuilding bombed-out structures. One of the first people he met here was Seymour Hersh, correspondent for *The New York Times.* Hersh brought out the journalist in him; in two weeks, he wrote fifteen thousand words, sitting down with typewriter and notes after Toshi fell asleep. He discovered the Vietnamese had a banjolike instrument, the dan-bau, and excitedly dashed off an article for *Sing Out!.* He strolled the streets of Hanoi with his notebooks and banjo, dressed in rubber-tire sandals of the kind worn by Uncle Ho. Children would stop and point at the tall, fair-skinned musician, and Pete would open his banjo case on the sidewalk and play for the amazed youngsters.

The Seegers again received VIP treatment. Despite their requests to travel like fellow workers, not diplomats, they were given a fancy car and a driver who honked bicycles and pedestrians out of the way. Pete felt like a white-skinned pharaoh. Once, unable to communicate his discomfort to their driver, he jumped out and walked alongside, rather than ride in the limousine. Reminders of the U.S. bombings surrounded him. The wounded filled the streets: newly crippled women, a child trying to run with only one leg. One afternoon the family visited an exhibit of "bombs and devices to carry on computerized electronic warfare from the air. Enough to give anyone nightmares." That night he shut his eyes and saw shrapnel, and platoons burned alive; he wrote that he "didn't sleep—not a wink all night."

Their two weeks ended momentously. After a farewell concert, Pete heard something that stopped him cold, which he later repeated hundreds of times, when asked about his work on the Hudson. He had ended his concert that night with songs of the Hudson Valley. Afterward, a Vietnamese novelist and war veteran came up. Hearing those songs had left a deep impression, he said. "That was when I decided I could believe you. Only when Americans realize that they too must stay home and fight to free their corner of the world—as we are fighting for ours—can the world live with America."

Pete had traveled ten thousand miles to be reminded of the importance of community organizing. "That was a very important story for Pete—for all of us," Arlo Guthrie said. "It became his way of saying: 'It's not a bad idea to go out and see the world, but you also have to do things at home.' " He carried the Vietnamese's speech like a medal.

The message was repeated at another dinner, when a guerrilla fighter said, "At one time I hated all Americans . . . but as you sang, I gradually realized that what Uncle Ho said was true—there is another America than the one we have known." At home, Pete was called subversive; it took foreigners, searching for something positive in America, to call him a patriot.

After all this excitement, China proved anticlimactic. His two weeks there seemed to distress more than enlighten him. (He remained sympathetic to the Soviet world view.) Pete gave only one major performance, a concert in Peking that he called one of his "signal failures," along with the Albany, Georgia, concert. It was the same throughout China: "They were so busy analyzing me that they couldn't join in one little bit. Analyzing this song, analyzing that one . . . they didn't even tap their feet."

Pete returned from his trip—as he had so often returned—brimming with enthusiasm. Out in his yard, he surveyed the water and heard the river's song afresh, echoing as it flowed to the sea. The projects piled on his desk now seemed manageable. The vindication carried from Vietnam eased his mind about his radical critics. The Hudson even looked clearer, and he worked on the *Clearwater* with new vigor. Then, in 1975, chemists hired by the *Clearwater* organization discovered contamination from PCB (polychlorinated biphenyl). This industrial chemical, manufactured by General Electric and others, was colorless, odorless—and an extremely toxic carcinogen. GE had dumped one and one-half million pounds of PCBs into the river, according to *The New York Times*. While the *Clearwater* project had been winning advances in sewer treatment and industrial wastes, the lethal chemical had been slowly seeping into the river bottom, lodging in the mud and entering the food chain; the fish ate it with their food, which poisoned them for humans. Pete was furious. He considered visiting General Electric and dumping PCBs on their desks. "The people of America must realize we've got to organize a defense against these chemical companies—they're getting away with literal murder."

After this, he continued to raise funds for the *Clearwater* and sailed occasionally, but he didn't connect with the project as before. He had a ready answer when old friends asked what he was up to, but he could not shake the association with yachtsmanship and his bitterness over the PCBs, which promised to pollute his golden river as long as he lived.

The *Clearwater* also hadn't caught on with local unions, who feared the loss of jobs and industry from environmental regulation. This effectively put Pete on the opposite side from labor. Environmentalism already had a reputation—often ill-deserved—as a middle-class, white cause; if union organizers had written topical songs in the Seventies, they might have satirized environmentalists. Controlling pollution created jobs, Pete tried to demonstrate, but most unions saw only a choice of jobs or environmental health. Sympathizing with both sides threw Seeger into a mild political paralysis.

The *Clearwater* had fulfilled his initial hopes; it had brought him closer to his community and publicized the Hudson's pollution. But publicity was not the same as social change, as Pete admitted, quoting Lenin's statement that change comes not in thousands but millions. When those millions failed to materialize in the 1970s, Seeger suffered. Without a movement for change, life for him grew static. Seeger resembled the pagan gods who became mortal once their last follower disappeared; now that he had outlasted his former enemies, he felt world-weary.

"Pete's always looking for the excitement of song and the movement" Jimmy Collier said. "When he can't find it, he addresses the young people and uses everything he has to make it happen. . . . And because he has money and success—well, no one's asked him to justify this, but it didn't happen that way with Woody. . . ."

At difficult moments, Pete had always turned to music, and this was no exception. His style had changed, however; he no longer stirred crowds into a frenzy, and he occasionally thought: "One reason I haven't been a better musician is that I've spent too much of my life organizing."

Pete was finally admitted to the Songwriters' Hall of Fame, alongside Gershwin and Berlin, but few writing on popular song paid him any attention. Rarely, if ever, did his name appear in scholarly works on American music; where he was mentioned, his politics, rather than music, attracted attention.

Pete also continued to have troubles with Columbia. In 1973 Columbia turned him over to Bob Johnson, Dylan's former producer. Lester Flatt, Earl Scruggs, and others played behind Seeger; but for some reason the tapes were never released, except for a few cuts on *Rainbow Race* (which finally included a moving rendition of "Golden River"). The song Pete most wanted to record was the anti-war "1, 2, 3, What Are We Fighting For?" When Columbia refused to release this as a single, Pete decided he was through with the company, and returned to Folkways. Collier detected another reason for the switch: "The need to make records had gone out of him." Even music seemed to have failed him: "Something's gone from Pete's performing," Don McLean commented. "It's gone perhaps because he let it go. Or it may have slipped away without him being able to retain it."

Starting about 1971, Pete Seeger had begun feeling ill. He had to have a hernia operation, which he kept postponing. His skin flared up, as badly as any time since adolescence. Pete found, to his great distress, that he couldn't sing as often or as long as before. In the Almanacs, he could play at parties and come home singing. Now he feared that he was losing his voice. Pete had never taken voice lessons—his father didn't want him to sound "trained." What Pete knew about preserving his voice had come from trial and error.

A lassitude overtook his actions, the absence of a reason for his art. Pete didn't want people attending his concerts to remember how it used to be; he tried to point ahead, to the next cause. Why sing, if people came only for nostalgia?

Seeger decided to take a year off from singing. He wanted to see if he could do it; and he had to heal his illnesses. In 1973 he told Harold not to accept any paid bookings and to cut down on his benefit concerts. The hernia operation laid him up in bed for two months, and his skin problems took another couple of months to clear up. He stayed at home, playing with Tinya or writing, the first time he had stopped singing professionally since he had begun in 1939.

This wasn't, of course, the first time he had *considered* stopping. In

1949—before Peekskill and before the Weavers entered nightclubs—he had sworn he would give it up. Then, after the Weavers had been blacklisted, he had resolved to teach or do research; instead he had wandered from one college to the next, searching for an audience. In 1968, after Resurrection City, he had felt little reason to go on—except for the *Clearwater*. But only when no social movement seemed to need him did Seeger actually stop.

The first change he noticed was that his health began to deteriorate: "As long as I have to perform, I can't get hoarse. Got to get sleep. The minute I don't have to perform, I say, 'Well, it doesn't matter if I catch a cold.' And one thing leads to another." It wasn't clear which was worse: the operation or not singing. "It was a year before I got back into the swing of things. I was very weak and out of condition. My voice got weak, my legs were weak, my hands were weak."

Pete discovered he could not survive without singing in public. He needed his audience more than they ever could need him. For his concertgoers, his singing meant a pleasant evening; for Seeger, it was a matter of survival: "For my health I know I've got to keep singing. I don't think I'd live long if I didn't."

He had come full circle, starting out in Patterson at his birth and traveling around the world to Beacon, fifty miles away. For most of these years he had followed the two paths of his childhood, his woodsy soul and his worldly duties. One led him to sketch, then become a musician; the other to journalism and community organizing. He tried to combine the two in the *Clearwater*, not always successfully. Even after the *Clearwater* took GE to court over the PCBs and won one of the largest environmental penalties awarded—a multi-million dollar penalty—some of his friends still scorned the project, asking, "How long will it take to get the last beer can out of the Hudson?" Nor were the criticisms limited to radicals: Pete received one of his worst concert reviews in 1978, when Robert Palmer of *The New York Times* wrote: "He has lost the ability to provoke. . . . Much of his political material has begun to sound unappetizingly shrill."

In the late Seventies audiences came to hear Seeger the living legend, flocking to a *Clearwater* festival, such as one in 1976, where the crowd spread over a grassy amphitheater sloping down to the Hudson. As the day turned to dusk, Pete played a familiar love song on his twelve-string guitar, "Kisses Sweeter Than Wine," and the audience relaxed. The fading rays of the sun rested for a moment on the vibrating strings, then spread out across the river's surface in a carpet of reflections. Pete's seadog beard was untrimmed. His lumber jacket, a few sizes too large for his slim, muscular arms, bunched up in the valley of his arm, beneath the guitar. His bushy eyebrows puckered like tiny wings when he sang. Kids ran up to say, "My grandmother remembers hearing you when she was a kid," and he just laughed. At the concert's end, his voice soared into the starry sky with a song about a dead hero, the sleeping lion who will some day return. Out across the river the harmony floated, a melodic wind on a cool summer evening.

Writing on his terrace by the river or hauling trash to the dump, Pete Seeger slowed down and cultivated his own garden, as Voltaire had advised. For forty years, his career had flowed from one cause to another, threading through the city and the woods. Like his golden river, his music had joined upstaters and downstaters, city folk and farmers. After four decades of singing, he still hadn't stopped appearing at benefits for Allende's Chile or at anti-nuclear rallies in Seabrook, New Hampshire, or in Manhattan's Battery Park. Most of all, Pete spoke out for localism and community control. "I feel like the revival preacher who led a wild youth," he joked, talking about how after traveling the world, he could sit contentedly around the stove at the Beacon Sloop Club, telling stories and picking his banjo.

When asked about his hopes for preserving the earth's ecology, he answered with dry optimism: "Environmentalists are like a few guys putting sand on one side of a scale with teaspoons, while on the other side a lot of industrialists are loading boulders with dump trucks. . . . You can never tell what might work if we had enough people with teaspoons."

In 1978 Pete revisited Spain with Toshi. The Catalonian singer Ramón had promised he could sing anything he wanted. "What a thrill! I sang to four thousand in Madrid and seven thousand in Barcelona. I sang 'Los Quatros Generales'; every verse they knew. The same thing happened when I sang 'Freiheit':

> We'll not yield a foot to Franco's fascists
> Even though the bullets fall like sleet
> Around us stand these men our comrades
> And for us there can be no defeat.

After the show, Pete asked a friend how everyone had known the words to songs forbidden for nearly forty years.

"We found your record; it was smuggled in."

"Isn't that fantastic!" Pete exulted. "That Folkways record was smuggled into Spain over the last forty years, and they kept the songs alive—and they knew my version of the song. Here I, who was never in Spain, me, with my hillbilly flamenco, mispronouncing the words and everything, kept those songs alive. They sang them beautifully. I was almost weeping."

It had been a long time since Pete stepped out from behind the Vagabond Puppeteers' curtain to play his banjo in public. He never succeeded in persuading the world to take songs as seriously as he did—not the Communist Party, who considered music as icing on a determinist cake; not the FBI, who heard only plots in his music. Seeger's place in the movements of his time rarely lasted, just as the songs themselves didn't last—music was lionized, then neglected once it was no longer needed. Nevertheless, he had succeeded in dragging his banjo into battle in Peekskill and Mississippi, into Henry Wallace's campaign and HUAC's courtroom, onto prime-time TV during the war in Vietnam—and his music helped win a few battles.

For all the advantages of his music-rich upbringing, he had blacked boots at Avon and accepted a third-choice career. Two qualities had protected him from his attackers, hope and endurance; with enough of these, people can move mountains. Perhaps he oversimplified his life when he wrote: "All you need to be a modern Johnny Appleseed is a guitar and some sticktoitiveness," but that was where Seeger had started, at age sixteen.

"Songs won't save the planet," Seeger once wrote. "But then, neither will books or speeches. . . . Songs are sneaky things. They can slip across borders. Proliferate in prisons. Penetrate hard shells." Pete also used to quote an admonition of Plato: "Watch music. It's an important art form. Rulers should be careful about what songs are allowed to be sung." He believed these teachings. All his life he labored under the impression that the right song at the right time could work wonders. "If rulers really knew how important songs can be," Pete Seeger once said, looking back on his life, "they would probably have done something to Woody Guthrie and me and other people long ago."

Epilogue

BY 1981 the strands of Pete Seeger's life had been woven into a whole. A new generation heard his voice on any of a hundred-odd records. The songs Pete loved, changed, or composed moved out into the world.

During a recent plebiscite on independence for Greenland, Danes and Greenlanders together sang "We Shall Overcome" on a torchlight parade. "Big Muddy" has found its way into dictionaries of slang as a reference to the war in Vietnam. "If I Had a Hammer" floats up from elevators and hotel lobbies; musicians as different as Perry Como, Aretha Franklin, and Ray Barretto recorded the song. Seeger heard "66 Highway Blues" sung by young unionists, who told him of finding it "in an old book." And, after four decades, he finally learned "John Henry" to his satisfaction, pitching it in a key where he could get his bell-like ring and still sing comfortably with audiences. Once, asked what his ultimate message was, Seeger quoted two lines from the song:

> *And before you let that steam drill beat you down*
> *Die with that hammer in your hand.*

Seeger's life is filled with ghosts, people from his past who reappear in the headlines or come backstage after concerts. Sheriff Jim Clark, the die-hard segregationist who guarded the highway between Selma and Montgomery, was convicted of smuggling three tons of marijuana in Alabama. Bascom Lunsford, who first played the five-string for Pete, told a mutual friend that Seeger could have gone a long way with his banjo playing if only he hadn't fooled around with unions. Even Johnny Appleseed reentered Seeger's life; Pete updated him as a "conservative" who would "probably look around 1978 U.S.A. in horror."

The Greenwich Village basement where Pete and the Weavers rehearsed is now a cafe. The Weavers have scattered. Ronnie Gilbert practiced primal therapy, then built a house in the woods of British Columbia; Fred Hellerman produced film scores and records; Lee Hays became a gardener. Bernice Reagon formed a political-gospel group, Sweet Honey in the Rock. Irwin Silber left *Sing Out!* to edit the ultra-left *Guardian*. Pete and Toshi even met Irving Younger, the attorney who prosecuted him for contempt of Congress: "I wasn't doing anything wrong," Younger volunteered. "I'd be willing to prosecute you again."

No one was going to prosecute Seeger any longer; he was so well known that, like an old song, he was parodied rather than banned. *National Lampoon* satirized his concerts as a ritual in growing up Left in America; the article had Pete revising "Frog Went A-courtin' " into a class-conscious ballad.

Pete remained fascinated by TV's possibilities; in the late Seventies, he outlined his ideal television program—using unobtrusive video equipment to record music in homes around the world. When West German television expressed an interest, he confessed he would "even give up the *Clearwater* to work on 'Songwriters Against the World.' "

Yet, at the beginning of the 1980s the old contradictions stood out more clearly than ever. Here was a man who contributed his art to every social movement of his time, even when activists dismissed his work; who thought himself a patriot despite a thousand attacks for subversion; who tried for union singing and ended up with unison singing, where each voice added to the whole; who yearned for a quiet woodland retreat but led a career of flaming controversy. Inevitably his music will be his judgment, just as the painter is remembered for his canvases and the judge for his decisions. Songs were Seeger's gifts, and many outlasted their recipients, as fine gifts do. In the Forties, his songs had helped unionize workers in the CIO; in the Fifties, his music had kept alive a struggling left-wing opposition and nurtured another generation; in the Sixties his anti-war songs may have hastened an end to the fighting; in Africa, he had demonstrated the universality of music; in the *Clearwater*, his songs had helped clean up a river.

At a dinner party in San Francisco recently, a group in their early thirties tried to pick a list of the ten living people they most admired; Seeger's name came up more than once. Pete's "children" have not vanished, though some think him as old-fashioned as Dickens's Christmas Past. "Pete Seeger—I remember singing those folk songs," said one woman, lounging in a hot tub in Colorado. "That was before dope and the Rolling Stones and all that." A former critic suggested that Seeger has known, like the farmer who toiled on barren soil, that most of his seeds will die, but the ones that grow to maturity will seem the sweeter for their hard-won victory. And perhaps he has been waiting not for his children, but for his grand-children before evaluating the fruit of his labors.

Other former fans joked about his optimism, so out of fashion in a world fascinated by apocalypse. Still others shook their heads and sighed when Seeger, in later years, missed a beat; he wasn't the musician they remembered him to be.

Indeed he was not. He had lost some of his dexterity—and changed his musical focus. The shift had begun in the Sixties, as he explored a maxim of Alfred North Whitehead: "Strive for simplicity and learn to distrust it." Pete simplified his art to the point where critics might call it minimalist: Instead of playing chords, he sounded selected notes to remind the audi-ence of the melody as they sang, a twang on the guitar instead of a loud strum. He focused attention away from the stage and withdrew from the music until only the skeleton of the song remained, alongside a trans-parency where he and the song and the audience were connected.

Audiences continued to be drawn to a singer who relished his work and who kept insisting the world was worth saving. His music had a way of making people feel better about themselves and more musical. His perfor-mances contained few flourishes; audiences either join in the music or sit silently, impressed from afar by genius, and Pete preferred the former. In *Rolling Stone,* Gene Marine summed this up well: "Many performers can turn on an audience as well as Pete can. What they can't do is turn on any audience the way Pete can. . . . In Moscow, Pete had 10,000 people who didn't speak English singing four-part harmony to 'Michael Row Your Boat Ashore.' I doubt whether Barbra Streisand and Mick Jagger *together* could do that."

One reason for this success was that his life corresponded to his songs; as Colman McCarthy wrote in *The Washington Post,* he wouldn't have the same magic, "were he a flashier fellow who would get out of his workshirts when he gets onstage or were he a singer who wouldn't clear his throat for less than $10,000 a performance. . . ."

But this integration of art and life was not without its liabilities. The pressure of public scrutiny was enormous. Instead of having a refuge in his art Pete felt obliged to live out his music. He often wondered if he couldn't have led a happier life if he had not been in show business, if he could have been a writer and hid behind a nom de plume, like Papa Banjo or Uncle Zeke: "Then I could be Pete Seeger/Uncle Zeke. The posters would say Uncle Zeke, and everybody would know Uncle Zeke is Pete Seeger; still, the posters wouldn't say Pete Seeger. . . .

"If I had had a grant early to be a researcher, I could have been one. But I wasn't willing to take the discipline. To be a real researcher, you have to get that degree and fulfill all the academic obligations. I've only recently realized how much I am a product of my family and childhood. One thinks that one creates one's own life. So there I was at nineteen . . . going out to do what I thought needed to be done. To my surprise, thirty-five years later, I found that I was practically carrying out what my family had trained me to do. Now it's true, I could have become a violinist—my mother wanted me to. I could have become a businessman—my grandfather wanted me to. I could have become a journalist; if I'd had more perseverance, I might have. Instead, I drifted into a particular niche I'd found for myself that no one else had ever found before."

This niche has so far lasted forty years. It is easy to forget, as Jimmy Collier said, that "it's the same guy who traveled everywhere playing his little banjo; who wrote all those great songs; who is now on Sesame Street; who was singing civil rights and folk songs, but couldn't appear on *Hootenanny*." It might be that a career like Seeger's will not reoccur in America, for his Popular Front patriotism belongs to a distant, less cynical era. Is America still a country where a southern farmer would call a wandering Yankee over for a glass of milk and teach him a banjo lick?

Perhaps when Seeger's controversy fades, so will his music. Future generations will judge the *Clearwater*'s importance in restoring the earth's environment. Today some call Seeger a blind optimist, others a great American. "We need people who still believe in what we once thought we were certain of," John Leonard wrote of Seeger in *The New York Times*. "Even the fish in the sea and the birds in the air would thank him if they knew," wrote Mike Cooney in *Sing Out!* "He is our music teacher. All of us who were so carefully taught to hate music in school then learned to appreciate and understand what it is for with Pete Seeger. He is one of the greatest of American patriots."

Patriots and nationalists from the Grimm brothers to Mao Tse-tung have used folklore and folk songs to bolster their cause. The most lasting contribution of Pete Seeger may come from his musical populism. If his compositions and influence on American music are ignored by textbook writers, that may be because of the general prejudice against anything "folk" as un-European, untutored, and unrefined. He and his circle have shaped the musical traditions that bind Americans together as a people. His was not the first make-America-musical movement, but it was the most nonelitist. If anyone in the United States had inspired people to make their own music, it has been Pete Seeger. He was, it will be remembered, a great believer in the magical powers of song.

Once, soon after Seeger had been sentenced to a year in jail, he told an audience in Providence his thoughts on why humans sing: "Some people sing because they're so happy they just can't stop. Some sing to keep their spirits from going five miles below Hell. And some sing just to keep their courage up." Then Pete said he wanted to sing them a hymn "made up years ago when people were getting thrown in jail for their beliefs." The lyrics summed up his life as well as any could:

> *My life flows on in endless song,*
> *Above earth's lamentation.*
> *I hear the real, though far-off hymn,*
> *That hails a new creation.*
> > *No storm can shake my inmost calm*
> > *While to that rock I'm clinging.*
> > *It sounds an echo in my soul.*
> > *How can I keep from singing?*
>
> *What though the tempest round me roars,*
> *I know the truth, it liveth.*
> *What though the darkness round me close,*
> *Songs in the night it giveth.*
> > *No storm can shake my inmost calm*
> > *While to that rock I'm clinging.*
> > *Since love is lord of Heaven and earth,*
> > *How can I keep from singing?*
>
> *When tyrants tremble, sick with fear*
> *And hear their death knells ringing;*
> *When friends rejoice both far and near,*
> *How can I keep from singing?*
> > *In prison cell and dungeon vile*
> > *Our thoughts to them are winging.*
> > *When friends by shame are undefiled,*
> > *How can I keep from singing?*

Notes

The major sources for this work are 110 interviews conducted by the author from 1976 to 1980, the writings and recordings of Pete Seeger, and the articles and books listed in the bibliography that follows these notes. At this writing, no collection of papers or letters of Pete Seeger exists, other than those compiled by Toshi Ohta and Seeger himself in their home and offices in Beacon, New York (which the author reviewed and catalogued). Harold Leventhal, Mr. Seeger's manager, also maintains scrapbooks and files, which he graciously opened to me. The author conducted ten oral-historical interviews with Pete Seeger over the period of April 1976 to August 1978, which yielded approximately 800 pages of transcript. Also valuable were Seeger's collection of journals and unpublished writings, amounting to another 1000 pages, and the 1600 documents released under a Freedom of Information Act suit, *Dunaway* v. *Kelley et al.*, U.S. District Court, San Francisco, over the singing groups with which Mr. Seeger was affiliated.

—D.K.D.

The numbers to the left of each citation refer to the page numbers of text on which the relevant passages appear. Each passage is identified by the key words. Unless otherwise identified, all letters are unpublished. In a very few cases—no more than a half-dozen—interviewees furnished information with the request of confidentiality.

Chapter One

Author's interviews with Pete Seeger, April 15, 1976, March 6, 1977; Bess Lomax Hawes, August 28, 1977; Mario Cassetta, September 26, 1976; Howard Fast, January 15, 1977; and Ronnie Gilbert, January 14, 1977.

page   *reference*

13   "I DON'T KNOW": Report of the American Civil Liberties Union, quoted in Howard Fast, *Peekskill USA* (New York: Civil Rights Congress, 1951), p. 116.

Chapter One (cont.)

page   *reference*

14   "SUSPECTING THE PARADE": Quoted in *Eyewitness: Peekskill USA* (White Plains, New York: Westchester Committee for a Fair Inquiry into the Peekskill Violence, 1949), p. 2.

16   "WE'LL FINISH HITLER'S JOB": Howard Fast, *Peekskill USA*.

17   "THE SPECIAL AGENT IN CHARGE": Documents released after a 1976 request under the Freedom of Information Act and a subsequent suit, *Dunaway* v. *Kelley*, U.S. District Court, San Francisco.

17   "IF THE POLICE": Quoted in Richard Reuss, "The Peekskill Riots: Domestic Cold War in Action," unpublished seminar paper, 1962; Reuss provides much of the detail used here.

17   "OUR OBJECTIVE WAS": Clipping in the Peekskill Public Library collection.

18   "THE DAY BEFORE": Letter dated September 3, 1949, from the Ku Klux Klan to People's Artists in the possession of Pete Seeger.

20   "UP AHEAD A STATE TROOPER": These two incidents reported in *Eyewitness: Peekskill USA*, Section 5, p. 2.

21   "YOU KNOW I WAS RAISED": The source of this information asked to remain anonymous; this conversation reported by Pete Seeger.

22   "HOLD THE LINE": As recorded by Pete Seeger on *Gazette, Vol. 2*, Folkways FN 2502.

22   "WHICH LINE": Richard Reuss, letter to the author, January 16, 1980.

Chapter Two

Author's interviews with Charles Seeger III, October 10, 1977; John Seeger, August 29, 1977; Pete Seeger, April 15, July 19, October 10, 1976; August 8, 1978; and Charles Seeger, April 6, 7, 8, 1976. Information on Charles Seeger's background also comes from his *Reminiscences of an American Musicologist,* a memoir of the UCLA Oral History Project, 1972.

page   *reference*

25   "ENORMOUSLY CHRISTIAN": Pete Seeger, 1961 concert in San Francisco, broadcast over KPFA-FM, Berkeley, California.

26   "THE NERVE": Pete Seeger, August 8, 1978.

27   "YOU DON'T LIVE": *Reminiscences of an American Musicologist,* p. 114.

27   "SHE COMMUNICATED": Charles Seeger III, October 10, 1977.

28   "WE TALKED": Charles Seeger, April 7, 1976, p. 115.

28   "DEEPLY SHOCKED": Pete Seeger, "Charles Seeger: A Man of Music," *Sing Out!,* June 1979.

29   "MIXING MY BOURGEOIS": *Reminiscences,* p. 130.

30   "TO ESCAPE": *Reminiscences,* pp. 134–35.

31   "THIN, ENERGETIC": William Archer, "Introduction," *Poems by Alan Seeger,* (New York: Scribners, 1917).

31   "PETE ALWAYS SAID": Toshi Seeger, October 6, 1976. His reworking of Alan Seeger's vision was "The Torn Flag," on *Pete Seeger Now* (Columbia CS 4717).

31   "IN ONE CAMP": *Reminiscences,* p. 136. A contemporary of Seeger's, Harold Story, tells of similar experiences in a memoir in the UCLA Oral History Project, 1967, pp. 280–84.

Chapter Two *(cont.)*

page   *reference*

31   "ROPES PUT ABOUT": Norman Thomas, *Conscientious Objector in America* (New York: B. W. Heubsch, 1925), p. 46.

Chapter Three

Author's interviews with Charles Seeger, April 6, 7, 8, 1976; Charles Seeger III, April 6, 1976; Pete Seeger, April 15, October 6, 1976; Don McLean, November 10, 1976; Bob Claiborne, December 13, 1977; George Draper, September 22, 1976; John Seeger, August 9, 1977; Dan North, May 23, 1977; Bill Leonard, December 9, 1977; Dr. David Boyden, July 14, 1976; Bess Lomax Hawes, August 28, 1977.

page   *reference*

33   "CHARLES HIT ON": Charles Seeger, April 6, 1976.

34   "THE FAILURE AT PINEHURST": Charles Seeger, April 6, 1976.

35   "HIS BROTHERS": Charles Seeger III, October 10, 1977; Pete Seeger, October 6, 1976; Charles Seeger, April 6, 1976.

36   "PETER'S MUSICAL EDUCATION": Charles Seeger III, October 10, 1976.

37   "YEARS LATER": The original "Abiyoyo" melody and story as Seeger learned it is on "Bantu Choral Folk Songs," Folkways FW 6912; the story appeared in *African Folksongs,* J. N. Maselina and H. C. N. Williams, editors, (Capetown, South Africa: St. Mathews College, 1947).

37   "A CLOSE FRIEND": Don McLean, November 10, 1976.

38   "SETON": Pete Seeger, October 6, 1976: *Two Little Savages* (New York: Doubleday, Page, & Co., 1903).

38   "ANOTHER FRIEND": Bob Claiborne, December 13, 1977; Pete Seeger, October 6, 1976.

39   "HE HAD ARRANGED": Pete Seeger, October 6, 1976.

39   "HIS EDUCATION": *The Education of Henry Adams* (Boston: Houghton Mifflin, 1918), p. 26.

40   "MUSIC IS A WEAPON": Charles Seeger, April 6, 1976. What inspired the Collective in the works of Hanns Eisler could be traced to German popular and folk music, though they didn't realize. See Dunaway, "Composers Collective," New York Folklore sum., 1979.

42   "BACK AT SCHOOL": M. Ilin, *New Russia's Primer: The Story of the Five-Year Plan,* translated by George Counts and Nucia Lodge (Boston: Houghton Mifflin, 1931); the book was designed for children from 12 to 14 years of age.

42   "PETER DIDN'T UNDERSTAND": This evening is described in Charles Seeger's obituary by Archie Green, *Journal of American Folklore,* October 1979, and by Charles Seeger, April 7, 1976.

43   "PLEASE, MOTHER": Correspondence reported by Toshi Seeger, October 6, 1976.

46   "BUT, PETER": Pete Seeger, July 19, 1976; letters from Adrian and Arthur Kantrowitz to author confirm this in part.

47   "REBELS": *What is History?* (New York: Random House, 1961), p. 65.

48   "WELL, FATHER": Charles Seeger, April 6, 1976. Had Peter's father been involved with radical groups less enthusiastic about New Deal folklore—the Trotskyites, for example—Peter might never have developed an interest in American folk music.

49   "IN ENGLAND": Maud Karpeles, *Cecil Sharp: His Life and Works* (Chicago: University of

Chapter Three (cont.)

page *reference*

Chicago Press, 1967), p. 25. Virtually every article previously written on Pete Seeger mistakenly places his visit in 1935; the sequence of festivals that summer and Charles's reports to the Resettlement Administration dates the summer Pete discovered the five-string in 1936.

50 "BUELL KAZEE": Seeger learned the banjo from recordings, not oral (from the mouths of others) but aural transmission (by listening). Folkways Records recorded and reissued many of Pete's inspirations, among them: Pete Steele (FS 3828); Dock Boggs (FH 5458, FA 2351); Uncle Dave Macon (RF 51). Bascom Lamar Lunsford is on Rounder Records 0065. Additional sources are: Bill Malone, *Country Music, U.S.A.* (Austin: AFS University of Texas Press, 1968), and Kristin Baggelaar and Don Milton, *Folk Music: More Than a Song* (New York: Crowell, 1976). A partial list of Pete's musical sources is found in *The Incompleat Folksinger* (New York: Simon and Schuster, 1972).

51 "JUST AS HIS FATHER": Spain makes an interesting test of the relative worth of songs and guns; though Seeger never fought, his recordings of Spanish Civil War songs outlasted many of his colleagues who died in (or returned from) Spain.

52 "REED": Material on John Reed in college from Robert Rosenstone, *Romantic Revolutionary* (New York: Knopf, 1975).

Chapter Four

Author's interviews with Charles Seeger, April 6, 1976; Pete Seeger, April 16, 1976; March 6, 9, 10, 1977; August 8, 1978; Jerry Oberwager, April 3, 1977; Gordon Friesen, April 14, 1976; Bess Lomax Hawes, May 6, 1977; Lee Hays, May 25, 1977; Mike Seeger, December 7, 1977; Mrs. Joe Gelders, December 8, 1979.

page *reference*

56 "A SMALL CROWD GATHERED": Much of this information on Seeger's New York life comes from his journals and interviews with John Seeger, August 27, 1977, and Charles Seeger III, October 10, 1977.

57 "LEDBETTER": Amazingly enough, no one has published a biography of Huddie Ledbetter. *The Midnight Special* by Richard Garvin and Edmond Addeo (New York: Bernard Geis Associates, 1971) is a "biographical novel"; the Lomaxes' book, *Negro Folk Songs as Sung by Leadbelly* (New York: Macmillan, 1936) was partially repudiated by Ledbetter. Perhaps the best essay is by Frederic Ramsey, Jr., "Leadbelly, A Great Long Time," *Sing Out!*, January 1965. Seeger devoted a chapter of his *Incompleat Folksinger* to Leadbelly. Material here is drawn from all these sources.

59 "I PLAY THE BANJO": Gordon Friesen, April 14, 1976, p. 26.

59 "HE FUMED": Jerry Oberwager, April 3, 1977. Information on the Puppeteers comes from "The Vagabond Puppeteers," a memo Pete Seeger wrote on February 6, 1940 (17 pages), and Warren Gardner (who wrote about the Puppeteers for the Federated Press Syndicate), who wrote Seeger on March 1, 1979.

63 "I WAS A BUST": Bess Lomax used to inspire her beginning guitar classes with this story.

64 "GO BACK": David De Turk and A. Poulin, editors, *The American Folk Scene* (New York: Dell, 1967), p. 214.

67 "THE COUNTERGIRL": "Low Levee Cafe," manuscript in the Woody Guthrie Archives in New York, dated May 28, 1947.

Chapter Four (*cont.*)

page   reference

68   "NOW PETE THINKS": Lee Hays, May 25, 1977. Hays probably included Seeger's later performances with the Weavers in this assessment.

70   "AW, HE JUST STOLE": Pete Seeger reprinted this as the epigraph to his semiautobiographical book *The Incompleat Folksinger.*

70   "PETE LOOKED TO WOODY": Lee Hays, May 25, 1977.

71   "AS ONE FOLKLORIST": Ray Lawless, *Folksingers and Folksongs in America* (New York: Duell, Sloan and Pearce, 1960), p. 211.

73   "TOO AMERICAN": Waldemar Hille, September 23, 1976.

74   "ANYONE COULD WRITE": Quoted in Tony Palmer, *All You Need Is Love* (New York: Penguin, 1977), p. 107.

75   "AN OLD MAN": This article, "Pete and His Banjo Meet Some Fine Mountain Folks," appeared in the Birmingham *Southern News Almanac* in 1940 (undated).

75   "THERE IS SOMETHING": *Born to Win* (New York: Macmillan, 1965), p. 29. When Guthrie wrote this, he was himself halfway through the long novel eventually published as *Seeds of Man.*

Chapter Five

Author's interviews with Pete Seeger, March 9, 10, December 14, 1977; August 8, 1978; Lee Hays, May 25, 1977; Mill Lampell, October 29, 1979; Gordon Friesen, April 14, 1976; Bess Lomax Hawes, May 6, 1977; Earl Robinson, March 18, 1976; Dorothy Millstone, December 29, 1977; Irene Paull, September 7, 1976; Peggy Seeger, August 29, 1977.

page   reference

79   "I LIKE CHURCHILL": Pete Seeger, interview with Dr. Richard Reuss, April 9, 1968.

79   "TALKING UNION": In *Talking Union,* the Almanac Singers, Folkways Records, FA 5285. The original version includes the phrase "God-damned Reds," later deleted.

82   "TALKING MANAGEMENT": *Bosses' Songbook,* Richard and Pat Ellington, editors. Second edition (New York: self-published, 1959).

83   "HIS ZEAL FOR UNIONS": This predated his Almanac experience by at least four years; it proved too much for his college roommate, a Mr. Holland Willard, who chided him: "Pete, I think I'll go into labor unions—that's where the real power's going to be in this country." Seeger interview, March 9, 1977.

83   "EVEN AT THAT EARLY AGE": Gordon Friesen, April 14, 1976.

83   "I SAW THEN": Earl Robinson, March 18, 1976. Seeger still resisted being a virtuoso, but he listened when his father wrote, in 1939: "If a composer is going to sing the American people anything new . . . he must first get upon a common ground with them, learn their musical lingo," a statement that may have served as an unacknowledged blueprint for the Almanacs. "Grassroots for American Composers," *Modern Music,* Volume 16, March–April 1939.

"INSPIRED BY THE ANONYMOUS MOVEMENT": By its nature, this group was ill-known. See Richard Reuss, *American Folklore and Left-Wing Politics: 1927–1957,* unpublished dissertation, Indiana University, 1971.

84   "NEWSPAPER WRITERS": *New Masses,* May 27, 1941; *Time,* September 15, 1941.

85   "THERE WERE THOSE WHO SAID": *The Un-Americans* (New York: Cameron Associates, 1957).

Chapter Five (cont.)

page   *reference*

86   "ON ACCOUNT OF THAT NEW SITUATION": Bess Lomax Hawes, May 6, 1977. Prior to World War I, many leftists made an equally abrupt switch to support the government's war effort.

87   "THESE WERE ONE OF THE FEW SESSIONS": There are, curiously enough, no more than two dozen songs released where Guthrie and Seeger play together. This was either because both singers were rarely in the same place for very long; because with Guthrie's disease developing in the late forties they were rarely at equal levels of instrumental skill; or because both were lead singers and instrumentalists, and their talents may not have blended.

88   "THE FBI IS WORRIED": FBI documents released under a Freedom of Information Act suit, *Dunaway* v. *Kelley,* U.S. District Court, San Francisco.

88   "THEIR HOST": Esther McCoy, *Los Angeles Times,* March 27, 1977.

91   "PETE LOVED THE ECHOEY": Joe Klein, *Woody Guthrie* (New York: Knopf, 1980).

92   "BOSSES HAVE HIRED": Quoted in *People's World,* October 28, 1941.

93   "WOODY HAD HIS OWN LITTLE RECORD PLAYER": Two of their most important records, in terms of sources, were *Listen to Our Story* and *Mountain Music Frolic,* two 1940 hillbilly albums that included the Monroe brothers and other bluegrass bands; J. E. Mainer and his Mountaineers; Lilly Mae Ledford and the Coon Creek Girls; and the Carter Family.

93   "JIM CROW": Richard Reuss, *American Folklore and Left-Wing Politics.*

97   "YOU'RE GETTING MARRIED": Richard Reuss, letter to the author, June 2, 1980.

100   "THERE WAS BIG DROPS OF SWEAT": Woody Guthrie, *Bound For Glory* (New York: E. P. Dutton, 1943). In Woody's account, he pretends he was alone, and that he walked off stage.

101   "THE WAY THEY GOT ON RADIO": Background information here is from Tony Palmer, *All You Need Is Love* (New York: Penguin, 1977).

106   "HE WORRIED": "Soldier's Diary," journal in the possession of Pete Seeger.

Chapter Six

Author's interviews with Pete Seeger, October 6, 1977 (with Toshi Ohta Seeger), March 6, 10, 1977; August 8, 1978; Charles Seeger, April 8, 1976; Alan Lomax, December 27, 1977; Jimmy Collier, July 10, 1978; Mario Cassetta, September 22, 1976; Bess Hawes May 6, 1977; Wally Hille, September 23, 1976; Leo Christiansen, September 22, 1976; Earl Robinson, March 18, 1976; Irwin Silber, May 26, 1977; Margaret Gelders Frantz, June 21, 1978.

page   *reference*

109   "YOU WANT TO KNOW": Jimmy Collier, July 10, 1978.

109   "THREE RECORDING SESSIONS": These were "Lonesome Train," 1943, Decca 29139-41; "Songs of the Lincoln Brigade," 1943, Asch 330 (reissued as Folkways 5436); "Solidarity Forever," 1944, Stinson 622.

110   "SEEGER'S FIRST HUAC MENTION": Report of the House Committee on Un-American Activities, second session. *Report on the C.I.O.-P.A.C. Committee, March 29, 1944* (J66 No. 10845), p. 97.

111   "OR THEY SANG ABOUT": Songs collected by Pete Seeger, catalogued in *Notes From the Marianas,* manuscript in the Library of Congress.

Chapter Six (cont.)

page   *reference*

112   "BY THE 1940s": Author's correspondence with Malvina Reynolds (an early PSI member) and Dr. Richard Reuss; Seeger might well have contented himself with founding a nonelitist cultural drive, banjos instead of symphonies. In the end Seeger and his political song movements may have begun to achieve this, however much hopes for labor were disappointed.

113   "PETE, IN HIS ISOLATION": Seeger, March 10, August 8, 1978.

113   "THE COMMUNIST PARTY": Material for this section was drawn from *American Communism in Crisis, 1943–1957* by Joe Starobin (Berkeley: Univ. of California Press, 1975); *The Autobiography of an American Communist* by Peggy Dennis (Westport: Lawrence Hill and Co., 1978); *A Long View from the Left* by Al Richmond (New York: Dell, 1972); and *The Decline of American Communism* by David Shannon (Chatham, N.J.: Chatham Bookseller, 1971).

      For the Communist Party's self-history, see "Fifty Years of the Communist Party U.S.A.," a special issue of *Political Affairs*, September–October, 1969.

113   "MARXISM WAS THE TRANSFORMING": Quoted in Vivian Gornick, *The Romance of American Communism* (New York: Basic Books, 1978).

115   "ONE LEGENDARY INCIDENT": Author's correspondence with Felix Landau, September 2, 1976; and Seeger, March 10, 1977, December 14, 1977.

116   "ALL HE WROTE IN HIS JOURNAL": This emotional distancing was so striking that years later, as Seeger reread his journals, he noted in the margin: "No mention of Pitou's death?"

116   "IN AN ARTICLE": "People's Songs and Its People," ten-page manuscript in the Woody Guthrie Archives, New York City.

116   "TOSHI PLAYED": Wally Hille, September 23, 1976.

117   "PLAYING THE BANJO": Leo Christiansen, September 23, 1976. People's Songs reflected this ambiguity of Seeger's: "Organized to create, promote, and distribute songs of labor and the American people," PSI vacillated between a music publishing house and a Communist/CIO organizing project.

117   "THE MEETING DISAPPOINTED HIM": Seeger, August 8, 1978. Richard Reuss writes about the Party's cultural policy on folk music in "American Folklore and Left-wing Politics," unpublished Ph.D. dissertation, 1971, Indiana University.

118   "PETE, HERE IN NEW YORK": Seeger, August 8, 1978. The Party may have been out of date, for the big bands so popular in New York in the 1930s were now disbanding; in 1946, Tommy Dorsey and Woody Herman both split up their groups. Seeger himself had periodic doubts about using folk music for the new "people's music," as he wrote the Almanacs during the war. "I wonder if we really have the right slant on the future of American music—us using so much folk music when jazz is so popular. But Kentucky would reaffirm anyone's faith . . . ."

118   "THIS CHEEKY COMMENT": Seeger, August 8, 1978. After the criticism Seeger received, the *Bulletin* actually did print several jazzy sounding tunes.

118   "MUSIC, TOO, IS A WEAPON": *New Masses*, July 16, 1946, p. 9. In a 1934 article for *Modern Music*, "On Proletarian Music," Charles Seeger used the same words: "Music is . . . one of the weapons in the class struggle." Years later this jingoistic adaptation of Communist cultural policy—"Art is a weapon, Writing is a weapon . . ."—would stick in Seeger's throat. He wryly repeated the words of Rockwell Kent: "Art is a weapon, but a breadknife is a weapon too—and it also cuts bread." (Interview with Richard Reuss, April 8, 1968.)

Chapter Six (*cont.*)

page   *reference*

119   "THE FBI": The surveillance discussed here was disclosed in the suit *Dunaway* v. *Kelley*, U.S. District Court, San Francisco. Through the Freedom of Information Act some 600 documents on People's Songs have been released or declassified. An additional 900 were released on the Almanacs, the Weavers, and People's Artists.

119   "AS EVEN EARL BROWDER": Starobin, *American Communism in Crisis*. Earl Browder's thinking may actually have been accurate but premature; years later the world saw the Russian-American wheat and industrial sales exchanges he anticipated.

121   "UNION LEADERS WERE": Because Seeger's happiness at PSI depended so much on success with organized labor, it is important to try and gauge the extent of union participation in People's Songs. Judging from newspaper clippings and PSI's list of bookings, union activities peaked in mid 1947 (during their collaboration on a filmstrip for the CIO Political Action Committee) and had largely faded a year later. Staunchly left-leaning locals naturally were the most interested. Among those with repeated contact were United Auto Workers; radio workers in the United Electrical Workers; the Oilworkers' International; United Office and Professional Workers; the National Maritime Union; the Transport Workers' Union; the International Typographers' Union; the Mine, Mill and Smelter Workers' Union; and the Newspaper Guild. Ads for People's Songs appeared in the *Trade Union Service Newspapers,* the *Department Store Employee,* and the *N.Y. Teachers News,* and the *C.I.O. Bulletin.*

122   "ONE WEST COAST MEMBER": Leo Christiansen, September 22, 1976.

122   "HE COMPLAINED": Seeger to Alan Lomax, July 16, 1946. Hays later contributed the wittiest columns in the *Bulletin*.

123   "WELL, THEY GAVE HIM HIS ORDERS": *Bosses' Songbook,* Pat and Dick Ellington, editors (self-published, second edition, 1959).

123   "TRIM, SLIM SINATRA": *Billboard,* December 21, 1946. In their subsequent review the following March 15, *Billboard* was less enthusiastic: "Seeger should make an effort to acquire more polish and smoothness. In addition, he should either wear make-up or the Vanguard should spotlight him with a diffused light. . . . "

123   "TO HEAR YOUR BANJO PLAY": The film is distributed by Audio-Brandon and includes footage of Woody Guthrie playing guitar, perhaps the only extant motion pictures of him performing.

124   "DOMESTIC INTELLIGENCE SUMMARY": Some idea of the accuracy of this report can be gleaned from the following excerpt: "Communism in the United States is no longer confined to the fellow with the thick-lensed glasses and tieless shirt preaching on a soapbox. Communists are now operating a section whose representatives wear full dress suits and top hats for the men and silver and gold spangled evening gowns for the fairer sex. . . . " People's Songs belonged to the workshirt-and-jeans set.

126   "A VISIT WITH HARRY": *Songs for Wallace,* August, 1948, song folio printed by People's Songs.

127   "THEN WALLACE DECIDED": Much of the material on Wallace comes from *Gideon's Army* by Curtis MacDougall (New York: Marzani and Munsell, 1965), particularly pp. 712–17, and Margaret Gelders Frantz, June 21, 1978.

129   "WE KNEW THE PRICE": Irwin Silber, May 26, 1977. Actually Silber was not alone in this feeling. "Lee Hays once said he wasn't in this thing to promote folk music, but the workers' cause," according to Wally Hille, September 23, 1976.

131   "UNION MAID": Headnotes from *Hard Hitting Songs for Hard Hit People,* compiled by Alan Lomax, notes by Woody Guthrie, music edited by Pete Seeger (New York: Oak

Chapter Six (cont.)

page   *reference*

Publications, 1967) p. 324. Words from *Talking Union,* Folkways Records FH5285.

131   "STICKING TO THE UNION": Joe Klein, *Woody Guthrie* (N.Y.: Knopf, 1980), p. 180.

132   "A PARODY": *Bosses' Songbook,* Richard and Pat Ellington, editors. Second edition (New York: self-published, 1959).

132   "THE REASON 'UNION MAID' ": Leo Christiansen, September 22, 1976.

133   "EVEN UNIONS": "Whatever Happened to Singing in the Unions?" *Sing Out!,* May, 1965.

134   "EMRICH": The Seeger-Emrich correspondence is in the Archive of Folk Song in the Library of Congress; the Emrich-FBI contacts are detailed in FBI memoranda on People's Songs, released under *Dunaway* v. *Kelley.*

134   "A FRIEND STOPPED BY": Joe Klein, *Woody Guthrie.*

135   "TOMORROW IS A HIGHWAY": As recorded on *Gazette Volume 2,* Folkways FN 2502.

Chapter Seven

Author's interviews with Pete Seeger, March 6, 9, 10, October 9, December 14, 1977; August 8, 1978; March 26, 1980; Lee Hays, February 11, 1977; Fred Hellerman, March 3, 1977; Ronnie Gilbert, January 14, 1977; Gordon Friesen, December 21, 1977; Arlo Guthrie, November 5, 1978; Mario Cassetta, September 26, 1976; Oscar Brand, March 27, 1980; Dave Garroway, January 14, 1977; Don McLean, November 10, 1976; Bess Hawes, May 6, 1977; Peggy Seeger, August 29, 1977; Charles Seeger, April 8, 1976; Pete Kameron, September 11, 1980.

page   *reference*

137   "WITH AN AX": "Timeless Troubadour," *Wall Street Journal,* June 21, 1973.

137   "FOR PETE AND THE OTHERS": Material here is from interviews with the Weavers and a letter of Ronnie Gilbert.

138   "GOING AROUND THE ROOM": Actually, the group had considered other members, including two young black singers, Hope Foye and Bill Dillard.

138   "IF I HAD A HAMMER": This was first issued as Hootenanny Records 101 (A), and first performed on June 3, 1949, at a testimonial for the Foley Square Twelve, as they were then called.

141   "AT A TYPICAL WEAVERS SHOW": This description is a composite of some of the Weavers' best-known performance pieces.

144   "CHALLENGED BY TV": Background material for this section from Erik Barnouw, *The Golden Web: A History of Broadcasting in the United States,* Volume II (New York: Oxford University Press, 1968).

144   "WASTING MY MONEY": This Reno engagement was one of the few where the Weavers felt direct censorship, the manager telling them, "Cut that political stuff out." The Weavers self-censored.

147   "ED SULLIVAN": This anecdote and much supporting information comes from an excellent, neglected history of blacklisting in the media, *A Journal of the Plague Years* by Stefan Kanfer (New York: Atheneum, 1973).

147   "FORMER FRIENDS ALSO ATTACKED": In fairness, not all radicals viewed the Weavers' success so dourly. Boots Cassetta, for instance, was more jubilant: "I was so happy for them. I wanted to stop people on the streets and say listen to that, those are

Chapter Seven *(cont.)*

page   *reference*

friends of mine, they're really radical as all hell, why didn't you recognize them before!" Seeger reviewed the Weavers' "When the Saints Go Marching In" in *Sing Out!* (September 1951), using the name of his grandfather, Nathan Charliere: he had his reservations about his own records.

148   "THE SPIRIT OF PEOPLE'S SONGS": Despite the relative insignificance of People's Artists, the FBI was asked by the Department of Justice to prepare a full-scale report for prosecution of PA before the Subversive Activities Control Board.

150   "DECCA LIKED GORDON JENKINS": A good example of this tendency was when the Weavers wanted to record "So Long, It's Been Good to Know You." Producers at Decca decided no one wanted to hear about the Dust Bowl anymore; at the Weavers' request, Woody visited Jenkins's hotel room and scrawled out new lyrics on brown butcher's paper spread out on the carpet.

150   "WHEN SEEGER ANSWERED": Pete Seeger, March 6, 1977; March 26, 1980.

150   "BRAND REFUSED": Irwin Silber reported on this speech in *Sing Out!*, November 1951. In 1963 Brand wrote: "The reason that I am now working for the networks, major industries, and even governmental agencies is the result of a happy discovery of the House Un-American Activities Committee. . . . When it was demonstrated that my anti-Communism predated that of most of the blacklisters, the doors were again open to me." Oscar Brand, *The Ballad Mongers* (New York, Funk and Wagnalls, 1962), pp. 135–36; author's interview, March 27, 1980.

151   "DEADLY BUREAUCRATIC REPRESSION": David Caute, *The Great Fear* (New York: Simon and Schuster, 1979).

151   "DAVE GARROWAY": In 1971 Seeger appeared on Dave Garroway's comeback show in Boston. His previous rejection may have continued to smart; Seeger was so outspokenly opposed to the war in Vietnam, the local RKO station regretted the spot, and eventually cancelled Garroway's show.

152   "THE MCCARRAN COMMITTEE": Documents released under a Freedom of Information Act suit, *Dunaway* v. *Kelley et al.*, U.S. District Court, San Francisco.

152   "TWO MEN, TWO WOMEN": Richard Reuss, *American Folklore and Left-wing Politics*, unpublished Ph.D. dissertation, Indiana University, Folklore Program, 1971.

152   "PETE RECEIVED WORD": Walter Lowenfels to Pete Seeger, February 26, 1951.

153   "SEEGER HEDGED": *Variety*, August 29, 1951.

154   "IT WAS THERE I GOT MY TRAINING": Harvey Matusow, *False Witness* (New York: Cameron and Kahn, 1955). While there is no telling when Matusow was lying—in his testimony or his later recantation—by recounting his experiences as published here, the ex-Communist opened himself to prosecution for perjury.

161   "REISSUING *TALKING UNION*": The story behind the reissue of what is now America's most popular record of union songs is a fascinating one. The masters had been lost, but Toshi Seeger had foresightedly bought an extra copy, which she kept in mint condition. There was one problem: the original six songs were only enough for one side of an LP.

Seeger formed an impromptu group, the Songswappers, including Mary Travers (of Peter, Paul and Mary) and Erik Darling (later to take Seeger's place in the Weavers); they recorded six labor songs arranged so similarly to the Almanacs' that many listeners have never noticed the difference.

162   "A THEN EIGHT-YEAR-OLD": Author's correspondence with Jill Reidel, September 11, 1979.

Chapter Seven (cont.)

page   reference

163   "EVADING QUESTIONS": Pete Seeger, December 14, 1977.

165   "UNFRIENDLY WITNESSES": Frank Donner, The Un-Americans (New York: Ballantine, 1961).

168   "I. F. STONE": *The Haunted Fifties* (New York: Vintage, 1963).

Chapter Eight

Author's interviews with Pete Seeger, October 6, 1976 (with Toshi Seeger); October 9, December 14, 1977; August 8, 1978; Bess Lomax Hawes, August 28, 1977; Moe Asch, May 8, 1977; Harold Leventhal, June 9, 1977; Lee Hays, May 25, 1977; Peggy Seeger, August 24, 1977; Don McLean, November 10, 1976; Ron Radosh, March 24, 1980; Myles Horton, May 2, 1980; Norma Starobin, January 20, 1980.

page   reference

169   "AN EIGHT-YEAR-OLD": This and other quotes in this section are from the author's personal recollection.

171   "I WANT TO GET UP THERE": This conversation from Pete Seeger, October 9, 1977, and December 14, 1977.

172   "A NEW GENERATION OF FANS": This group had a disproportionate influence on American politics. At a 1977 reunion of the once-militant Students for a Democratic Society, someone asked, "How many of you were red-diaper babies?" Three quarters of the audience raised their hands.

172   "HE FIT AN AMERICAN MOLD": Thoreau was the godfather to this mood of heroism-in-principle. David Mairowitz, *The Radical Soap Opera* (New York: Avon, 1974), pp. 150–54.

172   "INCLUDING PROGRESSIVE SOCIAL CLUBS": Estimates of Seeger's second-generation audience are speculative. In addition to the unions and social clubs, in the fifties he sang regularly at approximately fifty camps and fifty schools around the country; together their enrollment might add up to 30,000 people. A hundred or so colleges hired him, particularly after the headlines of his HUAC testimony subsided; that might make another 30,000 listeners.

172   "TEENAGER WHO TOOK BANJO LESSONS": Ron Radosh, March 24, 1980. Myles Horton, Director of the Highlander Folk School, told of another small but memorable gesture. On visiting Highlander for its 25th anniversary in 1957 (alongside Martin Luther King and other luminaries), Pete wandered off from the stage area to play banjo for the kitchen help while they worked.

173   "HAROLD VELDE": Walter Goodman, *The Committee* (New York: Farrar, Straus, & Giroux, 1968).

174   "AMID THE POPPING": Frank Donner, *The Un-Americans* (New York: Ballantine, 1961).

174   "WALTER": Charlotte Pomerantz, editor, *A Quarter Century of Un-Americana* (New York: Marzani and Munsell, 1963). Background on the Committee members is from Goodman, *The Committee*, and Donner, *The Un-Americans*.

174   "I MAKE MY LIVING": Seeger's testimony is reproduced in *Thirty Years of Treason*, Eric Bentley, editor (New York: Viking, 1971). HUAC members did not mention Matusow's perjured testimony on Seeger before the committee in 1952.

177   "HE IS INVOLVED": Trumbo, *Time of the Toad* (New York: Harper & Row, 1972).

179   "WALT WHITMAN": *Pete and Sonny at Carnegie Hall*, Folkways FA 2412.

Chapter Eight (*cont.*)

page   reference

184   "THE *DAILY WORKER*": Peter Fryer, *Hungarian Tragedy* (London: Dennis Dobson, 1956).

184   "HE DID NOT CRITICIZE": This might explain why Seeger, though far from Party discipline, could arrive at the University of Chicago folk festival in the Fifties and tell one of the students, "Oh good, you have the *Worker*—I'm two weeks behind."

184   "ON LEAVING THE PARTY": For every Louis Budenz or Benjamin Gitlow (one of the first fire-and-brimstone ex-Communists), a Joseph Freeman existed, someone who was expelled or drifted away from the CP but not from the movement or their ideals.

184   "A FEW SHARP CHORUSES": *Bosses Songbook,* Richard and Pat Ellington, Editors. Second edition (New York: self-published, 1959).

188   "AN UNDERLYING MILITANCE": Quoted in Pete Seeger to Lynn Rohrbaugh, undated (1956).

189   "MUSIC IS THE MOST POWERFUL": Stephen Spender, "Poetry and Revolution," *The Thirties and After* (New York: Vintage, 1979).

189   "A GENERATION OF FOLKLORISTS": Among the many Pete Seeger inspired were some of today's authorities on American folk song: Joe Hickerson of the Library of Congress, Richard Reuss, Kenneth Goldstein, Russell Ames, and many others.

190   "I COMMITTED NO WRONG": Circular letter in the possession of Pete Seeger, March 30, 1957; Seeger characterized newspaper reports of his "hassle with the government" as "incomplete, inaccurate, and sometimes downright malicious."

191   "A PAEAN TO PETE SEEGER": San Francisco *People's World,* February 8, 1958.

192   "THE DETROIT ARTS COMMISSION": *New York Times,* July 12, 1958.

Chapter Nine

Author's interviews with Pete Seeger, July 19, 1976; October 9, December 14, 1977, August 8, 1978; Bess Lomax Hawes, August 28, 1978; Malvina Reynolds, September 5, 1976; Jimmy Collier, July 10, 1978; Mike Seeger, December 7, 1977; Peggy Seeger, August 29, 1977; Charles Seeger III, October 10, 1977; Irving Younger, May 24, 1980; Mike Cooney, May 30, 1978; Don McLean, November 10, 1978; Charles Seeger, April 8, 1976; Mary Bernstein, December 29, 1961; Judy Collins, December 30, 1977; Howie Richmond, February 24, 1980; Harold Leventhal, June 9, 1977.

page   reference

193   "AMERICA THE BEAUTIFUL": Introductory statement to "America the Beautiful," on *Hootenanny Tonight,* Folkways FN 2311.

193   "NONE OF THE OTHERS WERE ENTHUSIASTIC": The Weavers experimented wildly with a commercial sound, including a rock and roll version of "Take This Hammer" called "Take This Letter and Carry It to My Darling," which featured a ripping sound for the opening of a letter. Ron Radosh, "Commercialism and the Folksong Revival," in David De Turk and A. Poulin, editors, *The American Folk Scene* (New York: Dell, 1967), p. 306.

194   "A VISION OF AMERICANS": What most disturbed Seeger was the *professionalization* of song. After World War II, as radio receivers and phonograph recordings became increasingly common, more and more of the "folk" heard professionals sing. The public was invited to listen, rather than invited to sing. Radio (and soon after, television) made it far easier to tune in entertainment than to make one's own.

Chapter Nine (cont.)

page   *reference*

194   "CHARLES SEEGER": Professionalism and Amateurism in the Study of Folk Music," *Journal of American Folklore,* LXII (1949), p. 112. Charles Seeger consistently forecast his son's career: Before the Almanacs he wrote "Grassroots for American Composers"; in the early 1950s Charles suggested that somebody—Charles didn't say who—should reopen oral communication by getting children and parents singing in their homes and schools. "Folk Music in the Schools of a Highly Industrialized Society," reprinted in *The American Folk Scene.*

195   "GOD HELP PETE SEEGER": Jimmy Collier, July 10, 1978.

196   "THE ATTACKS WORSENED": *Great Neck News,* December 11, 1959; *Los Angeles Examiner,* May 15, 1960; *Los Angeles Times,* May 13, 1960; *San Diego Union,* May 14, 1960; *People's World,* May 21, 1960.

196   "A SIMILAR INCIDENT": *Rockland County Journal-News,* November 22, 23, 26, 1960; *County Citizen,* November 23, 1960.

197   "TEXANS FOR AMERICA": Frances Fitzgerald, "Rewriting American History," *New Yorker,* February 26, 1979, p. 56.

199   "ALWAYS THE LAST TO LEAVE": Sara Effron to author, February 18, 1980.

200   "SEEGER WILL BE LUCKY": *Harvard Crimson,* March 29, 1961; *New York Post,* March 29, 1961. For coverage of the trial, see also *New York Daily News,* March 30, 1961, *New York Journal-American,* March 30, 1961, and *New York Times,* March 30, 1961.

200   "NEW YORK TIMES": Prior to 1961 Seeger was *The New York Times*'s invisible man of folk music. In the fourteen years between his first nightclub engagement and his trial, *The New York Times* index lists only three articles on Seeger, aside from mentions of the Weavers and his troubles with HUAC. To all but the most eagle-eyed reader, Pete's half-dozen concerts at Carnegie Hall never happened; People's Songs was a mirage; and Pete's sixty-odd albums were of no consequence.

202   "HAMMOND MET": John Hammond, *On Record* (New York: Summit Books, 1979), p. 346.

202   "MALVINA REYNOLDS": Reynolds subsequently left Columbia after being bitterly disappointed by her treatment there.

204   "THANK YOU, YOUR HONOR": Seeger's statement to the court is printed in *Sing Out!,* Summer 1961.

206   "BATTLE OF WASHINGTON SQUARE": Oscar Brand, *The Ballad Mongers,* p. 159; *New York Times,* April 10, 1961; "Hootenanny: Who Invented the Term?," Peter Tammony, *Hootenanny,* Vol. 1, No. 2, Oct. 27, 1963.

209   "A POEM ON HIS WEALTH": Manuscript in the possession of Pete Seeger, dated February 29 (sic), 1962.

210   "THE COURT FOUND": *U.S.A.* v. *Pete Seeger,* Second Court of Appeals, N. 27, 101; *New York Times,* May 19, 1962.

210   "SYNCHRONIZING LEADBELLY": Pete described this in an interview with Ralph Gleason, *San Francisco Chronicle,* May 7, 1963. Seeger's commitment to Leadbelly's memory remained high throughout his life. In 1964 he and Alan Lomax helped organize a memorial concert; in 1965 he and Jerry Silverman put out a twelve-string guitar guide "according to Leadbelly."

211   "GUANTANAMERA": Author's recording, July 15, 1962.

212   "SEEGER WALKED DOWN THE AISLE": "The Ballad of Pete Seeger," reprinted in De Turk and Poulin, editors, *The American Folk Scene.*

Chapter Nine (*cont.*)

page   *reference*

214   "LOOK, WE HAVE PETE SEEGER": Pete Seeger, August 8, 1978, p. 12. Bob Dylan's case is representative, as told in *Bob Dylan* by Anthony Scaduto (New York: Grosset and Dunlap, 1971).

215   "JOAN BAEZ REFUSED": *Billboard,* March 30, 1963. Other boycotters mentioned were Billy Faier, Ed McCurdy, and Erik Darling; two weeks later the Greenbriar Boys joined this list.

217   "PETE SEEGER JUST CAN'T HOLD AN AUDIENCE": Peter Lyons, "The Ballad of Pete Seeger," in *The American Folk Scene.* The original source for this quotation is a file of letters and notes on conversations about "Hootenanny" in the possession of Harold Leventhal.

217   "THE ABC NETWORK": Seeger gave his most vivid description of "Hootenanny" years later to a British interviewer: "The show was only a bunch of white college kids all clapping inanely, no matter what song was sung, big smiles all over, and never a hint of controversy or protest." Tony Palmer, *All You Need Is Love* (New York: Penguin, 1977).

Chapter Ten

Author's interviews with Mary Travers, January 19, 1977; Harold Leventhal, June 7, 1977; Pete Seeger, October 6, 1976 (with Toshi Seeger); December 14, 15, 1977; August 8, 1978; Bernice Reagon, December 7, 1977; Jimmy Collier, July 10, 1978; Mike Cooney, May 30, 1978; Irene Paull (Calamity Jane), September 7, 1976.

page   *reference*

221   "THE BANJO MEANT MINSTREL SHOWS": Dena Epstein, "The Folk Banjo—A Documentary History," *Ethnomusiciology,* September 1975.

222   "IF HE HAD KNOWN": The story of Pete's difficulties in Albany is from *The Incompleat Folksinger;* Bernice Reagon discussed the problems Carawan had in her unpublished Ph.D. dissertation, Howard University, 1975.

222   "WE SHALL OVERCOME": The history of the song is from Reagon's dissertation and an interview with Pete Seeger, August 8, 1978.

224   "WEAVERS' FIFTEENTH ANNIVERSARY": Vanguard issued two records from the May 2 and May 3, 1963, reunion concerts (VSD 2150—Part I, VSD 79161—Part II). The Weavers disbanded in the next few months, the end of a musical landmark.

225   "A FELLOW ORGANIZER": Jimmy Collier, July 10, 1978.

227   "PETE WAS AT HIS MOST PERSUASIVE": This and other songs and quotations from *We Shall Overcome,* Columbia CS 8901. A critic for the *New York Post* called the record "probably Seeger's best concert recording. It was obviously a highly emotional evening and Seeger was at his peak vocally." *Rolling Stone Record Guide* (New York: Rolling Stone/Random House, 1980).

228   "PETE'S SONG INTRODUCTIONS": One reason for the shift of platform personalities from oratory to concertizing was that records, TV, and electronic communication had reduced the power of speakers; audiences were more accustomed to listening to musicians than lecturers.

229   "HIS MIND CONTINUED TO DWELL": Journal in the possession of Pete Seeger, edited for publication by Joe Berger.

Chapter Ten (*cont.*)

page   *reference*

229   "THE GOVERNMENT": Seeger used virtually these words in an interview printed in *Outside,* May 1979.

230   "GANDHI, LIKE SEEGER": There are a number of other similarities: Both believed, as Seeger had written at Harvard, that no person is greater than his spiritual repute, and Gandhi is reported by his biographer, Erik Erikson, to have led strikers in processions singing improvised lyrics which showed "a transfer of traditional religious feeling to the new kind of social experience." *Gandhi's Truth* (New York: W. W. Norton, 1969).

232   "HE RELIED ON MUSICIANSHIP": A Soviet magazine later headlined: "SEEGER GOOD FOR FLU," after a number of people reported being cured by an evening of singing with Seeger. *New York Times,* April 11, 1964, *New York Post,* April 12, 1964. Interestingly enough, on his Russian tour, Seeger was told to sing only in formal concerts and eschew informal sing-alongs. Seeger answered that his voice was tired, but he would try to sing where he wanted.

233   "ONE VOLUNTEER": Paul Cowan, *The Making of an Un-American* (New York: Viking Press, 1970).

233   "A VOLUNTEER WROTE HOME": *Letters from Mississippi,* edited by Elizabeth Sutherland (New York: McGraw-Hill, 1971). In an interview on December 14, 1977, Pete Seeger downplayed his own role in inspiring the volunteers: "I never thought I had that much influence in getting people down there. I don't think [my concerts] meant that much."

236   "BERNICE, WHO TOLD HIM": Pete Seeger, December 15, 1977. Reagon has no copy of this correspondence.

237   "LYNDON JOHNSON ADDRESSED CONGRESS": This speech is included in one of the best short summations of the civil-rights movement, Francis Fox Piven and Richard Cloward, *Poor People's Movements* (New York: Pantheon, 1977).

237   "I LOVE EVERYBODY": This and subsequent songs are from a documentary with Pete Seeger, *WNEW's Story of Selma,* produced by Jerry Graham and Mike Stein of WNEW-FM, 1965, released as Folkways FH 5595.

238   "SHERIFF JIM CLARK": Reverend James McGraw, "Footnotes of a Marcher," *The Realist,* May 1965. In New York, a Selma support march took many whites to Harlem for the first time: "New Yorkers were looking someplace else while murders went on all around them," columnist Jimmy Breslin commented. "Not big open murders in the middle of a civil rights demonstration, but silent homicides, people's lives dripping away."

241   "TWO SHOTS TRAVELED": Fifteen years after Liuzzo's death, FBI files revealed that after the accident, FBI director J. Edgar Hoover began a campaign to vilify Liuzzo, ordering anonymous letters sent which called her a drug addict and claiming she was "necking" with a black man at the time of her murder.

242   "DURING THIS TIME": As SNCC went all-black it took its first international positions, opposing American intervention in Vietnam and supporting Palestinian nationalism. This was more than some former supporters could take. Theodore Bikel, who sang with Seeger (and Bob Dylan) at a SNCC benefit in Greenwood, Mississippi, in 1963, now sent off a bitter letter resigning (though he was never a staff member). It began: "You know me well. I've slept with you in the shacks in Mississippi . . ." according to Bernice Reagon, who remembered a flash of hostility at SNCC headquarters.

Chapter Ten (cont.)

page   *reference*

"Shacks in Mississippi? He'd been there two nights! If anybody tried to tell me they were down there to save me, it got me *furious!*"

242   "YOU CONSPIRE TO KEEP US SILENT": "The Movement's Moving On," in *Freedom Is a Constant Struggle,* Guy and Candie Carawan, editors (New York: Oak Publications, 1968).

243   "JULIUS LESTER": "The Angry Children of Malcolm X," *Sing Out!,* October 1966.

Chapter Eleven

Author's interviews with Bernice Reagon, December 7, 1977; Harold Leventhal, June 8, 1977; Pete Seeger, March 6, 1976; December 15, 1977; August 8, 1978; Danny Kalb, March 24, 1980; Gordon Friesen, December 27, 1977; Jack Elliot, August 27, 1978; Don McLean, November 10, 1976; Judy Collins, December 30, 1977; Jimmy Collier, July 10, 1978; Bess Lomax Hawes, August 28, 1977; Country Joe McDonald, March 30, 1978; Reverend Frederick Douglass Kirkpatrick, December 21, 1977.

page   *reference*

245   "TONIGHT LET'S SING": Background on the events at Newport comes from the articles on that 1965 festival in *Bob Dylan: A Retrospective,* Craig McGregor, editor (New York: William Morrow, 1972). Also useful is "Folk Rock: Thunder Without Rain," by Josh Dunson, in DeTurk and Poulin, editors, *The American Folk Scene,* and Anthony Scadato, *Bob Dylan* (New York: Grosset & Dunlap, 1971). Other material from the author's interviews with Bernice Reagon (Dec. 7, 1977); Pete Seeger (Dec. 15, 1977); and Harold Leventhal (June 8, 1977); Gene Marine also conducted an interview with Seeger, partly reported in "Guerrilla Minstrel," *Rolling Stone,* April 13, 1972. A live recording of the performances authenticated the audience-performer interaction.

247   "CRYING IN THE WINGS": Anthony Scaduto, *Bob Dylan.*

250   "A *NEW YORK TIMES* EDITOR": Pete Seeger, Aug. 8, 1978. *New York Times,* October 25, 1965. Second edition headline read "Seeger Critical in Moscow." The apology was printed in the *Beacon Free Press,* November 18, 1965.

253   "WHEN HE FINALLY SANG": "American Minstrel's Song of Success," *New York Times,* January 23, 1966. The East Meadow Case is best reported in *Newsday,* April 12, 1966, and *The New York Times,* July 8, 1966. *Who's Who* listed Pete Seeger as editor of *The New Lost City Ramblers Songbook.*

255   "EERIE INTERIOR MONOLOGUES": These notebooks belong to a series beginning in March, 1966, running through 1969, in possession of Pete Seeger. They are numbered, each one roughly corresponding to one month. These quotes from #4 and #3.

257   "IN FUTURE YEARS": Extended letter, Pete Seeger, May 10, 1967; "Lebanon/Israel, The Coin Has Two Sides," *Sing Out!,* June–July, 1968, and *The Incompleat Folksinger.* Seeger's conclusions on the Middle East were: "To the Lebanese I would say—keep up the pressure, but don't threaten war. To the average Israeli—don't allow 'em to push you out, but give the Palestinian Arabs first-class citizenship and see how Arab opinion will change."

258   "REJECTION OF PACIFISM": "A Portfolio on War," *Sing Out!,* December 1966. There was a strong pacifist sentiment in the Seeger family, which Pete had broken with. Charles Seeger had declared himself a conscientious objector in World War I; so had his son John, in World War II; and Mike Seeger, during the Korean War period.

Chapter Eleven (cont.)

page   reference

259   "SCHOLASTIC": Cliff Jordan (Superintendent of Schools, Coronado, California) to *Scholastic Magazine;* reply undated.

262   "THE NETWORK RECEIVED PUBLICITY": Harold Leventhal, June 9, 1977; *New York Times,* August 25, 1967; *New York Times,* September 4, 1967; *Delaware County Daily Times,* September 9, 1967.

263   "THE EDITOR OF A SMALL FOLK MAGAZINE": Dave Wilson, "Ramblin' Round," *Boston Broadside,* September 27, 1967.

263   "PETE SPECULATED LATER": Pete Seeger, December 15, 1977. There is some evidence that the censorship of "Big Muddy" reflected internal divisions in the network. The CBS broadcast standards office had advised that "Big Muddy" was "probably" unacceptable, but the producers had taped the song anyway.

265   "HE WROTE IRWIN": Pete Seeger to Irwin Silber, November 13, 1967; letter in possession of Irwin Silber. Pete's attack overlooks the very significant work Silber did in editing folk-music books like *Songs of the Civil War, Songs of the Great American West, Songs America Voted By,* and *The Folksinger's Word Book.*

265   "VIETNAM": The United States was not the only nation to find itself in this position, of course. French intellectuals suffered the same sort of crisis over their involvement in Indochina and in Algeria. And back in the 1920s, the French Surrealists' agony over French subjugation of the Berbers in Morocco pushed them to join the Communist Party.

266   "THE REVERSE OF HIP": Jeff Nuttall, *Bomb Culture* (London: MacGibbon and Kee, 1968); *Daily Pennsylvanian,* April 4, 1966, "Players and Seeger."

267   "INSTEAD OF THE CP": In the 1960s, young American radicals unknowingly relived the intergenerational tensions of the late 1920s between the (socialist-oriented) old Old Left and the (Communist) Old Left. The policies of older radicals were considered just as old-fashioned as those the New Left rejected a generation later, as an account of the radical labor college, Commonwealth College, makes painfully clear: Raymond and Charlotte Koch, *Educational Commune* (New York: Schocken Books, 1972).

270   "MY SONGS MUST BE": Seeger to a Mrs. Seki, undated.

271   "DUKE UNIVERSITY": Seeger reported this incident in his *Incompleat Folksinger.*

272   "THESE ZANY IDEAS": The metaphor of the wall is borrowed from John Berger in an interview printed in *In These Times.* A favorite topic for Seeger's flights of imagination was the nature of music, which he often argued with his father.

"You can translate words from one language to another," Pete's father said, "but no one, hearing a melody whistled from beyond a wall, would ask that it be translated. . . . Music does not have meaning; music is." Music does "signify," Pete countered. A group listening to the same music often receive a common mood: "The danger is in thinking that you can tell someone in words *the* meaning of a piece of music." In another exchange, Charles dissected the musical logic of one of Pete's favorite songs: "Peat-Bog Soldiers." Pete explained how he "audiencized" the song, sacrificing the musical effect of the original staccato rhythms to evoke the Nazi brutality for the audience as they sang.

The first exchange is reported in *Sing Out!,* December 1967; Charles Seeger to Pete Seeger, March 17, 1967.

273   "AN OBERLIN COLLEGE STUDENT": Steve Mayer, *Oberlin Review,* March 13, 1968.

273   "ECCLESIASTES": Ecclesiastes 3.1–8 (King James version); headnotes from "Turn,

Chapter Eleven (cont.)

page   *reference*

Turn, Turn," in Pete Seeger, *Bells of Rhymney* (New York: Oak, 1964). Pete actually updated Ecclesiastes with new verses.

274   "SINK THE SHIP": Bess Hawes, August 28, 1977. Notebook #17. Seeger wrote a song, "All My Children of the Sun," based on this vision.

275   "WE HAVE OVERCOME": *New York Times,* May 14, 1968. Much of the background information presented here is from *The New York Times,* March 20–June 25, 1968.

276   "HE DIDN'T KNOW WHAT TO SING": Background to this episode from "Resurrection City Reminiscences," in Pete Seeger's column in *Sing Out!,* October 1968, and interviews with Jimmy Collier, July 10, 1978, and Bernice Reagon, December 7, 1977.

277   "PETE CAUGHT THAT ANGER": Jimmy Collier, July 10, 1978; Bernice Reagon, December 7, 1977.

Chapter Twelve

Author's interviews with Harold Leventhal, March 28, 1977; Jack Elliot, August 27, 1978; Jimmy Collier, July 10, 1978; Gordon Friesen, April 14, 1976; December 27, 1977; Bernice Reagon, December 7, 1977; Don McLean, November 10, 1976; Bess Hawes, August 28, 1977; Peggy Seeger, August 29, 1977; Judy Collins, December 30, 1978; Pete Seeger, December 14, 15, 1977; August 8, 1978; Charles Seeger, April 7, 1976.

page   *reference*

279   "JULIUS LESTER": *Revolutionary Notes* (New York: Grove Press, 1969).

280   "FOR MONTHS STUDENTS AND TEACHERS": The episode at Beacon is covered by *The Village Voice,* "Non-Confrontation in Beacon, N.Y.," December 16, 1965. Seeger described the events in his interview of August 8, 1978.

280   "BEACON'S PAPERS": The *Beacon Evening News* was the forum for many of these letters, which appeared almost daily for three weeks from November 6, 1965. (The two letters quoted here are from that date.) See also the coverage of the *Poughkeepsie Journal* on November 11 and 18, and the *Beacon News* and *Beacon Free Press* for this period.

283   "A NINETEENTH-CENTURY TRAVELER": Excerpts from the 1826 Travel Journal of John Maude, reprinted in *Hudson River Sloops* (Dobbs Ferry, N.Y.: Morgan and Morgan, 1970).

283   "A LOCAL INDIAN LEGEND": This is from an article on the Hudson in *Parade,* November 26, 1978.

285   "LOOK AT THE WASTE WE MAKE": Interview broadcast over WPM in Cleveland, November 12, 1958.

286   "I FELT MY FINGERS CLENCHING": Quoted in "Can Music Save a River?" Marty Gallanter, brochure for the 1979 Hudson River Revival.

287   "LAURENCE ROCKEFELLER": Peter Collier and David Horowitz, *The Rockefellers* (New York: Holt, Rinehart, and Winston, 1976). This was before uranium's dangers were fully understood.

287   "THE *CLEARWATER* SLID": Details on the *Clearwater's* first cruise from *Songs and Sketches,* and "The Launching of the *Clearwater." A Hudson Slooper's Handy Guide* (Poughkeepsie, N.Y.: Hudson River Sloop Restoration, 1975) has the *Clearwater's* specifications.

288   "THEY ALL CAME DOWN TO THE WATER'S EDGE": Pete Seeger, Foreword, *Songs and Sketches of the First Clearwater Crew* (Croton, N.Y.: North River Press, 1970).

Chapter Twelve (*cont.*)

page   *reference*

289   "THE SHOOTINGS AT KENT STATE": Peggy Seeger, August 29, 1977.

291   "HIS 1970 TESTIMONY": *New York Times,* January 31, 1970.

293   "SHE RARELY TALKED TO REPORTERS": *Chicago Tribune,* March 3, 1974; *Denver Post,* August 15, 1974.

295   "HOPES FOR REFORMING TV": In the decade beginning in 1963, Seeger was extraordinarily preoccupied with television's social potential, as some of his projects suggest: In "The Air Belongs to Everyone" (*Harvard Alumni Bulletin,* March 16, 1968), he proposed an elaborate scheme to apportion commercial TV broadcasting hours to democratically elected local delegates, each representing interested TV viewers: Some would champion opera and others, children's programming. Another idea he had was a "Freedom of the Press TV Show," an international press review with commentary on how news is (mis)handled worldwide. Seeger also dreamed up a TV program on the 330 babies born worldwide in the time it takes to sing a song; as they appeared on the screen, the commentator would discuss their future: how many would grow up in semi-starvation in India, and how many in affluence in the U.S.

295   "THE *TODAY* SHOW": Of course, Seeger could be outmanipulated by TV professionals. Once Barbara Walters handled him slickly: On *Today,* when he said, "Mutter along with me for your mutter country," she fairly danced across the studio, saying, "Well, Mr. Seeger, we really are a country of mutterers, aren't we?"

295   "TELL A MAN WHAT HE MAY NOT SING": *The Praise Singer* (New York: Knopf, 1979).

299   "HIS THIRTIES VISIONS": Material here is from notebooks #26 and #27 and a journal Seeger kept in March 1972 (33 pages); the comments on Russia are from an interview with the *Daily World* in May 1974.

302   "FEW WRITING ON POPULAR SONG": Typical of this prejudice against folk-song materials is Alec Wilder's *American Popular Song* (New York: Oxford University Press, 1972). Of the eleven songwriters he discusses in depth, not one has roots in folk music. Arguing either by sales volume (particularly in the Weavers' 1950 arrangements) or by influence, Seeger (and Guthrie and Leadbelly) had considerable impact on American popular song; his compositional styles will probably show, on detailed study, common points with Berlin or Gershwin.

302   "SEEGER DECIDED TO TAKE A YEAR OFF": The exact dates of this sabbatical are uncertain, because Seeger could not resist singing for friends. According to an item published in *Sing Out!* (November 1972), 1973 was to be the year; yet on April 15 Seeger sang at Paul Robeson's 75th birthday; his operations took place at the beginning of 1974, and Seeger's first commercial booking of the year was probably on March 10, 1974, at the Opera House in Chicago. Seeger was apparently out of sorts, for the reviews of the concert were lukewarm.

305   "SONGS WON'T SAVE THE PLANET": Foreword, *Survival Songbook* (San Francisco: Sierra Club, 1971).

305   "IF RULERS REALLY KNEW": Quoted in *Outside,* May 1979.

Epilogue

Author's interviews with Irving Younger, May 24, 1980; Pete Seeger (with Toshi Seeger), December 14, 15, 1977; August 8, 1978; Jimmy Collier, July 10, 1978; Mike Cooney, May 30, 1978.

Epilogue (cont.)

page   *reference*

308   "IRVING YOUNGER": Pete and Toshi Seeger, December 14, 1977; Younger does not recall this incident.

308   "A FORMER CRITIC": Jon Pankake, "Pete's Children: The American Folk Song Revival, Pro and Con," in De Turk and Poulin, editors, *The American Folk Scene* (New York: Dell, 1967).

309   "INSTEAD OF PLAYING CHORDS": An example of this is a superb series of recordings made after the *Clearwater*'s maiden voyage by the musician crew. Seeger can be heard on a banjo solo on "Shenandoah," playing slowly and evenly a passage of 39 notes, more like a classical guitar than a five-string banjo.

311   "HE TOLD AN AUDIENCE IN PROVIDENCE": Providence *Evening Bulletin*, September 6, 1961; "How Can I Keep from Singing," by Doris Plenn, from *The Bells of Rhymney*.

Bibliography

This bibliography is divided into four sections: books and pamphlets by or with contributions by Pete Seeger; articles by Seeger; books that touch on his career; articles about Seeger. These last two sections are selected according to the sources for this book.

I. Books and pamphlets written, edited, or with contributions by Pete Seeger

Hard Hitting Songs for Hard Hit People. Originally compiled in 1940. Compiled by Alan Lomax. Notes on the songs by Woody Guthrie. Music transcribed and edited by Pete Seeger. New York: Oak, 1967. 368 pages. [Songbook]

The People's Songbook. Pete Seeger, associate editor. New York: Boni and Gaer, 1948. 128 pages. [Songbook]

How to Play the 5-String Banjo, third revised edition. Mimeographed edition, 1948. New York: Oak, 1962. 73 pages.

The Weavers Sing. With Ronnie Gilbert, Fred Hellerman, and Lee Hays. New York: Folkways, 1951. [Songbook] 48 pages.

The Carolers' Songbag. Pete Seeger, editor, with the Weavers. New York: Folkways, 1952. [Songbook] 40 pages.

"How to Make a Chalil." May 1955. 12 pages. Self-published (third edition, 1968).

The Folksinger's Guitar Guide, by Jerry Silverman. New York: Oak, 1967. Originally a booklet to accompany Seeger's instruction record, Folkways FI 8354, 1956.

"An Introductory Note About the Man and His Music," in Woody Guthrie. *California to the New York Island*. Pete Seeger, music editor. New York: Oak, 1958. 2 pages.

"Foreword." Reprints from *People's Songs Bulletin*. New York: Oak, 1961. 1 page.

American Favorite Ballads. New York: Oak, 1961. 94 pages. [Songbook]

The Goofing Off Suite. New York: Hargail, 1961. [Songbook]

The Steel Drums of Kim Loy Wong. New York: Oak, 1961. 40 pages.

"Leadbelly," in Moses Asch and Alan Lomax, editors. *The Leadbelly Songbook*. New York: Oak, 1962. 1 page.

Woody Guthrie Folk Songs. Edited and compiled by Pete Seeger. New York: Ludlow Music, 1963. 264 pages. [Songbook]

The Bells of Rhymney. New York: Oak, 1964. 128 pages. [Songbook]

Bits and Pieces. New York: Ludlow Music, 1965. 48 pages [Songbook]

The Twelve-String Guitar as Played by Leadbelly. With Julius Lester. New York: Oak, 1965. 80 pages.

Pete Seeger Singers Popular American Songs. Compiled by Grigory Schneerson. Translated into
   Russian by Samuel Bolotin and Tatiana Sikorskaya. Moscow: State Publishers Music,
   1965. 32 pages. [Songbook]
We Make Our Tomorrow. Beacon, New York: Glasco Press, 1965. Drawings by Anton Refreiger,
   verse selected by Pete Seeger. 22 pages.
Songs for Peace. Jeff Marris, Cliff Metzler, Pete Seeger, editors. Introduction by Seeger *et al.*
   New York: Oak, 1966. 112 pages. [Songbook]
"Introduction," in Jim Morse and Nancy Mathews, editors. *The Survival Songbook.* San Fran-
   cisco: Sierra Club, 1967. 1 page.
Oh Had I A Golden Thread. New York: Sanga Music, 1968. [Songbook]
"Foreword," in Don McLean, editor. *Songs and Sketches of the First Clearwater Crew.* New York:
   North River Press, 1970. 1 page.
Pete Seeger on Record. New York: Ludlow Music, 1971. 40 pages. [Songbook]
The Incompleat Folksinger. Edited by Jo Metcalf Schwartz New York: Simon and Schuster, 1972.
   596 pages.
Henscratches and Flyspecks: How to read melodies from songbooks in twelve confusing lessons. New
   York: Berkley Books, 1973. 256 pages.
Foolish Frog. With Charles Seeger. New York: Macmillan, 1973. Unpaged.
"Introduction," in Ed Robbins, *Woody Guthrie and Me.* Berkeley, Cal.: Lancaster House, 1979. 2
   pages.
"Introduction," in Ed. Renehan, editor. *The Clearwater Songbook.* New York: G. Schirmer, 1980.
   1 page.

II. Magazine and newspaper articles, reviews, and album notes by Pete Seeger

"Pete and His Banjo Meet Some Fine Mountain Folks." *Southern News Almanac.* Birmingham,
   Ala., October 1940. 1 page.
People's Songs Bulletin. January 1946–April 1949. Pete Seeger, principal editor. (Unsigned
   articles, letters, and notes, published monthly.)
"People's Songs and Singers." *New Masses,* Vol. 44, July 16, 1946, pp. 2–3, 9.
"A Menace to the Nation's Songs" (letter to the editor). *Daily Worker,* May 31, 1948. 1 page.
"Library of People's Music." *Sing Out!* July 1950, pp. 6–7, 16.
Review of *Ngoma: An Introduction to Music for Southern Africans* (by Hugh Tracey). *Music Library
   Association Notes,* Vol. 11, No. 2, March 1951. p. 314.
"The Weavers" (record review). *Sing Out!* September 1951, p. 16. By "Nathan Charliere"
   (pseudonym).
"A Contemporary Ballad-Maker in the Hudson Valley." *New York Folklore Quarterly,* Vol. 10,
   No. 2, Summer 1954, pp. 133–34.
"Johnny Appleseed, Jr." Column of 100—200 articles, in *Sing Out!,* beginning with Vol. 4, No.
   7, Fall 1954.
"The Coal Creek Rebellion." *Sing Out!,* Summer 1955, pp. 19–20.
"Introductory Notes." Album notes to *Bantu Choral Folk Songs.* Folkways Records, 1955. 6
   pages.
Testimony before HUAC, 1955, reprinted in Eric Bentley, editor. *Thirty Years of Treason.* New
   York: Viking, 1971, pp. 686–700.
"Introduction." Album notes to *Negro Prison Camp Work Songs.* Ethnic Folkways Library, FE
   4475, 1956. 2 pages.
"Introductory Notes on Community Singing." Albumin notes to *With Voices We Sing.* Folkways
   Records, FA 2452, 1956. 2 pages.
Review of *Sea Songs* (by Burl Ives). *Sing Out!,* Winter 1957, p. 21.
"The Steel Drum: A New Folk Instrument." *Journal of American Folklore,* Vol. 71, No. 279,
   January–March, 1958, pp. 52–57.

"Too Many People Listen to Me—and Not to the People I Learned From."*Caravan*, May 1958, pp. 13–14.

"Notes on Background of Songs." Album notes to *Pete Seeger at Carnegie Hall with Sonny Terry.* Folkways Records FA 2412, 1958.

"Play Parties." Album notes to *American Play Parties.* Folkways Records, FC 7604, 1959.

"On Singing Folk Songs in a Night Club." Album notes to *Pete Seeger at the Village Gate,* with Memphis Slim and Willie Dixon. Folkways Records, FA 2450, 1960. 1 page.

"Statement to the Court" (contempt of Congress case). *Sing Out!,* Summer 1961, pp. 10–11.

"Letter from the Editors," *Sing Out!,* April–May 1962, pp. 59–60.

"The Folk Process in Albany, Ga." *Sing Out!,* October–November 1962, 1 page.

"The American Folk Music Revival." in H. Grafman and B. T. Manning. *Folk Music U.S.A.* New York: Citadel Press, 1962, pp. 8–15.

"Remembering Woody." *Mainstream,* Vol. 16, No. 8, August 1963, pp. 27–33.

"The Integration Battle." *Broadside,* No. 30, August 1963, 1 page.

"In My Opinion." *Seventeen,* November 1963, p. 148.

"Pete Seeger's Farewell." *Hootenanny,* Vol. 1, No. 1, December 1963, pp. 15, 73–74.

"The Country Washboard Band." Album Notes to *Washboard Band Country Dance Music.* Folkways Records, FA 2201, 1963. 1 page.

"The Copyright Hassle." *Sing Out!,* December–January 1963–64, 2 pages.

"The Guitar Improvisations of Mwenda Jean Bosco." *Sing Out!,* April 1964, 2 pages.

"Footloose in Asia and Africa." *Hootenanny,* Vol. 1, No. 3, May 1964, pp. 20–21.

"Woody Guthrie—Some Reminiscences." *Sing Out!,* July 1964, 4 pages.

"Long Live Plagiarism."*Broadside,* No. 49, Aug. 1964 pp. 1–2. (Followed by a letter to the editor of Broadside, October 20, 1964.), 1 page.

"Some Songs of the Selma Marchers." *Broadside,* No. 57, April 1965, 3 pages.

"Record Review: Pete Seeger." *Sing Out!,* March 1965. pp. 85–87.

"Whatever Happened to Singing in the Union?" *Sing Out!,* May 1965, pp. 28–31.

"How Can People Talk to Each Other?" (letter to the editor). *American Dialog,* Vol. 2, No. 2, May–June 1965, p. 31.

"Folk Songs and the Top 40." *Sing Out!,* February–March 1966, pp. 13–14.

"On Protest Songs." Album notes to *Dangerous Songs!?.* Columbia Records, CS 9303/CL 2503, 1966. 1 page.

"Why Folk Music?" In David A. De Turk and A. Poulin, Jr.. *The American Folk Scene: Dimensions of the Folksong Revival.* New York: Dell, 1967, pp. 44–48.

"So Long Woody, It's Been Good to Know Ya." *Life,* November 10, 1967, p. 8.

"Sleep-time Stories and Songs." Album notes to *Abiyoyo and Other Songs for Children.* Folkways, FT 1500, FTS 31500, 1967. 1 page.

"Vietnam" (letter to the editor). *Harvard Alumni Bulletin,* March 16, 1968, p. 1.

"This Paleface Does a Double Take (Confessions of an American History Buff)." *Daily World,* July 4, 1968. 1 page.

"Let the Children Paint the Walls." *Daily World,* July 17, 1968, pp. 4–7.

"Lebanon/Israel: The Coin Has Two Sides." *Sing Out!,* June–July 1968, p. 37.

"TV: A Variety of Cream Puffs." *Daily Variety,* 35th Anniversary Edition, 1968. 1 page.

"Your Own Thing."*Seventeen,* August 1968, p. 92.

Interview with Pete Seeger at Ford Hall Forum. *PS Sings and Answers Questions.* Broadside Records, BRS 502, 1968. 8 pages.

"Woody Guthrie, Songwriter." *Ramparts,* November 30, 1968, pp. 29–33. (Excerpt from *The Incompleat Folksinger*).

"Parable of Uncle Sam." Album notes to *Young vs. Old.* Columbia, CS 9873, 1968. 1 page.

"The Air Belongs to Everyone." *Harvard Alumni Bulletin,* April 28, 1969, pp. 53–57.

"To Save the Dying Hudson: Pete Seeger's Voyage." *Look,* August 26, 1969, pp. 63–66.

"Sequoia: The Story of the Talking Leaves." *Sing Out!*, September–October 1969, pp. 9–10, 12–13.

"This Land is Your Land." *Village Voice*, July 1, 1971, p. 5.

"The World Flood of U.S. Pop Music Culture." *American Dialog*, Vol. 6, No. 1, Autumn 1971, pp. 5–6, 36–38.

"For Art's Sake." *New York Times*, December 1, 1971, Op-ed page.

"Hanoi Diary." *Eastern Horizon*, Vol. 11, No. 4, 1972, pp. 26–32.

"Pete's Pie." *Win*, December 15, 1972, p. 20.

"Strumming Banjo in North Vietnam," *Saturday Review*, May 13, 1973, pp. 28–32.

"Teach-In: Tuning the Steel Drums." *Sing Out!*, July–August 1973, pp. 23–25.

Untitled (on Walter Lowenfels). *Small Press Review*, Vol. 6, No. 2, November 1974. 1 page.

"Songs of Labor and the American People." *Sing Out!*, January 1976, p. 1.

Review of *The Poverty of Power* by Barry Commoner. *New York Daily World Magazine*, May 29, 1976, pp. 4–9.

"How the *Clearwater* Got Started." *North River Navigator*, 6-part series, Summer 1975–April 1976. 10 pages.

"A Thumbnail History of *Sing Out!*," *Sing Out!*, May 1978, p. 33.

"Why We Must Save the Hudson." *Parade (Washington Post)*, November 26, 1978, pp. 5–7.

"Charles Seeger, A Man of Music." *Sing Out!*, May 1979, pp. 18–19.

"Singalong." Album notes to *Pete Seeger Demonstration Concert*, Folkways Records, FXM 6055, 1980.

"Want a *Clearwater* of Your Own?" *Clearwater Navigator*, April 1980, 2 pages.

Review of *Joe Scott: Woodsman-Songmaker* by Sandy Ives. *Ethnomusicology*, Vol. 24, No. 2, September 1980, 3 pages.

III. Selected books with references to Pete Seeger

Baggelaar, Kristin, and Milton, Donald. *Folk Music: More Than a Song*. New York: Thomas Crowell, 1976, pp. 344–48.

Brand, Oscar. *The Ballad Mongers*. New York: Minerva Press/Funk & Wagnalls, 1962.

Denisoff, R. Serge. *Great Day Coming*. Urbana, Ill.: University of Illinois Press, 1971.

Dunson, Josh. *Freedom in the Air*. New York: International Publishers, 1965.

Elliot, Marc. *Death of a Rebel*. New York: Anchor/Doubleday, 1979.

Klein, Joe. *Woody Guthrie*. New York: Knopf, 1980.

Lawless, Ray. *Folksingers and Folksongs in America*. New York: Duell, Sloan and Pearce, 1960, pp. 210–12.

Marsh, Dave, and John Swenson. *Rolling Stone Record Guide*. New York: Rolling Stone/Random House, 1979, pp. 346–47.

Noebel, David. *The Marxist Minstrels*. Tulsa, Okla.: American Christian College Press, 1974. Originally issued as *Rhythm, Riot, and Revolution*, 1966.

Reuss, Richard. *American Folklore and Left-wing Politics: 1927–1957*. Unpublished Ph.D. dissertation, University of Indiana, 1971.

Roxon, Lillian. *Rock Encyclopedia*. New York: Workman/Grosset & Dunlap, 1971, pp. 442–44.

Scaduto, Anthony. *Bob Dylan*. New York: Grosset & Dunlap, 1971.

Seeger, Charles. *Reminiscences of an American Musicologist*. Los Angeles: UCLA Oral History Project, 1972.

Vassal, Jacques. *Electric Children* New York: Taplinger Press, 1976.

IV. Selected articles on Pete Seeger

Allen, Henry. *Washington Post*. "Pete Seeger After All These Years". August 17, 1980.

Auletta, Ken. "None Dare Call It Liberty." Syracuse University *Daily Orange*, November 18, 1964.

Barden, J.C. "Pete Seeger." *High Fidelity,* January 1963.

Barthel, Joan. "American Minstrel's Song of Success" *New York Times,* January 23, 1966.

Bell, Carol. "Pete Seeger: An Ideal to Cling to." *Denver Post,* August 15, 1974.

Bogdanovich, Peter. "Notes." *Story Songs,* Columbia Records CL 1668, April 1961.

Bracker, Milton. "Six More Witnesses Back Red Inquiry." *New York Times,* August 19, 1955.

Callaghan, J. Dorsey. "Folk Singer Boasts Revival-tent Fervor." *Detroit Free Press,* April 11, 1955.

Churchill, Michael. Series on Pete Seeger's Contempt of Congress trial. *Harvard Crimson,* March 28, 29, 30, April 14, 1961.

Cory, Christopher. "A Worried Man Sings." *Providence Bulletin,* September 6, 1961.

Cowan, Paul. "Non-confrontation in Beacon New York." *Village Voice,* December 16, 1965.

Dallos, Robert. "Pete Seeger Gets New Chance on TV." *New York Times,* August 25, 1967.

Friesen, Gordon. Series on life with the Almanac Singers. *Broadside* (New York), June 1, 30, November 1, 1962.

Gleason, Ralph. "Pete Seeger." *San Francisco Chronicle,* May 7, 1963.

Gold, Mike. "A Paean to Pete Seeger." *Daily Worker,* February 8, 1958.

Gould, Jack. "TV: Pete Seeger Makes Belated Debut." *New York Times,* Nov. 15, 1965.

———. "The Little 'List' Still Exists." *New York Times,* April 2, 1967.

Greenfield, Jeff. "The Party." *National Lampoon,* March 1976.

Hentoff, Nat. "That Ole McCarthy Hoot." *Village Voice,* March 14, 1963.

Hindustan Times. "Seeger's Folk Songs Charm." December 9, 1963.

Kempton, Murray. "The Minstrel Boy." *New York Post,* March 29, 1961.

Kwitny, John. "Timeless Troubador." *Wall Street Journal,* June 12, 1973.

Labor's Daily. "Pete Seeger Owes Much to Trade Union Members." December 14, 1957.

Leonard, John. "From Pete Seeger to the Sex Pistols." *New York Times,* December 6, 1978.

Life. "Minstrel With A Mission." October 9, 1964.

Little, Paul. "Seeger Helps Restore American Folk Heritage." *Downbeat,* May 30, 1956.

Lyon, Peter. "The Ballad of Pete Seeger." In David De Turk and A. Poulin, editors. *The American Folk Scene.* New York: Dell, 1967.

Marine, Gene. "Guerrilla Minstrel." *Rolling Stone,* April 13, 1972.

Mayer, Steve. "Seeger." *Oberlin Review,* March 13, 1969.

McCarthy, Colman. "Pete Seeger Sings for the Folks." *Arizona Star,* June 19, 1978.

Muns, Monty. "Pete Seeger: An Appreciation." *Sing Out!,* February 1961.

Nelson, Paul. "Newport Folk Festival, 1965." *Sing Out!,* November 1965.

New Yorker. "Pete Seeger at Vanguard." December 21, 1946.

New York Post. "Dangerous Minstrel Nabbed Here" (editorial). March 31, 1961.

———. "The Return to Reason" (editorial). May 20, 1962.

New York Times. "Seeger Explains Stand at Inquiry." March 15, 1961.

———. Coverage of Contempt to Congress trial, March 28, 29, 30, 1961.

———. "Seeger Song in Moscow is Anti-U.S.." October 25, 1965.

———. "A Timeless Seeger Gives Concert Here." February 28, 1970.

———. "Planned Songfest for Balmville Tree has Political Overtones." June 14, 1975. (These articles selected from 97 published 1946–.)

New York World Telegram. "OWI [Almanac] Singers Change Their Political Tune." January 4, 1943.

Palmer, Robert. "Seeger Sings of Fun and Politics." *New York Times,* August 16, 1977.

Pankake, Jon. "P-for-Protest" (with Paul Nelson). In David De Turk and A. Poulin, editors. *The American Folk Scene.* New York: Dell, 1967.

———. "Pete's Children: The American Folksong Revival, Pro and Con." Reprinted in *The American Folk Scene.*

Phine, Ken. "Pete's eager." *Sing* (London), February 1962.

Pittsburgh Press. "WQED Cancels Leftist Singer." April 13, 1962.

Ranzal, Edward. "Seeger Conviction for Contempt Of Congress Voided in Appeal." *New York Times,* May 19, 1962.

Rosenberg, Ed. "Pete Seeger: People's Artist." *Daily Worker,* June 19, 1949.

Russell, Don. "They Sing the Hard-Hitting Songs that Belong to America's Workers." *People's World,* August 8, 1941.

Schaef, A. Finley. "The TV Blacklist—A Case History." *Concern,* December 1, 1963.

Schanberg, Sydney. "L.I. School's Ban on Seeger Concert Ruled Unconstitutional." *New York Times,* July 8, 1966.

Seeger, Charles. "Grassroots For American Composers." *Modern Music,* March 1939.

Silber, Irwin. "The Weavers—New 'Find' of the Hit Parade." *Sing Out!,* February, 1951.

———. "Pete Seeger, Voice of Our Democratic Heritage." *Sing Out!,* May 1954.

———. "The Incompleat Folksinger." *The Guardian,* August 8, 1973.

Siminoff, Roger, and Doc Kissin. "Workin' At the Other End." *Pickin',* May 1976.

Smucker, Tom. "If Every Concert Were a Benefit, Pete Seeger Would be Frank Sinatra." *Village Voice,* October 18, 1976.

Soviet Life. "Pete Seeger's Tour—Music Good for Flu." April 1966.

Variety. "The Weavers." June 28, 1950.

———. "Catholic War Vets and N.Y. Journal Force Weavers' Cancellation." October 10, 1951.

———. "Weavers Deny Commie Link." March 5, 1952.

Vellela, Tony. "Pete Seeger vs. Pollution." *Christian Science Monitor,* November 3, 1975.

Discography

This nearly complete listing of Pete Seeger's recordings on commercial discs is arranged chronologically, in approximate order of the original recordings. The discography is divided into albums, extended-play discs, singles, foreign releases, anthologies, private pressing, and additional materials.

SAMPLE ENTRY

TITLE (other artists) songs	release data (recording data) [re-release data]	publisher ID# Release and recording information.
Albums		
SONGS FOR JOHN DOE (The Almanac Singers: Bess Lomax, Lee Hays, Mill Lampell, Josh White, Peter Hawes; Pete Seeger accompanies and harmonizes throughout. The Strange Death of John Doe Ballad of October 16 C for Conscription Washington Breakdown Liza Jane Plow Under Billy Boy	June 1941 (March 1941)	Keynote 102 (listed as Almanac Records)
TALKING UNION AND OTHER UNION SONGS (The Almanac Singers: Lee Hays, Mill Lampell, Bess Lomax, Pete Hawes; Pete Seeger) Get Thee Behind Me The Union Maid All I Want Talking Union The Union Train	1941 (May 1941) [1955]	Folkways 5285 originally released as Keynote 106; in 1955, the original 78s were paired with seven union songs arranged and performed by Pete Seeger and chorus.

Which Side Are You On?
(with the Song Swappers, an
eight-voice chorus including Mary
Travers and Erik Darling).
Recorded in 1955.

We Shall Not Be Moved
Roll the Union On
Casey Jones
Miner's Lifeguard
Solidarity Forever
You've Got to Go Down and Join
  the Union
Hold The Fort

THE SOIL AND THE SEA

(The Almanac Singers: Woody
Guthrie, Lee Hays, and Peter
Hawes; Seeger accompanies on
banjo and harmonizes
throughout.)

1941*
(June 1941)
[1964]

Fontana Mainstream
TL 5299
Originally issued on
General Records and on
Commodore BA 20, 21,
*Sod Buster Ballads, Deep Sea
Shanties.*

The Golden Vanity
Blow Ye Wind, Heigh-Ho
Blow the Man Down
Hard, Ain't It Hard
The Dodger Song
State of Arkansas
Ground Hog
The Coast of High Barbary
Away Rio
Haul Away Joe
I Ride an Old Paint
House of the Rising Sun

DEAR MR. PRESIDENT

(The Almanac Singers: Peter
Hawes, Sis Cunningham, Arthur
Stern, Bess Lomax, Mill Lampell,
Woody Guthrie)

May 1942
(February 1942)

Keynote III

Dear Mr. President
Round and Round Hitler's Grave
Deliver the Goods
Beltline Girl
Reuben James
Side by Side

SONGS OF THE CIVIL WAR—VOL. I

(with Tom Glazer, Baldwin Hawes,
and Bess Hawes)

1943
(August 1942)
[1961]

Folkways 5436
(also Stinson SLP 52)
Originally released as Asch
330, *Songs of the Lincoln
Brigade*

Jarama Valley
Cookhouse
The Young Man from Alcala
Quartermaster Song

* Throughout the Discography, the reader should refer to opening page for column heads.

El Quinto Regimento
Si Me Quieres Escribir

LONSOME TRAIN (with Burl Ives, Earl Robinson, and Raymond Johnson; Pete Seeger sings throughout the Cantata.)	1943	Decca DL-5054 10″
AMERICA'S FAVORITE SONGS (with Tom Glazer, Bess Lomax Hawes, Baldwin Hawes) Down in the Valley Casey Jones Go Tell Aunt Nancy Streets of Laredo Buffalo Gals Careless Love	1943–44 [1967]	Disc 607 Rereleased, in part, on *Asch Recordings* *1939–1945, Volume 2,* AA3
SONGS FOR VICTORY (The Union Boys: Tom Glazer, Pete Seeger [banjo and vocal], Burl Ives, Josh White) Hold the Fort We Shall Not Be Moved UAW–CIO Hold On Dollar Bill Jim Crow	1943–44	Stinson/Asch 346
FOLKSAY I Cindy Muleskinner Blues (with Woody Guthrie, Cisco Houston)	1943 [1963]	Asch 322 Rereleased on 3 LPs, Stinson SLPX 5, 9, 12.
FOLKSAY III Casey Jones		
FOLKSAY IV Cumberland Mountain Bear Chase T for Texas		
FOLKSAY V Teeroo, Teeroo		
FOLKSAY VI Young Man Who Wouldn't Hoe Corn		
AMERICAN BANJO Old Woman and the Devil Cindy Devilish Mary Reilly	1944 (June 19, 1944)	Asch 352

Erie Canal
Hard on the Farm

PETE! FOLK SONGS AND BALLADS	[1963]	Stinson SLP 90
Four Recorder Melodies		Rerelease of the above songs with four additional cuts
Money Is King		
Long John		
Erie Canal		

LONESOME VALLEY	1951	Folkways FA 2010
(with Tom Glazer, Bess Lomax, Baldwin Hawes)	(recorded 1943–46)	10″

Black-Eyed Suzie
Down in the Valley
Arthritis Blues
Polly Wolly Doodle All Day
(with Lee Hays, Dock Reese, Holly
Wood, Bess Lomax, Butch Hawes)

Lonesome Traveller

SONGS FOR POLITICAL ACTION	1946	CIO—Political Action Committee (PAC)
(with Tom Glazer, Lee Hays, and Hallie Faulk)		

Voting Union
Get Out the Vote
Dollar Bill
Oh, What Congress Done to Me
Four PAC Nursery Rhymes
DDT
Fare Ye Well, Bad Congressman
No, No, No Discrimination
Oh, Voter

BAWDY BALLADS AND REAL SAD SONGS	1946–47	Charter Records
(with Betty Sanders)		

Molly Brannigan
Young to Marry
Hey Donald
The Soldier Laddy
Wedding and Bedding
In the Evening
East Virginia

ROLL THE UNION ON	1947	Asch 370
(with Holly Wood, Lee Hays, Baldwin Hawes, Dock Reese, Lou Kleinman, Bess Lomax Hawes)	(December 10, 1946)	

Listen Mr. Bilbo
This Old World
Roll the Union On
Put It on the Ground
I'm Looking for a Home
The Rankin Tree

THE WEAVERS	1949	Charter—2 78s
(Pete Seeger, Lee Hays, Fred Hellerman, Ronnie Gilbert)		

Wasn't That a Time
Dig My Grave
Love Song Blues
Freight Train Blues

DARLING COREY	1950	FA 2003 10″

John Riley
Devilish Mary
East Virginia Blues
Cripple Creek
Penny's Farm
Danville Girl
Darling Corey
Risselty, Rosselty
Ida Red
Old Joe Clark
My Blue-Eyed Girl
Come All Fair Maids
Jerry's Rocks
Skillet Greasy
I Had a Wife

WE SING—VOL. I	(1950)	MDH records
		A "bootleg" album
		recorded live in concert at
		Reed College

Midnight Special
Two Irish Melodies
Kisses Sweeter Than Wine
Viva La Quince Brigada
Going Down the Road
Strangest Dream
Oleanna
Delia's Gone
All the Pretty Horses
Hey Zhankoye
All My Trials
Roll Down the Line
Wimoweh

SONGS TO GROW ON—VOL. 2	1951	Folkways FC 7020
		10″

By'm By
All the Pretty Little Horses
The Mailboat
Go Tell Aunt Rhody

SONGS TO GROW ON—VOL. 3	1951	Folkways FC 7027
		10″
		Originally issued on Disc

Young Man Who Wouldn't Hoe
  Corn

FOLK SONGS OF AMERICA AND OTHER LANDS	1951 (1950–51)	Decca DL-5285 10″
(The Weavers: Pete Seeger, Lee Hays, Ronnie Gilbert, Fred Hellerman, with Gordon Jenkins and his orchestra)		

Tzena, Tzena
The Frozen Logger
I Know Where I'm Going
Follow the Drinking Gourd
Around the World
Darling Corey
Hush Little Baby
Easy Rider Blues

BEST OF THE WEAVERS	1959	DL 8893/DXS 7173
Rock Island Line	(1950–53)	Rereleases from the above
Along the Colorado Trail		sessions, including
The Roving Kind		additional songs; also
Lonesome Traveller		rereleased as DL8909,
Down in the Valley		*Folksongs around the World,*
Kisses Sweeter Than Wine		DL4004, *The Early Fifties,*
So Long, It's Been Good to Know		DL7-5169, *The Weavers'*
Yuh		*Greatest Hits* (this record is
One for the Little Bitty Baby		a compilation of outtakes
The John B		and material originally
Goodnight, Irene		rejected); DL 4485, *All Time*
Old Paint		*Hootenanny;* and *The*
Sylvie		*Weavers' Gold.*
Bay of Mexico		
Wimoweh		
On Top of Old Smoky		
The Midnight Special		
Suliram		

WE WISH YOU A MERRY CHRISTMAS	1952	Decca DL5373 10″
(The Weavers)		

We Wish You a Merry Christmas
One for the Little Bitty Baby
The Seven Blessings of Mary
Twelve Days of Christmas
Go Tell It on the Mountain
Poor Little Jesus
Burgundian Carol
God Rest Ye Merry Gentlemen
Lullo, Lullay
It's Almost Day

AMERICAN FOLKSONGS FOR CHILDREN	1953	FTS 31501/FC 7601
Jim Along Josie		Originally issued on
There Was a Man and He Was		Folkways EPC 1–3,
Mad		extended play (45 rpm)
Clap Your Hands		records
She'll Be Coming Round the		
Mountain		
All Around the Kitchen		
Billy Barlow		
Bought Me a Cat		
Jim Crack Corn		
Train Is A-Coming		
This Old Man		
Frog Went A-Courtin'		

A PETE SEEGER CONCERT	1953–54	Stinson SLP 57
The House Carpenter		Reissued on Everest
I Had a Wife		Records FS 201; Archive
Oh, Hard Is the Fortune		of Folksong; Tradition
You Can Give Marriage a Whirl		2107
Greenland Fisheries		
Winsboro Cotton Mill Blues		
Paddy Works on the Railway		
Go Down Old Hannah		
The Road to Eilat		
Ariran		
Die Gedanken Sind Frei		
Bayeza		
Kisses Sweeter Than Wine		
In the Evening		
PETE SEEGER SAMPLER	1954	FA2043 10″
I'm On My Way		
Hey, Lolly, Lolly Lo		
Beans, Bacon, and Gravy		
Suliram		
Joshua Fit the Battle of Jericho		
Johnny Comes Down to Hilo		
Puttin' on the Style		
Deep Blue Sea		
El Día de Tu Santo		
Dig My Grave		
Delia's Gone		
Italian Christmas Song		
SING OUT! HOOTENANNY	1959	Folkways FN2513
(with "The Hooteneers")		Recorded live at People's
		Artists Hootenannys
All I Want Is Union		
Put My Name Down		
Talking Un-American Blues		
In Contempt		
Gray Goose		
Come All You Fair and Tender Ladies		
Raise a Ruckus Tonight		
I've Got a Right		
Jefferson and Liberty		
Another Man Done Gone		
Pie In The Sky		
Boll Weevil		
Popular Wobbly		
John Henry		
We Shall Overcome		
GERMAN FOLK SONGS	1954	Folkways FW6843
(Seeger accompanies Martha Schlamme on banjo and recorder throughout.)		10″
Wenne Alle Bruennelein Fliessen		
Da Dribn Am Bergal		
Rosestock, Holderbluet		
Dat Du Min Leeysten Bist		

Es Burebuebli
Muss I Denn
Ufm Berge, Da Geht Der Wind
Bei Mondenschein
Der Schwere Traum
Die Gedanken Sind Frei

GOOFING-OFF SUITE	1954	Folkways FA2045

Theme
Cindy
Blue Skies
The Girl I Left Behind Me
Jesu, Joy of Man's Desiring
Duet from Beethoven's 7th
   Symphony
Chorale from Beethoven's 9th
   Symphony
Russian Folk Themes and Yodel
Anitra's Dance (Grieg) and
   Brandy Leave Me Alone
Theme
Time's A-Getting Hard
Barrel of Money Blues
Sally My Dear
Oh! Liza, Poor Gal
Sally Ann
Woody's Rag

FRONTIER BALLADS—VOL. 1	1954	Folkways FA2175

Fare You Well, Polly
No Irish Need Apply
Johnny Gray
Greer County Bachelor
Cowboy Yodel
The Trail to Mexico
Joe Bowers
Wake Up Jacob
Cumberland Gap
Erie Canal
Blow the Man Down
Ox Driver's Song
The Texan Boys
Sioux Indians

10″
Some cuts rereleased on
*American History in Ballad
and Song* FH5801, 5802

FONTIER BALLADS—VOL. II	1954	Folkways FA2176

Ground Hog
Blue Mountain Lake
Paddy Works on the Railway
Young Man Who Wouldn't Hoe
   Corn
Joe Clark
My Sweetheart in the Mines
Holler
Arkansas Traveller
When I Was Single
Wondrous Love
Play Party

10″
Some cuts rereleased on
*American History in Ballad
and Song,* FH5801

Whiskey Rye Whiskey
The Wayfaring Stranger

BIRDS, BEASTS, BUGS AND LITTLE FISHES	1954	Folkways FC7610

Fly Through My Window
I Had A Rooster
Come All You Bold Sailormen
Old Grey Mule
Alligator, Hedgehog
Frog Went A-Courtin'
Raccoon's Got a Bushy Tail
I Know an Old Lady
Ground Hog
Mister Rabbit
Grey Goose
Teency Weency Spider
The Old Hen
Skip To My Lou
My Little Kitty

HOOTENANNY TONIGHT!	1959	Folkways FN2511
	(1954)	

Cowboy's Getting Up Holler
Muleskinner Blues
(with Jerry Silverman, Sonny Terry)

Talking Union
Wimoweh

America the Beautiful
Dark As a Dungeon

(with Bob DeCormier)

HOW TO PLAY THE FIVE STRING BANJO	1954	Folkways FI8203

THE FOLKSINGER'S GUITAR GUIDE	1955	Folkways FQ8354

BANTU CHORAL FOLK SONGS	1955	Folkways FW6912 10″

(with chorus)

Babevuya
Isileyi Sam
Manamolela
Abiyoyo
Bayeza
Hey, Tswana
Somagwaza
Bayandoyika
Hey, Motsoala
Here's to the Couple

FOLKSONGS OF FOUR CONTINENTS	1955	Folkways FW6911 10″

Bring Me a Little Water, Silvy
Ah, Si Mon Moine
Bimini Gal

The Greenland Whalers
Mi Caballo Blanco
Oleanna
Banuway Yo
Ragupati Ragava Rajah Ram
Hey, Daroma

CAMP SONGS	1959	Folkways/Scholastic
(with Erik Darling and the Song Swappers)	(1955)	Records SC7628

Children of the Lord
Bingo Was His Name
Daughter Will You Marry
If All the Rain Drops
The Younger Generation
John Jacob Jinglehaimer Schmitt
I Was Born 10,000 Years Ago
Kevin Barry
Putting On the Style

THE WEAVERS AT CARNEGIE HALL	(December, 1955) [1957]	VSD6533

(with the Weavers: Ronnie Gilbert, Lee Hays, Fred Hellerman)

Darling Corey
Kisses Sweeter Than Wine
Pay Me My Money Down
Greensleeves
Rock Island Line
Around the World (Flop-Eared Mule, Bright Shines the Moon, Artza Alinu, Hey Lily, Hey Lily Lo)

Wimoweh
Venga Jaleo
Suliram
Sholom Chaverim
Lonesome Traveller
I Know Where I'm Going
Woody's Rag and 900 Miles
Sixteen Tons
Follow the Drinking Gourd
When the Saints Go Marching In
I've Got a Home in That Rock
Hush Little Baby
Go Where I Send Thee
Goodnight, Irene

COUNTRY DANCE MUSIC WASHBOARD BAND	1956	Folkways FA2201 10″

(with William Cook, Sonny Terry, Brownie McGhee, Frank Robinson)

Cindy
Bottle Up and Go
Cripple Creek

John Henry
Old Joe Clark
Skip to My Lou
Green Corn

WITH VOICES TOGETHER WE SING	1956	Folkways FA2452

Deep Blue Sea
Risselty, Rosselty
Equinoxial
Oleanna
Chanukah
What Month Was Jesus Born
"Davy Crockett" parody
Que Bonita Bandera
Streets of Loredo
Brandy Leave Me Alone
Didn't Old John
Michael, Row the Boat Ashore
Senzenia
Wimoweh
Wasn't That a Time

AMERICAN INDUSTRIAL BALLADS	1956	Folkways FH5251

Peg and Awl
The Blind Fiddler
Buffalo Skinners
Eight Hour Day
Hard Times in the Mill
Roll Down the Line
Hayseed Like Me
The Farmer Is the Man
Come All You Hardy Miners
He Lies in the American Land
Casey Jones
Let Them Wear Their Watches
   Fine
Cotton Mill Colic
Seven Cent Cotton and Forty Cent
   Meat
Mill Mother's Lament
Fare Ye Well Old Ely Branch
Beans, Bacon, and Gravy
The Death of Harry Simms
Winnsboro Cotton Mill Blues
Ballad of Barney Graham
My Children Are Seven in
   Number
Raggedy
Pittsburgh Town
Sixty Per Cent

LOVE SONGS FOR FRIENDS AND FOES	1956	Folkways FA2453

Open the Door Softly
The Trip We Took over the
   Mountain

She Moved Through the Fair
Sally My Dear
No Sir No
Stranger's Blues
I'm Gonna Walk and Talk with
  Jesus
Study War No More
Passing Through
Over the Hills
Kisses Sweeter Than Wine
Little Girl See Through My
  Window
Strangest Dream
Listen Mr. Bilbo
Autherine
The Hammer Song
River of My People
Black and White

STUDS TERKEL'S WEEKLY ALMANAC ON FOLK MUSIC BLUES ON WFMT WITH BIG BILL BROONZY AND PETE SEEGER	1956	Folkways FS3864

(Seeger sings and plays)

The Frog
Cripple Creek
Old Joe Clark
Leather Britches
Sally Ann
Little Margaret
Hush A-Bye
Jesu, Joy of Man's Desiring
You've Got to Walk That
  Lonesome Valley
You've Got to Stand in Judgement
The Midnight Special

BIG BILL BROONZY AND PETE SEEGER IN CONCERT	June 1965 (1956)	Verve Folkways FV9008

(Seeger sings and plays)

Midnight Special
Green Corn
Mrs. McGrath
Hillel Instrumental
Goofin' Off Suite

SING OUT WITH PETE!	August 1961 (1956–61)	Folkways FA2455

Oh, Mary Don't You Weep
Michael, Row the Boat Ashore
Mrs. McGrath
Deep Blue Sea
Que Bonita Bandera
Wimoweh
(with group, including: Memphis
Slim, Willie Dixon, Big Bill
Broonzy, Bill McAdoo)

Hold On
Freiheit

The Hammer Song
Down by the Riverside
Oh, Mary Dont't You Weep
I'm On My Way

THE WEAVERS ON TOUR	1958	Vanguard
(Pete Seeger, Lee Hays, Ronnie Gilbert, Fred Hellerman)	(1956–58)	VSD6537/VRS9013

Tzena, Tzena
On Top of Old Smoky
Drill, Ye Tarriers, Drill
Fi-Li-Mi-Oo-Re-Ay
Over the Hills
Clementine
The Frozen Logger
The Boll Weevil
Talking Blues
I Don't Want to Get Adjusted
So Long, It's Been Good to Know
    Yuh
Michael, Row the Boat Ashore
The Wreck of the "John B"
Two Brothers (The Blue and the
    Grey)
Ragaputi
Wasn't That a Time
Go Tell It on the Mountain

THE WEAVERS SONGBAG	October 1967	Vanguard SRV73001
(Pete Seeger, Ronnie Gilbert, Fred Hellerman, Lee Hays)	(1956–58)	Compiled from Vanguard's (VDS2030), *The Weavers at Home;* (VSD6537), *The Weavers on Tour;* and (VRS9043), *Travelling On with the Weavers.* A different selection from these records was released as (VSD15116), *The Weavers' Greatest Hits* in 1972.

Aweigh, Santy Ano
Wild Goose Grasses
Erie Canal
Aunt Rhody
Old Riley
Howard's Dead and Gone
Greenland Whale Fisheries
Gotta Travel On
Bury Me
I Never Will Marry
Joshua Fit the Battle of Jericho
This Land Is Your Land

THE WEAVERS AT HOME	August 1958	VRS9024/VSD2030
(Pete Seeger, Lee Hays, Ronnie Gilbert, Fred Hellerman)	(1956–58)	

This Land Is Your Land
Aweigh, Santy Ano
Wild Goose Grasses
Meet the Johnson Boys
Aunt Rhody

Tina
Eres Alta
Come Little Donkey
Kum Bachura
All Night Long
You Old Fool
Every Night
the Midnight Special
Bury Me
Almost Done
Empty Pocket Blues
Howard's Dead and Gone

AMERICAN BALLADS	1957	FA2319

Pretty Polly
The Three Butchers
John Henry
Jay Gould's Daughter
The Titanic Disaster
Fair Margaret and Sweet William
John Hardy
The Golden Vanity
Gypsy Davy
The Farmer's Curst Wife
Down in Carlisle
St. James Hospital
Jesse James
Barbara Allen

AMERICAN FAVORITE BALLADS	December 1957	FA2320

Down in the Valley
Mary Don't You Weep
The Blue Tail Fly
Yankee Doodle
Cielito Lindo
Buffalo Gals
Wabash Cannonball
So Long, It's Been Good to Know Yuh
Skip to My Lou
The Wagoner's Lad
The Wreck of the Old '97
Old Dan Tucker
I Ride an Old Paint
Frankie and Johnnie
On Top of Old Smoky
The Big Rock Candy Mountain
Home on the Range

JEWISH CHILDREN'S SONGS AND GAMES	1957	FC7224 10"

(Seeger accompanies Ruth Rubin on banjo)

Shpits-Boydim
Du Maydeleh Du Fines
Oksn

Ketselech
Homntashn
Beker Lid
A Genayveh
Michalku
Tonts, Tonts!

PETE SEEGER AND SONNY TERRY	July 1958	Folkways FA2412

Goofin' Off Theme
Kum Ba Yah
Twelve Gates to the City
Coal Creek March
Pay Day at Coal Creek
Buddy Won't You Roll down the
    Line
Arkansas Traveller
Fox Chase
Right on That Shore
Pick a Bale of Cotton
Rozhinkes Mit Mandlen
In Tarrytown
Clean-O
Ladies Auxiliary
Bells of Rhymney
Reuben James
Old Lady Who Swallowed a Fly
Study War No More
Passing Through

TRAVELLING ON WITH THE WEAVERS	1959 (1958)	Vanguard VRS9043

(Pete Seeger sings and plays on
five songs:)

Erie Canal
Old Riley
The Keeper
Greenland Whale Fisheries
Gotta Travel On

AMERICAN FAVORITE BALLADS—VOL. 2	February 1959	Folkways FA2321

Oh, Susanna
The Riddle Song
Beautiful City
Sally Ann
House of the Rising Sun
Shenandoah
The Midnight Special
Careless Love
Hard Travelling
Poor Boy
Black Girl
Alabama Bound
Stagolee
Black Is the Color
Aunt Rhody

The Water Is Wide
The Fox
The Keeper and the Doe

GAZETTE WITH PETE   1958   Folkways FN2501
SEEGER—VOL. 1
Pretty Boy Floyd
Banks of Marble
TVA Song
Martian Love Song
42 Kids
State of Arkansas
Declaration of Independence
Teacher's Blues
The Wild West Is Where I Want to
  Be
Demi Song
Ballad of Peace
The Scaler
Newspaperman
Talking Atom
Battle of Maxton Field
Doctor Freud
There Is Mean Things Happening
  in this Land

SLEEP TIME   1958   Folkways FC7525
Green Grass Grows All Around   [1967]   Reissued as *Abiyoyo and*
Sweet Little Baby   *Other Story Songs for*
Sweepy, Sweepy   *Children,* FTS31500
Where Are My Pajamas
Sam the Whaler
Abiyoyo
One Grain of Sand

SONG AND PLAY TIME WITH   1958   Folkways FC7526
PETE SEEGER
Go In and Out the Window
Here We Go Luby-Loo
She'll Be Coming 'Round the
  Mountain
Mary Wore Her Red Dress
Skip to My Lou
Little Sally Walker
I've Been Working on the Railroad
I Wonder What Tinya Is Doing
Soon As We Cook Sweet Potatoes
Let Us Come In
Bob-A-Needle
Captain Jinks
Going to Boston
Red Bird
Ha Ha This Away
Bobby's Three Years Old Today

| **HOOTENANNY AT CARNEGIE HALL** | 1960 (1958–59) | Folkways FN2512 |

HOOTENANNY AT CARNEGIE HALL

Battle of Maxton Field
I Never Will Marry
Oh, Reilly
Kevin Barry
Wimoweh
Jacob's Ladder
United Nations Make a Chain

1960
(1958–59)

Folkways FN2512

AMERICAN PLAYPARTIES
(with Larry Einsenberg and Mika Seeger)

Mazoo, Mazoo
Skip to My Lou
Shake Them 'Simmons Down
Alabama Bound
Sally down the Alley
Turn the Glasses Over
Goodbye Liza Jane
Git Along Home
Paw Paw Patch
Betty Larkin
Jolly Is the Miller
Pig in the Parlor
Great Big House in New Orleans
Sent My Brown Jug Downtown

1959

Folkways FC 7604

FOLK SONGS FOR YOUNG PEOPLE

Skip to My Lou
Blow the Man Down
Working in the Weave Room
The Farmer Is the Man
Tree Chopping Song
The Washer Lad
Hi Lu Lu
Baa, Baa, Black Sheep
Sometimes I Feel Like a
    Motherless Child
Joshua Fit the Battle of Jericho
Oh Worry Care
On Top of Old Smoky
John Henry
Had'yenu
It Would Be a Wonderful World
So Long

1959

Folkways FC7532

AMERICAN FAVORITE BALLADS—VOL. 3

John Brown's Body
Girl I Left Behind Me
Mary Don't You Weep
St. Louis Blues
Swanee River
Camptown Races

February 1960
(1959)

Folkways FA2322

Swing Low
Goodnight, Irene
My Good Man
Clementine
Dink's Song
New River Train
Sometimes I Feel Like a
    Motherless Child
Wimoweh
Farmer's Curst Wife
When I First Came to This Land

NONESUCH   August 1959   Folkways FA2439
    (with Frank Hamilton)

Meadowland
Nonesuch
Ragtime Annie
I Know My Love
Rye-Straw
Lady Gay
Blues
Singing in the Country
Lord Randall
Chaconne
Pygmy Time
Pretty Little Widder
My Home's across the Smoky
    Mountains
Battle of New Orleans

FOLK FESTIVAL AT   1959   Vanguard VRS9062
NEWPORT—VOL. 1
    The Bells of Rhymney
    One Grain of Sand
    Abiyoyo
    Careless Love

    (with Pat Clancy and Tom Makem)
    Mountain Dew

FOLK MUSIC OF THE NEWPORT   1961   Folkways FA2431
FOLK FESTIVAL 1959–60   (1959–60)
    (with O.J. Abbott)

    Barley Grain
    Cumberland Mountain Bear
        Chase

INDIAN SUMMER (soundtrack)   1961   Folkways FS3851
    Horizontal Lines   (1959–60)
    The Many Colored Paper
    The Country Fiddle

    (with Mike Seeger)
    Indian Summer

THE UNFORTUNATE RAKE   1960   Folkways FS3805
    Ballad Of Sherman Wu

HIGHLIGHTS OF PETE SEEGER AT THE VILLAGE GATE WITH MEMPHIS SLIM AND WILLIE DIXON—VOL. I	1960	Folkways FA2450

I'm On My Way
Hieland Laddie
Tina Singu
Soon As We All Cook Sweet
    Potatoes
Worried Man Blues
O Mary Don't You Weep
Don't You Weep after Me
Pretty Polly
Jacob's Ladder
Times A-Getting Hard
Bayeza
The Quizmasters
New York City
The Midnight Special

PETE SEEGER AT THE VILLAGE GATE—VOL. 2	May 1962 (1960)	Folkways FA2451

Hold On
Jug of Punch
John Hardy
Another Man Done Gone
This Little Light of Mine
Big Rock Candy Mountain
I Never Will Marry
So Long, It's Been Good to Know
    Yuh

(with Memphis Slim and Willie
Dixon)
In the Evening
T.B. Blues

SONGS OF THE CIVIL WAR	1960	Folkways FH5717

John Brown's Body
Lincoln and Liberty
Clear the Track
Tenting Tonight
Marching Song of the First
    Arkansas
Kingdom Coming

(with Bill McAdoo)
Marching through Georgia
When Johnny Comes Marching
    Home

AMERICAN HISTORY IN BALLAD AND SONG—VOLS. 1,2.	1960–61	Folkways FH5801, 5802 Reissues of earlier recordings

Washer Lad
Shamrock
Buffalo Skinner
Sioux Indians
Greer County Bachelor

The Cowboy Yodel
Free Elections
No Irish Need Apply
Pittsburgh Town
The Blind Fiddler
Eight Hour Day
My Children Are Seven in
    Number
Let Them Wear Their Watches
    Fine
Cotton Mill Colic
Mill Mother's Lament
The Death of Harry Simms
TVA Song
Sixty Per Cent
Raggedy
Seven Cent Cotton And Forty Cent
    Meat
He Lies in the American Land
Sherman Wu
Roll On, Columbia
Teacher's Blues
State of Arkansas
Then We'll Have Peace

CHAMPLAIN VALLEY SONGS   February 1960   Folkways FH5210
Seneca Canoe Song
Isabeau S'y Promeneau
The Valiant Soldier
Elder Bordee
John Riley
The Banks of Champlain
Roslin Castle
Boyne Water
Un Canadien Errant
One More A-Lumbering Go
The Shantyman's Life
Les Raftsmen
Lily of the Lake
Vive La Canadienne
How're You On for Stamps Today
Clara Nolan's Ball
Young Charlotte
John Brown's Body

THE RAINBOW QUEST   July 1960   Folkways FA2454
Colorado Trail   Possibly recorded in 1958.
Spanish Is the Loving Tongue
From Here On Up
Texas Gals   .
Swarthmore Girls
We Pity Our Bosses Five
The Scabs Crawl In
Open the Door
Road to Athay
Why Do Scotsmen . . .
Hold Up Your Petticoats

O, There's 2 On Me Back
Seek and Ye Shall Find
Farewell, Little Fishes
Where Have All the Flowers
  Gone?
Fu-Ru-Sato
Step By Step
Joe Hill's Will
Oh, Had I a Golden Thread
There's Better Things to Do
The Dove
Five Fingers Has the Hand
To Everyone in the World
We Are Moving on to Victory
When I'm Dead and Buried

BILL McADOO SINGS	1960	Folkways FA2448

(Seeger accompanies on banjo)

I'm Gonna Walk and Talk for My
  Freedom
Wade in the Water
Caryl Chessman
John Henry
Fare Ye Well
Walk On Alabama
Let Me Hold Your Hand
I Don't Want to Have a War
Eight Hundred Miles

OLD TIME FIDDLE TUNES	1960	Folkways FG3531

(with Jean Carignan, Marcel Roy,
Denny MacDougal); (Pete Seeger
plays banjo)

Medley and Haste to the Wedding
Winnipeg Reel
Fishers' Hornpipe
Blacksmith's Reel
Reel of the Hanged One
Medley and Lord MacDonald's Reel
The Connaught Man's Ramblers

AMERICAN FAVORITE	1961	Folkways FA2323
BALLADS—VOL. 4		

Banks of the Ohio
You Are My Sunshine
Ballad of the Boll Weevil
Where the Old Allegheny
  and the Monongahela Flow
Oh How He Lied
Frog Went A-Courtin'
Johnny Has Gone for a Soldier
Go Down Moses
America the Beautiful
Hole in the Bucket
Erie Canal
Monsieur Banjo
No More Auction Block

What Shall We Do with a Drunken
   Sailor?
Gee But I Want to Go Home
Sweet Betsy from Pike
All My Trials

GAZETTE—VOL. 2	1961	Folkways FN2502

Tomorrow Is a Highway
The Dying Miner
Bourgeois Town
The Literacy Test Song
Fayette County
Peat Bog Soldiers
Hold the Line
When a Fellow Is Out of a Job
The Rand Hymn
The Crow and the Cradle
I Come and Stand at Every Door
The Easter Marchers
The Jack Ash Society

PETE SEEGER: STORY SONGS	(April 1961)	Columbia
	1961	CL1668/CS8468;

Way Out There
The Half Hitch
Hobo's Lullaby
Washington Square
Aimee McPherson
Buffalo Skinner
The Foolish Frog
Monongahela Sal
John Henry
Fayette County
Pretty Boy Floyd

rereleased as Odyssey
32-16-0266: "3 Saints, 4
Sinners, and 6 Other
People."

AMERICAN FAVORITE BALLADS—VOL. 5	1962	Folkways FA2445

Red River Valley
Foggy Dew
Molly Malone
Ida Red
Talking Blues
Lolly Too Dum
Riflemen of Bennington
Summertime
I've Been Working on the Railroad
Hallelujah I'm a Bum
Farther Along
Ain't It a Shame
Leatherwing Bat
St. James Infirmary
T. B. Blues

AMERICAN GAME AND ACTIVITY SONGS FOR CHILDREN	1962	Folkways FC7674

I Know a Little Girl with Red
   Pajamas
I Want to Be a Farmer

Skip to My Lou
Candy Gal
Ring around the Rosie
Here We Go around the Mulberry
    Bush
London Bridge
Shoo Fly
Liza Jane
Pig in the Parlor
New River Train
Yankee Doodle
Jolly Is the Miller

THE 12-STRING GUITAR AS PLAYED BY LEADBELLY (instruction)	1962	Folkways FI8371

Bells of Rhymney
The Water Is Wide
Freight Train

THE BITTER AND THE SWEET	January 1963 (May 1962)	Columbia CL1916/CS8716

We Shall Overcome
Living in the Country
Mister Tom Hughes's Town
Where Have All the Flowers
    Gone?
Barbara Allen
Turn! Turn! Turn!
Around and Around Old Joe
    Clark
Windy Old Weather
Ram of Darby
Juanita
Andorra
The False Knight upon the Road

HOOTENANNY	1963 (September 1962)	Prestige/Folklore 14020

Pete Seeger sings:
Here's to Cheshire, Here's to
    Cheese
I Don't Want Your Millions, Mister

PETE SEEGER, CHILDREN'S CONCERT AT TOWN HALL	1963 (April 21, 1963)	Columbia CS8747 Reissued as Harmony 30399

Little Birdie
Henry My Son
Here's to Cheshire, Here's to
    Cheese
Automation:
  Erie Canal
  I've Been Working on the
    Railroad
  Riding in my Car
Put Your Finger in the Air
It Could Be a Wonderful World
Michael, Row the Boat Ashore
Be Kind to Your Parents
This Land Is Your Land

THE WEAVERS: REUNION AT CARNEGIE HALL	1963 (May, 2,3, 1963)	Vanguard VSD2150

When the Saints Go Marching In
Banks of Marble
Woke Up This Morning
Ramblin' Boy
Poor Liza
Wimoweh
San Francisco Bay Blues
Guantanamera
If I Had a Hammer
Study War No More
Goodnight, Irene
'Round the World

THE WEAVERS REUNION, PART 2	1965 (May 2,3, 1963)	VSD79161

Hine Ma Tov
Frozen Logger
Brazos River
Sinner Man
Kisses Sweeter Than Wine
Rock Island Line
Roll On, Columbia
Get Up, Get Out
Yerakina
Miner's Life
Fyvio
Greenland Whale Fisheries
A. La Volette
On Top of Old Smoky
Fight On

BROADSIDE BALLADS—VOL. 1	1963	Folkways FH5301

Ballad of Old Monroe

WE SHALL OVERCOME	1963 (June 8, 1963)	Columbia CL2101/CS8901

If You Miss Me on the Back of the
    Bus
Keep Your Eyes on the Prize
I Ain't Scared of Your Jail
Oh, Freedom!
What Did You Learn in School
    Today?
Little Boxes
Who Killed Norma Jean?
Who Killed Davey Moore?
A Hard Rain's A-Gonna Fall
Mail Myself to You
Guantanamera
Tshotsholosa
We Shall Overcome

NEWPORT BROADSIDE	1964 (July 1963)	Vanguard VSD79144

(with Bob Dylan)
Ye Playboys And Playgirls

BALLADS OF SACCO AND VANZETTI Sacco's Letter	1963	Folkways FH5485

BROADSIDE BALLADS—VOL. 2   January 1965   Broadside Records 302
                                 1963

Little Boxes
Fare Thee Well
Never Turn Back
The Willing Conscript
Who Killed Davey Moore?
I Ain't A-Scared of Your Jail
What Did You Learn in School
   Today?
A Hard Rain's A Gonna Fall
The Thresher
William Moore the Postman
Business
Song of the Punch Press Operator
Ballad of Lou Marsh

LITTLE BOXES AND OTHER   1963   Verve/Folkways
BROADSIDES   FV/FVS9020

Little Boxes   Rerelease of the above
Ira Hayes   sessions, with additional
Bill Brown   cuts.
The Thresher
Who Killed Norma Jean?
A Hard Rain's A-Gonna Fall
Blowin' in the Wind
Lou Marsh
The Willing Conscript
Paths of Victory
Ol' Jim Crow
If You Want to Go to Freedom

THE NATIVITY   1963–64   Folkways FT35001
(Seeger narrates, sings and plays)

The First Noel
Mary Had a Baby
Glory to the New Born King
What Child Is This?
Rise Up Shepherd, and Follow
Lo, How a Rose E'er Blooming

STRANGERS AND COUSINS   June 1965   Columbia CL2334/CS9134
                             (1963/64)
Oh, Had I a Golden Thread
Manurah Manyah
May There Always Be Sunshine
Malaika
Peat Bog Soldiers
Ragaputi
Sourwood Mountain
All Mixed Up
Kevin Barry
Shtille Di Nacht
Masters of War
Talking Atom Blues

Uh, Uh, Uh
If I Had a Hammer

BROADSIDES	1964	Folkways FA2456

The Dove
The Flowers of Peace
Mack the Bomb
From Way Up Here
Tomorrow's Children
Get Up and Go
The New York J-D Blues
Coyote, My Little Brother
We Shall Overcome
To My Old Brown Earth

NEWPORT FOLK FESTIVAL 1964	1965	Vanguard VSD79184
(on 12-string guitar)	(1964)	

Oh Mary Don't You Weep
Never Wed an Old Man

SONGS OF STRUGGLE AND	January 1965	Folkways FH5233
PROTEST	[1968]	Probably recorded in the

Step By Step
Aimee McPherson
I Don't Want Your Millions, Mister
Joe Hill
Harry Simms
Los Quatro Generales
Bourgeois Blues
Pittsburgh
Talking Union
The D-Day Dodgers
Hymn to Nations
What a Friend We Have in
Congress

mid- or late 1950s;
rereleased as *Wimoweh and
Other Songs of Freedom and
Protest*

I CAN SEE A NEW DAY	January 1965	Columbia CL2252/CS9057

This Land Is Your Land
Oh What a Beautiful City
Healing River
Follow the Drinking Gourd
Viva La Quince Brigada
Oh Louisiana
The Bells of Rhymney
Go Down Old Hannah
How Can I Keep from Singing?
Mrs. McGrath
Mrs. Clara Sullivan's Letter
(The Ring on My Finger Is)
   Johnny Give Me
I Come and Stand At Every Door
I Can See a New Day

WNEW'S STORY OF SELMA	1965	Folkways FH5595
(with Len Chandler and others)	(March 1965)	

Hold On
We've Got a Rope That's a Berlin
Wall

I Love Everybody
If You Want to Get Your Freedom
Oh, Wallace
Which Side Are You On?
Ain't Gonna Let Nobody Turn
  Me 'Round
Do What the Spirit Say Do

GOD BLESS THE GRASS   January 1966   Columbia CL2432/CS9232
  The Power and the Glory
  Pretty Saro
  70 Miles
  The Faucets Are Dripping
  Cement Octopus
  God Bless the Grass
  The Quiet Joys of Brotherhood
  Coal Creek March
  The Girl I Left Behind
  I Have a Rabbit
  The People Are Scratching
  Coyote, My Little Brother
  Preserven El Parque Elysian
  My Dirty Stream
  Johnny Riley
  Barbara Allen
  From Way Up Here
  My Land Is a Good Land

DANGEROUS SONGS!?   August 1966   Columbia CL2503/CS9303
  Medley: Robin the Bobbin
          Mary, Mary Quite
            Contrary
            Little Jack Horner
  Die Gedanken Sind Frei
  Jackaro
  Never Wed an Old Man
  John Brown's Body
  Going across the Mountains
  Harry Simms
  King Henry
  Midley: Ode to Joy
          Goliath, Goliath
  Queen Anne Front
  Joe Hill's "Casey Jones"
  One Grain of Sand
  The Pill
  The Draft Dodger Rag
  Mao Tse Tung
  Walking down Death Row
    Two from Shakespeare:
    Full Fathom Five
    Perchance to Win
  Beans in My Ears

PETE SEEGER SINGS WOODY   1967   Folkways FTS31002
GUTHRIE   Probably recorded in the
  Deportee   mid- and late 1950s
  Pretty Boy Floyd
  Reuben James

Union Maid
This Land Is Your Land
Roll On Columbia
Round and Round
Clean-O
Miss Pavilchenko
Talking Dust Bowl
So Long, It's Been Good to Know
    Yuh

WAIST DEEP IN THE BIG   August 1967   Columbia CL2705/CS9505
MUDDY
Seek and You Shall Find
Waist Deep in the Big Muddy
Nameless Lick
Over the Hills
East Virginia
My Name Is Liza Kalvelage
My Father's Mansion's Many
    Rooms
Melodie D'Amour
Those Three Are on My Mind

(with members of The Blues
Project)
Oh Yes I'd Climb
The Sinking Of the Reuben James
Last Night I Had the Strangest
    Dream
Down by the Riverside

TRADITIONAL CHRISTMAS   1967   Folkways FAS32311
CAROLS   Rereleases, with new
'Twas On a Night Like This   material, from Folkways
Mary Had a Little Baby   FTS35001, *Nativity.*
Glory to the New Born King
What Child Is This?
Rise Up, Shepherds, and Follow
Carol of the Beasts
Traditional Tune
The First Noel
Behold That Star
Lo, How a Rose E'er Blooming
Masters in This Hall
Traditional Tune
Twelve Gates to the City

PETE SEEGER'S GREATEST   October 1967   Columbia CL2616/CS9416
HITS   Releases of previously
Little Boxes   recorded material for
Wimoweh   Columbia; some cuts may
Where Have All the Flowers   not be previously issued.
    Gone?
Abiyoyo
The Bells of Rhymney
Turn! Turn! Turn!
Talking Union
Which Side Are You On?

We Shall Overcome
Living in the Country
Darling Corey
Guantanamera

PETE SEEGER SINGS LEADBELLY	1968	Folkways FTS31022 Possibly recorded in the mid- and late 1950s.

The Midnight Special
Stewball
Pick a Bale O' Cotton
New York City
Ha, Ha This a Way
Bourgeois Blues
Bring Me Li'l' Water Silvy
Alabama Bound
Boll Weevil
Black Girl
Goodnight, Irene

PETE SEEGER SINGS & ANSWERS QUESTIONS AT THE FORD HALL FORUM IN BOSTON	1968	Broadside BRS502

Opinions and Social Justice
Background to Social Songs in
    Europe and the USA
Social Songs from the Colonial
    Times to Today
Songs of the Immigrants
Labor Songs in the USA
Songs of Prejudices and Protests
Black Revolts in the USA
Question and Answer Period
Anti-Vietnam Songs
The Big Muddy Controversy: TV
Arts in a Changing Society
Violence and Protest
Lisa Kalvalege
Union/Labor Songs
Bells of Rhymney
Woody Guthrie
Afro-American Songs

PETE SEEGER NOW	1969 (1968)	Columbia CS9717

The Torn Flag
Letter to Eve/Water Is Wide
Talking Ben Tre
Adam the Inventor
False From True

(with Bernice Reagon)
He's Long John
Michael, Row the Boat Ashore
Taint But Me One
Backlash Blues

A TRIBUTE TO WOODY
GUTHRIE—VOLS. 1 and 2
    Curly Headed Baby

    (with Richie Havens)
    Jackhammer John

    (with Judy Collins)
    Union Maid

1972
(1968–69)

Warner Bros. 2W3007

TELL ME THAT YOU LOVE ME,
JUNIE MOON (soundtrack)
    Old Devil Time

1969

Columbia CS 3540

CLEARWATER
    Old Father Hudson

    (with Jimmy Collier)
    Love Our River Again

    (with group)
    Haul on the Bowline
    Strike the Bell
    Sweet Rosyanne
    Sailing Up, Sailing Down
    Reuben Ranzo
    You Can't Eat the Oysters
    Good Morning, Brother Hudson
    Shenandoah
    Sea Man's Hymn

1974
(1969–74)

Sound House Records
PS1001

CLEARWATER II
    Golden River
    My Dirty Stream

    (with Tom Winslow)
    It's the Clearwater

1977
(1969–77)

Sound House Records
SHR1022

PETE SEEGER YOUNG VS. OLD
    Who Knows
    Bring Them Home
    When I Was Most Beautiful
    This Old Car
    Ballad Of the Fort Hood Three
    Cumberland Mountain Bear
      Chase
    Since You've Been Apart
    Lolly Todum
    My Rainbow Man
    Poisoning the Students' Minds
    All My Children of the Sun
    The Good Boy
    Be Kind to Your Parents
    Get Up and Go
    Declaration of Independence
    Both Sides Now
    Mayrowana

1971

Columbia CS9873

GREAT FOLKSINGERS OF THE
SIXTIES
    East Virginia Blues
    (with the Weavers)

1972

Vanguard VSD17/18
Rereleases

Erie Canal

(on banjo, with Tommy Makem)
The Whistling Gypsy

BALLADS OF BLACK AMERICA   1972   Folkways FC7751
(Seeger, banjo, and Jeanne
Humphries, bass, accompany Rev.
Frederick Douglass Kirkpatrick)

Harriet Tubman
Benjamin Banneker
Sojourner Truth
Leroy "Satchel" Page
Martin Luther King

RAINBOW RACE   1973   Columbia C30739
My Rainbow Race
Sailing down This Golden River
Words Words Words
Old Devil Time
Snow Snow
Uncle Ho
The Clearwater
Hobo's Lullaby
Our Generation

(with Bob Johnson)
Last Train to Nuremberg

MIKE SEEGER THE SECOND   1973   Mercury SRMI1685
ANNUAL FAREWELL REUNION
(with Mike Seeger)

Well May the World Go

HOMELESS BROTHER (Don   1974   United Artists LA315-6
McLean)
Seeger sings harmony on:
Homeless Brother

THE WORLD OF PETE SEEGER   1974   Columbia KG31949
We Shall Overcome   Anthology of previous
Where Have All the Flowers   recordings for Columbia
   Gone?
Turn! Turn! Turn!
Little Boxes
Who Killed Davey Moore?
A Hard Rain's A-Gonna Fall
This Land Is Your Land
The Bells of Rhymney
Masters of War
If I Had a Hammer
Coal Creek March
Barbara Allen
Guantanamera
Both Sides Now
Last Train to Nuremberg
The Sinking of the Reuben James
Last Night I Had the Strangest
   Dream

East Virginia
Hobo's Lullaby
My Rainbow Race

BANKS OF MARBLE   1974   Folkways FTS31040
Yodel
Don't Ask Me What a River Is For
God Bless the Grass
Joy and Temperance
Young Woman Who Swallowed a
   Lie
Three Rules of Discipline and
   Eight Rules of Attention
Estadio Chile
Well May the World Go
This Is a Land
My Father's Mansion
Pigtown Fling
Quite Early Morning

(with Fred Hellerman)
Banks of Marble

(with Nicky Seeger and Fred
   Hellerman)
Precious Friend

PETE SEEGER AND BROTHER   1974   Children's Records of
KIRK VISIT SESAME STREET   America CTW22062
Michael, Row the Boat Ashore
This Land Is Your Land
Skip to My Lou
She'll Be Coming Round the
   Mountain
Riding in My Car
Garbage
Old Lady Who Swallowed a Fly
Guantanamera
Sweet Rosyanne

(accompanying Fred Kirkpatrick)
Patty Cake Gorilla
Ballad of Martin Luther King

PETE SEEGER AND ARLO   1975   Warner Brothers 2R2214
GUTHRIE TOGETHER IN
CONCERT
Yodeling
Declaration of Independence
Get Up and Go
Estadio Chile
Henry My Son
Joe Hill
May There Always Be Sunshine
Three Rules of Discipline and
   Eight Rules of Attention
Golden Vanity

(with Arlo Guthrie)
Way Out There
Guantanamera

Well May The World Go
Deportee
Lonesome Valley
Quite Early One Morning
Sweet Rosyanne

CANTO OBRERO	1979	Americanto A1004
Harry Simms	(May 1975)	
Guantanamera		

FIFTY SAIL ON NEWBURGH BAY — 1976 — Folkways FH5257

(with Ed Renehan)

Kayowajineh
Fifty Sail on Newburgh Bay
The Burning of Kingston
The Phoenix and the Rose
The Old Ben Franklin and the
    Sloop Sally B
The Moon in the Pear Tree
The Erie Canal
This Is a Land
Big Bill Snyder
Tarrytown
The Hudson Whalers
Follow the Drinking Gourd
Hudson River Steamboat
The Knickerbocker Line
Of Time and Rivers Flowing

THE ESSENTIAL PETE SEEGER — 1978 — Vanguard 97/98
Coal Creek March — Rereleases "from Folkways
Oh What a Beautiful City — Records, 1950–74."
Clean-O/Ladies Auxiliary
The Bells of Rhymney
So Long, It's Been Good to Know
    Yuh
Viva La Quince Brigada
Suliram
Wimoweh
Bring Me Little Water, Sylvie
The Bourgeois Blues
Roll On, Columbia
East Virginia
Saint James Hospital
Harry Simms
We Shall Not Be Moved
Cripple Creek
Old Joe Clark
Ida Red
Come All Ye Fair And Tender
    Ladies
John Hardy
My Father's Mansions
God Bless the Grass
Where Have All the Flowers
    Gone?

Quite Early One Morning
Oh, Had I a Golden Thread

CIRCLES AND SEASONS	1979	Warner Brothers
Garbage		BSK3329
Sailing down This Golden River		
Mexican Blues		
The Photographers		
I'm Gonna Be an Engineer		
Seneca Canoe Song		
Maple Syrup Time		
Viva La Quince Brigada		
As the Sun Rose		
Sour Cream		
Tarantella		
Garden Song		
Harry Simms		
Allelulia/Joy upon This Earth		
EQUILIBRIUM: NATIONAL AUDUBON SOCIETY'S ALBUM OF NATURE AND HUMANITY	1980	Folkways FTS37305
One Grain of Sand		
SINGALONG	1980	Folkways FXM6055
(Demonstration record of song techniques)		2-12
THE GREAT HUDSON RIVER REVIVAL—VOL. I	1980	Flying Fish 214
(with the Sloop Singers)		
Roseanna		

Extended Play Recordings

YANKEE DOODLE AND OTHER SONGS	early 1950s	Children's Record Guild Originally called "Let's Join In," on Young People's Records
Yankee Doodle		
John Henry		
The Farmer Is the Man		
It Takes Everybody to Build This Land		
PETE SEEGER SINGS FOLK SONGS	early 1950s	Folkways FEP1
SEA CHANTIES	1950s	Young People's Records (3 EPs)
ALMANAC	early 1950s	Folkways Records
Folksongs		
I'll Sing Me a Love Song		
Kisses Sweeter Than Wine		
Wimoweh		
T for Texas		
East Virginia		

AMERICAN FOLKSONGS FOR CHILDREN	1953	Folkways EPC 1-3

All around the Kitchen
This Old Man
She'll Be Coming Round the
    Mountain
Train Is a Coming
Bought Me a Cat
There Was a Man
Clap Your Hands
Jimmy Crack Corn
Jim Along Josey
Billy Barlow
Frog Went A-Courtin'

SOUTH AFRICAN FREEDOM SONGS	mid-1950s	Folkways EPC-601

(with Robert Harter, Garrett
    Morris, Guy Carwan, Ned
    Wright)

Tina Sizwe (We the Brown Nation)
Nkosi Waqcine (God Save the
    Volunteers)
Asikatali (We Do Not Care If We
    Go to Jail)
Liyashizwa (Pass Burning Song)

Singles

Harry Bridges Babe O'Mine	1941	Keynote Records 304
Keep That Oil A-Rolling Boomtown Bill	1942	Keynote Records
Solidarity Forever (The Union Boys: Tom Glazer, Burl Ives, Pete Seeger)	1945	Stinson 622
Mule Train (with Burl Ives)	1944	Columbia Records Undated, no information
Newspaperman Talking Atom	1947–48	Encore Records 101
Cumberland Mountain Bear Chase Skillet Good and Greasy T for Texas	1948	Charter Records C-500
Johnny I Hardly Knew You (Seeger accompanies Betty Sanders on recorder)	1948	Charter Records C-500-A
Hallelujah, I'm a Travellin'		Charter C-25-B
Zhonkoye (with the Berries)	1948	Charter C-30-A
Black, Brown, and White Blues (with the Berries, the Grays, Goodson & Vale)	1948	Charter C-40-A
Death of Harry Simms Winnsboro Cotton Mill Blues	1948	Charter C-45-B

No Irish Need Apply
Unemployment Compensation Blues   1949   Charter RC-1
(with Mario Cassetta)

Conversation with a Mule   1949   Charter Records
Farmer Is the Man   (or private pressing)
Join the Farmer's Union

Utsu Etsa   1949   Charter Records
Schalome
(with the Berries)

Train to the Zoo   1949   Children's Record Guild
    Parts I and II

The Peekskill Story   1949   Charter Records C-502
    Parts I and II

Dig My Grave   1949   Charter 503
Wasn't That a Time
(The Weavers)

The Hammer Song   1949   Hootenanny Records
Banks of Marble   H-101
(The Weavers: Pete Seeger, Lee
Hays, Ronnie Gilbert, Fred
Hellerman)

Talking UnAmerican   1951   Hootenanny Records
    Blues   H-103
(Seeger accompanies Betty Sanders
on banjo)

WITH THE WEAVERS
Around The World   1950   Decca 27053
Tzena (Hebrew)   (May 4, 1950)

Tzena (English)   1950   Decca 27077
Goodnight, Irene   (May 26, 1950)

So Long   1950   Decca 27376
Lonsome Traveller   (October 24, 1950)

Wreck of the "John B."   1950   Decca 27332
The Roving Kind   (November 3, 1950)

Hush Little Baby/Suliram   1951   Decca 27727
I Know Where I'm Going   (November 6, 1950)

On Top of Old Smoky   1951   Decca 27515
The Wide Missouri   (February 25, 1951)

Frozen Logger   1951   Decca 27726
Darling Corey   (May 4, 1951)

Follow the Drinking Gourd   1951   Decca 27728
Easy Rider Blues   (May 4, 1951)

When the Saints Go   1951   Decca 27670
    Marching In   (June 12, 1951)
Kisses Sweeter Than Wine

Jig Along Home   1951   Decca 88075
Join into the Game   (August 23, 1951)

We Wish You a Merry Christmas Little Bitty Baby	1951 (August 23, 1951)	Decca 27783
Go Tell It on the Mountain Poor Little Jesus	1951 (September 19, 1951)	Decca 27818
It's Almost Day Burgundian Carol/God Rest Ye Merry Gentlemen	1951 (September 21, 1951)	Decca 27819
Wimoweh Old Paint	1952 (October 25, 1951)	Decca 27928
Around the Corner Gandy Dancer's Ball	1952 (February 27, 1952)	Decca 29054
Hard Ain't It Hard Run Home to Mama	1952 (May 6, 1952)	Decca 28228
Quilting Bee Bay of Mexico	1953 (September 17, 1952)	Decca 28542
Clementine True Love	1952 (September 19, 1952)	Decca 28434
Sylvie Rock Island Shuffle	1953 (February 26, 1953)	Decca 28919
Benoni Taking It Easy	1953 (February 26, 1953)	Decca 28637
You Are My Sunshine (with Jimmy Davis)		Undated, no information
Battle of New Orleans My Home's Across The Smoky Mountains (with Frank Hamilton)	1957–58	Folkways FA45-201
One Day As I Rambled Skip to My Lou	1957–59	Vanguard Records
Done Laid Around Aunt Rhody (The Weavers: Lee Hays, Ronnie Gilbert, Pete Seeger, Fred Hellerman, and Erik Darling)	1958	Vanguard Records
Little Boxes/Where Have All The Flowers Gone	1963	Columbia
Waist Deep in the Big Muddy/Down by the Riverside	1967	Columbia

---

Foreign Releases

Amadeo (France)

FOLKLORE AMÉRICAN   Originally Vanguard
PAR LES WEAVERS AU CARNEGIE   VSD 6533
HALL DE N.Y.
   Michael, Row the Boat Ashore
   On Top of Old Smoky

Drill Ye Tarriers
Clementine
Boll Weevil
So Long
Wasn't That a Time
Santa Claus Is Coming to Town
Go Tell It on the Mountain
Pay Me My Money Down
Darlin' Corey
Goodnight, Irene
Go Where I Send Thee
When the Saints Go Marching In
Sixteen Tons
Follow the Drinking Gourd

WEAVERS AT CARNEGIE HALL II		Amadeo 32 Originally Vanguard VSD 6237
HOOTENNANNY WITH PETE SEEGER		FWXM50103 Possible rerelease of "With Voices Together We Sing" Folkways 2452
	Amiga (Germany)	
WE SHALL OVERCOME	1966	Amiga 840038 Originally Columbia CL2101
	Aravel (England)	

LIVE HOOTENNANY—VOL. I AND II
  Lonesome Traveller
  Reuben James
  Shenandoah
  Kisses Sweeter Than Wine
  D Day Dodgers
  Greensleeves
	1959	Aravel AB 1003-5

	CBS-JAPAN	
THE PETE SEEGER STORY		CBS YS8334-C 4 12″ records
	Festival (New Zealand)	
FOLKWAYS AROUND THE WORLD		Festival FL7156 Originally Decca DL 5285
BEST OF THE WEAVERS		Festival FL7124 Originally Decca 8893
	Folklore (England)	

PETE SEEGER IN CONCERT—VOL. 1 and 2
  East Virginia
  Deep Blue Sea
  I Knew Leadbelly (Medley)
  Cumberland Mountain Bear
    Chase
  Pretty Polly
	(1959)	F-LAUT-1
		Also issued in Europe as Super Majestic Records (VOX) 1.580

He Lies In The American Land
One Big Fat Hen
Leather Britches
Jesu Joy of Man's Desiring
Suliram
Bells of Rhymney
I Never Will Marry
Water Is Wide
Others

Fontana (England)

THE SOIL AND THE SEA	Fontana TL5299 Reissue of *Sod Buster* *Ballads* and *Deep Sea* *Chanties,* Commodore BA 20, 21
TRAVELLING ON WITH THE **WEAVERS**	Fontana TFL6028
WEAVERS ALMANAC	Fontana TFL6011

Topic (England)

Peekskill Story Our Song Will Carry On	Topic TRC 28
PETE AND FIVE STRINGS Gerry's Rocks Little Dogies Fair and Tender Ladies John Riley Down on Penny's Farm Risselty, Rosselty	Topic Top33 EP From *Darling Corey,* Folkways FA2003
PETER SEEGER'S GUITAR **GUIDE** (instruction record)	Topic 12 T 20 Originally Folkways FQ8354
PLAY THE FIVE STRING BANJO	Topic 12 T 23 Originally Folkways FQ8354
HOOTENANNY NYC (with Sonny Terry, Bob DeCormier, Jerry Silverman) Mule Skinner Talking Union Dark as a Dungeon Wimoweh	Topic Top37 From *Hootenanny Tonight,* FN2511

Anthologies

THE UNFORGOTTEN MEN (a chronicle of the Roosevelt years) Talking Union Round and Round Hitler's Grave Union Maid	early 1950s	National Guardian Rereleases of earlier Almanac material

FOLK SONG AND MINSTRELRY (4 LPs featuring Vanguard artists; includes the Weavers from previous albums)	1962	Vanguard RL7624-3 Rereleases of earlier Weavers material

State of Arkansas
Eddystone Light
Greenland Whale Fisheries
We're All A'Dodgin
Git along Little Dogies
Wild Goose Grasses
Johnson Boys
Aweigh Santy Ano
Erie Canal
State of Arkansas

BORN TO LIVE (commemorative album on Hiroshima) Furusato	1965 (1960)	Folkways FD5525 (from FA2454)
THE BITTER END YEARS Where Have All the Flowers Gone?	1974 (1961–62)	Roxbury RCX 300
THE BAD MEN ("Songs, stories, book of pictures of the West's outlaws")	1964	Columbia Records legacy collection. Probably includes material from *Frontier Ballads,* FA2175-76
BREAD & ROSES Sailing down My Golden River	1979 (October 1977)	Fantasy F-79009

Private Pressings

SQUARE DANCE ALBUM	1940–46	Recorded for Margo Mayo's folk dance group, date uncertain; may be Library of Congress (M173A8, 673-6733)
PETE SEEGER ON SAIPAN	1944	Approximately 10 16″ transcription discs of Pete Seeger singing in the army over Saipan radio with the Rainbow Boys: bawdy material, collections of soldiers' songs, Chamorro songs
OPA SHOUT	1946	People's Songs Collection

PEOPLE'S SONGS FOR NATIONAL MARITIME UNION (with Holly Wood, Ronnie Gilbert, Tom Glazer)	1947	Transcriptions of soundtrack for filmstrip prepared by People's Songs

Solidarity
Commonwealth of Toil
Preacher and the Slave
Hold the Fort
The Whole Wide World Around
We've Got Our Eyes on You
Talking Union
Which Side Are You On?

GREAT DAY GLORY GLORY HALLELUJAH (Seeger's participation uncertain)	1948	Progressive Party

SOUNDTRUCK RECORDINGS (with Fred Hellerman, Lee Hays, Ronnie Gilbert)	1949	American Labor Party Recordings made for 1949 campaign of Vita Marcantonio for mayor of New York

Marc for Mayor
Skip to the Polls
Marcantonio
Now Right Now
New York City

Additional Materials

LULLABIES AND ROUNDS		Disc 78s 2 records, from the early 1940s
HUDSON VALLEY BALLADS (Seeger accompanies Frank Warner)		Disc 78s 3 records, probably from the late 1940s
SQUARE DANCES	1940s	Folkcraft Date of release and recording unavailable
THE WEAVERS AND OTHERS		CHI Institute Date of recording and release unavailable
CLANCY BROTHERS LIVE CONCERT (Seeger accompanies on banjo)		Columbia Records (undated)
PETE SEEGER—FREIGHT TRAIN	October 1964	Capital DT 2718 Date of (live) recording unavailable

Freight Train
Coyote
Dollar Ain't a Dollar Any More
T. B. Blues

This Train
Oh, What a Beautiful City
Careless Love
Banks of Marble
Red River Valley
Old Maid's Song
Jimmy Crack Corn
John Henry

PETE SEEGER ON CAMPUS　　　　June 1965　　　　Verve/Folkways
　Introduction　　　　　　　　　　　　　　　　　　FVS 9009
　Kum Ba Yah　　　　　　　　　　　　　　　　　　Date of original recording
　Reilly　　　　　　　　　　　　　　　　　　　　　unavailable
　Water Is Wide
　Kisses Sweeter Than Wine
　Bring Me Li'l Water Silvie
　It Takes a Worried Man
　Pretty Boy Floyd
　Pie in the Sky
　Dance Tunes
　The Bourgeois Blues
　Goodnight, Irene

FOLK GO-GO　　　　　　　　　　　　　　　　　Verve/Folkways
　　　　　　　　　　　　　　　　　　　　　　　　　Date of original recording
　　　　　　　　　　　　　　　　　　　　　　　　　and release unavailable.

AMERICA'S BALLADEER　　　　　　1973　　　　　Everest/Olympic 7102
　Michael, Row the Boat Ashore　　　　　　　　　Date of original recordings
　Big Rock Candy Mountain　　　　　　　　　　　unknown
　Working on the Railroad
　Down in the Valley
　Blue Tail Fly
　Black Is the Color
　Boll Weevil
　Joshua Fit the Battle of Jericho
　The Fox
　Casey Jones

FOLK FESTIVAL　　　　　　　　　　　　　　　Legacy 110
　Ariran　　　　　　　　　　　　　　　　　　　　Elektra/Everest rerelease

Index